ENGINES

OF WAR

ENGINES OF WAR

MERCHANTS OF DEATH
AND THE
NEW ARMS RACE

JAMES ADAMS

THE ATLANTIC MONTHLY PRESS
NEW YORK
◆

To Christine

First published in Great Britain in 1990 by Hutchinson
First Atlantic Monthly Press edition, April 1990
Printed in the United States of America

Library of Congress Cataloging-in-Publication Data

Adams, James, 1951–
 Engines of war: merchants of death and the new arms race / James
Adams.
 Includes bibliographical references.
 ISBN 0-87113-352-0
 1. Arms race. 2. Munitions. I. Title.
UA10.A33   1990   355.02'13—dc20   90-197

The Atlantic Monthly Press
19 Union Square West
New York, NY 10003

First printing

Contents

PART FIVE: THE IRAN-IRAQ WAR

PART SIX: NUCLEAR PROLIFERATION

PART SEVEN: CHEMICAL WARFARE

PART EIGHT: BALLISTIC MISSILES

PART NINE: CONCLUSION

Acknowledgments

Robin Pekelney did some very good research for me in the United States. Others have now recognised her talents and the work she did for me suggests she is perfect for the job she has taken.

Peter Wilsher and Peter Hounam shared with me the research they had done into Israel's nuclear programme. Peter Hounam played a key part in bringing the story of Mordechai Vanunu to the world and I am most grateful to him for correcting my mistakes and adding his own valuable insight to the story. Askold Krushelnycky kindly shared his knowledge gained while writing about the war in Afghanistan.

A number of people were kind enough to help in the preparation of this book and some of them then took the trouble to read an early draft of the manuscript. I hope I have corrected the errors of fact and interpretation that they pointed out. I am unable to mention any of these people by name because they all work either for governments or industry in sensitive jobs and publicity could do them or their employers harm. Nonetheless they have my thanks.

I am especially grateful to Rene Riley for smoothing out the rough spots and giving me encouragement and support just when it was needed.

Introduction

The start of the 1990s could well go down in history as the year peace broke out in the world. In 1989, Soviet forces completed their withdrawal from Afghanistan, peace became a possibility in Angola, the South Africans agreed to withdraw from Namibia and the ceasefire continued to hold in the Iran-Iraq war.

More importantly, the superpowers at last began to break away from an arms race that had continued unabated since the end of the Second World War. Intermediate range nuclear forces were disappearing from Europe, there was a real possibility of reductions in strategic nuclear forces and an early agreement on cutting back on conventional forces in both NATO and the Warsaw Pact seemed likely.

The new decade also brought with it important psychological changes in the perceptions of east and west. The Soviet bear appeared more benign than at any time since the Russian Revolution and even those in the communist bloc perceived their traditional capitalist enemies as people like themselves, divided not so much by ideology but by generations of ignorance about each other. The breaking down of the Berlin Wall, the overthrow in popular revolutions of communist governments in Eastern Europe, and the commitment of those new governments to democracy have further eroded barriers between east and west. At last, there is a real prospect of a complete change in relations between NATO and the Warsaw Pact.

To even the most cynical cold war warrior all these changes are for the good. Anything, after all, that reduces tension between east and west should be welcomed. Less tension means less chance of nuclear war. Aside from reducing tension, this rapprochement should mean that fewer arms are required, but arms dealers are confident this will not be so.

Conflict is taking different forms, from terrorism to more regional conflicts, and weapons will continue to be in demand. Arms producers are predicting a fairly steady market for the next five years which will be followed by a sharp increase as new weapons currently in the development stage reach an expanded market. It appears that the arms business remains relatively unaffected by the prospects of superpower peace.

Weapons and their use on the battlefield is not just about war but about the application of technology to the exercise of violence. For terrorists and narcotics traffickers, weapons have become increasingly specific. Where these criminals used to be satisfied by the $500 AK47 Khalashnikov automatic rifle for attacks, and oil and fertiliser to make their bombs, they have developed an appetite for sniper rifles with night sights and difficult to detect Semtex explosives detonated by remote control using lasers and sophisticated microcircuitry.

In the same way, nuclear warfare has evolved from the crude missile that goes up with a single warhead and comes down in the rough area of the target. Today any ballistic nuclear missile should have decoys and a number of warheads that can manoeuvre in space and be independently targeted. Such specialised requirements have not only increased the demand for a different weapon but differing marketing strategies bring about competition between arms manufacturers designed with non-state sales in mind. This in turn has given the second, third and fourth customers unparalleled influence on the design and development of new weapons.

As a high premium is now placed on exports to earn foreign currency and maintain jobs, governments have become directly and openly involved in the arms manufacturing and sales process. More important, however, exports also help fund the research and development into new weapons that allow a country to maintain an indigenous arms producing infrastructure to keep a place in the club of arms exporters.

Losing a place at that table is not simply a matter of status and money. Arms mean power. Arms exports bring influence far outside the defence arena. The country that buys guns may also be inclined to buy grain, and to provide diplomatic support for the arms supplier in forums such as the United Nations.

Developing countries recognise this and also realise that arms sales can be a valuable source of foreign income. As a result, the arms business is more diverse than ever before with more countries vying for the $50 billion annual market in arms exports. Newcomers such as China, Brazil, Israel, South Africa and North Korea have made significant inroads to a business that has traditionally been dominated by countries such as the United States, Soviet Union, Britain and France.

The newcomers in the market have thrived in the 1980s because of the number of 'small' wars ongoing around the world. Of these wars, the conflict between Iran and Iraq has proved the biggest bonanza to the arms business, and every arms producer has fed at the trough. Even with the ceasefires that are already in place, there are still some thirty-five or forty wars a year, from Peru, to Colombia and Afghanistan. These brushfire wars mean both government and black marketeers in the arms business have prospered.

In fact, this book will argue that while one arms race – between the Soviet Union and the United States – may at last be drawing to a close, another – between developing nations, and even between black marketeers – is only just beginning.

According to the US Arms Control and Disarmament Agency, worldwide sales of weapons broke through the $1 trillion barrier for the first time in 1987. While this is bad news, there is some ground for general optimism. Spending by the developed nations continued to rise but spending in

Third World countries dropped by 9.1 per cent in 1987 compared to the previous year. However, spending in South Asia rose by 10 per cent.[1]

The simple statistics suggest that, despite some small problems, the overall picture is much improved. In fact, the shrinking size of some arms budgets in some countries indicates not a reduced commitment to military investment but a change in the nature of that investment.

At every level of conflict from terrorism to biological warfare, new weapons are being developed that are accessible to a much wider market. Many of these weapons are both affordable and many times more effective than the weapons they replace.

In addition, technology has made it possible for many countries, previously denied access to such equipment, either to make weapons themselves or to buy them from their neighbours. This new market has been allowed to develop in part because industry in the developed nations is forced to find new markets or go out of business, and in part because governments have come to depend on arms sales for foreign exchange and jobs at home. This is nothing new. But what is new is the way other manufacturers and arms entrepreneurs have entered the market making it more imaginative, competitive and accessible.

This book began as a simple study of the arms business. But, as the research progressed, disturbing trends began to emerge: the proliferation of certain weapons, the secret development of new systems of devastating power that would be preferred by many developing countries denied access to nuclear weapons; the widespread disregard for international conventions by arms manufacturers in east and west; and the apparent impotence of governments to prevent the proliferation of weapons all consider dangerous to the security of the world.

[1]*Aviation Week and Space Technology*, August 28, 1989, p. 34–35; *Christian Science Monitor*, August 10, 1989.

To demonstrate the changes that have taken place and to show how new weapons are emerging and influencing the battlefields of today and tomorrow, I have looked in some detail at every level of conflict.

Much of the material that appears in *Trading in Death* is new and should help focus the debate on the nature of the arms business today. It should also draw the attention of a world lulled into a sense of false security by the good news flowing from Washington and Moscow to the real threats that still exist today.

Each section is chosen as an example of a larger issue: the development of the IRA as a terrorist organisation has been mirrored by other groups around the world and the lessons to be learned from the IRA can be applied elsewhere.

The book opens with a detailed examination of the IRA, and then climbs up the ladder of conflict to Afghanistan, the conventional war between Iran and Iraq and nuclear proliferation among Third World countries. The book concludes with a study of chemical and biological proliferation and the means being developed by some countries to deliver such weapons to their target.

The real danger for the future lies not in the arsenals held by the major powers but in the new weapons currently being developed that are just as deadly as nuclear weapons in their selective application, cheaper – and more readily available to any dictator, terrorist or drug trafficking organisation.

PART ONE: TERRORISM

1

Arming the Amateurs

In the long and vainglorious history of the Irish Republican Army, 1954 was a year to boast about. In June, a Dublin based IRA unit set off for the north on what was to become their most successful arms raid ever.

Twenty men rendezvous-ed in the Republican border town of Dundalk, where they expected to find a truck ready to transport them north over the border to Armagh and the headquarters of the Royal Irish Fusiliers in Gough Barracks. As happened frequently with the IRA in those days, no truck arrived and the team 'borrowed' a large red cattle truck leaving the driver under guard.

Arriving at the barracks in Armagh, a member of the unit approached the single sentry to enquire about enlisting in the British army. Once he was close enough the IRA man drew his pistol and ushered the startled sentry into the guardhouse where he was tied up. The truck then drove into the barracks and, using the guardhouse keys, the men broke into the armoury. Over the next half hour they loaded weapons into the back of the truck while others of the unit left on duty at the gate – complete with British army uniforms – escorted soldiers and visitors into the guardhouse where they were tied up. By the time the IRA men left, there were eighteen soldiers and one civilian under restraint.

After cutting the telephone lines, the IRA men drove unhindered to the border and then well south into the Republic before stopping to examine their booty. They discovered that they had stolen two hundred and fifty rifles, thirty-seven Sten guns, nine Bren machine guns and forty training rifles. It was a huge haul. They had also stolen a large number of keys from the guardroom.

Several things were interesting about the raid. The British were completely unprepared for such a brazen assault. The single sentry on guard duty had no ammunition for his gun; there was no effective method of raising the alarm; relations between north and south were such that it was several hours before news of the raid reached the border and by that time the IRA unit was safe in the Republic. The raid was also a major propaganda coup, by which the IRA were able to gain recruits (one hundred men were trained in two summer camps to use the weapons) and cash (the two hundred keys taken from the guardhouse were later auctioned to raise money in the Irish Republic and the United States). It is also striking that the IRA, rather than killing the British soldiers outright, tied them up and then left without injuring anyone. Twenty years later such a humanitarian approach would be unthinkable.[1]

The Gough Barracks raid was the first and last time the IRA would ever find the acquisition of arms so easy.

Eight years after that haul, the IRA's campaign to oust the British from the north and unite Ireland had collapsed. In the 1962 elections they polled less than three per cent of the vote, support in the north had virtually disappeared and the cash supply from America had dried up. The IRA army council meeting in Dublin on February 5 ordered a ceasefire and directed that all IRA army units should hide their arms.

Today the IRA is so clearly associated with terrorism of a particular bloody kind that it is important to remember that their campaign that ran for sixteen years until 1962 was, compared with today's, a relatively peaceful affair. Even with the arms they stole at Gough Barracks and other weapons they obtained from sympathisers in the Republic and the United States, there was none of the tactical sophistication that is the hallmark of today's IRA. Over sixteen years only six RUC men and thirty-two members of the British security forces were injured. Eight IRA men lost their lives and two hundred were tried and sentenced on terrorism charges.

Both the British and the IRA believed that 1962 marked the end of the military activism. For six years, there was peace between north and south and the IRA, while still existing in name and song, played no active part in local politics. But then, in 1968, simmering disagreements between the Catholics and the Protestants in the north boiled to the surface. On August 11, Catholics demonstrating against the Protestant government's unfair method of distributing housing were dispersed by the police. The next day, a Protestant Apprentice Boys' march turned into a riot. The trouble spread to Belfast and by August 14 the Catholics were under siege.

That night, the Belfast Brigade of the IRA was called to arms to defend the Catholics. Thirteen men answered the call and between them they could muster two venerable Thompson submachine guns which even when new were noisy and unreliable, a Sten gun, one Lee-Enfield rifle and nine hand guns. Few of the men had any serious training in how to use the weapons and they were of little value over the next twenty-four hours as the government sent in the hated Protestant B Special paramilitary troops to work with the British army to restore order.

That night, six people were shot dead, there was widespread shooting along the Catholic Falls Road, and by morning one hundred and twenty-one people had been treated in hospital, forty-two of them with gunshot wounds. Many members of the Catholic community felt they had no defence against the Protestant onslaught. At the time, there was some reason for their fears. The police were predominantly Protestant, as were the hated and tough B Specials. The British army at that time was seen as impartial but unable to control the Protestant militants.

The IRA was the Catholics' logical last resort and that night they had been found wanting. The following morning the Belfast Brigade met and agreed to send four parties south to the Republic to try to recover arms that had been buried there six years before. Unfortunately there had been no central record kept of the location of the arms caches so the men had to rely on local folklore and, in one case, a visit to an IRA man in jail, to help them find the dumps. Two days later, when the Belfast men met, again in Dundalk, they had mustered seventy-five weapons, the majority of them shotguns, with a sprinkling of .22s and .303 Lee-Enfields. It was a pathetic armoury.

This was an early lesson for the newly forming IRA. Without sufficient weapons they would be unable to defend themselves, and the Catholic community in whose name they were fighting would see them not as a protector but as yet another excuse for the Protestants to persecute them.

The IRA divided into two in 1969, with the Provisionals moving away from the Officials, who, they argued, were too prepared to compromise with the British. The Officials (OIRA), who were Marxist-Leninist, believed that they could use the electoral process to gain power. But the Provisionals (PIRA) violently disagreed with this and felt they could only achieve a united Ireland through armed revolution. Ironically, PIRA, who are now largely Marxist, presently have a policy of standing at local and general elections while at the same time continuing to employ terrorism.

The first place the IRA went for help to get weapons was the Irish Republic. Not only did the IRA have a network of supporters in place there but the Republic represented a safe haven for them, a place where they could import arms, hide them and then move them over the border in small quantities at their leisure.

In early 1970, a leading member of the Belfast Brigade of the IRA, John Kelly, organised a shipment of $50,000 of arms including 500 pistols and 180,000 rounds of ammunition, from Vienna. They were to be flown in to Dublin airport and after clearance through customs would be hidden in the Republic. British intelligence heard about the deal and alerted Jack Lynch, the Irish Prime Minister. The arms were intercepted and Kelly was arrested along with Neil Blaney, a member of Lynch's cabinet, and Charles Haughey, then the Irish Finance Minister. Lynch fired Blaney but both he and Haughey were acquitted at their trial. Charles Haughey is now Prime Minister of Ireland and supports efforts by both the Irish and British governments to fight the IRA.

From the start, the IRA had to obtain their weapons from abroad. Their legendary theft at Gough Barracks was an isolated incident never to be repeated. They did manage to steal the occasional weapon but never enough to arm their forces. To become a credible fighting force they needed plenty of guns and explosives coming in regularly. In fact, they never achieved regularity and instead had to rely on single operations along untested supply lines. This in turn led to serious security problems as the international arms market – which is populated almost entirely by men to whom discretion and loyalty are unusual attributes – had been well penetrated by western intelligence services.

Unlike many of the other terrorist groups that came into prominence in the late 1960s and early 1970s, in the beginning the IRA was never part of the international terrorist network. To other European groups such as the West German Red Army Faction or the Italian Red Brigades whose goals were difficult to understand, the IRA itself has always tended to be very insular and single-minded. They are suspicious of foreigners and uncomfortable abroad. So, contrary to what some commentators have suggested, the IRA have never established any meaningful links with other terrorist groups that have helped them with arms and they have never received any cash, support or training from the Soviet Union.

Until recently, the main source of outside support, particularly in the early days, came from elements in the United States. In 1970 there were 290,000 people living in the United States who had been born in Ireland and a further 15,000,000 Americans who claimed Irish descent. These Irish-Americans had a highly romanticised view of Ireland which had little to do with the dirty little war beginning in the slums of Belfast and Londonderry. But the IRA played the American card well and managed to portray the struggle as a fight against British colonialism, an argument which apparently struck a sympathetic chord with many Americans.

The most significant force in Irish American politics is Noraid – Irish Northern Aid, which was established in New York in 1969 by Michael Flannery, a veteran Republican who had emigrated to the United States in 1927 after spending several years in jail for pro-IRA activities. Noraid was officially established to raise money for humanitarian purposes, to relieve the suffering of Catholics hit by the war with the British. The organisation collected funds in bars and clubs around America and in a series of fund-raising events. It also acted as a focus for much of the anti-British sentiment among Irish-Americans.

Noraid swiftly grew to become a nationwide organisation with ninety-two chapters. As it became established, a myth grew up that Noraid was the key organisation that was underwriting the IRA. Without its support and the support of Americans, the IRA would collapse for lack of funds and arms. It was clearly in the interests of the IRA to perpetuate this myth: it showed that they were supported by the world's biggest democracy. At the same time, since the British government was anxious to undercut any potential broad support in the US Congress or even from an American president to support the IRA, they played up Noraid's significance and used the organisation as a stick with which to beat successive US administrations for allowing Noraid to support terrorism.

In fact, the organisation has never been that important in IRA affairs. They have never contributed more than around $250,000 and today out of an annual budget of around $7m, Noraid will contribute less than $100,000.

But, in the early days, Noraid did play a key role in getting arms through to PIRA. A large shipment arrived in 1970 from Philadelphia which for the first time included AR–16 5.56mm rifles. This was the Armalite which became part of IRA legend. With its twenty-round magazine, its great accuracy, and the ability of some ammunition to penetrate light armour, it gave the PIRA a significant increase in capability. The AR–16 in its Colt Commander version has a folding stock and is easily concealed, another reason why it was so popular. This particular weapon had not proved popular with the American military and was an interesting early example of how arms dealers will always find an alternative market for a particular weapon.

As with anything of permanence in the IRA, the Armalite quickly became part of the folklore, as is evident from a thirty-yard long inscription on the walls of Derry above the Bogside: 'God made the Catholics, but the Armalite made them equal'.

Eleven years after that first shipment, the Armalite, although superseded by other more effective weapons, was still playing its part. In Dublin in 1981, at the annual conference of Sinn Fein, the IRA's political wing, Gerry Adams, the then chief of staff and Sinn Fein vice-president, argued for a new strategy that combined terrorism with political campaigning. The strategy, agreed by the conference, was supported by one of Adams's close confidantes, Danny Morrison. 'Will anyone here object if, with a ballot paper in this hand and an Armalite in this hand, we take power in Ireland?'

But in the early days of the developing terrorist organisation, the arguments were not so sophisticated. All that mattered to the IRA was getting hold of as many guns and explosives as possible, of whatever kind, from whatever source. From 1970 on, cash was never a serious problem. Money came in from America (not only via Noraid) and was also raised locally by the terrorists, either from their own supporters or, more commonly, from Mafia-style operations such as protection rackets, bank robberies and kidnapping.

For the British, intercepting the arms was clearly a priority. Dealing with the IRA abroad was the responsibility of both the Security Service (MI5) and the Secret Intelligence Service (MI6). From the beginning informers were cultivated inside the IRA and British intelligence also attempted to infiltrate sources inside the organisation.

For many years the British have operated at least two very senior sources in the organisation who have provided valuable intelligence. But, over the years, the IRA has taken steps to counter these efforts by improving its security. The most important of these was the establishment of the complex cell structure where complete knowledge is restricted to a few — and few, if anyone, even senior officials in Dublin, have all the information. This has made the work of informers much more difficult as any specific leak is easier to trace.

To keep the edge in the war, various other covert methods have been used. For example, in the early 1970s British intelligence actually set up arms buys, and those stings, combined with intelligence supplied by informers, led to a number of arms shipments being intercepted.

In September 1971, British intelligence learned that David O'Connell, then the 33-year-old chief of staff of the PIRA, had left his usual haunts in Dublin for the European mainland. He was followed by the British and tracked first to Czechoslovakia and then to Amsterdam, where he stayed for six days. He was seen meeting with Ernest Koenig, an American arms dealer, and intercepted telephone conversations suggested that a major shipment of arms was on its way from Czechoslovakia to Dublin. In October, a 20-year-old Dakota transport aircraft flew in to Amsterdam airport. The Dutch police searched the aircraft and opened crates labelled as 'machinery'. Inside they found 104 tons of arms including anti-tank grenade launchers, automatic rifles, hand grenades, light machine guns and ammunition. It was a massive haul that had been purchased in Czechoslovakia and paid for by IRA funds brought over from the United States.

Other shipments at this time were allowed to go through after they had been doctored by British intelligence. A favoured trick was to allow the weapons to pass to the IRA while planting bugs that British intelligence could track to the hidden arms dump and even to the point where the weapon would actually be used.

These successes by British intelligence hampered the flow

of weapons to the PIRA but inevitably too many weapons got through the net. Supply outstripped the rate of recovery and weapons came in small numbers from the United States and detonators arrived from the same source – some of them from sympathisers working on building a tunnel in New York – since at that time, terrorism was not considered a significant worldwide problem and control of explosive stores at industrial sites was lax. Today, some stores are carefully monitored and explosives are marked so that forensic scientists can track the source. However, detonators and detonating cord are still easily accessible and much is smuggled in from Canada.

The IRA have also proved adept at making the best use of their own resources. According to British security sources, IRA bomb-making went through four distinct phases.

At the beginning of their campaign in 1971–2 they managed to obtain large amounts of commercial explosives from industrial sites and manufacturers in the Irish Republic. After security in the Republic was tightened, the terrorists turned to agricultural chemicals, which were widely available in the farming community, as a new source. In 1972, the IRA stepped up their bombing campaign using a volatile mix of ammonium nitrate and fuel oil, known as ANFO, and sodium chlorate and nitro benzine, known as CO-OP. By July 1972, the terrorists were using 50 tons of these mixtures a month, an enormous quantity that even the IRA had difficulty in sustaining. They continued to use commercial gelignite for booby traps, letter bombs and operations on the British mainland or against the British army in Germany.

In the five years up to 1978, the PIRA continued to refine their improvised explosives and managed to significantly reduce the size of bombs while achieving the same effect. In 1975 they introduced the blast incendiary, using home-made explosives mixed with or surrounded by petrol.

In 1986, the terrorists received their first shipment of Semtex explosive which is now used by PIRA for booby traps, small mines, filling for home-made grenades and mortars and small bombs that can be planted by hand. ANFO and a mixture of ammonium nitrate and nitro benzine, known as ANNI, is still used for large mines and car bombs.

Using their own resources, PIRA is able to manufacture a number of sophisticated weapons including large and medium mortars, hand grenades, anti-armour hollow charged projectiles, mechanical and electronic time and power units with settings that range from two minutes to 48 days, mercury fulminate detonators, pressure sensitive mines, cassette incendiary devices, booby trap car bombs, radio control and command wire bombs and unique booby trap systems.

Most terrorist organisations either manage to find regular sources of weapons or have a fairly low requirement. An organisation like the PLO, which needs to arm a large fighting force of several thousand men as well as to supply active terrorists with bombs and light weapons, has consistently had the support of various Arab nations and has been rich enough to buy its arms on the black market, generally from Eastern Europe.

Smaller terrorist organisations, like the Red Army Faction in Germany, have less than one hundred active members and need very few arms. Those that they need they can find in Europe, where the borders are lightly policed and moving weapons around is relatively easy.

The IRA are different. They are fighting a low intensity conflict that in scale falls between the PLO and the RAF. They have around three hundred active members and are opposed by a dedicated and professional police force as well as the considerable resources of the British army. They have an additional problem in that Ireland is surrounded by sea and any weapons arriving must do so initially by sea or air, both of which are well patrolled.

It has been a constant struggle, therefore, for the IRA to achieve a regular source of modern weapons with which to carry on the war. For most of the past twenty-two years, they have had enough weapons to fight, but not enough weapons to fight at the level they want. For example, from the early 1970s they have tried to buy a weapon, preferably a guided missile, able to shoot down British army helicopters. Control of the air gives the army high mobility and its effective use of helicopters provides it with an aerial reconnaissance platform that the IRA find difficult to combat. But until recently each attempt by the IRA to get surface-to-air missiles has been detected either by British intelligence or by the Americans.

The Provisionals have also been unable to take advantage of major technological advances that have been made in weapons in the past twenty years. Until recently they have still been using only rifles and explosives and this to some extent has dictated their tactics. In turn, this has made the work of the counter terrorists much easier.

Two arms smuggling operations organised by PIRA are worth looking at in some detail. One failed and the other proved stunningly successful. The first shows how inept the organisation was in its early days and the second shows why British intelligence and the British army now regard the IRA as one of the best equipped and most sophisticated terrorist organisations in the world.

Both these operations were made possible through the goodwill of one man, Colonel Muammar Gadaffi of Libya.

2

Courting the Colonel

Muammar Gadaffi was born in the family tent in the desert south of Sirte in Libya. Unlike his parents, Gadaffi was taught to read and write and after joining the Libyan Military Academy in 1964 was sent on a signals course to Britain. He had already gained something of a reputation as a revolutionary and it is hardly surprising that he found the course in Britain somewhat stifling – but despite later events, the experience does not seem to have made him particularly anti-British.[1]

Gadaffi came to power in a revolution that deposed King Idris in 1969. Only twenty-seven years old, he ruled over a country that had enormous oil reserves and over a population that was still largely feudal. Gadaffi is a devout Moslem and a firm supporter of the rights of the Palestinian people. He quickly embraced the cause of the Palestine Liberation Organisation and his rhetoric led other terrorist organisations to come knocking on his door for cash and arms.

Gadaffi viewed these supplicants with enthusiasm. He was young enough to believe he could change the world and sufficiently inexperienced to believe he could bring the world round to his particular brand of revolutionary theory by doling out guns to those who claimed to support revolution. In those early days, he appears to have been unable to distinguish between one terrorist organisation and another. As long as a group espoused the overthrow of imperialism then it was worthy of support.

One of the first contacts with Gadaffi was made by Brian

Keenan, a far-sighted and experienced IRA leader who travelled to Tripoli in early 1972. He received an enthusiastic welcome from Gadaffi who promised the IRA both cash and arms. He later described his support for the IRA in these terms: 'If we assist the Irish people it is simply because we see here a small people still under the yoke of Great Britain and fighting to free themselves from it. And it must also be remembered that the revolutionaries of the Irish Republican Army are striking, and striking hard, at the power which has humiliated the Arabs for centuries.'[2]

With the ground prepared by Keenan, the IRA decided to organise a major shipment of arms to Ireland from Libya. They set up a special unit which included Joe Cahill, a former head of the Belfast Brigade of the IRA and then the man in charge of finances, and David O'Connell, the mastermind of the abortive smuggling operation that had collapsed in Amsterdam two years before.

That two such prominent and well-known PIRA members were involved in such an important mission was a measure of the IRA's incompetence in those early days. Almost from the moment the mission began, British intelligence were aware of it and knew the identity of those involved. Such naivety, which gave the IRA a reputation for amateurishness, would soon be replaced by a new hard-headed professionalism.

But in January 1973, O'Connell travelled personally to Hamburg for a meeting with a German arms dealer called Gunter Leinhauser. The IRA had tried to use the German before as an intermediary to buy arms from Czechoslovakia, but, after their experience with the Amsterdam shipment two years earlier, the Czechs had refused to deal. Now with Keenan having prepared the ground, O'Connell had a new source for the arms but no method of transporting them. Leinhauser agreed to supply his own ship, the *Claudia*, to transport the arms from Libya to Ireland for a flat fee of $35,000: $20,000 in advance and the balance on delivery.[3]

The *Claudia* was a 298-ton coaster registered in Cyprus and owned by the Cypriot company of Giromar which in turn was 90 per cent owned by Leinhauser's wife, Marlene, who ran a small stationery and toy shop in St Ingert, Saarland. The remaining 10 per cent was owned by a West German businessman, Peter Mulak.

At the time O'Connell travelled to Hamburg, the *Claudia* was doing a brisk business selling duty free cigarettes in international waters in the Mediterranean. While the ship finished selling her cargo, O'Connell flew to Tunis with Leinhauser where they had made reservations at the Hotel Africa. On March 12, the *Claudia* put in to Tunis where the ship's captain was briefed to set sail for Tripoli. O'Connell flew on ahead and met up with Joe Cahill and two other IRA men, Sean Garvey and Gerald Murphy, who had come along as guards.

The *Claudia* arrived in Tripoli harbour at 11 am on March 15 and twenty-five crates of arms were loaded from a Libyan army truck onto her later that day. Both O'Connell and Cahill arrived in a chauffeur driven limousine to supervise the loading from the quayside.

The *Claudia* set sail from Tripoli before dawn the next day and headed west towards Gibraltar. She passed through the Straits on March 21 under the watchful eyes of the British Royal Navy. She was then under constant observation by a Royal Navy submarine as she made her way up the Bay of Biscay. At one stage during the journey Cahill actually spotted the submarine's periscope but was reassured by the *Claudia*'s skipper who told him that it was probably that of a Soviet vessel.

The British government now alerted the Irish that a major arms shipment was coming their way. All leave was cancelled at the Irish naval base at Haulbowline near Cork. On Saturday, March 24, the minesweeper *Fola* left harbour to be followed the next day by the minesweeper *Grainne* and the fishery protection vessel *Deirdre*.

The IRA plan called for the *Claudia*'s cargo to be transferred to a smaller boat that would land the arms at Muggles

Bay near Waterford. But, when the *Claudia* actually arrived on Tuesday, the weather was too rough to carry out any transfers of the cargo. For the next twelve hours the *Claudia* steamed back and forth in international waters under the constant observation of the Irish Navy and RAF surveillance aircraft from St Mawgan in Cornwall.

During the night the weather moderated, and a launch came out to meet the *Claudia*. O'Connell returned to his cabin and emerged with a black case which the British now believe was filled with cash from Gadaffi. O'Connell boarded the launch which immediately headed for the shore at speed. On board the *Claudia*, the crew had picked up four returns on the radar and they watched two of the Irish navy ships they represented turn to chase the launch. However, the Irish vessels were too deep-draughted to go close inshore and before the navy had time to launch one of their own small boats, O'Connell had landed and made good his escape with the black case.

It was now clear to the IRA that their mission had been compromised but even so Cahill ordered the *Claudia*'s skipper to move inshore to rendezvous with a launch owned by the Dungarvon Boat Company, a local sea angling group. The two ships were in the middle of transferring the cargo when the Irish navy moved in. After firing a warning shot both the launch and the *Claudia* and their crews were arrested and taken to Haulbowline.

On board the *Claudia*, the Irish discovered five tons of weapons including 200 AKM 7.62mm assault rifles, 50 7.62 AKM rifles, 243 handguns, 100 anti-tank mines, 100 anti-personnel mines, 500 RG4 grenades, 20,000 rounds of ammunition and 600 lb of TNT. It was the biggest consignment to date intercepted by the British and the Irish, and its loss was a serious blow to the IRA.

Today Joe Cahill believes the mission was betrayed by the *Claudia*'s skipper who he alleges was in touch with British intelligence. This is typically unrealistic. In fact, security for the whole operation had been a disaster. Not only had the

IRA sent abroad two of their most well-known figures but they had allowed them to appear in public with known arms dealers. They had then personally travelled to Tripoli to oversee the arms shipments. Such 'hands-on' management is directly contrary to standard operational security and it is hardly surprising that British intelligence was plugged in to the operation from the start.

As Cahill now admits, the interception of the arms was a disaster. 'At that time, the sources of weapons in Ireland had dried up and we needed to look further afield. The IRA depended on those arms and we believed that this was a new market. We pinned a lot of faith on those particular weapons and it took the IRA a long time to get over it.'[4]

The interception of the arms was a disappointment to Gadaffi as well: he saw the postponement of his dream of bringing about a successful revolution in Ireland. His relations with the IRA now collapsed into something close to farce. In 1974, impressed by a strike in Northern Ireland organised by the Protestant Ulster Workers' Council which had reminded him of the bloodless coup that brought him to power, Gadaffi invited a delegation from the Ulster Defence Association to visit Tripoli to discuss Libyan economic assistance to the province. When news of this reached the IRA, they immediately sent their own delegation to argue the Catholic cause. To Gadaffi, who clearly had a very simplistic view of the Ulster situation, a swift history lesson from committed Protestants and Catholics must have been very confusing. He clearly found it all too difficult and the result was that he severed all contact with the IRA for more than ten years.

It took the IRA four years to open up new supplies of arms from the United States, the Middle East and Europe. But these supplies were never reliable and they never managed to establish an effective arms network. What they needed was one supplier who, behind the backs of British intelligence would give them what they needed. Only then could they hope to get the firepower they needed to put the British government on the defensive.

3

The Semtex Revolution

To the French customs service, Operation Cracker was just another routine patrol aimed at the drugs smugglers bringing hashish by sea from North Africa to France. On such missions, a spotter plane equipped with high resolution photographic equipment works in tandem with a well-armed fast patrol boat.

On the evening of October 27, 1986, the plane flew over a small ship heading north from Spain into the Bay of Biscay towards Ushant at the northwest tip of France. The aircraft flew low over the vessel to take photographs and record its name, the *Eksund*. Checks back at customs headquarters in Nantes showed that the 237-ton *Eksund* was registered to Coral Springs Navigation, a previously unknown Panamanian company.[1]

The following day, the plane returned and noticed that the *Eksund* had changed direction and was now heading on a northerly route to the west of normal shipping lanes. Its present course would take it to the Scilly Islands off Britain's southwest coast and then on to Ireland. Further checks on the ship revealed that she had left Malta on October 11 heading for Gibraltar but she had never arrived. Clearly, the vessel had stopped off somewhere along the way and French customs believed that the diversion might have been to load a cargo of drugs.

At 2pm on Friday October 30, French customs again flew over the vessel. The *Eksund* had changed course again to head up the English Channel. But she was now inside French waters heading for the small French port of Roscoff. 'We saw some movement on the deck. The hold was open and the crew were preparing to launch a dinghy,' said Alain Nicholas, the director of operations at the Customs HQ in Nantes.

A fast patrol boat from the nearby port of Lezardrieux, which had been shadowing the *Eksund*, was ordered to board her. Maujis Pascal, the second-in-command of the French vessel, boarded the *Eksund* with two other armed customs men. According to Pascal, the *Eksund*'s crew were taken completely by surprise. 'First when we came onto the bridge we found five persons. Three of the persons had diving suits and one of the three had a battledress on underneath his diving suit.' Pascal asked to see the ship's log book and cargo manifest and when he was told they did not exist, he ordered the vessel into Roscoff.

At nine that night, the French customs began a search of the boat. When the hold was opened, they found twelve bundles of explosives connected by wire to a detonator with a timing device. By the bridge underneath a pile of lifejackets there were five cocked and loaded AK-47 Kalashnikov automatic rifles and a machine gun.

But the real find was in the hold. Loaded in crates marked 'Libyan Armed Forces' were enough weapons to equip a small army, which was precisely their buyer's intention. The French unloaded 20 Surface to Air (SAM) 7 missiles, 1,000 AK-47 assault rifles, 10 Soviet 12.7mm Kalashnikov machine guns with ammunition and anti-aircraft mounts, 1,000 82mm mortar rounds, 120 RPG–7 portable rocket launchers, 3,000 rounds of ammunition for an American-made 106mm M40 recoil-less rifle, up to 100 tons of ammunition and 2 tons of Semtex explosives with detonators and fuses. The 110 tons of weapons had a total value of around $5m.

The French customs men, expecting to find a relatively innocuous haul of drugs were astonished and baffled. They had received no intelligence from any source suggesting that an illegal arms shipment was in the offing. Further inspection of the *Eksund* revealed that the customs men had boarded just before she was about to be scuttled. In between originally being spotted by the customs plane, the crew had first tried to escape by moving outside the main shipping lanes and then when they saw the aircraft flying over them once more had panicked and headed for the French coast. On the way they had carefully erased the ship's name from her bow and stern, destroyed all documentation and lashed down the liferafts. The charges had been laid to scuttle the vessel and they were about to launch the one remaining liferaft, with its name changed to the *Zoe II*, before setting the timer on the explosives when the French moved in. An hour or two later, all trace of the *Eksund* would have vanished and the crew would have disappeared into the French countryside.

Under questioning, the crew gave their names as Adrian Hopkins, 49, of Blackberry Lane, Delgany, near Greystones, Bray, Co. Wicklow, Eire; Henry Cairns, 44, also of Bray described as a 'bookseller'; William Finn, 43 of Co. Mayo; Denis Boyle, 42 and Edward Friel, 34, both of Co. Donegal.

As soon as the Irish connection was known and the arms discovered, the French alerted both the British and the Irish. The Irish police immediately sent Assistant Commissioner Eugene Crowley, the head of Garda intelligence and security and Chief Superintendent Tom Kelly to France to interrogate the suspects.

For the British Security Service, whose responsibility it is to gather information on such arms smuggling operations, news of the *Eksund*'s cargo was a complete surprise. They had received no earlier intelligence of any kind suggesting that such a massive shipment was on its way. They did not even have any hard information that the IRA had renewed its links with Colonel Gadaffi. The closest they had come to any such evidence was a close analysis of Gadaffi's speeches, which suggested a new support for the IRA. But this was simply intelligence analysis; there had been no real information.

The Security Service despatched their own representative to France and in a matter of hours a disturbing story began to emerge, particularly from Adrian Hopkins who talked freely to his captors.

The Irish police discovered that Boyle, Friel and Finn were in fact James Coll of Rossnakill, Fanad, Co. Donegal; James Doherty from Cruit Island, Burtonport, Co. Donegal and Gabriel Cleary from Priorstown, near Tallaght not far from Dublin. Boyle and Friel were both using false Irish passports which were part of a batch of one hundred stolen in 1984 by an IRA mole working in Iveagh House, headquarters of the Irish Ministry of Foreign Affairs. All the passports were thought to be in the hands of the Provisional IRA. Other passports from the same batch had been found in a Glasgow safe house being used in 1985 by an IRA team on a bombing mission in Britain.

In 1981, Doherty had been detained and questioned for forty-eight hours at Ballyshannon in the Irish Republic under the Offences Against the State Act after police found a major IRA training camp and arms dump on Cruit Island. Boxes of ammunition, twelve rifles, radio sets and ammunition were found and Doherty, who was known locally for his IRA sympathies, was pulled in. But police had no real evidence to link him to the find and he was released. For three months prior to his capture, Doherty had not been seen around his usual haunts. To anyone who asked he had 'got a job in Cairo working on the buildings'.

James Coll, a trained electrician, had moved to Eire from Coleraine twenty years before and had no known links with terrorists.

But the real surprise among the crew was Gabriel Cleary. A known IRA terrorist, Cleary had last been in the hands of the Irish police in May 1977 when he appeared before the Special Criminal Court in Dublin charged with possessing two tons of high explosive found in a cache near Athy in Co. Kildare. However, Cleary had not been convicted because of a lack of technical evidence.

After the case, he moved swiftly up the IRA ranks until at the time of the *Eksund* seizure he was a member of the PIRA

headquarters staff in Dublin as director of engineering. Cleary was responsible for acquiring arms for PIRA and ensuring the men received training on the modern weapons he shipped to the Republic.

Ironically, he was only on board the *Eksund* because he was returning from a training mission in Libya where he had learned how to fire the SAM–7 missiles that were in the ship's hold. His capture meant the IRA still had no one able to train their men in the use of a piece of equipment they had recently acquired, after seeking it for nearly twenty years.

Under questioning the IRA men, who are trained to resist interrogation as a matter of routine, refused to say much. But Adrian Hopkins, the *Eksund*'s skipper, was the hired hand and talked freely. As his story unfolded, his listeners realised that they were hearing a tale of arms smuggling on a scale they would not have believed possible; of an IRA mission that had been stunningly successful, until this final journey; and of renewed support for the IRA from Colonel Gadaffi who in consequence has transformed the military capability of the IRA for the rest of this century.

Exactly when and how Gadaffi renewed his contacts with the IRA is still not known. However, British intelligence believe that the most likely cause was the shooting of Police-woman Yvonne Fletcher on April 17, 1984. She was gunned down in St James Square, London after police had been alerted by a security guard who saw Libyan diplomats carrying rifles into the People's Bureau, only partly hidden inside blankets.

Fletcher was killed without warning by a machine gun fired by a diplomat inside the bureau. The British government reacted swiftly and expelled all the Libyan diplomats and cut off diplomatic relations. At the same time, there was an outpouring of fierce criticism by the British media against the Gadaffi regime. Exhibiting the rather childlike emotions that are characteristic of Gadaffi, he seems to have decided to punish Britain for criticising him and his diplomats.

Gadaffi sent a message to the PIRA offering arms and cash.

Remembering their previous experience with Gadaffi and the ill-fated *Claudia*, the IRA were not immediately enthusiastic about the Gadaffi offer. They already had other plans in hand to smuggle one of the biggest arms shipments of all time into the Republic, from the United States. But in September, after a joint intelligence operation involving the British and Americans, the *Marita Ann* from the US was seized by the Irish navy off the coast of County Kerry. On board were 156 tons of arms and at a stroke yet another IRA attempt to equip themselves with modern weapons had been thwarted.

Immediately after that disaster, the IRA army council in Dublin decided to take Gadaffi up on his offer. But, this time, security had to be paramount.

Cleary was given control of the operation and charged with liaising with the Libyans, recruiting his team and preparing hiding places for the weapons in the Irish Republic. He handled the operation brilliantly. His contact in Libya was Colonel Nasser Al Ashour, a senior officer in Libyan intelligence. Al Ashour arranged all the arms shipments and was always on hand whenever any arms were handed over to Cleary.

The members of Cleary's small cell were all from the south and none of them was apparently active in the IRA. Cleary had once lived in Bray, Hopkins's home town and it may have been there that the two first met.

On the surface, Adrian Hopkins, later to serve as the *Eksund*'s skipper, was an unlikely confederate. In 1981, his travel company, Bray Travel, had gone bankrupt with debts of more than $1.5m leaving hundreds of holidaymakers stranded abroad. Hopkins then went into business buying and selling boats. At no time was he thought by the British to be involved with the IRA and it was certainly his clean record combined with his knowledge of boats that made him an attractive recruit to Cleary.

From late 1985, it was Hopkins who was the front man for all the IRA operations. The first vessel he bought in June 1985 was a 65ft Irish fishing boat, the *Casamara* at a cost of

$70,000. The ship had been built at Arklow, in Co. Wicklow, fifty miles south of Dublin, but Hopkins moved her to St Katherine's Dock in London telling anyone who was interested that he was planning to use her to cross the Atlantic.

In August, the *Casamara* sailed for Malta where three IRA crewmen joined her. On August 9, the ship left Valetta harbour and rendezvous-ed with a Libyan ship five miles off the island of Gozo. Seven tons of arms were taken on board, including AK-47 semi-automatic rifles and a consignment of pistols. The ship off-loaded the arms in Ireland at Road Stone Pier inside a small bay at Clogger Strand just south of Arklow.

As part of the planning for the operation, Cleary had gained the support of a local farmer who in the first instance supplied vehicles to distribute the arms to pre-arranged hiding places around the Republic.

After dropping off the arms the *Casamara* sailed a mile up the coast and docked at Arklow. The customs there had picked up some local gossip about the ship and its skipper and suspected that she might be involved in running drugs. They boarded the ship and searched her but found nothing. Even so, she was placed on a customs 'watch' list of suspect vessels. It was here that the first intelligence failure occurred. There was apparently no exchange of information between the Irish customs and the Garda, so the Garda never heard about the customs' suspicions regarding the vessel and its crew. If they had, it may be that these suspicions, when pieced together with other intelligence, would have hardened into certain knowledge about arms smuggling.

The success of the first, trial, run encouraged the IRA and the Libyans to try again. In October 1985 the identical trip was repeated, this time with ten tons of arms, including one hundred AK-47s, 10 machine guns, some Webley revolvers and one hundred boxes of ammunition. Once again the arms were successfully offloaded at Clogger Strand.

Until now the weapons supplied by the Libyans had been pretty unexciting: old, and with none of the sophisticated missiles or explosives that the IRA really wanted. The

Libyans kept promising such modern equipment but failing to deliver. Then, in April 1986, the Americans bombed Tripoli in retaliation for Gadaffi's involvement with terrorism, and British Prime Minister Margaret Thatcher had actively supported the American bombing missions by allowing US jets to take off from bases in Britain. Once again, Gadaffi responded swiftly.

In July 1986, the *Casamara* set off once again from Malta for its rendezvous off Gozo with the Libyan arms shipment watched over by Colonel Al Ashour. But, for this trip, Hopkins had changed the name of the *Casamara* to the *Kula* and, to confuse the authorities further, he had re-registered it in Panama. This time, Hopkins collected fourteen tons of weapons, including 4 SAM-7 ground to air missiles.

Cleary was told by Al Ashour that next time they could have as many arms as they wanted but they would need a bigger boat.

In Norway, Hopkins bought a former oil-rig servicing ship, the *Sjamor*, for $70,000 and sailed it to Malta where it was renamed the *Villa* and registered in Panama. The *Villa* left Malta on October 6, 1986 and met up with the Libyan mother ship just off Tripoli. More than 105 tons of arms were transferred including SAM-7s, several tons of Semtex explosives, pistols, heavy machine guns and rocket propelled grenades. It was probably the biggest single arms shipment ever received by the IRA, and when the ship reached Clogger Strand there were around thirty men waiting with a fleet of trucks to unload the weapons through the night and distribute them to their hiding places. Once again, Cleary demonstrated how effective his security was. In the past such large numbers of people would inevitably have led to a breach of security. In this case, not a whisper of the shipments reached the authorities.

Once again, the Libyans promised Cleary even more arms if he could find a boat big enough to carry them. That winter the *Villa* stayed in the Dublin port of Howth and then sailed to Malta in April 1987. The previous month, Hopkins had contacted Bengt Hellberg, a reputable Swedish ship broker, with a story that he needed a merchant ship to trade in the shallow waters in Nigeria. In fact, a shallow draught was essential if the ship was to enter the bay at Clogger Strand.

Hellberg sent out a telex to his brokerage clients: 'Do you know of a 250-ton shallow draft cargo freighter suitable for use on rivers of West Africa?'

On May 2, 1987, Hopkins flew to Stockholm to finalise the purchase of the 50-year-old 237-ton *Eksund* for $75,000.

'Hopkins told me he planned to ply general cargo on the rivers of Nigeria. The story struck me as a bit odd – particularly when he spent $13,000 replacing the ship's navigational instruments with a sophisticated satellite system,' said the boat's former owner Bruno Gustavsson, when questioned a few months later.

The vessel sailed from Sweden for Malta skippered by Iain Kerr Hunter, a professional delivery captain from Midlothian in Scotland. Six days out, the engine's cooling system broke down and the ship put into Lowestoft, Suffolk for repairs. A local firm of marine engineers fixed the problem and on August 12, the *Eksund* sailed down the coast to Shoreham in Sussex to collect a cargo sent by Hopkins. The container held two rubber dinghies, three outboard motors and block and tackle. The ship then headed for the Mediterranean arriving in Gibraltar on August 15 and Malta on August 27. The crew then left the ship and Hopkins took command.

During the first week in October, the IRA crew arrived in Malta to join Hopkins. On October 12 the *Eksund* left for Tripoli where she arrived two days later. The vessel was escorted to the military section of the harbour where she was loaded with her cargo under cover of darkness. She then sailed for Clogger Bay only to be intercepted by a chance encounter with a French anti-drug operation.

In the ten days immediately following the capture of the *Eksund* Irish police launched the biggest search for arms ever seen in the country. More than 50,000 houses were searched, 7,573 under warrant and 42,559 without. Also, 164 cruisers on the River Shannon and 775 caravans were searched without a warrant. A total of 33 people were arrested and five of those were charged with various minor offences. The total haul from this massive operation was hardly significant: 22 rifles, 15 revolvers, 13 shotguns, 4,312 cartridges, 2,277 bullets, 43 detonators, 2 timing devices, 1cwt of suspected explosive mix, 7 gas cylinders of the type used in mortars and 25 cylinder bombs.

One of the first places to have been raided was the farm of Gabriel Gleeson whose land fronts on to the beach at Clogger Strand. In 1986, Gleeson had built a new silage pit beneath a barn on his property with the aid of a government grant, and the police suspected that the arms may have been stored there before being moved out to other hiding places. However, nothing was found at the farm.

Over the next few months a number of arms caches were discovered throughout Ireland. In the past, most IRA arms caches had been crude: plastic bags filled with weapons and buried in a dustbin or hidden in the cellar of a house. What made these caches particularly significant was that they had clearly been well constructed and designed to store weapons for a long time. In one case the underground bunker had been fitted with wooden shelves and electric light. Leading off the central chamber was a 70-foot tunnel with a room at the far end for storing explosives.

Such sophistication was the hallmark of all stages of the arms smuggling operation from Libya. From the start, the smuggling had been organised so that security was absolute. For nearly three years the IRA had been buying boats, travelling in and out of Libya, shipping weapons to Ireland and moving them around the country, and in all this time, not a hint of what was going on had been picked up in Libya – surely the most well observed country in the world – or in Ireland by British intelligence. This was a significant failure for the British and the success of the operation was testimony to just how far the terrorist organisation had evolved since its crude operations back in the 1970s. And since the overall structure of the PIRA had clearly improved to match the calibre of its average terrorist, the 120 tons or so of modern arms that did get through from Libya were obviously going to make a significant difference to their military prowess.

There are three interesting aspects to the weapons shipments. First, much of the equipment that was supplied appeared to be unsuitable for the IRA. For example, they had no need for M40 ammunition as they did not have a weapon suitable for the shells and anyway nor would they wish to have such a bulky, old-fashioned item in their armoury. To the intelligence analysts poring over the lists they had carefully put together it appeared, in fact, that the Libyans had given the IRA a job lot. It was as if Colonel Al Ashour had walked into the warehouse in the military section of Tripoli harbour, pointed to a pile of surplus odds and ends in the corner and told the dockyard workers to load whatever was under the tarpaulins on board the IRA ship.

Second, while much of the equipment, such as the AK–47s, was useful, it was only the SAM–7 ground to air missiles that really gave the IRA a significant weapon to tackle the much hated helicopters. Immediately after the British realised that the IRA might have the SAMs, all British aircraft flying in Northern Ireland were fitted with electronic and other decoy systems designed to confuse the SAM's heat-seeking guidance system. These included the US-made Sanders AN/ALQ–144 infra-red counter-measure system which uses flares and jamming to decoy the missile. This system is linked to the Tracor AN/ALE–40 chaff dispenser.

The IRA have not yet used their SAMs, in part because Cleary, the only man with the training, has been in jail. However, others in the IRA have now been trained in their use and the British expect them to be used in the near future.

Finally, the IRA received several tons of what is in many respects the perfect terrorist weapon – Semtex high explosive. It is highly explosive, cheap, virtually undetectable, can be moulded to fit any shape and can be set off using a simple detonator. It is hardly surprising that it has become the weapon of preference for every major terrorist group in the world.

The explosive is manufactured by the Czechoslovakian government at Pardubice, sixty miles east of Prague. The factory first produced the explosive for military and civilian use at the end of the 1960s, and by the beginning of the 1970s it was being sold outside the Warsaw Pact. Today it has been sold all over the world, including Africa, Central and South America and the Far East.

Semtex was first used in Northern Ireland in late 1976 when a booby trap bomb planted by the Irish National Liberation Army was discovered in Londonderry. Since then the IRA have used the explosive regularly, but the Libyan shipments have allowed them to make it their main explosive of preference. They now have sufficient stocks to last them for many years.

But all the weapons in the world are only as good as the people that use them. Many terrorist organisations have proved to be inept with their weapons, blowing themselves up or missing their targets. The IRA, too, have made their share of mistakes but those who have worked against them have nothing but respect for their military expertise.

The marriage of Libyan arms with IRA skills makes, quite literally, a deadly combination.

On Sunday, March 6, 1988, four members of the Special Air Service shot dead three IRA terrorists in the streets of Gibraltar. The terrorists had planned to plant a bomb on the island timed to explode as the band of the Royal Anglian Regiment conducted their regular Tuesday morning parade in the main square.

Some exceptionally good intelligence enabled the British to foil the plot, and the terrorists were killed while the SAS men were attempting to arrest them.

The shootings proved to be one of the most controversial incidents in the history of the long war between the British security forces and the IRA. There were allegations that the soldiers had been sent to murder the terrorists – allegations which were unfounded. However, even an exhaustive inquest failed to allay the suspicions of those who saw a British government conspiracy to 'shoot to kill' IRA terrorists.

Those who understand how today's British intelligence and the SAS work realised that these allegations were nonsense. But deeper questions did remain unanswered.

Gibraltar was an extraordinary target for the IRA to choose. It was a long way outside their normal area of operations which was generally restricted to Northern Ireland, England and West Germany.

The IRA had made a number of serious mistakes in the months prior to Gibraltar where innocent civilians, many of them Catholics, had been killed. Yet Gibraltar would have caused extraordinary devastation, certainly killing or maiming all the bandsmen but very probably killing dozens, perhaps hundreds, of local residents and tourists.

It seemed to the intelligence analysts who tried to understand just why the IRA had chosen Gibraltar that the whole operation was very out of character and could easily do immense damage to the Republican cause if too many civilians had died in the attack.

Then, some intelligence was collected that explained the apparently inexplicable. It can now be revealed for the first time that Gibraltar was the price demanded by Colonel Gadaffi for the arms he had supplied to the IRA.

According to both British intelligence and army sources, Gadaffi told his IRA contacts that he wanted Britain to pay for the humiliation they had heaped on his country, first by expelling his diplomats after the shooting of WPC Yvonne Fletcher and then by allowing American bombers to fly from Britain to attack his country.

'Gadaffi told his IRA contacts that he wanted a spectacular attack that would cause a great deal of damage and that would embarrass Britain in the eyes of the world,' said one intelligence source.[2]

It is not clear exactly who suggested Gibraltar. It could easily have been Gadaffi himself who came up with the idea.

He has a fairly narrow view of the world and Gibraltar is the nearest British target to Libya.

It is unclear at this stage whether the IRA's failure to deliver their part of the bargain has fractured relations between the terrorists and their sponsor. To some extent this has become irrelevant. While the IRA would certainly like a steady flow of weapons from Libya, Gadaffi has already supplied enough to keep them going for a long time.

This particularly applies to the tons of Semtex the IRA now have, for it is in the field of electronics and detonators that the IRA are justifiably known as the best terrorist organisation in the world. And it is in this area, far removed from the headlines, that there is another, particularly dirty little war going on that will in the end decide who holds the edge in Northern Ireland.

4

Electronic Warfare

On Remembrance Day, November 8 1987, the IRA detonated a thirty pound bomb in the main square of the largely Protestant town of Enniskillen in County Fermanagh. The bomb exploded as Girl Guides, Boy Scouts and old soldiers gathered at the Cenotaph in the square to pay their respects to the dead of two world wars.

Eleven men, women and children were killed in the blast which largely destroyed the square and buried dozens of people in the rubble. The secondary school headmaster was left paralysed and more than sixty people were injured. Even in a country where violence had become a tolerated part of life, the brutality of the Enniskillen bombing caused outrage. In Dublin, thousands signed a book of condolence and the Russian newspaper *Tass* denounced the 'barbaric' murders.

In an attempt to mitigate this public relations disaster, the IRA army council took the unprecedented step of issuing a statement expressing 'deep regret' for the loss of life in the bombing. But the statement also tried to lay the blame for the bombing on the British army. The IRA claimed that 'HQ has now established that one of our units placed a remote control bomb . . . The bomb blew up without being triggered by our radio signal. There has been an ongoing battle for supremacy between the IRA and the British army electronic engineers over the use of remote control bombs. In the past, some of our landmines have been triggered by the British army scanning high frequencies, and other devices have been jammed or neutralised. On each occasion, we overcame the problem and recently believed that we were in advance of British counter measures.'

The allegation that the British had detonated the bomb was swiftly denied by the army and the RUC (the bomb was actually set off by a simple mechanical timer) and the excuse if not the incident was swiftly forgotten. But it was important not because of what it said, which was crude – and inaccurate – propaganda, but because it was said at all. The IRA statement gave a very brief glimpse behind the security curtain hiding the most secret part of the military and intelligence war against the IRA. This is not so much a war of agents lurking on street corners or spying on covert meetings of terrorists or indeed of trapping arms shipments or shooting terrorist gunmen. It is instead a highly sophisticated war of technology, and challenges the army's best scientists to counter the increasing reliance on technology by the IRA.

The result has been the development of the IRA as the most technically proficient terrorist organisation in the world and the development of the British army as the acknowledged world expert at countering modern terrorist weapons.

From the start of the current campaign in the late 1960s, the British understood the value of accurate and timely intelligence. In the early days surveillance devices were fairly basic: voice activated bugs and video cameras concealed in known IRA areas were the most common sources of intelligence. Bugs were planted both north and south of the border and the information they relayed back to the listening intelligence agents proved important in allowing the army to predict likely IRA targets or the movement of terrorists.

But it has been a singular characteristic of the IRA that they are extraordinarily patient and thorough in the way they gather their own intelligence. Over the years, the British have discovered documents which show that some potential targets have been kept under sporadic surveillance for months and occasionally years. The IRA use all their resources to build up a detailed picture of the operating habits of all branches of the security forces. Photographs of officers serving in Northern Ireland are taken as a matter of routine, so that they can be matched against photographs of suspected members of the Special Air Service or undercover agents at some time in the future. All local and national newspapers are culled for articles and photographs that might help identify people working undercover in Northern Ireland or those who might make future targets for assassination in Britain.

Of course, this is all routine intelligence gathering. What makes the IRA different from the majority of terrorist groups is the commitment they bring to the task by dedicating intelligence agents to the job for periods of more than ten years. But what also sets them apart is their understanding of the role that technology has to play in war. So, while the British were doing their best to listen in to as many conversations between IRA terrorists as possible, the IRA, too, had understood the value of Communications Security (COMSEC).

At a very early stage in the war, the IRA learned that ordinary black and white television sets operating on VHF could be tuned to pick up military audio transmissions by switching to a spare channel and retuning the coils.[1]

Each local IRA military commander was given responsibility for listening in to army and police messages, which were often transmitted in clear speech using only the most basic codes. For example, 'rucksack' meant the RUC, 'watchdogs' were military policemen, 'foxhounds' were ordinary soldiers and 'sunray' meant a unit commander. In addition, as much of the British army is organised in groups from specific areas, the accents of the voices speaking on the radio gave an indication of the troops involved and therefore of their possible mission.

It was not until a raid on the Belfast unit's headquarters in 1974, that the British fully understood by how much they had underestimated the technical prowess of the IRA. The British recovered recordings of conversations between military commanders, including calls between army headquarters in Lisburn and outlying commanders. These recordings had been obtained by phone taps.

The find was an early lesson to the security forces that complacency breeds slack security and death. Steps were immediately taken to sweep all telephone lines regularly for bugs and the security forces tightened up their COMSEC to make the interception and interpretation of conversations more difficult.

To further confuse the IRA, the security forces started to use frequency-hopping radios which jump from one frequency to another in a random pattern making them difficult to intercept. These radios often incorporated a scrambling device that either turned the message into garble or into a digitised signal or both. Even with these precautions, the IRA developed their own counter measures that involved the theft of equipment used by the security forces themselves and the monitoring of messages, some of which could be unscrambled using oscilloscopes and spectrographs.

The knowledge that the IRA regularly listen to radio messages permitted an advantage to the security forces. False or deceptive signals could be sent out by the British that might suggest an army raid on an IRA unit at one address while in fact they were planning a raid elsewhere. Or, messages could be sent giving the IRA information that might lead them to launch an attack and walk into a trap. Aside from directly affecting the ability of the security forces to arrest or monitor the IRA terrorists, there has been an additional benefit to this 'phony' war. It has forced the IRA to dedicate more personnel, time, money and effort to non-violent intelligence gathering and analysis.

The IRA's capability in the area of passive radio and telephone interception has led them to develop a more active capability in the safe detonation of bombs. At the start of the current campaign, the IRA used any materials that were readily available to use as explosives. These were generally commercially available explosives and detonators which the IRA either stole from building sites and quarries or were given by sympathisers in the Irish Republic. The simplest way of exploding a bomb was a safety fuse which when lit with a match or cigarette would provide a short delay before the blast. The burning fuse is the most reliable method of initiation for improvised explosive devices (IEDs) and once ignited is virtually impossible to counter. But it also means the terrorist has a limited time to escape, especially when warnings have to be given to minimise civilian casualties.

The introduction of modified alarm clocks and kitchen timers provided the bomber with an opportunity for the covert delivery of a bomb and up to twelve hours to make his escape. This extra delay between the planting of a bomb and its detonation gave the security forces a chance to find the devices and defuse them. Nearly a third of the 1,022 devices planted in 1971 were defused by the army. This success rate was unacceptable to the IRA and thus started a technical war between the bomb makers and those whose unpleasant task it was to counter them.

This technical war obliged the security forces to gather intelligence on bomb makers, sources of explosives and components, logistic supply routes, forward explosives dumps, bombing group members and their future targets. Technical intelligence on the construction of devices enabled specialised equipment and disposal procedures to be devised. The police and forensic scientists applied themselves to the exacting task of linking hard evidence to suspected terrorists.

The PIRA were to prove both resourceful and innovative in the construction of sophisticated devices and in their use. It had no shortage of sympathisers and recruits with the necessary brains and training to make the most modern and effective terrorist weapons. But the bomb making industry was complex and fraught with danger and the PIRA lost a number of their members through premature explosions. They tried to standardise the manufacturing process and thus reduce the risk. One of their most successful efforts at standardisation started in 1971 with the aid of a Belfast Post Office engineer. He introduced the IRA to the GPO Type

44A fuse which allowed the bomb to remain inactive until a switch was tripped at the last minute. For the person planting the bomb the final act of tripping the switch required particular courage as any mistake in the making of the bomb would mean instant detonation and death for the terrorist. As a result a number of bombs were found by the security forces without the switch tripped.

To overcome this problem, the GPO engineer introduced a further safety device based on a simple timer known as a Memopark which is normally used as a simple parking meter timer. This readily available gadget gave an elapsed time of up to two hours before triggering a small buzzer to alert the motorist that his time on the meter had expired. The IRA adapted this so that at the end of the set time instead of a buzzer going off, a circuit was completed to detonate the bomb. The Memopark was first used in conjunction with the GPO 44A fuse on July 6, 1971 and since then has routinely appeared in most IRA bombs. In fact, it was such a successful innovation that it has been adopted by the IRA's most feared enemy, the British Special Air Service, as an effective safety device for use with their explosives.

At the same time as the Memopark was introduced, the GPO engineer revolutionised the overall design of IRA bombs. From 1971, most IRA bombs were designed so that once they were armed, they could not be lifted or opened without being detonated and any interference with the electrical circuits would also cause the bomb to explode.

Such clever design work by the GPO engineer intitially caught the security forces by surprise. In two years the army lost four bomb disposal experts to booby-trapped bombs prepared by the engineer, including the officer commanding the bomb squad, who was killed in March 1972. The GPO engineer was never convicted of the killings and is today living openly in Ireland.

The widespread use of the Memopark meant that the IRA needed a large supply of them to meet the demands of their bombmakers. Their prayers were answered by a quiet, unobtrusive Catholic priest, Patrick Ryan.[2]

Ryan was ordained a Catholic priest in 1954. He went as a missionary to Africa and then as a priest in East London in the late 1960s. He appears to have become politicised around this time and began to spend more and more time working for the IRA. When his church was contributing to central funds, he admitted to having sent the money to the IRA and he refused instructions to stop.

In 1972 he was suspended by the Church from his normal duties and given six months leave of absence which he spent back in Ireland establishing his position with the IRA. To the terrorists he was a unique asset: a priest with no known links to terrorism and a man who had never been seen in Ireland since the outbreak of the troubles. He was swiftly put to good use, first as one of the IRA's links with Libya and later, in 1973, when he was moved first to Switzerland and then to Le Havre in France, acting as the IRA's money launderer and arms buyer, setting up a network of bank accounts in Switzerland and Luxembourg. But perhaps his most important contribution was the regular supply of bomb making equipment he sent back to the IRA. He supplied hundreds of electronic timers and Memoparks although British intelligence do not believe that Ryan himself knew very much about bomb making. He was simply a man with a shopping list.

In May 1975, Ryan delivered his first batch of Memoparks to the IRA. They worked so well that on July 21, 1979 he bought 50 Memoparks in Switzerland for 900 Swiss francs and seven days later returned to buy 500 more for 6,000 Swiss francs.

In the eighteen months from May 1979, Memoparks were used to detonate 185 bombs in Northern Ireland and in Britain.

Ryan was careful never to set foot back in the United Kingdom, so the British knew nothing about him. But a Canadian tourist who had taken a room next to Ryan in a

Le Havre hotel was suspicious of the man who claimed to be an ordinary seaman but had enough cash to live well and make international telephone calls. The tourist lifted papers from Ryan's wastepaper basket and handed them to British police when he arrived in Britain a few days later. This chance find alerted the British, and Ryan was put under surveillance.

On July 26, 1976 Ryan was arrested by Swiss police after allegedly committing a minor motoring offence while driving his camper van in Geneva. A search of the camper van revealed a mass of documents detailing Ryan's covert life in Europe over the previous four years. Ryan readily admitted to being a member of the IRA but he had committed no offence in Switzerland and after ten days he was released. But he was now a marked man: he was arrested in France and expelled in December 1976; refused entry into Italy in February 1977 and arrested in Luxembourg in March 1977.

Although his cover was blown, Ryan continued to supply Memopark devices and to act as bagman for the IRA in Europe. British intelligence believes that he supplied the switch used in the bomb that exploded in Hyde Park, London, on July 20, 1982 killing four soldiers and seven horses.

But to the IRA hierarchy he was now reduced to the status of messenger boy. They knew of his boasting about his IRA membership while under arrest in Switzerland and he was seen as insecure. He was never again used in any really sensitive operations.

The British lost sight of Ryan in the mid 1980s when he went to ground in a small studio apartment in Benidorm in Spain. Then in June 1988, Ryan travelled to Belgium where he rented a flat at 6, Avenue D'Overghem in the Brussels suburb of Ukkel. Ryan's name was still on the watch list given to all European customs posts and he was picked up crossing the Belgian border. Queen Elizabeth was due to visit Belgium later that month and as a routine security precaution the Belgians, who normally take a fairly relaxed view about terrorists operating on their territory, decided to arrest him. 'They were worried that he might be about to assassinate the

Queen and they couldn't take the risk of allowing him to stay loose,' claims one intelligence source.[3]

When Ryan was arrested on June 29, he had with him a number of circuit diagrams showing how to use the Memopark in different kinds of bomb, along with explosives manuals.

The British government were notified immediately Ryan was arrested. The British had, of course, received such news a number of times in the past and had never bothered to attempt to get him extradited. He had committed no offence in Britain and the evidence against him was nearly all circumstantial. So when the Belgians proposed that the British apply for extradition, the British replied that they might not have a strong enough case.

Clearly embarrassed at having Ryan on their turf, the Belgians then said that however weak the case, the extradition request would be granted. On the basis of that assurance, the British government then prepared their case and submitted an extradition request to the Belgian government. At first, all went well and the Justice Ministry kept their word and recommended Ryan's extradition.

But, in the event, Ryan went on hunger strike while in jail and the Belgian cabinet lost its nerve, overruled the court which wanted to allow the extradition and ordered him to be deported to Ireland. The British had no choice but to apply once again for his extradition.

In December 1988, the Irish government refused to hand Ryan over to the British for trial. The Irish Attorney-General, John Murray, argued that he would not receive a fair trial in Britain because the extensive publicity given to the case would prejudice any trial in Britain. The British Prime Minister, Margaret Thatcher, dismissed this argument as 'an insult to all the people of this country.'

In his sixteen-page judgement, Murray acknowledged there were 'serious charges' against Ryan which should be investigated by the court. As a fallback, the Irish suggested that Britain take advantage of a little used provision in the 1976

Irish Criminal Law (Jurisdiction) Act which allowed for certain serious offences committed outside the Republic to be tried there. The British Government agreed and over the next few months, all the evidence available to the British was handed over to the Irish Government.

In October 1989 the Irish Director of Public Prosecutions announced that there was insufficient evidence to prosecute Ryan. While the British had supplied a substantial quantity of documentary evidence, information from witnesses prepared to testify in court was critical to the case. In the event, two key witnesses, one a retired Swiss shopkeeper who had sold Ryan Memopark timing devices and the other a British businessman who knew Ryan in Libya, refused to testify in Dublin.

The Ryan affair was a shabby episode in the fight against terrorism. Although there is no doubt whatsoever of Ryan's extensive involvement with the IRA over a number of years, his role was difficult to prove in court. This was recognised by the British when he was first arrested in Belgium. There was no intention to ask for his extradition until the Belgian government suggested the idea. Then, the British applied for his extradition and the Belgian government lost their nerve and expelled him to Ireland. The Irish, who always have to be scrupulously fair in matters relating to the IRA, rightly concluded there was insufficient evidence on which to try Ryan. Despite the widespread criticism that resulted from the Irish government's decision, it actually caused little surprise to the British government when the weakness of their case against Ryan was recognised.

The impotence of the law in the Ryan case provided a clear illustration of just how easy it is for known terrorists to escape justice.

Ryan supplied the IRA with a safety device that made their bombing campaign safer for the terrorists. But the IRA also needed to be able to set bombs off by remote control, to hit targets, such as moving cars, that required precision timing. In the early 1970s, this was achieved using a command wire which was a simple wire leading from the bomb to the site a few hundred yards away. By sending an electrical current down the wire the bomb could be set off. This method had two disadvantages.

Often bombs had to be planted hours or even days in advance of the target coming within range. A command wire, however well concealed, could be discovered and could lead security forces both to the bomb and to the team hidden at the other end of the wire.

Even after the bomb had exploded, the security forces knew they only had to find the wire and follow it to find where the terrorists had been hiding. This gave them a vital edge and made escape difficult.

The PIRA began to use radio control devices to detonate bombs in 1972. Initially, they used equipment designed to control the flight of model aircraft. A simple pulse sent on one frequency was enough to blow up a bomb. This was cheap and effective and gave the bombers a lot more flexibility in setting up their attacks.

For the security forces this was a new and worrying development. The army's bomb disposal teams were trained to deal with a static bomb complete with booby traps. Before moving in to defuse such a bomb, the army would sweep the area and check for command wires. Once the bomb disposal unit was given the all clear then they could move in and, using a number of unpublicised devices, freeze the timer on the bomb.

But remote control bombs introduced a new factor into the already dangerous business of bomb disposal. With the help of specialists from the Royal Corps of Signals, the Royal Army Ordnance Corps devised a piece of equipment that would send out a jamming signal on the same frequency as the model aircraft control units. In this way, the security forces could make sure a bomb would not be detonated by remote control just as they moved in to defuse it.

To deal with this new electronic factor, every five-man team of bomb disposal experts, known as Felix, had one man whose sole job was to operate the counter measures. With typical army originality he was known as the 'Bleep'.

The IRA has recognised the way of the future. Its general headquarters is now divided into several departments, including an engineering department which deals with the latest bomb-making devices and electronic counter measures used to neutralise the army's own equipment.

With the development of a counter to their model aircraft detonators, the IRA began to lose both men and equipment. The army were able to detect the radio signals and either jam them or discover their source. There were also a number of premature explosions of radio controlled bombs, some of which killed the terrorists planting the devices.

The PIRA had no idea of the cause of these failures and the result of their internal investigations, later revealed in their own propaganda, was that the army was either using some kind of 'Death Ray' or a special device to scan radio frequencies and detonate the bombs as soon as they were armed. Both these conclusions were almost certainly wrong. First, the PIRA almost invariably use a delayed arming circuit in their radio controlled bombs to protect the terrorist while planting the bomb. Second, any radio controlled receiver is able to pick up spurious signals from a number of sources, which are always present in the ether. PIRA experts are well aware of this and it is more likely the premature explosions were due either to incompetent handling of the bombs by those planting them or spurious radio signals arriving after the bombs were laid and armed.

It is most unlikely that the army would authorise any signal likely to set off a bomb unless the exact location of the device was known and the prospect of civilan or military casualties minimised.

As a result of these counter-measures, the IRA designed a simple but reliable encode/decode defence system which, with improvements, remains in service today. The PIRA have used a wide variety of transmitters and receivers but have now standardised on a VHF transmitter and receiver operating in the two-metre band. Their basic piece of equipment is the Japanese-made ICOM walkie-talkie. The IC2 model, which is used by PIRA, can be easily adapted by anyone with a working knowledge of electronics. In the standard unit, changes in air pressure created by the speaker's voice are converted by the microphone into electrical pulses and transmitted to the aerial on the receiver. These signals are reconverted by the handheld set and relayed in the form of electrical pulses which vibrate the loudspeaker to replicate the words or sounds transmitted.

However, IRA electronics specialists fitted the receiver with a decoding circuit which compared the coded transmitter signal to its own. Only when the two codes matched would the receiver activate a firing trigger attached to an electronic detonator to explode the bomb.

This system, too, the security forces have been able to counter. But for every counter there is a response and the IRA continue to modify their equipment with technological advances, briefly gaining a slight edge before the army once more moves ahead.

Since 1972, the IRA have used remote control devices some two hundred times, including at Warrenpoint in 1979 when eighteen soldiers were killed with two bombs; the murder of Lord Mountbatten and his family while fishing off the coast of Donegal in August 1979; and the murder of Lord Justice and Lady Gibson when their car was blown up at Newry on April 25, 1987.[4]

The nature of this particularly secret war is never discussed by either side. The issue of remote control detonation was one of the central aspects of the inquest into the killing of three IRA terrorists in Gibraltar in March 1988. It was the British government's contention that the terrorists were going to plant a bomb which could have been set off by remote control. To convince a jury of this, the government were forced to reveal something of what they know about the IRA's techniques, while the IRA used the opportunity to deny that they ever set off bombs by remote control.

But by the time the inquest was over, the IRA had already introduced a new and more deadly method of setting off their bombs. This was made from the radar detection devices fitted to some American cars to detect a police speed trap. These devices work entirely on line of sight and the signal is difficult to interrupt. But within a few months the British had developed an effective counter – and without the IRA being aware that the British even knew they had the device in the first place. Once again, the British had achieved a vital edge in the underground war.

This is an area where both sides invest considerable amounts of cash and manpower. For the British, intelligence about a new IRA system is vital and the mere knowledge that such intelligence has been gained is a closely guarded secret. This gives the security forces time to develop effective counter measures without the IRA being aware that their new equipment has suddenly become vulnerable.

What impresses the security forces is that this generation of IRA terrorists has an understanding of the technology of warfare that no other terrorist group in the world has demonstrated. Despite the restrictions of operating on an island where all their arms have to be imported, they have managed to fight a war which, while not conclusive, has in their terms continued to be effective.

Since the late 1960s, the IRA has evolved from a few street corner hoodlums, supported by some old men who remembered how once it might have been, into a sophisticated and competent fighting force. They began with a handful of weapons and considerable popular support. Today, they have enough weapons for their needs in the foreseeable future, and a fraction of their earlier popular support.

The IRA have almost come full circle. Today they are now a Mafia-type organisation that owes its existence not to political support from a disenfranchised minority, but to systematic exploitation of the community it once served, with all the corruption that implies.

An accurate assessment of the financial resources of the IRA is difficult to establish, but the current best estimate by the security forces is that they need over $10m for their annual budget, of which around 20 per cent is spent on military operations. Increasingly, the IRA have invested in legitimate business to bring in a steady income on which they can rely, and the organisation now owns a chain of estate agents, some restaurants and hotels. But the new Prevention of Terrorism Act that came into force in 1989 is specifically designed to make it easier for the authorities to seize cash and close down businesses belonging to the IRA.

This is a major step in the right direction, but unfortunately these moves come at a time when the major military expense that the IRA have faced in the past – the purchase of weapons and explosives – is no longer a factor.

The massive injection of arms that the IRA received from Libya will last them for many years and, unless the security forces get lucky in their finds, probably until the end of the century.

At the same time, the hard core of the IRA that remains has a great deal of experience which it puts to good use when planning its operations. While the actual figure of people who will pull a trigger or press a detonator may be less than 300, there are between 500 and 1,000 activists who are prepared to go on a terrorist operation; there are 1,000 terrorists in jail, some of whom are released every week to rejoin the ranks of the IRA; the families of those in jail or currently serving form a hard core of around 10,000 supporters; to which can be added the 100,000 or so Sinn Fein supporters in north and south.

That this hard-core group have learned from the experience of the past twenty years can be seen from the way they handle their arms and deploy their troops. Weapons are closely guarded and security is so tight that even those agents British intelligence still has in place in the senior ranks of the organisation are never able to tell the full picture. It is striking that few of the weapons delivered by the Libyans three years ago have been recovered. Indeed, they have already been put to use. Between 1986 and 1988, the number of deaths from terrorism increased from 61 to 93, the number of weapons recovered rose from 270 to 543, ammunition found rose from 29,000 rounds to 104,000 rounds, shooting incidents increased from 285 to 448 and bombings from 220 to 448. The only statistic that showed a fall was the number of terrorists convicted which fell from 531 to 431.

PIRA gunmen are all well-trained, not just in security but to resist interrogation and deception. The days when teenagers with a long record of violence would be sent on sensitive missions have long gone. The terrorist unit that was sent to Britain in 1987 with a brief to assassinate the Northern Ireland Secretary Tom King was divided into two sections for reconnaissance and assassination.

In fact, the IRA practises cell security as a matter of routine and has established complex organisations for its units active in Northern Ireland, mainland Britain or Europe. (See Appendix, page 291). This organisation can involve up to seventy people with a number of sub-units having specific tasks. None of the terrorists involved know each other and each controller of a sub-unit only knows the controller to whom he or she reports. The unit at the beginning of the chain which carries out the very early reconnaissance has no idea of the eventual target or who will carry out the attack or when. This kind of security means that even when one arrest is made, there is little impact on the activities of the whole group.

In the King case, the reconnaisance unit was captured but the terrorists who were actually going to carry out the kill remain at large and the identity of the members of the logistics support unit responsible for supplying weapons, documents and safe houses is unknown.

The weapons they planned to use were smuggled to Britain months or possibly years before the team actually arrived. All IRA units operating outside Northern Ireland are today issued with a standard pack which includes weapons, ammunition, explosives and detonators.

Despite the efforts of the police, the members of the unit have escaped the search for them because the IRA chose men with no criminal records who have stayed well clear of their usual haunts among the Irish community in Britain. The IRA is aware that the British Special Branch has heavily infiltrated the Irish community with informers so has carefully established a completely new support network in Britain. Over a number of years, left-wing activists who voiced support for the IRA in the early 1970s have been contacted and now form part of a new underground support system. It will take the police several years to penetrate and develop an informant network in this new section of society and in the meantime the IRA have safe havens and an advantage.

The combination of experience, refined tactics and modern weapons make today's Provisional IRA a potent force. There is no prospect of them winning the war against the British – not least because the Irish government has no wish to see the IRA gain any form of power in the north or south. But reality is unlikely to temper the enthusiasm with which the PIRA will fight the next round of their battle against the British. They have always played the long game and now they have the weapons and the experience to make the British pay a heavy price.

5

Repression and Retaliation

The Soviet invasion of Afghanistan in December 1979 was a textbook operation. On Christmas Eve, advance units dressed in civilian clothes flew into the Afghan capital, Kabul, on scheduled Aeroflot flights from the Soviet Union. At the same time KGB agents put into action a carefully laid plan designed to immobilise potential threats in the Afghan armed forces. They persuaded two armoured divisions to put their tank batteries in for routine maintenance and invited a number of key officers to a cocktail party at the Soviet Embassy the following day.

On the day after Christmas the troops that had arrived in civilian clothes two days previously moved to secure the radio station, the presidential palace and, most importantly, the airport. As soon as the airport control tower was in their hands, the first giant Antonov transport plane landed. Over the next two days, more than two hundred transport aircraft arrived at Kabul airport bringing regiment after regiment of troops who would eventually make up an occupying army 115,000 strong.

In the north, meanwhile, Soviet tanks and armoured personnel carriers moved over the border and headed down the Salang Highway – later to be a target for many bloody guerrilla attacks – towards Kabul.

Within twelve hours President Hafizullah Amin had been assassinated, leading political figures had been arrested and loyal elements in the Afghan armed forces had been killed.[1]

The Soviets had used tactics they had practised before in both Hungary and Czechoslovakia: the sudden overwhelming use of force; the ruthless assassination or arrest of key political and military figures; the use of special forces to prepare the way for the conventional troops. But it was the too rigid application of these tactics to the Afghan case that was to prove the downfall of the Soviets. In both Hungary and Czechoslovakia, the Soviets had seen that control of the centre of power was sufficient to overwhelm the nation. But Afghanistan had no such central control. Nominally Kabul was the capital of the nation and levied taxes and implemented a central political and economic policy. But in fact the Amin government's writ was narrow at best and failed to cover vast tracts of the inhospitable countryside, where traditional tribal fiefdoms were far more important than the government in Kabul and where loyalty to the local chief took precedence over loyalty to a president living in a remote palace that most people had never even seen.

Over the next nine years the Soviet forces floundered, out of their depth in a war they never clearly understood, and where their tactics appeared increasingly outdated.

Initially, the same thing could be said about western governments. The invasion had been carefully timed to catch all but the most diligent of western intelligence agencies by surprise. In fact, the US government had received good intelligence from satellite reconnaissance that up to 30,000 Soviet troops were massing on the border but, as is so often the case, there was disagreement between different departments in the administration about the significance of the move. The US therefore failed to issue any clear warning to the Soviets not to invade. The lack of that warning backed by real sanctions may well have been seen by the Soviets as a tacit agreement to the invasion. In the event, they sorely misjudged the response it would evoke from the Carter administration.

Immediately after the invasion, disagreements between the doves in the State Department and the hawks – in the most visible form of National Security Adviser Zbigniew Brzezinski

"Sure," said Dan eagerly. The corner of a little table nipped at Dan like a terrier as he followed his old buddy, the great man, into a high, dark, glamorous room filled with books and papers. Dan was thrilled to have McDonald call him "son."

"Real leather," said Dan agreeably, as he settled onto a sofa.

"Yes," replied McDonald.

"Sure good cigars."

"Would you like another?"

"Great."

McDonald offered Dan another cigar from a polished wooden box. Dan felt a warm partnership as the great man lit it for him. As he reached up to pluck the cigar from his mouth, he realized the one from dinner was still going in his other hand. McDonald looked puzzled. Dan held a cigar in each hand — how stupid! To cover the gaffe, Dan raised the blazing Havanas like a pair of six-guns and said, "Bang! Bang!" McDonald didn't respond.

"What are your plans, son?"

"Well, I'd sure like to see the Big Apple," answered Dan, as he awkwardly stamped out one cigar.

"Ro's told me about the problem."

"Oh, right, right."

"What are your plans?"

"Well, my uncle has a finishing camp — I mean a fishing camp — in the Rockies, and he always said any time I wanted to guide and stuff. I guess he thinks I'm pretty good. I'll tell you one thing, I do know how to fish. I can feel them sometimes, and they know it. It's like we both know it's time to get caught."

"May I ask what the hell that has to do with my daughter?"

criminal team, thought Dan, the woman deflecting his attention so the man could grab the jewel of Mrs. McDonald's company. He had another draft from the magic wine glass that was always full.

"Oh, just about family and horse-racing."

"Ah, you have horses."

"Who, me?"

"It's such fun."

"Yes."

"My husband will not let me buy a horse. I've been dying for years to have a racing horse, but he only buys art. He tells me not only does art appreciate, its race is already won, and you don't have to buy it hay."

Dan laughed. This woman was attractive too, tits as big as football helmets. Is there any line so mystical as that formed by big breasts shelved together by a low-cut evening gown? Not to get caught staring at them, Dan concentrated on her face. "It's the first time I ever saw most of these things."

"What is your favorite?"

"Here?" (The true answer was too idiotic to admit: Jane McDonald.) "Well, I think that Léger painting is perfect for the stairs, because his paintings are real constructed-looking, like buildings going up, so it gives you confidence on the stairs. Like the stairs are well built."

This woman did not laugh. Dan had another sip of shadow. He was sure Jane McDonald would have understood. Having a remark like that out before a woman who simply stared blankly made Dan feel desperate, especially when he considered the possibility that she might think the phrase "well built" had to do with those redoubtable breasts she presented.

"That's Picasso, I bet."

"Yes it is. Nineteen fifty-seven."

"Boy, it's a great piece."

"How do you know so much about art?"

"I major in History of Art. I mean, I did. I just graduated."

"What are you going to do?"

Dan thought of her naked, in a lascivious pose, pitched forward slightly, wagging those wonderful immense tits slowly back and forth.

"I want to see New York."

"You haven't?"

"No, ma'am."

"Well, you must visit us when you do. We are one month at the Pierre." Did she know he thought she meant by "us" those breasts? Somehow she seemed to have a sense of his interest and not to mind it. Dan was surprised. After all, she was married. When he glanced around for her husband, Dan was surprised to find Paul Steigen regarding him. In fact, Steigen was pointing at Dan's wine glass to the butler. He looked quickly away.

John Russell McDonald couldn't help considering his daughter and Novitski naked, doing it. The thought made him shudder. At least the boy looked clean, even athletic. Novitski from Idaho, impregnating her, Rowena Clark McDonald. The son of a bitch. He certainly was full of himself, talking away about anything, like a goddamn salesman. America was a great country, so great it had made room for a lot of tinhorns and cheaters, salesmen and power-boat people, tasteless nobodies the powerful had to take care of with ridiculously high wages and various other free rides. But they were, after all, the voters, the consumers, the public. John Russell McDonald was

all for them, of course. He just didn't like seeing th spill over into his house, into his daughter.

All the women had mysteriously vanished. McDon the prince, the art dealer, and Dan were there alone. F Steigen poured cognac for Dan. A box of cigars ca forth. The men all seemed to have expected to be al together. The prince and Steigen were chattering c erly. Dan, grinning with drink and flushed with the ef of women's smiles, had a cigar with the rest of th John Russell McDonald had begun to seem to Dan li cross between Abe Lincoln and George Washington.

The men and women separating after dinner — course! Dan got it; he'd heard of it somewhere. It like so much of this remarkable evening, actually b in a situation you had seen only on TV.

A tool lay in the cigars to clip the tip off. Dan did fine. The others slipped the rings off their smokes. Dan, thinking it was both kind of pretty and reminis of engagement and marriage, left his on. The com tion of cigar smoke and cognac was something Quaaludes. He listened to them get exercised ove President, being by this time only slightly surprised McDonald said things like "I told him last week it w going to work," speaking, of course, of the Preside the United States. Dan expected he'd be chatting the President pretty soon, too.

"Dan," said McDonald, suddenly coming into from the softening spectacle Dan had begun to ma his surroundings.

"Yes, sir?" Dan felt as if he were treading wate pleasant reverie of sex and luxury.

"Let's go in the library, son."

"Oh, well, I was thinking we could start out there after we get married."

"I see."

"She likes it up there. We went out a lot at school. Boy, she's OK, Mr. McDonald. She's terrific."

"Your plans are to guide fishing expeditions in the Rocky Mountains? Live in a tent?"

"But I think first see New York. I've got five hundred dollars, almost. So see New York for a while, then go back to Arch's, that's my uncle, Arch Friebick, who's got the camp. Mountain Water Fishing. You ever hear of it?"

"No, I haven't. Well, I'm delighted to hear you have things so clearly thought out, Dan."

"Then after that, I don't know."

"I see."

"I like History of Art and I know how to fish. I figured I'd just take it from there."

"Start a family on those two principles."

"Well, sir, the family got started by itself."

Once again, McDonald revolted himself by contemplating obscene combinations of his daughter and this slouching lout who looked to be sinking into the quicksand rather than sitting on a couch, holding up the cigar like a little boy pretending his toy airplane was flying. John Russell McDonald wanted Ro to marry someone like the son of his friend Lord Cove, or one of those handsome boys of the president of France. He couldn't even see this one any longer; only that arm aloft, flying the cigar.

"She's just great, sir." Fatherless Dan felt another happy rush of kinship with this magnificent man.

"What do your parents do, Dan?"

Dan sat up, grinning. *The bastard was drunk.* Was John Russell McDonald supposed to take care of him now? Buy the boy booze and a bed so that he could ruin his daughter's life?

"Mom sells real estate. My dad took off when I was five. He plays the horses. Once he sent me this postcard from Santa Anita that said, 'Happy birthday, wish I was here.' "

*

McDonald was gone when Dan woke up. A dead cigar had stayed in his fingers. He sat up and shook his head. When Dan tried to stand, one of his legs had gone to sleep, and he fell, cracking his head on a table. The blow rang in his head, the background music for rushing red waves of pain. It was dark in the library; the door was closed. What had Dan said? It was all going so well, and then suddenly it was all wrong. Some fear spilled in Dan's stomach, a panic over where he was and what he had done. He opened the library door. The house was silent, ticking with sleep. He had passed out! What a godawful, stupid thing to do!

Dan turned on a switch; all the pictures lit up. It was dark except for the paintings, all alive and brilliant in spotlights. Now they *were* like slides in the dark — bright crazy windows to paradise. Dan's head rang with a high harsh noise. Was it coming from the chorus of masterpieces? All the beauty now seemed terribly painful and cruel. Dan's head throbbed; it was wet. He was streaming blood.

In a bathroom, bright light and mirrors revealed an appalling sight. The Creature from the Black Lagoon was seeing his reflection for the first time. How unspeakably awful. Dan washed as best he could. There were no Band-Aids in the spotless bathroom cabinet. Dan held a wad of toilet paper to stanch the wound. It stuck there like the gardenia in Dorothy Lamour's hair.

With a washrag, Dan mopped at the brilliant red blood drops in the shining white bathroom. The pinkened washrag testified against him no matter how often he rinsed it. He left it to soak and limped upstairs. Ro's room was closed and locked. A note flapped on the door. It directed him elsewhere.

Dan pulled open the alien loaf of a strange, unwelcoming bed and got in, ashamed to be soiling their sheets, to be using anything in the house. When he thought of sleeping in his van, it was too late; he was too tired. He remembered he'd left the lights on downstairs. *Passed out in front of the father.* Jesus, had anyone in the history of man ever been so obnoxious? He fell asleep.

FIVE

ohn Russell McDonald had breakfast with news tapes going on his cable channel, the *Times, Wall Street Journal, Le Monde, Figaro,* and *Washington Post.* He also made telephone calls. Somehow, he never got egg yolk or marmalade on the papers, nor did he ever have to swallow in midsentence. Making calls and taking in the first news was a favorite passage of the day for him. He accomplished it unshaven, in his dressing room, served by his valet in proper, male fashion. He knew that Winston Churchill, Marshall Tito, Mao, de Gaulle, all the old boys would understand this hour incorporating the world and the awakening body.

"The state is I," said the old French king; information and breakfast coming, shit and commands and whiskers going out. Edwards knew perfectly how to serve his master during this hour. It was for both of them a ritual of great and noble reality in a world every day further distorted into lunatic fiction by women and children.

The dressing of the toreador concluded, McDonald in a cat-gray London suit came downstairs to get papers from his library and drive into New York.

The bloodstains, glasses, spilled ashtray, and unventilated funk of Dan's misadventure startled McDonald. Until this moment, he had forgotten the whole ugly matter of his daughter's condition. He had been thinking of petroleum, nuclear-warhead deployment, the changing face of Eastern Europe, and a bauxite investment, when he saw the punk spoor in his library. His face twisted with disgust. Drugs, fornication, homosexuality, and that stridently moronic music infesting the modern air all occurred to him as he looked at the little fouled nest of depravity from which the fledgling fornicator had apparently fallen.

Lamps burning in daylight are a sordid sight. All the pictures were lit. The son of a bitch was in that house somewhere. McDonald was half-tempted to pull him, from wherever he'd dropped for the night, by the scruff of the neck and drop him on the highway to be hit, broken, and gradually erased into the asphalt by passing cars.

But he hadn't time. About to get in his car, he remembered a file he wanted to bring into town. Cursing the boy for the run he'd snagged in the silk of McDonald's morning concentration, one of the most valuable mental passages of his day (and, he considered, valuable not just to himself personally, but to his country as well), he said to his driver, "Goddamn it."

To which the man replied, "Yes, sir." And watched his employer stalk back to the house.

The chauffeur reopened his *Racing Form* and puzzled over the tea leaves of Past Performances, seeking the winner's configuration.

As McDonald entered the house, he heard someone

coming downstairs fast. This displeased him. He liked to see only his valet in the morning. Family, even Doris, were not sights McDonald relished before lunch.

Ro appeared in a rush.

"I'm so glad I caught you, Daddy."

"Good morning."

"Can I come into town with you? I want to talk to you."

"Of course, dear." There was no escape from family life today, McDonald decided. "Let me just finish dressing," she said. "I'll meet you in the car."

McDonald found his file, weighed it in his hand while looking again at the boy's mess, hit the folder lightly against the desk, a little ax stroke that broke the kid's neck in McDonald's mind, and went out to his car.

"Wait a minute, Dan," ordered McDonald as the chauffeur made to leave. *Another Dan* — McDonald considered what a common name it was as he pushed the buttons of the phone in the limousine. Waiting for his call to connect, he noticed for the first time how long his driver's hair was. A pregnant daughter, a sloppy chauffeur — McDonald reflected that he was going to have to take command before the weeds took over completely. Rowena rushed across the gravel and hopped in. Her father was once again there and not there, looking at her blankly as his mind danced cheek to cheek with his phone call.

McDonald raised the panel of glass between them and the driver so that he could talk with Ro as they negotiated the antiquated parkway with its scenic curves from a period that confused transportation with travel.

"It's sure confusing to come back this way," said Ro.

"It's ridiculous, Ro. You're twenty-one years old."

"Mummy was only twenty when you got married."

"That was a long time ago."

Another long phone call halted progress in the dialogue. Ro had lost his attention again. He'd adjusted something that put her to the side of his perception. Ro looked angrily at the back of the chauffeur's head. He was new to Ro, a long-hair. Ro smiled. Her father being driven by a long-hair? Times were changing.

"Come help me in France," her father had asked her last night. If he really meant it, he was going to have to work harder to stop her from marrying Dan.

"I'm sorry, darling, about all the phone calls. Look — let's have lunch. I'll be all yours for lunch — I just have to make these calls now."

"OK, Daddy."

"Meet me at one at 'Twenty-One.' "

"OK."

McDonald lowered the window between them and the driver as they drew up before his office building.

"Come for me at twelve-forty, take Miss McDonald wherever she wants, and pick us up at 'Twenty-One' at two-fifteen."

"Yes, sir."

"And while we're at lunch, get a haircut."

"Sir?"

"If you're driving for me, that hair must be gone by two-fifteen."

With that dismissal, McDonald strode angrily into his building.

When Ro heard the driver say "Shit," she put the glass back up between them. He looked in the rearview mirror. She lowered the glass only long enough to give him the address of their apartment in New York, and looked away from his glance. He should have short hair. This was New York. Her father was John Russell McDonald. This wasn't a Colorado pickup with a gun hung behind the seat and Coors cans rolling on the floorboards.

At the McDonalds' New York apartment, the doorman's obsequiousness picked up right where it had left off. The housekeeper's, too. It was wonderful to be back from the sticks, to see uniforms and polishing — to see all the class-conscious nuances of life in New York that just weren't there out west, at least not so meticulously and flagrantly practiced as they were here.

Ro had gone west to be done with snobbery, but she didn't mind a little when she came home.

She called friends and shot the breeze. She was invited to cocktails with one and dinner with another. When she hung up, she allowed herself to realize she hadn't mentioned Dan to her friends. In her rush into New York, she'd forgotten Dan, still asleep in Connecticut. How strange that was — she was going to marry him. She was pregnant by him. Ro felt guilty. She could call back and fix it if Dan was still around when she went back to Connecticut. But of course he'd be around! What was going on? Ro worried about her sincerity. Pregnancy, at least, was real. Pregnancy didn't forget or change its mind.

*

"Muff, listen I forgot to tell you my boyfriend is here, Dan Novitski. I-T-S-K-I. A while. Are you coming over? See you, Muff."

Muffy probably thought Novitski was a funny name. Good; wait until she saw him. He certainly wasn't one of those dancing school retards who would wind up in the money business like Muffy's typical boyfriends. Ro wished Dan had brought his cowboy boots. Those sneakers were so awful. He'd been so awful last night. Passing out in front of her father — what a disaster. Mummy alone pronounced him utterly divine.

He was wonderful in many ways. He looked wonderful, he made wonderful love, he was quite original and independent — of course he was heaven. He was going to be her husband! They were going to live in a way people like Muffy couldn't even imagine. She wondered if his drinking was going to be a problem. He was really wacko at dinner. She hadn't ever seen him like that, and at such a crucial, critical moment: meeting her father. Meeting both her parents. Of course, Mummy would go for it; she drank like a fish.

Muffy arrived and they went into Ro's room. There again was that feeling of a previous time, the moment she was last there meticulously preserved by the curator-housekeeper. Ro's last departure was still in the room, if she cared to recall it. She did care to recall one detail of it. Ro stood on a chair and reached back in her closet. There it was, the slick little origami-folded stash of Rico the dealer. There was enough for three lines apiece. They headed out to do a little serious shopping. Park Avenue looked completely fabulous now.

In the happy glow of high, Ro told her wonderful, truest, oldest, bestest friend Muffy about how fabulous Dan was, how she was going to marry him, how she was pregnant. Muff thought it was incredibly fabulous, wildly original, and typical of McDonald, who had been the most incredible girl in their whole school. Ro insisted

Muffy come to lunch — at least for a drink — with her father, with whom Muffy was completely infatuated, of course.

They were shown to the best table with the breezy unctuousness that had built the restaurant. They chattered a bit about inconsequential things, pleasantly aware of their image as a pair of young rich girls, and decided they would be best friends for absolutely ever. When John Russell McDonald entered, many people whispered and smiled, and a few waved. Muffy felt a tingle, and Ro beamed with pride.

"Well, hello, Muffy. How are you?"

"I can only stay a minute, Mr. McDonald — I came to keep Ro company."

Congratulations on his appointment as ambassador to France brought a couple of the richest men in the world over to the table. He joked, laughed, sent the heralding eyebrows up and down for them, exemplified success and charm for the entire restaurant. Ro was extremely proud and still quite high. Muffy was ready to sleep with him.

"Well, wonderful to see you, Mr. McDonald. Bye, Ro. I can't wait to meet Dan."

At that word — Dan — McDonald's glow went out like an old television set, into a little bright pinhole of fury. Muffy's exit camouflaged it, but Ro felt her father's anger like a jolt when he sat back down. McDonald looked at her as violently as he had when she announced her pregnancy.

He was about to say something when the basset-faced captain leaned worshipfully in to take a drink order. McDonald smiled charmingly at once and asked for a Tab.

Ro wished she weren't high. Her father's total attention scared her. He would detect it. She was afraid to say anything.

"What are you having," he repeated to her. She almost confessed, "Cocaine!" but she saved herself, realizing it was an offer, not an interrogation. Her father was looking directly toward her. The waiter studied her desperately, as though she were deciding for or against his life. Why couldn't she think of what to say?

"Tab, too," she squeaked. McDonald smiled finally at the waiter, who left to see to their order at once. McDonald's smile went away as quickly as the waiter.

"The first thing to do, Ro, is get rid of it. Whatever you want to do about marrying or not marrying is, of course, up to you. But it's wrong to be forced into a thing like this by circumstances that are still within your control. Always study your options before you make a decision. If you're satisfied with the freedom of your choice, you'll live with it far happier and longer than you will if it's forced."

"Uh-huh."

"I've been thinking a great deal about it, dear, ever since you told me. A father can offer a daughter only two things in life, advice and support. I'm giving you my advice. You have my support no matter what you do."

"Oh, Daddy!" suddenly she cried against his abrasive wool shoulder. He patted her with his big, clever, protective hand.

"Everything all right?" queried the waiter indiscreetly as he brought the drinks.

"Oh, yes," said Ro with manic enthusiasm, as though she were the heroine in a play, hearing the first words of her deaf-mute pupil.

SIX

Sunlight on wallpaper, on a rug pretty as a creel of trout, on a chair that would be handsome if it weren't for the clumsy, sordid shroud of clothes over it, the pants spewing out underpants, twisted and fallen like a dead soldier. One sneaker lay on its side, the other facing backward, an auto accident involving two sneakers in which two socks were killed, one thrown clear onto the chair, the other limp on the open rug. Dan looked at the scene, recognizing the casualty clothes like next of kin at a morgue. A horrible hangover filled him. His palms were cold and greasy; his body felt run over. The worst damage seemed to have been wrought inside his skull. The worst events of the evening before were delivered one at a time to his wounded memory as he washed in a spotless bathroom. This was Ro's house. The fall, the pass-out, the father — oh God.

A medicine cabinet was stocked with all one needed to convert the hulking, sleep-soiled beast into a shining citizen, under normal conditions. But Dan's condition was not normal. Dried toilet paper stuck to his head wound. Blood-caked strands of hair there felt like wire. His eyes were a pair of flesh wounds; his mouth gaped for air like a grouper's. Inside that awful head were those depressing memories of the fool he'd made of himself.

Dan sure didn't want to put on the foul clothes littering the floor, but where were his bags? What time was it? He found a phone and discovered it was 2:30 P.M. Out the window, the gardener worked across the lawn. Dan envied the distant figure's useful toil. Even more, he envied the man's position. The gardener had a reason to be there. He belonged there. He helped the place. Dan had none of those attributes. He was crabgrass. Dan had to talk to Ro.

The aromas of booze, cigars, and sweat wafted from the bloodstained shirt. He had to find his bag. The tie was bloodstained too — John Russell McDonald's tie! Dan held it like Macbeth's knife. Anywhere he put it, it shouted for justice. Should he flush it down the toilet? To hell with it. He'd buy a new one, replace it. Find a clean shirt, pay for his sins, talk it over with Ro, live through the hangover — that's all Dan had to do.

Ro's room was not just empty; it was clear of any sign of habitation. His bags weren't there. The cute beds looked chaste and smug. Ro wasn't just not in her room; her existence had been erased by the expert servants. No admission of sexual frolic came from any object there.

Dan looked at two photos of younger Ro with other boys. The males grinned happily; Ro beamed with a touch of naughtiness that suggested both subjects were sexual liaisons. He found another, a coming-out party picture with another happy partner. Dan placed himself in a long line of grinning boys she had taken to her side. The question that bothered him was whether he was the end of the line or somewhere in the middle.

She was tilted toward each boy in each picture, resting on his strong love, but only resting, apparently; soon to spring away from them and head back onto the track. It was insane to think of marrying her, with all this money and power. She'd use him up like a Popsicle and drop the stick in a wastebasket. He had no more to offer Ro than the same common gift of skin the boys in the pictures must have presented her.

Stinking Dan in the flouncy, perfect girl's room wished he hadn't left college. He'd guided fishing parties where the women had money. You could tell in a minute. The men were court jesters or empty martinets or fashion plates. They were never whole; the final command always came from the female tent: "I want to see you a moment." And everyone waits until the hired husband returns and announces the trip is over. Dan looked at the Chagall, lovers flying, cow's eyes, a world of emotion free of circumstance. Unfortunately, marriage to Ro would be oppressively circumstantial. He wished he could find a clean shirt.

Dan's mother's boyfriend, Gene, was a cowboy, gone for weeks at a stretch, always supremely confident of his position in her affections.

"Yes, sir," he told Dan once as his mother drove to the liquor store to get his brand of bourbon, "she's a great lady. They all can be if you keep ahead of them. Putting a woman on the lead brings out the worst in 'em."

Ro had deserted Dan and probably gone into New York City — that's where that guy's art gallery was, the guy who kept talking to her in a low voice with a grin, all dressed in black, all slick, like a magician.

A further examination of the note on Ro's door advised Dan that his clothes were in the very room in which he'd slept. They were all put away, washed and folded. Dan felt himself sliding into hopeless debt to this house, the company store. He put on a green shirt Ro had doted on, hoping she'd come back from New York City, wondering where it was.

*

New York City's sharp glitter became, after her high lunch with Daddy, crueler as Ro came down the other side of cocaine's bell curve. To escape the legions of tough strangers on the street, Ro took a cab back to the apartment. Not only was there no more cocaine; there was no company. Even the housekeeper was gone. Ro's depression thrived on her sudden solitude.

The gloss was gone off Ro's Manhattan return. The desolated apartment clicked as Ro hugged her knees in fetal solitude.

But was she alone? There was that thing in her. She was pregnant — a little yechnoid glob in some awful bag of skin was in there, absorbing life from her. Ro sobbed. No one knew where she was, no one would call unless she called, and she was too depressed to do anything. She wept and prayed for the phone to ring, for instructions from the gods.

abies rage with the most perfect indignation about any affront to their persons, appetites, or expectations. In time, doubt, sin, and guilt take the certainty out of such displays of emotion. What was bald anger turns inward, becomes depression. John Russell McDonald's secretary, Doris Laitch, even though she believed no prosecutor with access to every fact of her life could pin a thing on her, suffered from these ingrown rages to a frightening degree.

The nips of "Russian quicksilver," as the man at the package store where she purchased her own little bottles called it, stung this serpent of despond to temporary recoil, but every so often it was all around her, tightening. If people came and cocktails appeared among them, the serpent ran off in fright and she was fine. But waking in the morning alone in her bed, she was wrapped head to toe in its terrible coils.

Pride and self-discipline made Doris inevitably attend to her toilette, no matter how ghastly she felt. She wanted her body to be coifed, tailored, washed, and powdered. If the despair won, they would not find a slat-

tern. Hers would not be a cheaply dressed or inade-
quately attended corpse. Doris had been raised in dire,
ignorant, West Virginia poverty. She was enormously
proud of how meticulously she had erased every smudge
of that gaunt, toothless, dirty, rickety past — first on
the Corrasable bond of secretarial training, and then on
the creamy stationery of one of the greatest figures of the
Western world.

It was Doris Laitch who had once correctly advised
John Russell McDonald that the secretary of state was
lying to him. McDonald had come to trust Doris' opinion
in many areas. She understood what he wanted to know.
She was like a great surgeon's best nurse.

Her talent, industry, and ambition had brought her to
this suite of rooms in a grand house, an apartment of her
own on Park Avenue, luxurious hair and skin care, and
three mink coats. But this bonanza of prizes never was
enough to keep the awful thing away completely. What
made it worse now was an intuition that John Russell
McDonald was going to get rid of her.

There were days when she couldn't get through the
enemy lines to the safety of a few hours at Elizabeth
Arden's. There were days she just lay there, thinking of
the noose, wondering if there were any viscous injection
of potent fluids that could save her before she herself arranged the rope.

This morning was one of these. She felt the pistol in
the drawer watching her with its little blue steel eye. She
waved her head from side to side on a pillow no longer
plump, sleek, and washed, but crushed and granulated
from the battle of the night.

She was sure McDonald wanted to fire her. That little
bitch, Ro, the apple of John's eye, was in the house

again, talking about how Doris drank too much. That ridiculous wife, Jane, who knew how much closer John was to Doris than to herself, was also there to inflame the lynch mob. The two of them together, Goneril and Regan, were undoubtedly scheming against Doris, the fair Cordelia of King Lear McDonald.

Because one was his wife and the other his daughter, Doris was reduced, when they were in the house, to the mere rank of McDonald's employee. Doris loathed and feared the tenuousness of this bond. She could be fired, dropped, or severed (they were all words describing medieval torture). It seemed horribly unfair. The daughter had never been close, and the wife had never shown any respect for what John Russell McDonald, with the help of Doris Laitch, had done with her money. That enormous fortune McDonald had built of Jane's money was something Jane took for granted, as though it had been accomplished by the sun and rain.

In a *Racing Form* the new chauffeur had tracked in, Doris had read of the battle between the owners of a champion racehorse and their trainer. Clearly, the owners, new to racing and incandescently lucky, had come to resent the trainer's share of a glory they felt was meant for them alone. The horse's desire to gaze on nothing in front but home stretch had become their own jealous identity. They had begun to believe it would have happened with any trainer, or even with no trainer. The trainer had become a dangerous, frail, interloping intelligence, and they fired him, to his own and the profession's dismay. The horse continued to win anyway, and Doris felt the ingratitude and bitterness of the trainer personally, on two counts that reminded her of her own case.

First, it reminded her of Jane's fortune, which McDonald, with Doris' assistance, had trained to championship. Second, she thought of herself, no longer necessary to the fortune's now inevitable victory. The very instinct that had so brilliantly guided John Russell McDonald through twenty-seven years of acquisition now informed her he was tired of her, that he wanted her gone.

McDonald's impeccable timing of buying and selling that had yeasted Jane's inheritance to a great golden loaf had more than once been based on Doris' instinct. "I don't trust him"; "Not yet"; "I think so." How often these signals had changed his mind correctly! And how often when he disobeyed Doris' instinct he came to regret it: getting rid of that natural gas well, that Cézanne landscape (he still didn't seem to realize what a mistake that one was), that cook who baked as well — those were examples the rueful Doris had nodded at in the dark as she touched her lips to the glass circle of her flickering highball. How dare he fire her!

As Doris rubbed fifty-dollar unguent into her mortal flesh, more events from the night before recurred unpleasantly. After dinner, Doris had not joined the ladies in the drawing room, not because she couldn't (despite Jane McDonald's failure to invite her), but because she simply didn't want to sit with those two bitches, Ro and Jane.

She had instead gone straight to her room and had those highballs, looking out at the great shards of green lawn showing on the dark outside the downstairs windows.

She had waked up awfully, on the floor where she had apparently been lassoed and dropped by her own girdle as she'd tried to undress for bed. It was grimly quiet and accusingly late. Doris pulled herself up with an arm glowing in the dark with pain, and finished undressing. She even got a nightgown on (backward) and tried to hang things up before she got into bed.

Then there was no sleep for hours. The overdraft announced by the clock grew toward bankruptcy. Doris could find no stripe of longitude in the entire 360° of her revolving body that would allow her rest.

Toward dawn, she sat up and drank from a bottle in a drawer in the dark. (Bottles in drawers, guns in drawers, Bibles in drawers — are there any lonelier symbols?)

That was the horrible night that had brought her to this hangman's morning. She brushed her teeth and put them back in. She sent a little cobra bite of vodka after the great constrictor of despair and swathed her body in beige cashmere.

Doris went downstairs, fearful and agonized, her head bumping weakly on every step, deciding like a lover plucking the petals of a daisy whether to live or die. The last step, she realized five from the bottom, would tell her to die, so she stepped over one, sighed, and went into the office, where McDonald had left work for her and the servants had left a thermos of coffee.

*

Downstairs, Dan found Doris Laitch presiding over some paperwork. A palm tree of smoke bloomed from the ashtray at her varnished fingertips. The smell of coffee and cigarettes made Dan homesick for his mother's mornings in Boise.

"Good morning, Dan. Would you like some coffee?"

"Yes, please, ma'am."

"And a little Alka-Seltzer?"

"That would really be great."

Doris knew the drinker's morning. She chuckled sympathetically and settled Dan in the breakfast room. He kept thinking how much he was costing Ro's family. The English muffin package Doris was opening said 89¢ right on it.

Dan wondered how much an hour Doris cost and whether this part of her bill would be annotated "Making breakfast for Dan Novitski." But if she didn't do it, he wouldn't have dared, and he was starved.

"Ro went into town with her father."

"How far is that?"

"Under an hour. They're having lunch. You can probably reach her at the apartment pretty soon. It's after lunch."

The father. Dan was relieved to know she was with her father and not the slick art dealer. But it was unpleasant to consider what they must be talking about, the great pass-out scene in the library last night.

Stalactites of hangover came down from Dan's head to meet the stalagmites growing up from his stomach. He could feel the food spelunk into his tormented digestive tract. Breakfast at three in the afternoon, unwelcomed in Ro's parents' house. If the police arrived for him, he would admit everything and expect the gas chamber.

"Ma'am?"

"Yes, Dan."

"Could I ask you something about, umh, Ro's dad?"

"John Russell McDonald?"

"Right."

"Funny, I don't think I ever heard anybody call him that before. Ro's dad. Adorable."

Doris had fixed them both Bloody Marys along with Dan's food. Making Dan's breakfast had been just the excuse Doris needed for the day's first public drink. The well-named "nips" that bit her stomach with silver vodka teeth throughout the morning could now be joined by a real drink.

Dan looked at the Bloody Mary she handed him as she raised its twin, said cheers, and knocked back an audible glug of it.

"Like, what does he do?"

"You don't know?"

"No, ma'am."

"Ro's boyfriend doesn't know what Ro's dad does?"

"No, ma'am."

"Well, for instance, he's the new ambassador to France."

"Foreign service?"

"Oh no, Dan. Ambassadors aren't foreign service. Ambassadors come from the private sector."

"Oh."

"John Russell McDonald is terribly important in the private sector, Dan. In fact, he is, you might say, a prince of the private sector. He owns a great deal of it."

"Far out."

"And I have helped him for twenty-seven years, Dan."

"Right."

"Twenty-seven years."

"What's Ro's number, ma'am?"

"I don't think it would be inaccurate to say I had a very great deal to do with where John Russell McDonald is today."

"Yes, ma'am. If you have her number, I'd like to give Ro a call."

"A *very* great deal, Dan."

"Far out."

"Of course, Jane had money. But he's the one who built it, Dan. Everybody talks about her money. Her money was just a little pipsqueak compared to what we've done with it, Dan."

"Real fine."

"Let's have one more drink, shall we? There's absolutely nobody here but us chickens. You didn't drink yours."

"Actually, I don't think I better."

"Waste not, want not," said Doris, sweeping up Dan's glass.

Doris didn't leave after she finally gave Dan Ro's phone number in New York. She sat smiling and staring at him as if he were a television set.

Fuck it, thought Dan, and dialed anyway, smiling stupidly at Doris' glazed regard.

"Oh my God, it's a miracle," said Ro when she heard his voice. "Thank God, Dan — God, I love you! — I love you!"

Dan was at once astonished and enormously relieved by Ro's reaction to his call. Even Doris' stare vanished in the flash of happy hope that so suddenly replaced the gloomy doubt that had plagued him. Her love was bright fresh paint that made Dan's trip brand new again. She loved him; how could he ever have thought anything else?

"I'm coming out on the next train to be with you, my darling — my husband."

"I'm sorry about last night . . ."

"No, *I'm* sorry, darling. I shouldn't have shut you out — please forgive me. Tonight I'll be in your arms, my love."

"Great." Now Dan was aware of Doris again. He turned away from her. She was obviously too much in the bag to leave him alone.

"And I want it, Dan, I really want it."

"The baby?"

"That too, my darling. I'm coming on the next train. Oh, I love you. Good-bye."

She hung up. Dan smiled and nodded at Doris.

"What baby?" Doris asked.

"Ma'am?"

"I heard you say the baby."

"If you'll excuse me, ma'am, I'd like to go for a run." Doris blocked the door.

"What baby, you adorable young man?"

"Me and . . . Ro and I are going to get married."

"You don't say."

"Can I please get by?"

"Is our little Ro in a family way, young man?"

"Yes, ma'am."

Doris faded gracefully from a barricade and reformed as Dan's dancing partner.

"Oh, you divine thing." She laughed. "Does he know?"

"Who?"

"Ro's dad," she said ironically.

"Yes, ma'am."

"I think it's all too hysterically divine," said the tipsy Miss Laitch, releasing Dan to float back to John Russell McDonald's study.

*

Cheered by Ro's love, which was a sort of ratification of his presence in these swell surroundings, Dan forced himself into a trot down the graceful curve of the McDonald driveway, despite his ghastly hangover. He put on a face of heroic endurance and squinted down the row of trees bordering the road like a wounded general inspecting ranks despite personal pain. This brave scrutiny caused him to miss seeing one of the cautionary driveway bumps, and he almost twisted his ankle. He grimaced at the second of these menacing seams and passed by the gate onto the public road.

This world was stupendous and strange. Cortez was jogging on his first morning through Tenochtitlán. Ro was in New York, but in the grand houses of this enormously wealthy suburb she was abstractly present to Dan. This was her world, as unexpected and grand to Dan as the Rockies must have been to her. He had watched her change from someone whom he had let tag along, to girlfriend, to fiancée. Now he almost felt he'd been passed by her.

Thank heaven she sounded so loving on the phone! As he ran, he heard grand shouts of organ music. He loved her madly; he ran faster, his head weaving in rapture — he saw the two of them climb to the top of the highest peak of the Rockies, which had become a wedding cake on which they stood — a perfect, sugar couple. It was green and humid, abuzz with insects in the mansion land through when he ran. Dan's hangover beat rhythmically. He was examined by the contents of passing cars; the dark, expensive cars of the suspicious natives.

In the distance, another jogger appeared, disappeared behind an intervening hill, and appeared again. He was of John Russell McDonald's breed and vintage. He wore an old dark red sweater with an H on it that Dan just knew must stand for Harvard.

"Good afternoon," said Harvard as he passed. It was such a fancy and unexpected greeting, the man was on by before Dan was ready to return it.

Ro's lovestruck phone call had brought back Dan's lost confidence. He didn't feel like a despised freeloader anymore. He waved at the next car that passed. Another jogger appeared, heavier and younger than the first, a beefy squire in a proper jogging ensemble, striped like a race car. When he was near enough, Dan said to his potential new neighbor, "Good afternoon," to which the man replied, "Lovely day."

EIGHT

Ro thought of Dan's call coming at the exact nadir of her depression as a sign from Fate to reconsider their engagement. All that was fine about him came to mind as she rose, smiling, and set out to buy a dress she'd looked at with Muffy that morning, before rushing back to Connecticut and his good-looking arms. Sitting alone feeling sad is its own reward. Things were moving into truer and better perspective since his perfectly timed call.

The chic rush of Manhattan shoppers invigorated Ro. A woman glanced at Ro with the impersonal appraisal of the clothes-conscious, and Ro stood a little straighter and looked a little haughtier. It was great to be in New York again, away from the quilted vests and jeans of Colorado.

She found the wonderful dress. Ro decided to wear it out of the store straight to the train and Dan. It was one of those lucky garments that is so immediately right that Ro felt an increase in the intensity of her presence which others quickly ratified with admiring glances.

The call, the dress, and soon Dan's arms were all wonderful things just around the corner from her grim gloom of an hour earlier. She was happy, really; organically happy without a single drug. The right dress and the right man were agents of a true natural high.

Ro considered how unfair it had been to leave Dan quite so on his own his first night in Connecticut. He hadn't finished the evening well, but there were some memorable successes in his behavior, notably the African mask. She reviewed the way Dan had waded right into her father's little aesthetic séance with the mask. Dan had spoken up so unexpectedly, and with such unabashed equality, that Ro saw her father study him. And when he found the bullets and ruined Paul Steigen's sale, he had taken the moment from even her father. She sighed happily.

"It's really fabulous," said the saleswoman, mistaking Ro's exhalation for sartorial pleasure.

"I'm in love with a fabulous man," gushed Ro, surprising the saleswoman.

"You poor kid," said the clerk before she could stop herself. "What am I saying, as long as it makes you look great," she added.

Ro found herself looking at a dining room table as an aesthetic object for the first time in her life. Even the name of that part of the store sent a thrill through her: Home Furnishings. This red thing in a loft in SoHo, ringed with all her astonished old preppy friends roaring and eating fabulous food — she and Dan would do things like really put little Barbie Doll shades on fishes, serve real banana splits for dessert, have masses of flowers and soft places to sit. And then she and Dan would mysteriously disappear from a scene clamoring for their pace-setting presence. They would be in Idaho together, kissing softly and lying together in a meadow, hiking, fishing, quietly renewing their souls and cleaning their bodies of city excess.

All her friends, stuck with wimpy lawyers and inherited furniture, would lie awake at night, thinking enviously of Ro McDonald.

"Could you put a hold on it? I'm getting married."

"Yes, of course. What name?"

"John Russell McDonald."

Ro was pleased to see that her father's name caused a flicker of attention in the chic, gay salesman.

"Oh, of course."

"But I guess under Rowena McDonald."

"We'll take care of it, Miss McDonald."

"Thanks."

"And would you please congratulate your lucky fiancé for me?"

That's the way Ro liked it, when they knew about who she was if she cared to let them. It was a small but undeniable disappointment when the name meant nothing.

*

Dan pulled up from his jogging at the McDonald driveway. The run had successfully reclassified the pain of his hangover from its less bearable spiritual source to a physical one. Now he envisioned a cold turquoise splash in the pool and Ro's return. He hoped she would get back while he was still swimming, because it had been such a special pleasure the day before.

The McDonald house didn't look as big as it was until you were close. An American flag in the courtyard beyond it made its great but discreet luxury seem somehow almost patriotic.

It was so different from his old conception of riches, largely got from a Boise millionaire named Big Mike Mangurian, whose daughter Miriam was an awkward but bounteous classmate of Dan's. Big Mike had half a dozen real pinball machines in a playroom. At Miriam's memorable parties, he fractured roll after roll of quarters, popping them out like Life Savers to kids to work the machines. Dan could not imagine John Russell McDonald passing out quarters.

This was a very different situation. Orderly gardens and lawns mapped the grounds as far as Dan could see.

"With those legs, she's going to need every cent," said Dan's mother of Miriam Mangurian. Ro had tons more money and great legs. She was smart enough to graduate with honors. She spoke perfect French. Was there some flaw Dan had overlooked? Some mortalizing balance for her wealth?

Wealth, wealth, wealth; riches. The glittering green hedge was made of freshly printed greenbacks; the giant lawns were lakes of bills. The trees in the distance were mountains of moolah, and Dan was diving in and out of it like an otter.

Everyone seemed to be gone. It was so still, Dan's footsteps on the driveway sounded like a horse chewing. He looked at the palace and felt a moment of private triumph. He had taken the castle. For the moment, as its solitary inhabitant, the place was his. Ro had just said she loved him so much she couldn't see straight — Dan decided he could handle it. He wouldn't wind up an ornamental husband. He could live with all this as naturally as if it were just a tent. He trotted toward the pool, into which he decided to cannonball naked, yelling "Wahoo" to celebrate his sudden glory.

Dan pulled off his clothes as impulsively as if he were jumping into the sack with Ro. He flung open the gate to the pool and took one step of what he had expected to be a six-step run into the air above the pool.

Ro's mother was by the water in an encampment of suntanning equipment. She lowered a magazine and raised the brim of her straw hat, revealing a pair of sunglasses staring big, blank, and black as moth's eyes at Dan's frontal nudity.

"Sorry, sorry," he said, mortified, trying to get his pants on and closed. Why hadn't he even considered that there might be someone at the pool?

"Hello," she said in the warm voice he had felt to be so friendly at dinner. There was no trace of disapproval.

"Sorry," he said again.

"For what?"

"I was just going to take a swim," said Dan, plunging for the dressing room, where he was relieved to find a wide choice of bathing suits.

He peered at his face in the dressing room mirror.

"You asshole," he whispered to it. He stepped back to appraise himself for presentation to Ro's mother. He flexed his stomach muscles. He checked the effect of a clenched fist on the machinery of his forearm.

Dan was off the ground, on his way into the wet blue, when he realized Mrs. McDonald had spoken some civility that expected a reply. Any respectable human being would have paused to exchange greetings before launching himself into the pool. With only his vulgar splash for a reply, Dan stayed under water for a length, cursing himself for bungling this audience with his future mother-in-law.

As though wrestling his own bad manners before her,

like a gladiator, Dan did five laps in a violent butterfly stroke. Then he did ten more in a strong, suave racing crawl. Two things occurred to him as he rolled smoothly up and down the pool: that he was showing off for Ro's mother and that he was in some way betraying Ro right where they'd made love the day before.

Dan heard a splash. He slowed his pace, but continued lapping the pool. The fact that Jane McDonald had joined him in the water elated and excited him. Was she going to do laps, too? He remembered how he had sexually ambushed Ro's laps. Might the beautiful Jane be heading toward him like a torpedo? Of course not! What a base and ridiculous thought! Dan somersaulted in a racing turn and avoided looking in the direction of her splashes. Then it happened: she grabbed him. Dan was overcome with a heart-stopping, electric thrill until he realized in an appalling moment it was not Ro's mother but the old Labrador retriever who had joined him. The first glimpse of black and claws Dan took to be psychedelic hallucination over the unbearable, ecstatic realization that Ro's mother was hugging him. But it was the dog.

"Jack! Jack come out of there. Bad dog!" shouted the real Jane McDonald from her suntanning encampment. The old dog turned for the shallow end. Dan was blushing so badly, he had to submerge to regain his composure.

"Are you on the swimming team?"

"Oh, I was," answered Dan, with his elbows hanging him from the swimming pool, at her feet. "But I'm too old now. It's a teen-age sport."

"How old are you, Dan?"

"Twenty-one."

Dan pulled himself gracefully out of the pool. Jane stood up and moved her chair to talk with him. Her fingers were long and slim and bent gracefully back and forth several times on the way to perfect clear nails. Her legs were even more disturbingly beautiful. Dan's heart beat more than it should from a swim.

"How long have you and Ro been together?"

Ro's name quickly checked Dan's infatuation. What a dumb way to feel! He was ashamed.

"Last semester. She's certainly a fine person, Mrs. McDonald."

"Oh, good."

"Very smart and terrifically decent."

"She is?"

Ro's mother seemed to be looking at Dan with genuine curiosity, as though she had never met Ro. Once again, Dan felt baffled.

"Yes, sure she is."

"In what way?"

"Intelligent. She graduated cum laude."

"Good for her. And how is she decent?"

"How?"

"Yes."

Dan figured he was being slipped the old Socratic-dialogue technique: feigned ignorance from Plato to expose completely the student's thinking.

"Well, to other people. And me. She's nice to people. She doesn't let you down."

"I'm so glad to hear this. She can't stand me."

"Ma'am?"

"You know how it is. She adores John Russell McDonald, so she's jealous of me. It's one of those classical psychological situations. You must have heard her talk about it."

"She never talked about any of it. I didn't even know she was loaded — I mean, I didn't even know it was like this where she came from."

"Didn't she tell you about her family?"

"Hells bells, Mrs. McDonald — I don't get any of this!"

Dan's voice startled him. It sounded like a dog suddenly barking at some mystery. He was talking on before he even caught up with that first outburst.

"I didn't even know she was pregnant. If she didn't want to get married, I wouldn't be here. I feel stupid most of the time."

Jane pulled up her shades and stared at Dan. She had blue eyes and black hair. She was so beautiful, Dan couldn't even remember what he was trying to think about. He wished he weren't talking to her at all. He wished he had a guitar and were singing her the most beautiful song in the world.

"You and Ro are getting married?"

"Well, that was the idea."

"She's pregnant?"

"Didn't they tell you?"

"No."

The relationships of this family were constructed in some new mathematics in which Dan couldn't figure out the simplest equations.

Dan didn't want to stay with Jane McDonald another minute. Neither did he ever want to spend another minute without her for the rest of his life. Her towel was a leopard skin. Her shades were a tiara. She was the queen of nature, twice as long as Ro and without a single flat surface, just beautifully filled volumes of skin flashing with sheen from the ointments in the straw basket by her side. Straw basket? Ivory maybe, or amber. Even her toes were perfect, not knobby, not twisted; toes that touched the earth as if it were a jewel.

What the hell was this all about? Dan was breathing through his mouth. He quickly touched it to make sure he wasn't drooling. The spots of water were cooking off the cement around him. Was he heating them up, or was it the sun?

"She's a really, really fine person," shrilled someone using Dan's voice box.

"I think she's a fabulous person. But you can't make people like you, and I made every mistake in the book with her, raised her with nannies, forgot about her too often. I don't blame her for loathing me."

"Oh, she doesn't *hate* you," retorted Dan, who had never heard Ro even mention this unreal female for what appeared to Dan to be the most obvious reasons. Ro was a mortal girl. Her mother was a goddess.

"Just the other day she was telling me about what fun she had with you looking at those cave paintings at Lascaux."

"I wasn't there."

"Oh."

"I think she's a very lucky girl, Mr. Novitski."

"She handles it real well. She never talks about any of it. I never heard about any of it until yesterday, when I saw this place."

"I mean lucky about you."

"Oh, thanks."

Dan was mortally chagrined to realize how far from the mark this kind judgment of himself was. He was betraying Ro with every thought and feeling attached to him at that moment. By the pool at this creature's feet. He felt like rolling over on his side and whimpering like a dog, or spreading his arms in a swan dive upon her. It was an effort to keep a lid on the hallucinatory gases rising within him.

"She's just smart as hell and awfully good in the mountains," said Dan to the perfect toes.

"Going out west was her own idea," said Jane to the horizon as Dan looked up. "She's brave and independent, and you might tell her some time that her mother admires the hell out of her."

"Oh, right. She really is a terrific person. She's just a natural about fishing. I just told her a few things and she was terrific."

"What did you study?"

"History of Art. I met Ro in Chinese painting. Mr. Woo. The first day he showed us this slide of, you know, regular old Chinese painting and he said, 'Ancient painting, no?' And then he said, 'But see here, a truck, on closer inspection, a Dodge truck, not ancient Chinese painting — a new painting of modern communist painter.'

"Mr. Woo's pretty funny without meaning to be. Ro and I laughed about that. That's how I got to know her. She got a ninety in that course and she's not even a History of Art major. She's just terrifically intelligent."

"I'm so delighted to hear it. I feel so guilty about her."

"Me too."

"You do? Why?"

"Oh no, I don't mean guilty. She's a terrific, terrific person, and sometimes I don't even know if I even deserve her."

"Do you love her?"

"Oh sure, of course. Like mad." Dan heard the shrill clang of the Liars bell suddenly ring in his brain.

"Good. That's important. At least it gives you something to fall back on — the memory of love. At least you know why you did something, even if it's all changed. I can't tell you how important it is, Dan, to your self-esteem, to know you loved someone."

"Right."

"Cimabue," said Dan to the old Lab, Jack, who had arrived again like Charon, the boatman on the River Styx, some pilot between worlds. The old bastard of a dog poked at Dan with his nose, like a doctor tapping for bronchial echoes: *Yes, Mrs. McDonald, this boy is riddled with lust.* This was no dog; it was an augur, a wizard, a troll.

"I was so impressed when Ro wanted to go west on her own. I was never so daring," said Jane McDonald.

Dan was glad the dog didn't laugh out loud and reveal he had been sent to ferry Dan across the blue, chlorinated, unmoving River Styx next to them, to the bright pointy flames of hell he so richly deserved for thinking what he was thinking about Ro's mother. Just as this prosecuting vision came into accusatory focus, the gate opened and Ro herself came running across the lawn in a new dress, her arms out like Christ's on the cross. He hugged her when she landed on him. She picked up her feet and Dan whirled her insincerely in a circle.

"I love your dress," said Jane.

"Isn't it great?"

"Ro, could you come up to the house and help me get dressed? I want to talk to you."

"Oh yes — I want to talk to you, too. Would you excuse us, my love?"

When they walked off toward the house, Dan was surprised to see that Jane and Ro were the same height after all.

NINE

I t was an unlikely walk from the pool to the house for Jane and Ro, who had never been close. For Ro, it wasn't entirely unlike the table she had thought about buying for the marital loft.

"I'm going to need your help, Mummy."

Involuntarily, Jane squeezed her daughter's arm. The form was taking on substance. There was a sudden bolt of maternal love. Jane blushed.

"What are his objections?"

"That I'm doing it because I'm pregnant."

"Ro dear, are you?"

Jane didn't want to upstage her daughter's announcement by telling her Dan had already made the annunciation. Once again the artifice of their intimacy struck her.

"Yes. And I'm very happy about it."

"I can't tell you how much I like that boy. He's very different and attractive and independent."

"I think we'll start out in New York — get a loft — he

majored in History of Art — maybe Paul Steigen could give him a job."

"I think you ought to stay away from Paul Steigen."

"Why?"

"Well, for one thing, he's a little too close to home. Too close to your father."

"So?"

"I don't like him. I don't trust his advice. He's the one who talked your father into selling that Cézanne from Mother's estate."

"Well, maybe he knows somebody else."

"Maybe. I think he knows lots of people," said Jane with a touch of sarcasm.

Ro kept to herself the notion that her mother didn't like Steigen because Steigen was close to her father. In the long parental war that boomed and flashed through the background of Ro's childhood, she had always rooted for her father. After all, what with her mother's beauty and money, he was the underdog. She made up her mind to get Dan together with Paul as soon as possible.

"His family owns a fishing thing; his uncle guides people in the Rockies. He wants to do that, so maybe some kind of school where he'd have time to do the fishing thing. I love it in the mountains with him. They have a camp that's just to die over, all these meadows and streams and stuff."

"You've told your father all this, too?"

"Yes."

"I don't think it's what he had in mind."

"I know, but so what?"

"Good for you."

"Daddy always has something in mind for everybody

and everything. Sometimes everybody and everything have something in their own minds!"

Jane stopped and took both of Ro's upper arms in her hands. There were tears in her eyes and a wide smile that wiggled a couple of times from the emotion running through her.

"I am so proud of you, Ro!"

"Oh — Mummy!"

Ro pressed herself against her mother, excited at how many ways she had discovered access to adult conventions (marriage, serious talks with one's mother, furniture-shopping) and yet slightly suspicious about all of them. Was her mother truly proud of her, or was she just happy to hear Ro knock her father?

Jane felt the defenses she had constructed against Ro (who had only just finished a vituperative adolescence, during which she had relentlessly and mercilessly had at Jane) sliding away like spring ice into the Volga. Choruses sang hymns of renewal. Jane would help Ro realize a happy marriage with Dan in the face of McDonald's disapproval (which Jane was sure was based in McDonald's own Olympian ambition for the best possible everything, including sons-in-law). She would guide her daughter through the minefield of matrimony with all the tricks and wisdom time and failure had taught her. If only her feelings of love and sympathy for her daughter were as pure as this great moment of reconciliation deserved!

TEN

oft-shelled crabs are an Atlantic Ocean phenomenon available for a limited time as spring becomes summer. The soft, succulent delicacies the waiter sets before you are shaped like the same horn-hard, prehistoric-looking little monstrosities whose brutal claws figure in nightmares. But a light touch of the fork is sufficient to pop open these savory oceanic treats. Their claws, legs, bellies, and backs are as soft as ours. They are not a separate species from the hard-shelled panzers scuttling across the sea bottom the rest of the year, but those same creatures, caught in what must be a singularly humiliating natural process called molting. Because they outgrow their carapaces as children outgrow shoes, they must step outside them by some legerdemain and spend a few weeks soft, while their new, weak skin hardens into armor. Their great claws are only rubber knives. Their steel armor is tissue. They are weaker than any of the soft little bits of life they spend the rest of the year gnashing to bits. They must spend this vulnerable, embarrassing time hiding in shadows, hoping their frightening shape will trick predators into presuming it is composed of armor, as usual.

The expression on John Russell McDonald's face as his car pulled away from "21" was likewise best hidden in the shadows of his limousine. When he was looking forward to Vanilla, his face, which even in sleep was worthy of a place on Mount Rushmore, became vacant, vapid, even a little goofy. He smiled. He had stars in his eyes. He was a mooncalf, a teen-age idiot, a puppy standing happy and guilty in a puddle of pee.

He called Ellen Weld "Vanilla" because her hair reminded him of the richest vanilla ice cream. She didn't mind the sex-object implications of his nickname for her, because she thought he was terrific. He'd *given* her a Cézanne. He was enormously knowledgeable about art, handsome as the men in any advertisement attempting to assert wealth, distinction, and breeding, and richer than chocolate.

The great man, looking like a plate of fried eggs, sunny side up, was pleased to see a new-mown orb under his chauffeur's cap (just as well he couldn't see the fuchsia-tinted pigtail coiled under that cap, all that remained of the morning locks of this modern man). He was pleased by lunch with Ro (he had not only said the right thing, but phrased it handsomely). He was pleased to see people strolling under a building they couldn't know he and Jane owned, on a mall he had given them under it (to improve the quality of their lives). But these were only attendant pleasures to the grand one that lay ahead.

Not only did McDonald feel the same intense pleasure and satisfaction with Vanilla that he felt for the finest art, the richest deals, and the noblest gestures; he also felt it for himself as he sat alone in her apartment, waiting for her to wend her way through New York City's underground entrails from the Columbia library, where she spent so much time extracting information and putting it on file cards for her dissertation. He felt like a student again, a young bachelor again, just plain young again, as he looked around the place.

Her books were jammed so helter-skelter in an overstocked bookcase along one wall that it looked like a great cubist work itself. The pretty, pretty Cézanne (so subtle and deeper than its own prettiness that McDonald thought it had to be hers who was so like it) was of a perfect proportion for the little Victorian upstairs fireplace it hung above. There were many photographs, snapshots, and portraits of her family and vacations that bespoke upper-class American life in what McDonald felt was a sound and modest form. In the photographs, one could detect wealth a couple of generations ago, thinning to well-off in the next generation, and enough in this one. Someday, she would probably marry a man who would bolster her present status (and she'd make up some unprovocative explanation for her Cézanne); would use her doctorate in some part-time museum capacity. (This was more or less how McDonald the protector would have it go for her after he departed this life.)

McDonald went to the bathroom. Its untidiness uncharacteristically appealed to him. The hurried preparations for dates and dinner parties after a busy day, suggested by the clutter and disorder there, delighted him because it reminded him of her. She was at a stage of life he remembered totally, hurrying to get all the best of it while the opportunity and interest were at their most intense.

They had met at a dinner party. She knew of his collection. She was dying to see it. Pretty girls know they can see whatever they want, but pretend to be surprised and touched when they are in fact invited to realize their wish. She had been like a pretty fire in a pretty fireplace in the tuxedo gloom of that dinner party. Her eyes were bright as a fox's and her breasts like a pair of fresh tennis balls. Her piece of family jewelry gave her gentility, and her eager, educated conversation gave her anything she might want from John Russell McDonald.

Face creams, nail files, hair machinery, perfumes, spermicidal jelly, toothpaste, sponges, and powders; this collection made him laugh softly as he looked around. The apartment was so small compared with the usual spaces surrounding McDonald that it reminded him of the navy, of a submarine, even.

She produced little meals for him from a kitchen the size of the galley on a racing yacht. Her cuisine was simple and expensive, from the New York food boutiques that bring the purest, most obscure and authentic comestibles from Europe and present them in chicly decorated stores at impressive prices.

McDonald's vintage wines, the Cézanne, silk-satin draperies, and a queen-sized bed were the signs of his intrusion in her apartment. He was sitting on this last, drinking a glass of this first and looking at a big book of plates of paintings, one of which belonged to him, when he delightedly heard the rustlings of her arrival.

"Hi," she said as easily and cheerily as she would to a lover of her own age. He held her pretty domes and hollows against him, smiling idiotically. "Vanilla," he said softly.

She set about arriving home again, putting away her

books and bags with the graphics of expensive stores emblazoned on them, kicking off her shoes, and lighting a cigarette.

"I can't stay tonight, dearest," said John as he saw something airmailed from France emerge from one of the bags.

"Oh damn, this is real pâté de campagne, fresh."

"My daughter, Ro, is here from college. Actually, she graduated and there are problems."

"Oh."

It felt awkward for McDonald to say "my daughter" to Vanilla. He realized Ro and Vanilla weren't far from the same age. The anger he had felt over imagining Ro fucking the kid at dinner came back as a different pain when he spoke of Ro's existence to this contemporary of hers, with whom he had been hoping with every fiber of his being to have that very pleasure shortly. Her "Oh" announced a little cloud in the room. The joy that had quickened from a gallop to a dead run when he heard her rustle outside halted. She kept moving as though nothing untoward had happened, but McDonald knew she was annoyed. The inevitable intrusion of his other life would grow as their relationship progressed. He feared there would be a time when the two lives challenged one another mortally, and which would probably have to mean the affair would end. The ominous cloud had begun to form.

"She's pregnant. She came home with him. It's a very touchy and unpleasant situation."

McDonald told Vanilla this not only to get it off his chest, but to divert her attention from the unhappy prospect of the inevitable showdown between an affair and a marriage to a sort of common enemy, the more respectable dilemma of a responsible father. Vanilla's sympathy for McDonald the father's plight would deflect of a scrutiny of her own.

"Oh, dear. What's he like?"

"Who?"

"The boyfriend."

"Perfectly awful. He's a silly, drunken hillbilly who obviously likes what he sees when he looks around the house."

"Oh, God. Is he completely wrong for her?"

"Oh, he's her age," said McDonald, with a note of reassurance that surprised him; "a classmate."

McDonald brooded over his rush to approve of the lout's age. Did it mean he disapproved of himself with Vanilla? How unpleasant it was to taint the joy that had grown all the way over here to paradise.

"He's not there to marry her?"

"Yes, he thinks he is."

"Poor Mac."

She stood on her bare toes and kissed him. That moist taste eradicated all else. There were no worries; the conversation stopped by the kiss was then hurled by it into oblivion. Clothes and moans, limbs and lips, orifices and things to insert in them covered the big bed like a crowd milling at a county fair. Then the ferris wheel began to rise and drop them, and finally came the fireworks display.

Although he disapproved of cigarettes, Vanilla's postcoital smoke was for McDonald one of the most supremely romantic moments he could recall. She seemed like a wise and total woman when she stared at the ceiling, spuming tobacco smoke at it, her arm under her head, a sheen of cooling perspiration and the rank fragrance of lovemaking about her. He kissed the lobe of her ear.

"I have a present for you."

Vanilla's response was instant, electric attention. Those were the words and this was the same occasion as the time he had given her the Cézanne. She even looked around the room. He pulled on his big creamy shirt and went to the jacket hanging on a chair. She watched him eagerly, smiling. She pulled a sheet over herself. He handed her the key.

"To what?" she asked.

McDonald chuckled at the big-eyed Christmas child who had replaced the sensuous woman of the world in the cute clutter of the love nest. Vanilla looked at the key and at McDonald.

"Thirty-two rue de la Bruyère," he said.

"Paris?"

"You'll love it; two rooms and a balcony on the Left Bank. Twenty minutes from the embassy."

"Mac!"

"It's about the same size as this."

"I can't just pick up and go, can I?"

"Why not? Write your paper there."

"Give up my job at the gallery?"

"Darling, it's not a problem. In fact, Paul will help you get a job in one there. I've already talked to him."

"Mac — please don't always be two steps ahead of me."

"What do you mean?"

"You can't just move a person's life around to suit your plans."

"Of course not. I'm sorry, I meant it as a surprise."

"I'd be a French mistress."

"Vanilla, forgive me."

"That's funny. I think my grandfather had one. What would he say if he knew his granddaughter would be one?"

"So damn presumptuous of me. I just didn't think."

"You've told Paul Steigen?"

"I did."

"So my job is already gone. I'm a French mistress. I'm a fait accompli."

"Of course not. Forget the whole thing."

"Can Cézanne go back to France?"

"Vanilla, I was thinking only of myself as usual. It's not until September anyway, dearest. Why don't we both get back to it in a couple of days?"

"I want to think about it."

"It's sure as hell not a very good beginning."

"What?"

"To my career as a diplomat. I've bungled my first negotiation."

"No you haven't, darling."

What a pleasure it was to have this vital part of life in place! thought McDonald, leaving. How many other old goats had girls like that? McDonald could almost be certain he knew which of his colleagues had girls and which didn't — but he was utterly positive none of them had prizes like Vanilla. She was that thing so infernally unattainable even when he was young — a nice girl.

John Russell McDonald plunged youthfully down the narrow, warped, carpeted stairs, out of the old brownstone containing Vanilla's apartment. A block away, his car was waiting. As soon as he was on the sidewalk, the armor was back, glistening, glorious, harder than ever. Mad molting with Vanilla was over.

ELEVEN

an shampooed his hair in an effort to look his best at dinner. He'd learned the trick of hair conditioner from Ro, some kind of unguent that kept one's locks from locking out the comb. There was none of this magic smoother in his bathroom. His hair was raveled as a doormat. Dan put on a towel and peered out into the long quiet gloom of hallway. He walked briskly to Ro's door, feeling particularly, ludicrously wet, naked, and out of place in the dressy formality of that hallway. As he got his hand on the knob of Ro's door, Doris Laitch's voice opened a trap door under his feet.

"Oh good, a bedroom farce," cooed the grinning Doris.

"Oh, good afternoon," said Dan, as though his new Eastern possession, this quaint, formal term of address, were the suit he wasn't wearing.

"Little Ro is not in there, young man. She's with her mother — no fun in the haystack."

"I just wanted to get something out of the bathroom."

"A little birth control thingie?"

"Hair conditioner."

Doris laughed. "That's right — you don't need your little thingies now, do you?"

"Excuse me." Dan blushed and pushed open the door. His pulse was working hard, he noticed in the isolation of Ro's bathroom. He read the conditioning directions to get Doris' remarks out of his head. When he passed back out, she was still there, leaning against the wall, arms folded, head back, smiling like a hooker. Dan held up the tube of conditioner in salute and returned to his room.

"Shit," he said aloud as he got back in the shower, "they've got dragons and witches in this castle." (That thing in her hand, cigarette case or little purse or whatever it was, had looked for a minute like a pistol.)

A shower is a wonderful place to meditate. The mantra of falling water brings the washing one to undistracted solitude. The first rupture of peace, the lack of conditioner, was healed. The next, the unfortunate interview with the crazy beige lady, closed over. Dan threw his head back and sent the lances and sabers of the water cavalry to chase the sluggish conditioner out of his hair.

"I'm just here to meet Ro's parents," said Dan to his shower. It was a much better made shower, he noted, than the flimsy one at home. "Ro and I are getting married," he further explained to the soap.

Marriage represented to Dan, among other things, a unification of the erotic urge, a final solemn twist that would bring a single image into focus. There, on the phone, in the marital crosshairs, sharp and clear, was Ro. Jogging that afternoon, he had run with Ro's face before him, like a Mexican peasant crawling fifty miles on his knees after a pure image of Nuestra Virgen de Guadalupe. He had expected to be baptized in this faith when he jumped in the pool.

Instead of baptism, the pool had brought him to Jane McDonald. In the next mere piece of an hour, Dan's resolve to live happily ever after with Ro was cracked and aged. Jane McDonald sat by the pool — Cleopatra on the Nile — and Dan's clear, sharply focused future was a blazing pile of shards, the smashed lens of certainty glittering next to a bottomless swimming pool of sexual mystery.

Once again Dan pitched these thoughts out and concentrated on the purpose of being where he was: meeting the parents. He rubbed the towel harder than necessary. Ro, of course, would want to meet Dan's parents. She was used to successful, brilliant, well-dressed parents. Dan's mother didn't even always make the bed. She went with a cowboy. His uncle Archie never took off his hat. Worst of all, who was Dan's father? The postcard was all Dan knew. His mother had expunged all traces of her one-time husband.

What would it be like when these clans came together, this grand and beautiful paragon of American home life and his own strange little pumpkin patch of "folks"? Maybe he and Ro could elope.

A limousine so expensively quiet that its tires' abrasion on the gravel driveway made more noise than its engine pulled in below Dan's window. The chauffeur rushed around to open the door, emitting John Russell McDonald in an imposing gray suit, a steel skyscraper of international business and politics with a briefcase and a blazing halo of sterling silver hair. Looking down upon this halo, Dan shuddered, considering his inevitable audience

with this superhuman, before whom he had ignomin-
iously gone down, waving a cigar and bleating like a goat,
the night before. After McDonald disappeared into the
house, the chauffeur did a funny little jig, swept off his
hat, and bowed like a courtier, mocking his departed employer. What made the gesture particularly ludicrous was
the man's purple pigtail — a punker hiding in a chauffeur's black serge!

Dan pulled out his only other clean button-down shirt
like a man on the wrong end of an old movie chase pulling out his last bullet. He realized he wasn't going to be
able to hold out much longer at the castle. He remembered he had no tie, that he had, in fact, destroyed one
belonging to the king who had just clomped in over the
drawbridge. It was all becoming impossible again.

His door opened and Ro stepped in. She smiled, her
eyes shining, her arms held forth. The front of Dan's last
clean shirt rose, and welcome spread quickly up from his
groin into his brain, erasing all doubt.

"What a coincidence, darling," said Ro. "Neither of
us is wearing underwear. Wait; I want to wear this dress
for dinner."

Dan didn't want to wrinkle his last shirt, either.

Making love to Ro was wonderfully familiar to Dan,
who needed some such postcard from home in this
strange land. Ro thought this particular piece of lovemaking was as fine as the table she would show him tomorrow in New York for their loft.

"Ro, I really fucked up last night."

"Don't worry, darling."

"I mean, I even wrecked that tie. I wrecked everything, didn't I?"

"Mummy *adores* you."

"It wasn't her tie."

"I'm taking you into town tomorrow, Dan. I want you to meet my friends. There's going to be a cocktail party — I thought we might talk to Paul Steigen . . ."

"That old bastard at dinner you liked so much?"

"Paul's not old. Dan — are you jealous?"

"No."

"He's a wonderful man. Wait until you see his gallery."

"I don't like guys like that."

"He might help you."

"Why, so he could see you?"

Hot huffs of unpleasantness kept steaming through Dan as he recalled the old smoothie's alligator grins at Ro in the candlelight.

"I love it. You're jealous!" said Ro.

"Oh, forget it."

"We're going to stop and see him."

"Great."

"What's the matter?"

"Nothing, only this tie is wrecked — I mean look, I wrecked your father's tie."

"I'll get another one."

"Ro."

"What?"

Dan sat down, flushed and frustrated. It was so easy for Ro here and so hard for him.

"I don't know."

"I love you, darling. Wait here — I'm going to get you a new tie."

Dan nodded. Ro smiled, dropped the dress back over her utter nudity with the effect of a film cut, and scampered out. Dan resumed his shirt, again feeling like a

confused outsider, a freeloader, and some new unpleasantness, the feeling of being a toy. What did she think he
was? Her Ken Doll?

*

John Russell McDonald's ties were the province of Edwards, the valet. Their solemn, military order made Ro
smile. Her father's dressing room was like the inner
sanctum of the malest male club. It tut-tutted, grumbled,
muttered, and twitched miserably as she entered, clad
only in the thin pretty cotton of her new dress, bare-
footed, just fucked, adorably happy.

Ties, Ro concluded, obviously had a complex and neu-
rotic connection with the male member. They hung from
the neck, the throne of the brain, an arrow pointing
straight to the cock. Her daddy and all the old big shots
at a top-level business powwow, all wearing brightly col-
ored silk arrows pointing at their penises, as ludicrous as
South Sea island warriors tying theirs up with feathers
and fibers to assert their virility to one another.

Daddy's ties were generally ponderous, conservative,
somber ones. Ro picked through them for something
suited to the powerful young knight she had just left. She
found a fabulous one from long ago (when Daddy was a
young knight). Ro considered that she ought to look at
her horoscope and discover why today was a day she was
able to find exactly what she wanted every time. She slid
it out and held it up just as her father entered, jacketless,
with his suspenders down, expecting, of course, to be
alone as he changed for dinner. In some hideously comical bit of choreography, the father lowered his trousers
just as the daughter pivoted, wearing his tie.

"Jesus."

"Oh, excuse me, Daddy."

He pulled up his trousers. Both of them realized something Ro put into words before she could stop herself.

"Daddy, where are your underpants?"

John Russell McDonald pictured the site where that garment undoubtedly reposed: the chair in front of Vanilla's little Olivetti typewriter, with its inevitable index card of facts about a painting.

"What?"

Ro would have withdrawn the question immediately; in fact, she probably never would have asked it at all, if it hadn't been for what she had been doing fifteen minutes earlier with Dan.

"Don't you wear underpants?"

"What are you doing in here?"

"Borrowing a tie for Dan."

"Oh."

"Daddy!"

She kissed her embarrassed father. Sex gave Ro that democratic insight whores feel for the absurdly simple truth of masculinity. She left at once, leaving McDonald squinting into the middle distance, realizing it was time to take a moment with the charts and find out where he was before going down to dinner.

*

Dan watched Jack, the old black dog he had recently suspected of supernatural origins, saunter into the grand living room and drop like a banana peel on the floral glory of a great English Aubusson rug.

It could have been a meadow, the linoleum floor of a Boise kitchen, or the back of a pickup, and the dog would have lain down in the same way. That, Dan decided as he stood there alone, slicked down and dressed for dinner, was the key to behavior here. Treat these things as surfaces, these people as regular humans, this kingdom as earth, or you will feel like a tightrope-walker suddenly remembering the part that isn't the rope.

"Would you like a Manhattan," asked Doris Laitch in a coy pose in a doorway.

"Ma'am?"

She held up a pretty cocktail.

"Manhattan."

"Sure."

Dan, for want of anything else to do, crossed over and watched Doris prepare the cocktail in that bar where he'd made the mistake of ordering a beer the night before.

"Manhattans are nice," said Doris Laitch, airily, dealing bottles with pharmaceutical detachment. "I just started drinking Manhattans again in October, or maybe it was November — that warm week in November — what a surprise that was! I'd forgotten about Manhattans. John Russell McDonald always has two martinis —Russian vodka — and I just put my foot down and said, 'Doris, remember Manhattans? Why don't you just have a Manhattan for a change?' I gave John one, and you know what he said?"

"No, ma'am."

"He said, 'What's that for?' Just like that — like a growly old dog. 'What's that for?' And I said, 'It's a Manhattan, John. I thought it might be fun to try a little change.' And you know what he said?"

"No, ma'am."

"He said, 'I don't want a Manhattan, Doris.' "

"Right."

"I don't want a Manhattan, Doris," said Doris in a sour voice, twisting her face to add scorn to her performance.

"I think a person should stay flexible," she commented next in a voice of Athenian reason; "otherwise, you get all old and sour. Have you noticed that, young man?"

"Oh sure. It's real good."

Only a few hours before, Dan had decided never to have another drink his whole adult life. But then that was also about the time he had vowed to keep only unto Ro, forsaking all others. It was before that confusing swim. Besides, the name of the drink appealed to him.

Dan stood up so fast, he slopped his Manhattan when Jane McDonald walked into the room in a caftan white as a burning light bulb against her glittering tan. What a different pair she and Doris made, like a before-and-after ad, these two poles of the female possibility. Doris opened her painted nails in a little fan and threw back a few planks of her plywood hair in a gesture of miffed acknowledgement of Jane's entrance.

"Sit down, Dan. I'm going to make a drink," said Jane. As Dan did so, he realized too late that he was sitting down right on top of Doris. He heard a little despairing cry and then felt a great slap on his butt.

"You might just watch where you're going, young man!" said Doris, furious at being so quickly and completely eclipsed by Jane's entrance.

*

John Russell McDonald was accustomed to dignity and grace. The opposite of such is getting caught with your pants down. His private parts lolled out like a tongue in a fun house. His knees were two clowns' faces in the beautiful old Georgian dressing mirror. He pulled up a pair of sleek, fleecy drawers and quickly reached for the trousers Edwards had laid out. It was not only embarrassing; it was troubling to find Ro in his dressing room, to have her find he'd forgotten his what she called "underpants." ("Drawers," McDonald called them, a much less cheap, noisy, and vulgar name than "underpants.")

He had never seen her in there before. No one but Edwards was expected to be in among his clothes, his bathing things, his nakedness. What troubled him about it was her reaction, like a tart laughing at him. The little bastard somewhere in this house had not only violated his daughter, but pimped her into whoredom. McDonald pulled a tie viciously from the rest and snapped the lash, ready to beat the son of a bitch raw as soon as he was tied to the mast and the crew assembled.

Did Ro seem a whore to him especially because he had just been with Vanilla? Vanilla never seemed like a whore to McDonald. She was a romance. She loved him. She was crazy about the best things about John Russell McDonald, so crazy about his virtues that he felt refreshed and quite sure of hers. If only he hadn't discussed Ro with Vanilla. It was putting those two women together for the first time in his mind, realizing how close they were in age, even in background, manner, point of view, and ambition, that had appalled McDonald.

Either Ro was no longer a little girl or Vanilla was a little girl, which made McDonald a dirty old man. Ro's leer and knowing laugh outraged him again. He held the tie like a garrotte to strangle the sleazy pander who had punctured and dissipated his daughter's virtue.

McDonald issued an irate "Goddamn it" to the empty

room and resumed dressing. Dressed for dinner, except for a jacket and shoes, he brooded over the news on television in his dressing room while a glass of Scotch kneaded his taut nerves.

The news sons of bitches were a pleasant diversion for his anger that the whiskey encouraged him to follow. There they were, popping around to all the world's disasters, popping off at the people who actually made things happen.

Prim, powdered, combed, and self-righteous, they sat prettily in their anchor rooms like gods looking down from Olympus on bungling, corruption, murder, and devastation. McDonald had walked often enough with this hydra of a thousand microphones striking at him, the laboring camera elephants backing clumsily before him with their electronic howdahs, the salesmenlike reporters in sharp suits asking sharp questions — none of them caring or understanding a damn thing about humanity — he knew this circus well because he had often walked in its center ring. The reporters formed instantly around the newsworthy and left just as quickly, buttoning up and rushing off like soldiers after a gang bang when they, and their subject, were finished.

McDonald particularly scorned the fatherly, pious central son of a bitch with a salary in the millions who sat in a set designed to make the viewers think it was the war room of a great military campaign in which this man — whose only real decision was what color tie to wear — was enduring the responsibility of sending thousands of men to their deaths. McDonald chuckled at the inevitable symbolic lawn scenes, where the field reporters (generally blacks and women — would there soon be gays?) stood looking intense on lawns in front of the Capitol, the

White House, the home of the bereaved family or the mass murderer, holding their damn microphones on those newsworthy lawns like cast-iron jockeys.

Partly because of his boundless scorn, McDonald thoroughly enjoyed the news. He liked the gap between what he knew about it and what they knew about it. This little vacuum supplied the energy for financial manipulation as well as the pleasure of measuring his distance above the herd. McDonald personally knew most of the world figures rushing by the mike-bearers, camera-carriers, and shutterbugs, going to cover in limousines as the news-crazed pack barked helplessly on the curb.

He was, after all, one of these great figures about whom these preening parrots squawked. Looking into his television set was, for McDonald, something like looking out the window of his car at the familiar newspeople faces holding the tin peckers of their trade and yearning to find out what McDonald knew.

He looked at himself in the mirror. His coloring was excellent, his features becoming: Vanilla made him look great. It was a look he liked to parade in front of his wife.

TWELVE

O n his first trip into the famous New York City, Dan wondered if people who saw him in the limousine thought he was rich. It was a pleasant sensation to dwell in the luxury their flash of recognition decreed. He didn't smile and wave at them like a beauty queen on a float. He scowled at them, slightly annoyed, the way Ro did. It felt infinitely grand, a wince at the gap separating the rich from the poor. It was large and quiet in the back of this thing. Chauffeurs, appropriately, wore outfits that, if you added a badge and a pistol, were the same as guards'.

The personality of the chauffeur interested Dan because he'd seen him dance in mockery of John Russell McDonald the night before. Did this man feel bad, driving the rich brats into New York? Dan had seen the punker's pigtail, now hidden under the black skillet of subservience, so he felt there was some crazed spark of defiance in this servant, a Spartacus among McDonald's slaves. Coming down out of that black visored bat sitting on Spartacus' head were two sinister probes that went into his ears. Of course, they were those new ear prongs wiring total sound into the cranium, so the wearer is not where he is, where some grim necessity of employment places him, but soaring in disco sound space, beyond the reach of mundane wage slavery.

Had Alex told Dan what was in store for him when Dan went east with Ro, Dan would have laughed at his old friend. What if Alex could see him now, sliding along in limousines, humping among masterpieces, smoking cigars made of tobacco (rather than bubble gum), chatting with the sort of people one sees only in the news or ads or on daises — he would die. Dan wanted to guffaw and slug good old Alex in the shoulder, hand him a cigar, and show him the Picassos.

He wished his mother could see him, dressed in some of John Russell McDonald's clothes (borrowed without permission by Ro), a handsome youth in a limousine (was he a prince, a financial prodigy, a rock star?). Not that Dan was lonely; he just wished someone who could appreciate his accomplishment could witness it. Ro probably didn't know people didn't live this way. She probably thought school was a quaint way to live, lining up for food on trays, hearing people complain that they didn't have enough money to go to the movies — just a game, like the French court of Marie Antoinette pretending they were shepherds in those gay, intricate, sugary paintings of Antoine Watteau.

"What are you thinking?"

Ro's question startled Dan. "I thought you were asleep."

"Half."

"I don't know — about a picture, actually — a Watteau."

"Remember not to get weird at Paul Steigen's, Dan."

"Did you ever sleep with him?"

"Of course not! Hey, kiss me, you. I love you!"

They were getting along fine. At dinner the night before, she had called him "darling" in front of her parents, even though it made her father squint at her. She visited him in the room he'd been assigned before she went to bed and in the morning, too. He smiled at her.

He smiled at all of it. For some reason, God or Fate had decided to give Dan the best of everything right away.

New York City was much more enormous than Dan expected, if you just counted the windows and figured there was a person to look out every one, and then realized every one of them was going to have a hamburger and then considered all those hamburgers in a single pile — the pile would probably rise above the timberline of the Rocky Mountains.

An elderly doorman with hair as white as his gloves touched the beak of his hat and called Ro "Miss Ro." That wacko chauffeur, his earphones retracted into his hat, stood grinning behind India ink shades, offering a wildly insincere version of respectful subservience in concert with the doorman's. Dan couldn't guess what that driver was on, as they entered the funeral parlor lobby of Ro's apartment house. Would the driver do that Three Musketeers bow after they were out of sight, informing anyone passing what he thought of his patrons?

There were more masterpieces in this apartment. Out the window, across a river, some industrial city stretched like a plain of rust, as far as the eye could see.

Dan was feeling more and more a part of this formerly unthinkable grandeur. The apartment in Boise where he was raised already seemed obsolete and far, like the corny birthplace of a President.

Ro and Dan had the McDonalds' New York apartment to themselves. Jane had seen to it after her intimate walk and talk with Ro the day before. Ro was touched and pleased. It was theirs to try civilized life together for the whole weekend. She showed Dan into her father's dressing room to change (after all, Dan was the man of the house).

Dan tried out everything in McDonald's dressing room: the scale, the shower shooting from every wall, the exercise bicycle, and the steam bath. He smelled some cologne from a manly looking bottle, shook a little on his palm, and rubbed it in. On the walls were photographs of John Russell McDonald with Presidents, dead animals, children, and yachts.

When Dan was a child, he imagined his father returning in a magnificent and munificent way — a patriarch along the lines of Uncle Sam, Santa Claus, and George Washington, with wealth, wisdom, and love for his regained scion. Time and bits of information from Dan's mother replaced the happier fantasies of the paternal return with something closer to dread. In John Russell McDonald's dressing room, all the glory of the rich and successful possibility recurred. Maybe Dan's father lived like this, too. Maybe at the wedding, two great chiefs could stare into the crystal clarity of one another's magnificent gazes and bless the union of Dan and Ro.

But that one recent bit of evidence Dan had from his father, the postcard from the race track he'd turned into a light anecdote, didn't suggest elevation to such glory as Dan was presently inhabiting. What if some monstrous bum found Dan at the wedding, and curled the guests into cinders of revulsion, ruining everything?

Dan's missing father, a gap only intensified by his

mother's refusal to recall anything about it, had led Dan to work harder on the invention of his own identity than more completely parentally outfitted children. He had, for instance, pretended to himself, after reading *Paris Match,* that he was the illegitimate son of an important Frenchman. This French possibility had led Dan to smoke Gaulois cigarettes while wearing a beret behind the privacy of his locked bedroom door, listening to an Edith Piaf album that sounded so sad, he feared the needle was hurting the record.

In the swell circumstances of McDonald's dressing room, Dan was pleased to realize that, while he might not have a father, he was about to be one, and, standing in this present splendor, one of which a child could be proud.

How incredibly coincidental it was when the radio he turned on replied with Edith Piaf! A jackpot on the first nickel.

THIRTEEN

ane hadn't spent a Connecticut weekend with John Russell McDonald in quite a while. She had adjusted her life imperceptibly but thoroughly in ways that caulked the seams of their undeclared separation. These adjustments were never so apparent to her as they were this morning, as she felt McDonald's presence on them. That familiar clearing of the throat, that authoritative connection he made through the telephone to a world that agreed with him about his importance, just the unexpected spectacle of him in a room reading a big white newspaper like a ship undersail — all these perceptions of his presence were surprising.

He reefed the newspaper and tapped the cigar ashes of his eyebrows. He saw Jane, still damn good-looking, in pink pants, a shirt, and a hat, carrying a basket, passing through the room where he sat, headed for the pool. A strange expression hit her face like a pie when he lowered the paper — she was surprised to see him there. Why should he feel embarrassed, of all things, to be seen reading a newspaper in the living room of a house he'd owned for twenty years by a woman to whom he'd been married for twenty-five? But he'd felt that funny chill draft from underneath, such as you get in an outhouse. His eyebrows butted together like warring rams. He unfurled a fast, cheap smile. She returned an equally insincere one and continued through the room as though ten thousand eyes were upon her.

What struck Jane was the newspaper. She'd never seen him reading one, in a chair, like a man killing time. He was always connected to the world. He was never in its waiting room, never left outside its lighted windows. Jane had no such connection. She didn't just read newspapers; she did the crossword puzzle. She read escapist, useless novels, watched television, and shopped. She was time's confessed, convicted killer, married to a man who seemed to think he created the stuff.

John Russell McDonald was always working; operating, deceiving, urging, seeking, performing. He was not a man who sat in an easy chair with the newspaper. It struck Jane that he really didn't know what to do alone there with his wife, that the newspaper had been a sudden inspiration, an effort to behave like other men and make the situation look ordinary.

McDonald looked at the surprised scowl of the little Rembrandt portrait next to him. There was a dog here, too, someplace, he believed. He put down the paper and walked to the kitchen to ask Edwards if there was still a dog at his Connecticut house.

"Edwards, is that dog . . . ?"

"Sir?"

"The dog, you know . . ."

"Jack, sir."

"Yes. Well, how is old Jack?"

"Jack's at the pool, sir, with Madam."

McDonald was disconcerted. Of course the dog wasn't dead. He'd seen it around. Jack was its name. Of course.

This morning he was caught in a warp. He had arranged to wake in his own house with his wife, alone. Edwards, taking advantage of the comparatively rare chance he had to play the country butler, was in the old-fashioned, formal dishabille of his trade: a striped apron, white cuffs folded back over cherubically pink English skin, clipping roses in the garden for the table.

It was only morning. The day stretched before McDonald like the sea before Columbus. His treasured privacy was no treasure without demands upon it, guests, calls and appointments waiting — Vanilla to sneak to. He hadn't watched television this morning, had not scoffed at the news. He'd chosen a newspaper in a chair an English gentlemen must have employed for the same purpose two hundred years before and impatiently awaited the effects of his pantomime. He hoped for the jolly, imaginative, genteel musing of his eighteenth-century forerunner in the chair. He awaited a dose of something like that century's elegant, eager meditations to arrive and instruct and entertain him. But all that had happened was the nonsensically disturbing appearance of his wife in pink pants, passing to the pool by which he reckoned she spent most of her domestic exile.

No jolly thoughts came to the current resident of the civilized old chair; only that chill, that outhouse draft from under him when he saw her studying him, seeing through him, as she always did. If the old chair wouldn't bring him the eighteenth century, and the dog was unavailable (a relief actually. What would he and the dog do?), passage into McDonald's study became inevitable. Perhaps he should have gone there directly, but some combination of curiosity and sense of form made him try some of the customs of a country home — the paper, the walk with the dog — before descending from the conning tower, closing the hatch, and giving the order to dive.

His files held hundreds of pounds of letters to him, incised on the best stationery by the best secretaries at the behest of the world's best people — proof aplenty of the urgent, vital importance of the man at that desk, the addressee of pleas, offers, congratulations, and surrenders. But even a perusal of these didn't raise McDonald's flags this day.

*

Suntanning was never gone in for by any culture until ours, recently. The poses are Egyptian both in stillness and complex pharmacy. The water blazes with the stars of eternity. Perspiration and chemicals make a gleaming sheath for the body browning like a roasting chicken. The mind's requirement is to entertain or find entertainment while this morbid repose passes through darkening time.

Suntanning was for Jane a temporary scaffolding on her body that came down in the evening to reveal her darkly glowing in a dress at a dinner, smiling and gliding in to roost with men and women who entertained one another.

Her encampment by the pool was engineered with precision and authority. She opened her novel on the lectern of her unguent-burnished knees and reached for the traditional location of her cigarettes. But today, she found she couldn't read. She could only think how he was there, in the house, that man whom she married long ago, reading the paper as if he were at home.

He had seemed out of place and embarrassed, caught reading the paper in the chair. It was shocking to realize that neither of them even had a routine through which to deal with each other anymore. They saw each other rarely and formally and officially now. That's how he wanted it.

McDonald was still the man of Jane's dreams, which is why she hadn't left him. No matter how much money he made, he seemed to feel penitent because most of it was made possible by hers. This penitence made him distant and guilty. Would it ever subside? By the pool, studying the shimmering ladders of reflected sunlight, Jane began to want to run to him, to hold him and hear the sentimental roar of Hollywood music well up as they found one another at last, again.

She decamped and headed back for the house. The chair where he'd been was empty, a toss of newspapers left on it like a victim. Jane went straight to his study.

Unusually, McDonald was neither on the phone nor reading. He was disarmed by inactivity, startled by her intrusion.

"What's the matter?"

"Nothing. How are you?"

"Fine."

"You know, I think about the only time I've been alone with you like this in years is once or twice on elevators."

"Jane, for Christ's sake."

"Here we are, Mr. and Mrs. McDonald, at home."

The titles appalled McDonald. "Mr. and Mrs." They

reminded him, chillingly, of his parents, whose memory he confined in his imagination to a pair of names conceiving him in *Who's Who*. Jane instantly regretted her tone of mockery. She had planned otherwise, but the chemistry of their awkward encounter brought out the teasing, defensive jibing that camouflaged her vulnerable feelings toward him.

"I don't like it any more than you do, believe me."

"I didn't say I didn't like it," said Jane, increasing the unpleasant confusion that had beset McDonald all morning. He was a man who knew what he wanted to do; always had. He wasn't one of those you see up on shoeshine stands, gazing glumly and blankly at nothing, like that statue of Abe Lincoln in Washington. He was a man who loathed the impotence of elevator rides, the impudence of traffic intruding on his destination, tardiness, any interruption to the life of success he feasted on as single-mindedly as a cow eats grass.

He hadn't realized he was so obviously doing nothing until this second appearance of Jane. Her acute perception of him, titillating when he knew it was of his manly campaigns with Vanilla, now unmanned him by informing him that he had been seen doing nothing, the very thing of which he disapproved most. She stood smiling at him. It was awkward.

Jane closed the door. McDonald rose, confused, then sat back down.

"What is it?"

"The children, I guess."

"Ro?"

"Yes, Ro and Dan. They are why we're here, aren't they?"

"Yes, yes, it's a damn nuisance. I want her to get an

abortion as soon as possible. It's crazy nonsense to marry this kid, no matter who he is. They're too damn young. She couldn't possibly know what she's doing."

McDonald rapped his knuckles on his desk in judgment and turned away from Jane. Her hand suddenly closed over his forehead. She gently pulled his head back onto her breast. McDonald was baffled. The sensation of emptiness changed to bewilderment. He sensed her complete confidence that he would do her bidding. She had come to fill his emptiness.

His head was against her breast. The giddiness that swept through his loins reminded him of Vanilla. He suddenly wanted to show Jane the man he was! The moment that occurred to him, his desire turned from the erect trophy he was about to thrust her way to a hole in the sand through which the sand began to run, the hourglass of the old man instead of the heroic erection. McDonald deliberately thought of Vanilla's pussy, hoping the prayer he sent this inspirational vision of flesh, hair, and moisture would give him back the fine flashlight he wanted his wife to use on her dark interior. But thoughts of Vanilla only stole more of his lust. Now his wife was no longer a sexy woman. She was only movement and textures, a sack of gerbils, a pair of hounds in a bag — not the fantasy flesh that sends armies of blank men into drab porn stores to peek at pictures of strangers playing doctor. Furious that Jane might suspect him impotent, McDonald broke from the maternal hold she had descended on him from above and behind, Samson breaking the chains, and the moment crumbled as he pushed over the columns.

Jane stared down, humiliated. McDonald walked away from her.

"She's a twenty-one-year-old girl who thinks lust is love. I'm not letting Ro go down the tubes."

It had seemed natural, graceful, moving under its own momentum to leave the pool, walk to him, hold him. For a moment it had worked; then her arms, instead of circling around her husband, held an armful of firewood falling, breaking her toes. She searched the memory of that moment of loss for what caused him to rise, throw her off, walk away, and talk about Ro. Whatever caused it all would not show itself. Something within him had refused her again.

Jane had had several affairs in twenty-five years of marriage to John Russell McDonald. One had gone on longer than the others. It grew, got to the point where the difference in station between herself and the bearded man with whom she sat in a car on a country lane being shelled by a summer shower became an insurmountable obstacle.

"We both love the same music."

"I'm too poor."

"I don't understand you."

"It drives me crazy. The only times I don't feel it is when we're making love or listening to music. I'm a goddamn schoolteacher — that's all I am. It would be so grotesque — all the scandal and snickering — and I couldn't stand living off your money and you couldn't stand living on mine."

Watery craters winked on the windshield. The rain on the roof sounded like gravel. A tear ran down her cheek. The bearded man kept shaking his head. It was the end of the road.

"Do you love me?"

McDonald was jolted by this ancient, self-answering, doomed question. "Of course."

He was afraid she might approach him again. "You're all for it?"

"What?"

"Ro marrying this Dan Novitski."

"I'm crazy about him."

"Why?"

"He's lovely. He's very special — don't you think? Being from Idaho and studying History of Art. Why not? He says the funniest things sometimes."

"It's not a reason to get married."

"What is?"

"Well, the family, love."

"Like us?"

McDonald had never had a worse morning in his life.

His office in New York was where he wanted to be, in the middle of a week: events balancing on his decisions; men to deal with, to negotiate with, to analyze, outwit, learn from, join, recruit, and impress. Cornered in this country house by Jane suddenly pulling at the seventh veil of their marriage was where he wanted not to be. The phone rang, and McDonald was relieved to hear the crackling, gassy hiss of long distance.

McDonald's luck had not gone out. It was a Brazilian banker. McDonald was relieved to watch Jane become two dimensional again, like a fine painting on his wall, as the banker engaged the self he'd been searching for all morning.

His features smoothed into order as he spoke on the phone, watching her like a picture he enjoyed. Jane sighed. The momentum of this marriage was too great to jump off. She backed toward the door, watching him busy and oblivious, invulnerable again. Her joints and muscles were all out of kilter, as though she'd been beaten in her sleep. She cried on the way back to the pool.

*

For thirty-five dollars (a sum Ro seemed to regard as a cute midget) Dan traded most of the monetary power in his wallet for some old clothes she assured him were divine. The jacket, a pattern of pink birdlimes splatted on a gray field, the snake tie, and hospital-green shirt caused enthusiastic comments from the girls at Muffy's party and bemused, scornful glances from the males. But it made Ro happy, even if Dan would rather have appeared in McDonald's clothes.

Dan had a good time anyway. He made the Eastern girls laugh and discomforted the males, which pleased both himself and Ro, who held his hand a lot, proud of his iconoclastic effect. Muffy's party gave Dan confidence. Even in a clown's outfit among cliquish strangers, he had won admiration.

Tailoring, tie pins, monograms, seal rings, and accents so bizarre that Dan took a while to understand what the males were saying to him. (A harmonica, he reflected, can be played by either blowing out or sucking in air, just so the manner of their speech proved to Dan that English also could be spoken on the intake.) All these things marked the young men as a breed different from his Western contemporaries.

Muffy's parents' apartment was done up in startling pastel shades and appointed with small porcelain dogs, Scots, and shepherds. It looked plenty expensive, but it wasn't at all grand, like the McDonald domiciles. For some reason, Dan felt less at ease in this home for daisies and lap dogs than he did among the masterpieces. In fact, Dan soon began to feel slightly superior to these surroundings, even though he sprang from a home that boasted only one sofa and usually featured several unmatching, partly filled coffee mugs in the locations that were populated here by Staffordshire statuettes.

"I always liked mongrels," Dan told Muffy. Then she told him the dog he had just dismissed was a Westminster champion.

When Ro looked over to see how Dan was doing, Muffy signaled her friend with a smirk and a roll of the eyes, so Ro crossed, took Dan's arm, and got the happy raconteur out of there before the curiosity and admiration he had excited turned to disdain.

Ro decided Dan was going to need a little work on his social graces. She was curious to see how his professional aptitude would look the next day.

aul Steigen's gallery was no longer a store to which the Sunday aesthetes, clutching their Gallery Guides, came to catch the art scene. It was more of a private office. The more expensive things get, the more privacy their transactions require. Discretion is one of the attributes of luxury; the dimmed-out windows prevent the public from ogling the inhabitants of the expensive limousine.

Ro, hand in hand with Dan, initiated their entrance by speaking with a guard. Dan noticed the electronic locks, like a passage over a drawbridge, with a murderous gate lowering behind them, fencing out the surly peasants, restless hordes, hungry crusaders, and jealous competitors.

Steigen moved with the times, but not so avidly as to appear trendy. The fashion of industrial interior decoration, like preceding fads of glass and chrome, and the jigsaw puzzle piece–shaped tables and chairs of the fifties, always appeared at the height of its season in his place of business, but never stridently and exclusively; only in passing, the way his hair style and clothing and location kept up. His merchandise was always the same:

primitive pieces, old masters, only those dead and dying moderns whose work had reached the six-figure measure.

Dan admired the tight-napped gray rug, white walls, strong, bleak hardware fittings, and antiromantic furniture. The florid, ice cream cone, poodle-dog frames on the dappled old impressionist masterpieces were in almost embarrassed contrast to these stark, metallic furnishings.

"Hi?" asked a pretty blond girl whose clothing was also stark and handsome, citified in a way that made Ro look a little corny. She rose from a desk with no typewriter. She wasn't a secretary.

"Hi, is Mr. Steigen here? I'm Ro McDonald."

Because Dan was studying the girl at this moment, he saw her quick blush. Dan figured it was simply the ordinary New York reaction to what he had come to realize was Ro's famous name.

"Oh, yes," said the girl, a tone too loud, looking around as though something were missing. "I'm Ellen Weld."

"Dan Novitski," introduced himself.

"God, well of course," said Vanilla pointlessly, two fingers on her forehead as if she were about to pluck a jewel from it, walking back to her desk to see if it, and the earth, were still there.

"Paul is at his apartment. Shall I give him a ring?"

"Oh, no. He said to drop in if we were in the neighborhood, so I thought I'd take a chance. My, well, my friend Dan here wanted to see some of these things, so we stopped by. My dad buys a lot of stuff here."

"Well, yes, I know," stammered Vanilla. "Oh. Come in the other room and see the new Balthus."

The inner room was of a completely different style

from the other. It was very grand, and yet much smaller than it looked. Paneling, cascading satin draperies, an ancient floral rug, a carved fireplace, books — it had all the accoutrements of a home. This fancy old room was filled with inanimate guests — menacing sculptures, longing portraits, gorgeous landscapes, intellectual abstractions, and glorious nudes, all at their best moment, as if this were a party.

It was, oddly, much cozier than McDonald's home, even though it was only a showroom. Steigen had magazines on his tables. Unlike the house in Connecticut or the apartment, this place even had wastebaskets with crumpled contents.

The blond girl proceeded quickly to a painting of a girl who, although yet to sprout her first bodily hair, plainly knew the art of love.

"Balthus," she said. They all looked at the picture obediently, like people at the zoo. Vanilla almost instantly regretted choosing this subject, but it was too late. The others seemed riveted.

"There was a girl like that back in Boise," said Dan jokingly. Ro nudged him reprovingly. "We figured she learned from ice cream cones." Ro kicked him in reprimand. It's true he didn't know the blonde well enough to make such jokes, but something about her made him eager to proceed with it.

"Are you crazy?" asked Ro, when they hit the street.

"What?"

"I sure don't want to have to worry about you making dirty jokes every time I introduce you to someone."

"She laughed."

"She had to."

"What's the matter?"

"You did it at the party, too."

"What?"

"I heard about it."

"What?"

"You told some awful ranch story about something."

"What?"

"Muffy told me. About castrating a dog. What are you trying to do, anyway? You pass out in front of my father and tell some disgusting story to my friend. What is your problem?"

"You mean the story about Cream?"

"What?"

Dan the raconteur began at once with a tested piece of his repertory: "Cream was the owner's dog at this ranch I worked at, and Harold, this cowboy, couldn't stand how Cream acted so superior to his dogs. What made it worse was Harold's dogs were purebred and that old Cream was a mongrel."

Dan, bright-eyed, winsome, and smiling, gestured and talked as they walked a fashionable avenue. People always laughed at this story. He didn't notice Ro was scowling at store windows as he talked.

"We were laying sheet metal on a roof. Harold and another cowboy named Bob Ferny and me."

Dan had already noticed the word "cowboy" as a familiar term disarmed Easterners.

"And old Cream came sauntering down. Harold stopped hammering, and Bob and I looked at him. He was just staring at old Cream coming to the barnyard. Then Harold's two purebred Australian sheepdogs curled their tails under and went under the barn. Harold said, 'Bob, we ought to smooth that dog.' See? 'Smooth' means castrate."

Dan turned, expecting his story to be received as quaint and funny. Ro stopped, scowled, and looked at Dan squarely.

"I'm just getting a little tired of you."

"Huh?"

"Maybe," said Ro with a quick, arch glance at her abdomen, "the world already has too many Idaho cowboys."

Dan heard a buzz as if he'd been slapped. People stalked relentlessly by in every direction; he felt caught in the middle of a square dance he didn't know and couldn't leave. He looked at Ro. She had a victorious, angry smile.

Dan wheeled and stalked off, ordered by honor to leave. His stomach, the seat of emotional disturbances, was like a pinball machine. The city was half ripped open, half filthy, a highway carcass after an hour. He'd never seen such ugly people in his life. A bag lady picked up her skirt to study it and make pedestrians wish they hadn't noticed she wore no underwear. Mean black kids gave murderous looks. Old people with shattered nerves walked as if wading through an infernal river. Hopelessness, ugliness came around every corner like a mudslide on the urine-veined sidewalks.

All that cool elegance of McDonald wealth rushed haughtily off, a carriage rolling over the scum, footmen beating back the rabble.

From the promising youth noticing subtle details, the nuance man, Dan was in an instant the land-mine victim, staggering alone in bloody ribbons.

Once, when he was lost in Boise as a child, Dan had promised himself, "You've slept in bed every night of

your life so far, so you will tonight." Had he? He must
have, but he couldn't remember how he'd managed it, as
he took another bad street where filthy winos reached at
him.

Dan knew no one he could think of in New York. Was
it really he who had been gazing out of a limousine window only a day before?

He checked his wallet and found he had seven dollars.
He was no doubt expected to return to the apartment.
That metropolitan beast through which he'd walked all
the way to darkness could be just a view out a high window again — their window, the McDonalds, who, he now
knew, could turn on him, turn on a dime.

Eighty more dollars were in the apartment, and fifty at
the house in Connecticut. His van was out there, too; his
own planet in alien space.

As he walked back to the apartment, Dan found himself alternately chastising and forgiving Ro. He re-
hearsed savage, noble, rational, and loving things to say
to her when they met. She would no doubt be in a state.
He'd been gone for hours (he checked: four hours and
ten minutes). He decided he would have to leave her, go
back to Idaho. She would have to come out there, to him
this time.

It took yet another hour to find the McDonalds' apartment building. Several looked like it; he hadn't remembered the number. He tried seven awnings before he
found Ro's. He recognized the lobby. A different doorman peered at him, opening the door with reluctance and
self-importance.

"McDonald?"

"Yes."

Dan started for the elevator. Another uniformed man stood up, not specifically, but possibly, to guard that elevator.

"Who is calling?" asked the doorman.

"Dan Novitski."

"Just a moment, sir."

The doorman stepped into a closet off the lobby, turning his back discreetly as he spoke into a house phone. The man between Dan and the elevator looked away. Dan felt like a suspicious character. That outfit from secondhand stores Ro thought was so divinely punk wasn't as easily understood by the stratum of society with which he was now dealing. Dan looked forward to the approval descending into the doorman's ears from the seventeenth floor (he did remember the floor). He wanted to give him a quick, reproving, corrective smile before he rose up with the elevator man, admitted to a world they could only guard.

"There's no one in, sir," said the doorman.

"McDonald?" chirped Dan in a voice that squealed like a binding saw in green wood.

The doorman already had the door to the street open. The elevator man had fallen into a military pose, parade rest, and inhaled deeply.

"I'm staying there," offered Dan, plucking at the sleazy fifties' sport jacket that had looked so fabulous to Ro the night before.

"There's no one up there."

"But I'm staying there."

"I can't let you in without permission."

He wasn't even saying "sir" anymore. The bully that had first glowered at the stranger seeking admittance had returned, swollen with justification.

"What am I supposed to do? Look, phone them —
phone the house in Connecticut."

Mention of this knowledge of another house stalled
the bully's evictive work with the big door.

"What's the name, sir?"

"Dan Novitski."

"I'll see if there's a message."

The doorman returned to the intimate communications closet. The elevator man rocked back and forth on
his toes, still at parade rest. This period in the lobby
seemed longer than the hours Dan had walked the
streets.

"There's no message," said the doorman finally, shaking his head and returning wearily to the door through
which they would pitch Dan into the darkness of nowhere.

Dan walked out, hearing, just before the big iron door
shut, a chuckle.

The housekeeper of the apartment had served Dan
breakfast that morning on a little tray lined with a soft
white napkin. What wasn't perfectly polished silver was
china, light and thin as a potato chip. There were eggs,
bacon, muffins, jellies, butter, a pitcher of coffee, and a
crystal beaker of real orange juice. It was, as it turned
out, Dan's only meal of the day. The part of town where
he now walked was empty except for the brief bright passage of the inhabitants of these fortress apartments in
and out of cabs and cars. Dan was starving. If he hadn't
remembered that breakfast, maybe he wouldn't be so
hungry. But he had remembered it.

"Would you like some more, sir?" the housekeeper
had asked, and Dan, to his poignant present regret, had
refused because he didn't want to appear to be an animal.

The emotional sting from Ro was the alternative thought to food. He could get so mad that he wasn't hungry, walk furiously farther, feeling terribly wronged, and await the dawn. Or he could think of food and have to start bailing out his watering mouth like a lifeboat, almost going under. He had to find a train, get to his van, get away from this awful place, this awful situation.

"Hey," said a girl's voice next to him, causing Dan to jump and four people he hadn't seen to snuffle and bark with laughter. He had walked into their midst in a dark, empty plaza.

A nervous, giggling little girl with a big head, wearing cowboy boots and a blond porcupine punker's hairdo, a tall, lissome black girl with a hairdo that reminded Dan of a telephone receiver, and two young men with loose, wrinkly, expensive clothes had surrounded him.

"We've been following you," she said, and they all laughed. "We saw you twice in way different parts of town. Are you trying to get anywhere?"

The club where they took Dan was in a parking garage. They had the air of insiders guiding the greenhorn. Bored greetings wove them into the bizarre fabric of the place. They were known. Dan was new shoes at school, the outsider appearing halfway though the year.

Smoking grass only made Dan even more ravenous. At last they left the spastic riot of the club. By calling it "crashing," Dan could fold his homelessness unpathetically into the courtesy of modern times. The tomato he ate from the big-headed little girl's icebox was a magnificent wet explosion of flavor. When he smelled the eggs frying, water from his mouth ran down his throat in a torrent. He could taste every grain of wheat in the bread.

No bottle of beer was ever more perfectly brewed and chilled than the one washing it all down.

"Hey, Half Dozen," she said when Dan woke.

"Huh?"

"We named you Half Dozen because that's how many eggs you ate last night."

She was joined in mirth by the black girl. There was no one else in the place, which was big enough to graze a couple of sheep.

"I'm Dan Novitski."

"Cheryl Schultz."

"Eartha Mann."

Dan memorized their names out loud, sensing instantly he was the morning's entertainment. "Cheryl Schultz and Eartha Mann," he repeated.

Uproarious laughter.

"Not Eartha Mann, fool; Eartha, man."

Dan laughed obligingly. It had become apparent to Dan the night before that manic Cheryl was the queen of the court. The awkward and demanding role of parasite thrust on him by the McDonald hospitality had sharpened his study and instinct for the identification of such hierarchy.

Looking at large plants by the loft windows, Dan reflected that New York City was all people and no nature, the opposite of fishing with Uncle Archie.

"Thanks, really," he said to the girl.

"My God, where are you, darling?" said Ro on the phone, in a voice frayed with perceptible torment.

"Where am I?" Dan asked Eartha, who cleaned up while Cheryl took a bath.

"That's in SoHo."

"Could be."

"Darling, I want you to come right away."

"Yeah?"

"It was all screwed up, darling. I left a note for the housekeeper to let you in. I was coming back; I didn't know it was her day off."

"Oh."

"Oh darling, what could you think? I've been up all night waiting for you to call — I called the police, Connecticut, everything. I even called your mother and your Uncle Archie."

Dan was at once gratified and worried — the scale of his disappearance had grown too big. People worrying about him crossed his mind: his mother with a line between her eyes and her knuckles to her lips, Archie shaking his head slowly, his tan wrinkly neck folding back and forth, and Ro, frowning, on her toes with concern.

"Are you OK?"

"I'm fine now."

"You know what I kept thinking when you were lost?"

"What?"

"But he can't be lost — we're going to have a baby!"

Dan had just been a little paranoid, as Ro would later tell him. All the *Sturm und Drang* of eviction, all the terrible feelings of class cruelty and rejection, of turning into a parasite, of being a toy, were all wrong. Dan, even when he didn't realize it because of some stupid mixup, was still the fiancé of the only daughter of John Russell McDonald.

Bidding his new friends good-bye and heading back to his forthcoming kingdom, Dan felt not unlike Babar.

FIFTEEN

That's incredible! SoHo's right where I want us to live, darling. I was going to take you down there today."

"It's great."

"You didn't, I mean really, not that I would blame you after the way I treated you — really — but you didn't sleep with her, did you?"

"No. Everybody was too burned out."

"You mean you would have?"

"No — I just mean the situation never came up."

Dan had. Cheryl had screeched dirty words and pinched him at the climax. Her scratchy little hands; had she left a mark? Why was he already exiled by a lie? It was Ro's fault, and he could do anything he wanted. But he lied to keep her pleased, to keep everything darling again.

Ro's pregnancy was a subtle, amorphous bonding to her that Dan had violated by sleeping with Cheryl. That's why he'd lied — because Ro was still his biological wife. He was quite sure it had nothing to do with that elation he'd felt riding back up to the fancy part of town in a cab, not giving a damn about money, to that great apartment. He wasn't just trying to say the right thing to marry the rich girl — of that he was quite sure.

Ro was cute and bright-eyed — Bushy Tail, the squirrel. Dan ruffled her hair and she laid her head across her collarbone and smiled at him. Their intertwined hands hammered the mistake into the sofa with slow, soft blows. They kissed; Ro opened her mouth. Dan didn't really feel like it. Maybe he didn't love her anymore. Maybe he never had. He sent his tongue against hers like a brute wrestling a tackling dummy. He heard her sigh and felt her tilting. Of course he loved her! She was terrifically cute and pregnant by him and she was terrifically — he didn't want to think about it but he did, all the time now — rich.

Whatever else fornication accomplishes, it performs the service of punctuation in relationships. Dan smiled down at the new paragraph of his experience with Ro. Her eyes were closed. She reached up and read his face in Braille. It was all going to be fine. He could see her at fifty doing the same thing with old freckled fingers. He just hoped Cheryl didn't have V.D.

Ro looked at Dan and thought he looked particularly great. At the party she'd gone to with him the night before last, she'd seen how right she'd been to choose Dan. The obvious choices, the well-bred, privately educated, monogrammed boys who grew up to join clubs and the hunting parties operating out of Wall Street were all there in all their boring splendor. Too easy, too obvious. They had floated by at the party like tin ducks in a shooting gallery awaiting the chance hit by someone who could afford the ticket. Ro hadn't gone west because she wanted to live happily ever after on Park Avenue.

Ro felt ready to make her domestic arrangement with life. Her biological clock said it was time, even if her father said it was too soon.

Dan seemed fine. She liked the way his quirky individualism had survived the intense radiation of John Russell McDonald. He looked divine. She would just have to get rid of some of the rough edges (for instance: "We figured she learned from ice cream cones") and start him on the way to becoming director of the Metropolitan Museum of Art. Once they were married, Daddy would have to help him advance. After all, Daddy wouldn't want a nobody for a son-in-law.

Paul Steigen's gallery would be the perfect place to start Dan. She'd taken him there to see how he'd react. Ro did wish the girl working there wasn't pretty and single. Dan had made that awful remark, not even knowing her. Was that an expression of subliminal desire? He certainly liked to do it. Ro looked at her lover. His eyes were closed in a serene expression, like a death mask. His clothes lay in pools on the floor. Would he drive her mad with other women? With drink? Dining room tables were much more stable investments.

Dan's eyes opened and looked surprised.

"What is it?"

"Forgot where I was."

"You're here, darling, with me."

"I've been so many places lately, I lose track. It's like we're on a hike with different camps every night."

"You don't think I wanted to ditch you yesterday, do you?"

"No, no."

Ro nuzzled Dan with her love-warm pink breasts. Miss Brasenose the old housekeeper walked in, pointed straight for the clothes on the floor, her controls aiming her relentlessly at disorder in the apartment.

"Lord a mercy," she said and ran out of the room with Dan's pants gripped in panic.

Miss Brasenose was forever setting things right, removing the daily stains and refuse. She had spent her life one step ahead of the great beast of the human mess. Today she had come upon it directly, the beast with two backs, the monster she cleaned up after without ever seeing. It was about as she expected, only stupider. Their eyes looked at her from their mixed-up limbs in a strangely beseeching way. They were lost, but that was no business of Miss Brasenose's.

SIXTEEN

oris had discovered it when she wrote the chauffeur's check. It seemed an impossible coincidence, but Doris almost depended on it as she walked to the garage in the evening, the check flapping in her hand. She'd called to make sure the chauffeur was in. He often wasn't — it was such a cushy job, being McDonald's chauffeur. McDonald was gone most of the time. A housekeeper was supposed to keep the staff busy, but the focus of entertaining had long ago shifted away from the Connecticut house, and most of the time it just waited, polished and idle, like the rooms behind ropes in museums.

There was only one, very silly thing the chauffeur had to do besides drive. He had to break in John Russell McDonald's new shoes, which arrived once a year from his London bootmaker. Chauffeurs were chosen for their foot size. Perhaps because shoes and cars both transported McDonald, he had assigned the operator of the latter to the maintenance of the former. Edwards, the flawless English manservant McDonald had more or less inherited from a mentor who had been ambassador to the Court of St. James's, was of the wrong foot size to serve his master in this pedestrian matter, so the task had evolved on chauffeurs twenty-five years ago.

The chauffeur was asked to walk five times around the estate, every evening for a week, in the great man's new shoes, and then to present them to Edwards, who polished them with a bone to the genteel glow that would be recognized by other gentlemen of high estate at top-level conferences, royal audiences, and the very finest whorehouses.

The chauffeur was on one of these marches when Doris went in search of him. A man in an orange jump suit, with his head shaved except for a fuchsia pigtail, strolling painfully in black wing-tipped London shoes, he cut a bizarre figure on the well-groomed grounds.

The chauffeur didn't see Doris waving his check at him because the priority of his perceptions had been radically altered by a psychedelic mushroom he had consumed, along with a television game show, an hour earlier. The sight and sound of Doris approaching, talking, flapping the check were being received on separate channels by the chauffeur, one of sound, the other of vision, which the Mayan mushroom prevented from fusing into information. The messages coming in over the two sensory receivers, instead of abetting one another, eradicated each other.

When she halted him and repeated herself again, he thought she was a waterfall of, of all things, tiny chrome jacks such as little girls play with. With an effort he perceived her as she did.

"Where are you from?"

"Lord Krishna." He bowed.

"Where?"

"America."

"Don't be smart, young man, or you will find yourself on the job market very shortly."

"I'm sorry, ma'am. I was born in San Diego, if that's of any help. It was a green room, and the doctor had bristly black hairs on his fingers. It was quite a shock."

"Were you ever married?"

"Why do you want to know all this? The agency just said I had to be eleven D."

"If John Russell McDonald saw the way you look now, I assure you you would be seeking other employment."

He bowed again. "Jesus God, did you ever see anything so unbearably beautiful as this tree — this flow of life? Let's touch it — feel the charge of its beingness!"

"And you are on drugs, aren't you?"

Self-preservation gripped the chauffeur. He saw the flapping check and recalled the economic system that had him there, walking in those shoes, which, although black, he saw as two red cactuses of pain.

"I'm terribly sorry, Miss Laitch, but, except for breaking in Mr. McDonald's shoes, I believe I am on my own time, as it were. Is that for me?"

"Yes, and it is going to be your last if you don't answer me in some reasonable way."

"Anything, O Kali."

"Were you ever married?"

"I was."

"Have you children?"

"Yes."

"What?"

"A son."

"Yes! How old?"

"I don't know, twenty or so."

"Yes! And you haven't seen him, have you, in years? Since you left him in Boise when he was five."

"Correct, O Kali. But I did send him a postcard."

"Here is your check, Mr. Novitski."

Doris was thrilled to the marrow by what she had just discovered.

The orange man with the purple pigtail, yellow check, and black shoes stood still, studying the watermark and paper fibers of his check as Doris half-loped back to the house, a hand on her beating heart, charged with the fizz of discovery.

*

Doris made a nice little drink and sat alone on a terrace, facing the pink west of sundown. She raised her glass to this geographic direction which had sent her a father and a son who didn't know their relationship. This spectacular scoop was exclusively Doris'; the Pulitzer Prize–winning reporter who had so often in the past come up with these great stories for her famous editor, John Russell McDonald. When McDonald heard Doris' astonishing news, he would be once again in her debt, again saved by her. He would remember how many times in the past she had found information that had changed everything for him, inspired him, guided and warned him. Doris could see the black eyes glitter, the jaw drop. There would be astonishment and then gratitude and humility: *John Russell McDonald Saved Again By Doris Laitch.*

This sensational bit of information could not have come at a better moment for Doris. The real cause of her terrible depressions, her deepening gloom, and sleeplessness was the growing feeling that McDonald was going to get rid of her. His French appointment was a real threat to Doris, who spoke no French and distrusted those who did. He had not asked her to recruit a staff for him. He hadn't told her what her title at the embassy would be, or whether she would have anything to do with his official functions. She'd soothed herself by deciding he might only want her to work on his private interests, his business deals.

Doris always felt confident of her position when McDonald and she were working on a deal. She was the memory bank, researcher, and prompter he had always used — the alter ego he needed like a shaver's mirror while he worked it out. But when the deals at last rose out of their hands into the sky, Doris always had a terrible spell of worry. She inevitably tortured herself with the possibility that he would let her go, too. And the bauxite deal on which they'd spent half a year had closed a week ago, just when these two rival women, Jane and Ro, appeared on the scene to whisper detracting things about Doris in McDonald's ear.

"Would you like a tray, Miss Laitch?" asked the housekeeper. Doris had assessed it too dark to be found on the terrace. The two or three little refills had left Doris oblivious of time, pleased for reasons that had abstracted into a simple but soaring pleasure fueled by the drinks. Doris rose from her chair as awkwardly as an adult disentangling from a child's bicycle. She looked at the furnishing she'd dismounted, at the interrogative housekeeper, at the lawn gone gray with night. The instinct that kept Doris from a pauper's grave advised her that it would do her no good at all to ber interviewed in her current state of mind by any member of the McDonald family.

"Bring me a tray," she said thickly to an apparition of the housekeeper apparently located about three feet to the right of that actual personage. Doris hurried to the safety of her room. She couldn't quite remember what had made her so happy, but she was grateful for the pleasure she felt.

*

In the morning, Doris woke, awaiting, as was her custom, the hangover that sprang on her like a panther a split second after painless sleep deserted her. Only a kitten of it came. She felt so much better than she expected, she was apprehensive. When it became clear she was not to suffer as awfully as usual, she turned up the reason: that juicy secret, that the chauffeur was the fiancé's father, and the reward she expected it to call forth from McDonald, had passed her into an unusually deep, curative, untroubled sleep.

Sunday morning still had for Doris a religious implication, or at least a religious aftereffect. It was a less worldly day than the workdays and a less fleshly day than its party-time neighbor, Saturday. It still took place for Doris under a high Gothic arch.

Would the McDonalds, who were spending their first weekend in years together at the Connecticut house, go to church? Doris decided they would. Since the appearance of their union was important to McDonald's dignity, he wouldn't waste the opportunity to show the community his reverence for God and the American family. The time to hit him with the news was after church, on the way back to the sins of town.

Sure enough, out her window Doris saw John and Jane, in churchgoing outfits, climb into the car to be

taken into the community for a show of humility and de-
votion, blissfully ignorant that their pilot on this Protestant pilgrimage (who Doris knew was bald as a candle
burning a fuchsia flame) was soon to be their new rela-
tive. The car crawled off at a religious pace. Jane's head
turned profile in the back window to say something to her
coworshiper. Doris began to laugh.

*

After the weekend, riding back into town with McDonald, in the car driven by her secret scoop, Doris was cool
and patient. The window between the seats was up. Doris
started the trip by talking shop and politics with McDonald. She didn't want to give up the fun of her secret the
first minute she was alone with him. It was delicious to
see her secret in the flesh at the wheel. McDonald's relationship to his chauffeur was not so simple as it
seemed — and only Doris, in all the world, knew why.

Working alone with McDonald in his office had always
been Doris' happy time, just as twisting in the dark on a
sleepless night was her unhappy time. Here she was with
John Russell McDonald, helping him with business, his
closest associate, trusted more than any other person in
his life ever had been. She loved his hands, one laid out in
a spray of fingers holding the page of checks flat, while
the other, with a pen, looked like a hen's head, pecking
out signatures. A hen? No, an eagle!

"Oh, write one to — where the hell — here it is."

He produced a paper from Paul Steigen's art gallery.
On it was an address in Paris and the name of a real estate firm.

"How shall I enter this?"

McDonald smiled. "You know I have always needed

private assistance even in my public capacity, Doris."

Doris laughed, and McDonald laughed with her. She thought he meant the address on the memo was to be her apartment. He thought she laughed because she simply admired the old rogue she knew so well.

"Is that it? Because I've got something I'm dying to tell you — about Mr. Dan Novitski!"

"What is it?"

Doris looked again at the apartment address on the memo.

"Rue de la Bruyère — is this the Left Bank, John? What fun! That's my favorite part of Paris. I'm so glad. The rest of the city is so formal. I just love the idea of an apartment on the Left Bank — like Audrey Hepburn or something."

"Yes — and for Christ's sake don't let that ever appear where Jane might find out about it."

"This apartment?"

"Yes, that's a private matter."

"It's not . . ."

"What?"

"I thought it was mine."

"Doris, I want to talk to you about that."

"Yes?"

"I want you to stay on here — maybe at your apartment."

Doris' jaw and her stenographic pad dropped open at the same moment.

"What's the matter?" asked McDonald.

"I just want to know how this check should be entered," replied Doris, closing her flaps.

"You'll stay and keep an eye on things here."

"Not come to Paris?"

"Run things here for me. I think we're all set with that bauxite now."

"Yes."

"And I don't plan on doing any more deals just now."

"What was it you were going to tell me?" he asked with a smile.

It had happened! The dismissal she'd feared, that she'd felt stealthily approaching for years, had sprung for her throat.

"About that damn boy — Novitski?"

Doris kept her eyes away because she didn't want McDonald to see her tears. "Novitski": that name shut off the flow of tears at once. *She had almost told him, but she hadn't.* Somehow, knowing, being the only one who knew the chauffeur's relationship with the fiancé, was going to serve Doris. It mustn't be given away. Her redoubtable survivor's instinct told her it was something that would serve her if she kept it secret, like her pistol.

"Only that we're all so happy for them."

"What are you talking about?"

Doris dried her eyes with her back to McDonald so that he couldn't see, and turned beaming, radiant, and composed. Heroic by her own measure in the awful circumstance of McDonald's betrayal and dismissal. Stay here with no deals? How long before her unnecessary presence became too annoying to continue on his payroll? First he would leave her, go to Paris. Then he would cut her off, wither up what connection was left, raise up one of his tarts to fill Doris' shoes, shoes that had followed him over the long march only to be refused admittance at this later, posher date. *Stay at her apartment.* He was already clearing her out of Connecticut!

"Dan is perfect for Ro."

"I couldn't disagree more."

"Why, John?"

Doris' voice was low and mature, smooth and wise. She heard it with a detached, admiring approval. It was the voice she knew convinced him. Doris wanted Dan and Ro married, because it raised the value of her unique information inestimably. The cause of Dan's engagement had just found a violent champion. She continued in that timbre whose very arrival gave her confidence about her course.

"He's attractive and really quite brilliant."

"What do you mean?"

"He had the highest grades ever given in History of Art at Colorado."

"Really?"

Doris nodded. It was an utter lie, but the right one to tell the man who'd got the highest grades ever given at Yale. Medals, high grades, titles, pedigrees, and fortunes were all tickets McDonald accepted solemnly to the private and exclusive showing of his personal admiration. Doris' campaign for Dan's elevation in McDonald's opinion marched forward before she even thought about it, as if it had its own intelligence.

"You really ought to talk to him some time."

"The time I tried, he passed out."

"They'd been traveling. And the wine and all."

"He just seems to me like a little opportunist."

"He's as tall as you." Doris laughed warmly (knowing as well as McDonald that Dan was in fact taller than McDonald, a man vain about his exceptional height).

"I thought you had something special to say about him just now."

"It was the high grades."

"You don't know anything else about him, do you, Doris? Who his people are?"

"Novitski was a name given to emigrants from Poland."

"Emigrants?"

"Yes, the real name was something like Gorski, de Gorski. When the ancestor left, the Polish government ordered that he lose his title and take a new name."

"Title?"

"These Counts de Gorski go back to the third crusade, apparently."

"How did you discover all this?"

"I did some research."

"Did the boy tell you?"

"No. In fact, he doesn't know. I've had the most extraordinary conversations with a priest in Boise who knows the family."

"Doris, how did you ever discover all this?"

"You know how I feel about you and your family, John. I wasn't going to say a thing about it, unless something was wrong. I just made some calls."

"You are a wonder."

Doris watched him hurry out. For the first time in her life, she'd tried to fool the man she had protected so totally. It was so easy. And it would no doubt soon be easy for others, too.

oris, who had always despised any attempt to utilize her secretarial skills to social ends, went about the engagement party with the enthusiasm of a politician and the intensity of a chain saw. For the whole week at the office in New York she'd prompted McDonald every day about this celebration of what he still considered a big mistake. Now he was supposed to go back out to Connecticut for yet another domestic weekend. He was beginning just to want the whole bloody thing over with.

McDonald had begun to consider Doris' seriousness of purpose about arrangements for Ro's dubious party as final proof of how much he needed a new secretary. It seemed to him that he was observing how Doris thought she was going to spend her declining years with him: talking him into entertainments he didn't want to give to show she was still of service to him. He was grateful for the French post. It would be a relief to work with a professional diplomatic secretary in another country, where Doris' lack of language skills made her technically useless enough for him to remove without an emotional review. He wanted her gone years ago, but she had hung on like a terrier. The recent bauxite deal was more an attempt to keep Doris occupied and useful than it was something he needed. He was glad to be away from all of them. He looked forward to this next domestic weekend no more than a reluctant dishwasher entered a kitchen forested with filthy stacks of plates and pans.

McDonald had always felt grander than business. The constant reminder that his was a business success fueled by a wife's wealth was only reinforced by the physical presence of his old war horse. Put Doris out to pasture. Go to France and buy art with beguiling Vanilla. It was such a civilized, private country. France would close about him with exclusivity, elevation, and flattering elegance. Becoming ambassador to France was not a mere vulgar business award. It was adoption into the line of that American prodigy McDonald had admired all his life, Benjamin Franklin.

He looked through the *Almanach de Gotha* for the Counts de Gorski. On the way to that entry, he passed many names that invited reveries. He stared at the family name of his friend, the president of France. Two months before at the Elysèe Palace, engravings of the knotty old carbuncles of armorial bearings had made the new ambassador to the Old World reflect to the French president how these devices were reborn in the USA as rootless designs created in art departments to dignify cars and refrigerators. The president of France had loved that. McDonald felt his ability to joke about his country without betraying it was a reason he was admired by this well-bred aristocrat, whose son McDonald wished were where he imagined the cowboy at the house in Connecticut was at this very moment.

The Counts de Gorski didn't exist in the *Almanach de*

Gotha. Where the hell was Doris? In Connecticut, of course, with the rest of his problems.

*

Above the garage in Connecticut was the chauffeur's apartment. The hubcaps on the wall were arranged in mysteriously significant-seeming constellations. It was much neater than Doris expected. The man even played the stock market, she thought, approaching a table covered with newspaper stock pages, a calculator, and tablets furred with numbers. Only the newspapers proved to be *Racing Form*s. The man was a horseplayer! Doris laughed carefully (for her teeth had rocked loose that morning) and reflected how all the man's destiny, from driving McDonald to breaking in his shoes to horse-racing to the wandering he must have done between deserting his family and arriving here, involved transportation.

She called his name again and heard it strike the vacancy of the place like a hammer on iron. She appraised his rooms like a fellow loner. She so approved of the unexpected neatness. He was personally clean, after all, she reflected. You can tell the dirty ones at once, as if only part of a scene is being filtered through dark glasses, the part that is the filthy person. The film of personal filth both darkens and fades them, like an old stain on the fabric of landscape. Doris knew too well from her childhood what dirty people looked like.

His bed was covered with one of those bright, cheap, slave-labor, third world cloths of embroidery and little mirrors. Undoubtedly, decided Doris, this was the sort of thing he stared at when he smoked pot, or whatever he did. Drugs, felt Doris as an advanced and traditional alcoholic, were depraved and antisocial.

Above his twinkly bedspread, on the wall, were pasted small pictures of a bizarre pantheon: a lurid, languid Jesus pointing to his stylized, exposed, and radiant heart; a cheerful young black baseball player on a trading card; a Buddha-looking thing with more limbs than a lobster; a pouty, oily, slickly lit photographic portrait of the late James Dean; a grinning, balding old swami; and the red-eyed, storm-gray head of Spectacular Bid: all boys!

Doris' heart leaped with the inspired hope that he was homosexual. She could ask for no more to humiliate totally and finally the other father-in-law of the forthcoming nuptials.

McDonald's shoes creaked behind her, and Doris whirled. Mr. Novitski was standing in them.

"Get out of here, you old bitch," he said by way of greeting. Her heart was too full of love for how much he meant to her in her present circumstance vis à vis John Russell McDonald to be affronted.

"I was just poking around in your things," she replied pleasantly.

With a pained pair of twinges, Mr. Novitski removed his tortuous wing tips.

"Yeah?"

"Leonardo da Vinci, Marcel Proust, Alexander the Great — where would our civilization be without them?"

"Huh?"

"Practically my best friends are down at Elizabeth Arden's. Such wonderful, sympathetic boys. The only people I can really talk to."

"What the hell are you doing in my place?"

Doris pulled out a check. The chauffeur's expression smoothed. She sniffed it like a flower and held it to him. It was for five hundred dollars. Unexpected money surprises only for a moment. We all, after all, deserve at least as much as comes our way. Giving it a neat crease, he slipped it deeper into his possession before asking Doris why she had handed him five hundred dollars.

"Engagement bonus — the boss's daughter is getting married." Doris didn't say to whom. She might bring Mr. Novitski into her little plan later, if she could figure a way to do so that welded him into alliance with her through the adamantine bond of self-interest.

The man relaxed. The check was fully assimilated; five hundred dollars.

"You want something?" he asked in a host's voice, looking left and right for something to celebrate with.

"Oh, whatever," said Doris. He handed Doris her first joint. It was a very strong one. She laughed and laughed. She asked him to shake the bedspread again. He laughed too. His orange jump suit opened like a pea pod. Doris reached in for the peas. Her big, scented saggy body didn't bother him. Her first fuck in years slammed on and on in an endless time she'd never known. She could feel the throb and squirt, and she squealed like a girl on the roller coaster — it was happening to her, too.

"I thought you were gay," she said after they tumbled back down into mortality.

"Nobody's perfect, man," he replied, enigmatically.

Doris held the bedspread gracefully over the aurora of her pink nipple; her other hand kneaded his gooey member (which she never wanted to release again in this lifetime).

Life is so discontinuous. The ash heaps on which Doris was abandoned had turned rich with bright, gorgeous fruit. She felt plums, grapes, flowers, and peckers everywhere she turned. It was for this moment every laughing baby on this earth is born.

They had a tasty fried dinner at a table splattering with candle light. His head was in the dark. His body was a gulf in the open orange jump suit. She reached her fingers in to pluck and squeeze at the dark hairy chest that had covered her. His throat shone; his chin moved; his head was now the black silhouette of a tree. Doris' fingers were white tubes with the red lipsticks of her fingernails exposed like dog hard-ons.

She couldn't think what to say. The drugs had shaved her mind down to perception and sensation. She had originally set out for the garage to pay him more, anything, to make sure he stayed until she could, at the right instant, aim who he was at McDonald, pull the lanyard, and watch the toy soldier, our new ambassador to France, blown into gaudy pieces. But her intention was gone. She was in a dark, fire-dancing room, among gold smoke, musky smells, and a man who had physically wanted her. She could only make a noise she had never heard in her life when his finger hooked over her trigger and stretched the surprised hole again. Doris went backward, looking through the big white fork of her thighs as the angel flew down again, his blue eye passing like a fish's in an aquarium. There was the weight and grunt and connection; once again, he was slamming Doris to glory.

"I roll, keep rolling, but I roll in perfect triangles, straight forward, the triangles are only cross-sections, invisible rods extending through my eyes, my navel, my testicles, my asshole from behind forward from oneness to nothingness," explained Doris' lover about the hubcaps. She ladled her big soft breasts into the beige hives he'd searched for honey, but he took them out again and played with them in both hands, like mud pies. He loved the body she had so long scorned.

"I take off all my clothes and jump in the air every morning to be disconnected from the manmade world," he further explained; "then I bitterly regret the fillings in my teeth. I think how if they weren't there, when I was in the air, I'd just be a dust mote floating in all the air."

The remark made Doris worry about her own teeth. Defensively, she reflected that she had most of them. She did care for her teeth as she cared meticulously for all the things sprouting from her skin: teeth and hair and nails — it wasn't ignorance that had lost her teeth, the way stupid white trash around her saw theirs go green, erode, go black, be gone. Her father had knocked Doris' teeth out when she was sixteen. He was a drunk. (Doris drank too, now, but at least she was an alcoholic.) Would this holy atom bomb of a lover be aghast at her missing teeth? He'd loved her hated corrugations of flesh, her cauliflower thighs, and puffy buns. He called her body clouds, and he dived in and out of them, seeking pink eyes, red buttons, carmine lips. She wouldn't tell him yet her teeth were somewhat artificial. He was too much of a hippy, she figured, to understand. He would make her take them out, live in a hut, and stink. The hippies were too close to the hillbillies she'd escaped.

Anyway, he had, after all, dyed that crazy sprout of hair on his head some unnatural violet color, so he couldn't blame her for the expensive rinse on her own. He'd sucked her fingertips, so he must not disapprove of nail polish.

That was enough for now. She would just hang on to the teeth secret — and the other secret. The false teeth

and the fiancé were still unrevealed deep in Doris, although he'd peeked in every orifice on her body.

*

The next morning at breakfast, Dan looked up to see
Doris smiling insanely and staring at him as if he were
magic.

"More coffee, darling?" she asked.

"Thanks," he said, dipping his lips to his napkin, wondering why she was doing this. He figured it had to do
with his growingly official engagement. The coming party
was a measured advance toward the big promises that
would legalize the unexpected results of one of those
many little thrills he'd had with Ro at college.

They'd both speculated about which tryst had impreg-
nated her: in the car in the parking lot (they had lain im-
mobile as the dean of the college himself suddenly got
into the very next car in the lot — one twist of this motorist's head would have shown him Dan's buns, Ro's
knees, Dan's back, Ro's wide-eyed face)? In the stacks of
the library (the little-used geography section)? Or just
one of the regular bed ones? They hoped it was a funny
one. It seemed far away and long ago, the college part of
this romance.

Doris kept staring at him. She wasn't bombed. Dan
gave her a smile. She cocked her head to one side and
gave a light pat to his head (right where the chauffeur's
pigtail sprouted).

Doris was pregnant, too — not with a child like the
hot little bunny this young breakfast-of-champions eater
sitting before her had mounted — but pregnant with a
secret, a messiah, a Dalai Lama of a secret! Only Doris
knew the chauffeur was his father. She contained the

bond of these two men as deeply, secretly, and mysteriously as nature itself. Scientists peeled at nature to discover genetic bonds. They would have to peel at Doris to discover this one: she held it deep inside, like strata holding a fossil.

To think she had held this very secret out to John Russell McDonald and, just before her fist bloomed into fingers handing him the jewel, he had betrayed her! Quickly she had stuffed it back in her pocket. It would come out again, at the right moment — only next time it would be a pistol.

She hadn't told the chauffeur, either. She wanted to see what sort of man he was. Would he join her in blackmail? She had gone to look at his place, size him up, make sure he would stay on, use her famous intuition on him. And then she opened the door on magic. Alice had walked through the looking glass. She gave herself to him, or he took her — she wasn't sure which had happened. She did know that when it was over, she had managed to save two things from the world she had stepped out of: the secrets of her teeth and his paternity.

Last night she had slept in gorgeous, furry oblivion for the first time in ages. The first person she saw on waking sat before her, here in the kitchen. The boy who had in some way become her child in the apartment over the garage.

"Do you take vitamins, Dan?"

"Oh, yeah."

"Good, darling. You look fine."

"Thanks."

"You must have had a very, very handsome dad, Dan."

"I guess."

"Very."

"Would you excuse me?"

"Of course, darling."

This old broad was getting too weird, Dan decided. He was glad Ro didn't like her. They wouldn't have to see much of her after the wedding.

He looked at the scene on his breakfast plate being revealed as the clouds of scrambled eggs lifted: men in red coats, leaning back as horses stylized into lizards jumped fences, following hounds.

When the whole thing was settled, when Dan was married and working at the Metropolitan Museum of Art (Ro's idea, why not?), when they had children, and after he gave his mother some fabulous present (maybe a Renaissance drawing), Dan thought how he might hire detectives to find his father. He pictured that mysterious father-stranger leaning on the rail at a race track, with two men in suits and hats closing in on him from behind.

"Dan Novitski?"

"Who wants to know?"

"Sent to look for you, sir, by your son, the director of the Metropolitan Museum of Art in New York City."

They would dine together. The craven, wide-eyed father would be looking at his radiant young host the way the peasants looked at their Guest in Rembrandt's *Supper at Emmaus.*

"Hi, darling," said Ro, bouncing in to breakfast with her robe not quite closing. Dan shuddered, shaking off his sentimental reverie. He smiled and kissed her in the grown-up, married-couple way they'd been treating each other all week. Without her, Dan reflected, he would never be thinking of glamorous reunions with his missing father.

EIGHTEEN

"My love is a river,
My love is a razor
..." sang Doris
to Jane's surprise
in the turquoise
electric dappling of the pool. It was the chauffeur's current musical favorite. When he cooked their fried delights, he sang this song, bending his parallel knees to the beat, and throwing his face back in mock agony, like a man being flogged.

Jane had never seen Doris swim. Doris jerked across the pool in a dignified side stroke that kept her white helmeted head focused clear out of the water while her sturdy pink body was shattered into shimmering pink pieces following in propellant spasms.

"Doris!"

"Hello, Jane."

"I didn't know you swam."

Doris took Jane's remark to be a snide reference to the gaunt, hick poverty of her origins.

"Oh, yes, the whole family swam," she replied in a quick lie. In fact, Doris had gone to her first swimming class in New York when she was eighteen, just escaped from West Virginia. The dour, indoor, formaldehyde pool of the Y was yet another classroom in which the plain, determined girl had worked to better herself. She was drawn back to the water now possibly because the swimming instructor at the Y had been her first lover in the big city.

He was a Bengali who, in his native land, had killed snakes with his bare feet. He ate only vegetables and worshipped other gods than the miserable tortured family presented to Doris by the drown-happy Baptists of her childhood. (Doris never forgave the Holy Family for being poor. The figure on the cross, all skin and bones and sorrow, was all too familiar to her. Doris, even then, preferred the Romans.)

On those distant, hot Manhattan nights, the swimming instructor pulled his brown body over her like earth while his gopher ran in and out of her hole. This unwhite lover, the cigarette propped between her painted nails, swimming, drinking, eating his peppery vegetables, and him — these were all bright prizes stuffing Doris' arms at the happy party celebrating her escape from the hills and hollows.

It all came back to her now for the first time in years, through the door that had opened in the orange jump suit.

"Shiva!" said Doris in the shallow end, remembering the name of her lover.

"What did you say?" asked amazed Jane, who in the twenty-five years of their acquaintance had never seen Doris in anything but a dress.

Why haven't you ever had a swim before in the twenty years you've spent here? Jane wanted to ask. Instead, she gestured to an attachment on the side of the pool. "Have you tried that Jacuzzi?"

Doris' cries as she shot water at her front were sensual and abandoned. Jane realized, and corrected the fact, that her own mouth was hanging open in astonishment at seeing something so familiar that it has become plain and banal, transformed so utterly as Doris Laitch cooing at the Jacuzzi as if it were a seduced boy.

"How've you been, Doris?" she asked with affected casualness. Doris' laughter seemed to be bumping downstairs, the trunk of a fan dancer jumping the bill late at night in a tank-town hotel.

"Fine," said Doris, with an emphasizing crinkle of her shining nose, and her thumping laugh descended another flight.

"Are you brushing up your French?"

It wasn't unarguably certain that Doris had replied, "Fuck France," as she dropped her head back on the water and sank, but it sounded awfully close to that. Doris' knees breeched like a pair of identical white whale twins, Moby Dick and Moby Rick, before following the rest of her under water.

Jane didn't want to get in the water with all that madness; it might spread like polio in a public pool.

Doris got out and sat with her legs spread and her painted toes scratching the air.

"I haven't done that in a while," she said with private double meaning that gave her a laugh, "but you don't forget how, after all."

"How are the invitations coming?" asked Jane, more to affect reality in a fantastic situation than to obtain information.

"Fine. About twenty acceptances already. People

want to say farewell to the new ambassador, so they're all making an effort."

Jane was pleased to hear reason issuing from this suddenly unpredictable creature.

"Lots of politicians?"

"Of course."

"God."

"He's such a fabulous young man."

"Dan? Yes, I'm crazy about him."

"He's a god."

"What?"

"He's a young god, Jane."

*

Doris, in a brand-new silk blouse opened far enough to reveal the crack between her breasts, stood in the doorway as the limousine crackled in over the Rice Krispies of the driveway.

The car stopped and the driver jumped out. He looked at Doris over the black roof. He crossed his eyes and hung out his tongue. After reordering his facial expression, he circled to where his employer, oblivious of the obscene shenanigans gyrating all around him, scowled as he put away papers he'd been studying.

Doris compared this odd pair who had both won her heart, one from the brain, the other from the opposite end. For McDonald, she'd been loyal, chaste, and singularly devoted for almost thirty years. For the chauffeur, she'd been molten for thirty minutes, a piece of West Virginia, black-lung coal squeezed into a diamond. And McDonald had betrayed her. There was no question which of the two men on the driveway now had Doris Laitch.

McDonald was handsome, tailored, vain, and successful. The chauffeur, stone-faced and moving with a faintly mocking awkwardness that exaggerated his unfamiliarity with subservience, seemed to be a character from an animated cartoon who had wandered by mistake into a heroic war movie starring John Russell McDonald.

The chauffeur bowed all the way to a right angle as McDonald strode away from him toward Doris at the door. McDonald's face was gripped with the tactical seriousness of a general entering Supreme Command Headquarters, an expression reinforced by his sight of Doris, all in beige, holding a beige file for him. McDonald appreciated this martial tinge to his arrival. It was the best way he could think of to approach the emotional minefields of family life.

As McDonald nodded a handsome scowl at damn Doris, the chauffeur's hat fell off. The bald pate with the twist of dyed hair in its center was exposed a moment, aimed right at McDonald's back: a pecker-pink cannon exuding fuchsia smoke. Doris roared with laughter, astonishing McDonald and popping loose her false teeth. In the confusion at the door, the chauffeur scurried back to the wheel and pulled out. McDonald was disconcerted by Doris bent double, still laughing, shoving at her mouth.

She turned her back to him, and with one hand splayed above her shoulder to express "excuse me" and the other at her mouth, she galloped down the hall.

NINETEEN

In the tub, Ro heard her father arrive downstairs. She looked at her abdomen as though she expected to see a thread of volcanic smoke twining out of her navel. Pregnancy had begun to make her feel rotten in the morning. Discomfort brought depression, which in turn brought doubt. If only Dan were different, older maybe, or working. Out west, he had had so much more command than he had here.

Alongside her father, Dan looked particularly ludicrous. Her father had come out from town at Ro's behest to join the council planning her big engagement party. She had dragged him out of town for an event he was against, yet he came, for her. Ro wanted to cry out and hug her father, to thank him for caring, for accepting her wish. She wanted him to be happy. As she thought about it in the tub, wringing a hand towel, more than anyone in the world, Ro wished to make her father happy.

Ro dressed for her father's eyes, in a demure, mature, elegant dress that she could imagine wearing with him at dinner in Paris. She descended the stairs with self-conscious grace, and went to visit him in his study.

He always looked just as he should. He regarded her over his glasses, smiled, and pushed away the world's documents.

"Get you a drink, dear?"

"No thanks, Daddy."

"Well, how's the big party coming?"

How kind it was of him to be nice about the party! How really superb he was. He didn't want her to marry Dan, but he would support her out of principle — like those patriots defending to the death the right of others to say things with which they totally disagreed — that was her father; her founding father interrupting his draft of the Constitution of the United States to be with his little daughter, his sweet baby darling, who truly, madly loved and admired him, the golden eagle who protected her, his little golden egg.

"You don't want me to do it, do you, Dad? Marry Dan."

"No, I don't."

"Why?"

McDonald walked to her and held out his hands, which she took like a baby committing herself to learn to walk.

"Because it's all wrong, Ro. You come over to France with me, see some of the world. You just haven't seen enough, and you're going to regret it like hell if you start complicating your life way back in the beginning."

"Mummy married you then."

"Ro, that was practically pioneer days," he said, with a wonderful, winning chuckle.

When McDonald wanted charm, it came. Ro smiled bashfully at her father's joke on himself. They were truly close. She felt it. It wasn't cold and clammy, the way it was with her mother. Her father so often seemed to Ro to be a boy. Just now, he even made his own marriage seem like a frog in Tom Sawyer's pocket.

"And I wouldn't say young marriage turned out so absolutely magnificently for your mother," he admonished.

("Your mother" — "Your father." Both her parents had long ago taken to assigning Ro ownership of their spouse.) Ro smiled coquettishly. France might be more fun than that table, that loft in SoHo. Screw parties for Muffy. The damn table now reminded Ro of an operating table. "Open wide, this won't hurt." Screw it. Ro did feel lousy in the morning. She was too young to feel lousy. Life wasn't for feeling lousy.

McDonald smiled and raised his eyebrows at Ro. He chuckled for no more reason than the fun of a conspiracy that was wordlessly forming between them. She shook her head with a big smile, feeling it too. He put his arm around his daughter and laughed. She laughed with him.

Since Ro's birth, McDonald had felt an automatic sympathy with her. If she were less dazzlingly beautiful than her mother, he felt it was because of the subtraction by his own genes. And he was pleased with this physical effect of himself on the child — his gravity drawing her away from Jane.

"You go into town with me first thing tomorrow, Ro. We won't say a word to anyone. We'll leave early and we simply won't be here when they wake up."

It was exhilarating to feel suddenly that she was looking at her father across an equation, the two of them balanced, conspiring. She had all his concern, intention, and intelligence. She felt a flash of adrenalin burn her cheeks with a blush. She was going partners with him.

McDonald began thinking of fun and Paris — walks in tweed suits, showing his handsome, intelligent daughter the wonderful little pleasures of Paris.

The two of them laughed out loud again.

McDonald could suddenly taste sauces, smell Paris air, see dead leaves scuttling across old boulevards. Ro would have a sweet frozen lick of cassis ice cream. He would smoke a small cigar (a thing he did only in Paris). The generations of gentlemen who had made a Parisian promenade with their daughters before him passed through his imagination. What a pleasant fancy! It was dear and genteel and rational to love a daughter the way McDonald loved Ro.

Daddy was so fabulous. At his best he was grand. He looked, acted, and spoke in ways that were simply and completely grand. He did it in public, at parties; thrilling, moving, and rendering envious the men and women of occasions. Privately, he was more often only difficult. He was a show horse not always great to be alone with in a stall. But when he did exercise this capacity to make life seem a sojourn to ennoble rather than simply endure, when he did it one on one, he was magnificent. He paraded with Ro about his study. The abortion was a fait accompli.

Doris had announced she was dining elsewhere. (A surprise — no one thought Doris had an elsewhere.) McDonald was supremely cordial and relaxed at dinner, solicitous of everyone. He patted Ro's hand often. He talked of art and great men. Dan was thrilled by this almost father-in-law talking beautifully in a beautiful room. He felt as if he were in a cathedral.

"Museums have just gotten too damn smooth for me," said McDonald. Dan felt a thrill — this was to be his family! "They're too damn public. The pictures are too preserved-looking. The buildings are too anonymous. The public is trained by the department stores to hunt for value, and that's what they do in these awful modern icebergs where some anonymous bastard's tax write-off hangs on the trigger of a burglar alarm. The Musée Guimet in Paris is my idea of what a museum should be. It still looks like some old rich bachelor uncle's place. You feel like a kid being shown something precious and private. The people in the place don't look like shoppers. God, I like that!"

Ro turned to Dan and cocked her head. She looked concerned.

"I want to talk to you," she said privately to Dan.

At the conclusion of this beautiful, civilized dinner, no hymn was sung. McDonald was called to his phone before dessert, and he simply never returned. Jane left after one more smile.

"Let's go outside," said Ro. She was taciturn, like a teacher choosing a punishment. Dan embraced her in the dark.

"I want to talk a minute," she said. He let go. Ro hopped up on a garden wall like Humpty-Dumpty. An extraordinary wail came from the windows over the garage.

"Mountain lions?" asked Dan.

"We've got to talk about it," said Ro. Another wail, followed by a string of short, operatic notes interrupted Ro's high seriousness.

"Dan, darling . . ."

"Isn't that where that guy lives, the driver?"

"Listen, I hope you understand. I'm going into New York alone with my father for a while."

"How come?"

"I want to talk to him."

"I thought he came out here to talk."

"I'm going in with him."

"OK."

"Do you understand?"

Dan understood. "Look, Ro. I'm going back to Boise."

"What?"

"Yeah."

"What's the matter?"

"Nothing."

Dan walked directly away from her. He went to his room and began to pack. A rush of freedom swept through him — to hell with them. It was crazy here, like the phantoms in old Chinese stories — the temples that weren't really there, the feasts that were hallucinations, the beautiful girl who turned out to be the White Bone Demon.

Green hell — that's what lost travelers called the Amazon Rain Forest. That's what this was — a green hell of cash so dense, you couldn't even see the sun. Dan had to sit on his suitcase to get it closed, so swollen with excess were its contents.

He carried his luggage down to the garage. Back in his room, he had been prepared for Ro to burst in, but she never came. He couldn't stand being there another minute anyway, feeling he was costing money to feed and house, feeling Ro didn't love him anymore, feeling he didn't belong there, feeling that thing he didn't even want to feel about Jane. (That last made it hard for Dan to feel simply and purely a victim.) How great it would be to be alone again!

The dark garage ticked. The van door made its good

old binding screech. It was so wonderful to enter his own property again. Dan found Ro sitting in the passenger's seat. Wordlessly, they kissed and hugged. Hot saliva glowed like lava at the mouth of the volcano. In the back, lengthwise like stiffs in a hearse, they lay. It was all so eternal and familiar. The fleshy piston pounded the skin cylinder. They groaned and hugged, locked, trading turns powering the engine of love.

Doris was on the point of turning on the garage light when she heard the sounds coming from the van, which rocked like a moored boat on a passing wake. It amused her enough to race back up. With a red fingernail latching her lips in the signal of silence and gesturing her lover to follow, she and the chauffeur, with silenced laughter causing violent grimaces, watched the van quake. Climactic groans came first from a female voice, and comic Doris silently applauded. When they came a second time, the male voice tromboned a bewildered cry of orgasm, and the chauffeur raised his thumb in a victorious signal. Arm and arm, Doris and her lover went back up to his apartment and turned out the lights. In pale moonlight, they saw the younger lovers, hand in hand, move up the gravel aisle toward the altar of the big house.

TWENTY

onah woke up and looked around. He was still in-side the whale, but he felt better than he ever had since being swallowed. In old tales, knights wake from curative swoons. Glittering days spread before the grin of the happy man. Indomitable, accompanied by vic-torious stabs of brass music, astride a magnificent steed, to the cheers of the populace, the hero went to the bath-room. Was this the face of a handsome young man? Today it seemed so.

Just before reaching for his razor from a steamy shower, Dan noticed a certain bareness about the bath-room that explained itself as he drew back his hand: all his stuff was in the van. He recalled the night before: he had been on the point of fleeing back to Boise. How ridic-ulous that night had been, him about to storm off into the night, headed home like a cur with a tail end full of buck-shot.

Ro's last dear kisses before she disappeared behind the white slab of her bedroom door returned as wet mem-ories. He smiled and blew the thought of her one. Would it arouse an erotic dream in her? Dan imagined Ro groaning and touching herself in her sleep.

In the kitchen, the frail, lacy old housekeeper with a white scribble for a face ventured out to take Dan's breakfast order with the timidity of a fawn in a clearing.

Dan noticed the virginal firmness of the newspaper. Was he the first one up?

Dan was having a fine time scoffing at the world's notions of importance in the newspaper, lifting the dew-glazed tumbler of fresh orange juice to his love-kissed lips. "My wife and I . . ." was a phrase that ran through his mind as he turned the pages of the *New York Times,* imagining he was chatting with these players on the world stage. A limousine would pull him from one important place to the next as circumstances in desperate need of his guidance, opinion, and repairs lay ruinous before him one minute, and then glittered fixed behind.

The handle of Dan's fork slipped complacently into the egg yolk. He pulled the little whore gingerly clear. There was no napkin. He couldn't bear to disturb the fragile old porcelain housekeeper. He tore off a corner of newspaper and wiped the fork. What to do with the yellowed, translucent scrap of newspaper? It would foul his pocket — why not call the woman? She would, of course, see exactly what he'd done, how he had wrecked John Russell McDonald's *New York Times* because he was too timid to order the servant to bring him a napkin. To hell with it — he would call. Then he saw the napkin ablaze at his feet. Dan held the corner of dark, yolky newspaper like a dead mouse. His lip curled. The print on the back of the page came clearly through the shining grease, only backward. "dlanoDcM llessuR nhoJ, yadoT," read the panicking murderer. He'd destroyed the very story the subscriber to this ruined journal, the owner of the property he had abused, would most prize.

The cocky dandy who owned the world was suddenly a fugitive again, a rat in the palace sewer.

"Jesus," whispered Dan disgustedly. He balled the paper and carried the sticky gaffe to the nearest bathroom, washing his hands after hurling it in the maelstrom. Should he face up like a man to his crime:

"Sir, I couldn't find my napkin and my fork slipped into the yolk and I didn't want to call the old lady who makes breakfasts because she looks like it pains her to walk just to get me a napkin so I tore off a piece of your newspaper to wipe it off and, after I'd wiped yolk all over it, I found out it was a story about you. I can't begin to express how sorry I am."

"Why didn't you call Mary and get a napkin, Dan? That's what a gentleman would do. Gentlemen don't destroy property because they're afraid to give orders to servants."

"I don't know, sir."

"Do you really think you can be a director of the Metropolitan Museum of Art if you're afraid to ask a housekeeper for a napkin?"

"Well, sir, I was going to, but just then I found the napkin had fallen to the floor. It was there all the time."

"And you think I would allow a coward like you to marry my daughter? To sire my grandson?"

"No, sir."

"Let's see how you handle this!"

The great man throws the boy a saber, and backs off, brandishing its twin. McDonald has spent his entire life fencing, winning duels, being awarded fencing medals; Dan has never held such a weapon in his life. They square off. At first, with a mordant smile, the great man plays with his doomed quarry like a cat. But Dan begins to hear powerful, distant, but audible symphonies. He is beginning to see a pattern in fencing. He who knows the finest touches of the fly rod begins to understand in deep and mystical ways the properties of this brutal machine sprouting from a fist flecked with his own blood. McDonald is taking piece after piece out of the boy. They litter the carpet like feathers from a pillow fight. But the wisdom of the fly rod is beginning to find use in Dan's hand. The flashing, flailing blade has begun to send intelligence about the enemy up through Dan's chipped arm to the same instinctive faculty of his brain that has, in the past, so often arranged the successful capture of major American trout.

McDonald is mildly surprised to find his stabs predicted and impeded. He draws back a moment to assess the change in the kid's fight. Then, with a snarl, he lays back into the duel, pulling out every trick in the book. But now Dan knows how to duel. He parries every thrust; he astonishes the old champion by an offensive stroke that nicks and draws blood from McDonald's shoulder. McDonald bellows and attacks with deadly brutality . . .

"Is anyone in there?" The door handle of the real world cocked its head back and forth.

Dan recognized Jane's voice. He answered, pitifully, "Just a minute." Could any juxtaposition be more ludicrous? A beautiful woman, a creature who draws every drop of what nectar of poetry exists in a young man, calls out to him in the clear, beautiful, reed-instrument voice of which he dreams. Only a door stands between them. And at this exquisite moment, the young, ardent squire happens to be midway through his morning movement.

Dan waited until he figured Jane was well away before he emerged from the bathroom. He foresaw her at the breakfast table, puzzling over the missing fragment of the story about her husband.

Jane tucked a point of jam-sparkling toast into her mouth as Dan walked in, smiling idiotically and trying not to stare at her.

"What would you like?"

"Oh, I ate," he replied, wishing he'd said, "No thank you, I've had breakfast," in the manner of Leslie Howard.

"What time did they go?" asked Jane.

"Who?"

"Ro and John. Doris went with them; she left a note."

Dan was startled. He felt something breaking inside him, spilling some unbearably hot liquid down through him. Despite the night of love, she'd gone with her father. She'd rejected him. What fool's play it all was, especially the part about Jane. Dan felt exactly like what he was — a dumb bastard.

TWENTY-ONE

ike a man of importance, pushing through onlookers with his aides, McDonald's limousine elbowed its way through the New York traffic.

Doris shook back a plank of hair and placed the receiver to her ear.

"Yes. Would you tell Dr. Saks that John Russell McDonald would like to speak with him?"

Doris smiled and passed the phone to the boss. It was fun to show the chauffeur her business side. She was glad the window between the seats was down so that her divine lover, Apollo driving this sun chariot, could hear her counsel, organize, and connect John Russell McDonald to the rest of the pantheon of modern power. Doris smiled at McDonald in a patronizing way, amused at how the slightest gas bubble caused him to call Dr. Saks. He was such a baby — terrified his prostate would blow like a fuse, emptying the scabbard between his legs. John Russell McDonald was vain as a drum major, reflected Doris, for all his conservative suits.

The little bride-to-be was there too, looking adolescently tense and knotted. Oh well, she was young, and the mother was admittedly beautiful; maybe she would grow into something worthy of the divine Dan, the spiritual progeny of Doris' ecstatic couplings with the very man guiding their big smoky limousine through the yolky taxis and brutally awkward trucks coagulating thicker as they approached Manhattan.

"Hello, Sam. Is it all set? Good. Should she eat anything? I see."

McDonald placed a hand on the phone.

"What did you have for breakfast, darling? She just had juice and coffee, Sam. Swell, Sam. OK. OK, Sam, see you at one.

"Don't eat lunch, Ro."

Ro gnawed her fist and looked out the window at a car full of eyes peering to see who was riding in the swell limousine.

An alarm went off in Doris.

"Is Ro all right?"

Tears welled in Ro's eyes; she turned away.

"Yes, yes. Call Superior Oil. What's his name — you know."

"Hugh. Hugh Stockton."

Doris answered McDonald in a voice so different from the smooth sleek business purr she'd exuded thus far that the chauffeur glanced in the mirror and wondered why the scene back there was so weird, Doris staring at the old man and the kid as if they were ghosts, the old man lifting his chin and clearing his throat, the kid crying and looking out the window. A car honked, and the chauffeur pushed his foot back into the gas. This old son of a bitch was so loaded he didn't care how much you used, as long as he was passing the rest of the cars wherever he was going.

As soon as the limousine stopped, Doris rushed to call Dan.

"You must come right away. You've got to talk to Ro. She's going to have an abortion at one. Hurry, Dan; whatever you do, hurry."

The shock absorbers on the filthy taxi had collapsed, and the jarring Dan took fitted perfectly with his clobbered heart and his beaten wallet. The East was trying to shake him to death, like a terrier with a rat. He staggered getting out of the cab as the untipped driver insulted him and the cold formal hospital sneered before him. Doris was right there at the door, reaching for him like an impatient kid in a relay race.

Pulled along by her, Dan reflected how unexpected Doris' alliance was. Why was she so helpful? Human antiquities in baby color pastel blankets were wheeled brusquely past Doris and Dan, their old eyes on misty visions far from the cheerless blank of the architecture. Speaking through holes in Plexiglas to the bored, superior mandarins, Dan and Doris got to a waiting room said to be near where Ro was being prepared for the operation. Dan looked desperately at linoleum skidded by wheelchair tires and pacing shoes. A nurse with a face like a bicycle seat hung on a door she'd suddenly opened.

"She's fine," said the nurse cheerily. It was all over. The anti-father of the negative birth was congratulated. Cigars were taken from him; he backed out of the room, the hospital, time, until he was pulling his organ from between Ro's closing legs, spending less and less time with her, glancing at her for the first time, never having met her.

If Dan had just not had a baby, Doris now felt she had given true, personal, hospital birth to her first, him. She took him to her apartment. Now she was the mother, the chauffeur the father, and Dan the baby. They could live happily ever after, taking Dan to the zoo, to the movies, Disney World — of course, he was a little old for all that, poor thing. He sat quietly, like a student puzzled by a math problem. She was on the point of making him a Bloody Mary when she decided that, in view of what had just transpired, it would be a particularly inappropriate drink.

Doris' apartment was small, neat, and impersonally attractive. No more than six should really dine there; no more than one should really live there. Two chintz chairs squared off across a mirrored table that had reflected ten thousand drinks, almost all in exactly the same place, by the chair where Doris now sat, where she so often sat alone, having served herself a drink on a napkin emblazoned with her own initials and started a magazine or a book that would gradually become invisible as the drinks faded it into oblivion.

Doris kicked off one shoe and tucked a leg under her. She shook her hair and drew at a cigarette. Dan sat in the other chair, trying to make out the future in the crystal ball of vodka and ice she'd set on her monogram before him. She'd taken charge when she saw the spirit go out of him in the room of the grim congratulations at the hospital. He'd turned and walked out, toward nowhere. Doris had come after him. No, he didn't want to see Ro, see McDonald, any of it.

"Send some flowers, Dan," she'd advised. She paid for them. He found himself signing a card, which Doris held for him, wishing any sufferer speedy recovery. Doris watched her poor baby digest the unhappy taste of the world at her apartment. He looked up for the first time.

"Can I borrow a hundred dollars, ma'am? I could leave some security."

"Oh, of course, son. You don't have to leave anything, darling — and especially in that glass! Cheers!"

"How come you've been so nice?"

"Dan, I think you're a wonderful young man, that's why. And I'm going to help you, dear. I'm going to help you marry the princess even if the wicked old king doesn't want you to. Even if he just talked her into this little operation, it doesn't mean the battle is lost. Everyone wants the marriage except him, and everyone's tired of always seeing him get his way. I'm going to see to it that he just lets Ro make up her own little mind from now on. Now the first thing, dear, is not to give up. Sometimes little abortions are just a girl's way of being coy."

The intercom of Doris' apartment buzzed. The announcement she heard appeared to delight her. "Send him up," she purred.

"Do you really think you might be able to lend me that money?" asked Dan, encouraged by her blossomed mood.

"Of course, darling."

"I've got to get home," he explained.

"Is that why you want the money?"

"I've got some there; I can pay you back."

"You want the money to go home?"

Doris' doorbell gave an unpleasant ding-dong.

"Yes, ma'am."

"But, Dan," said Doris, grinning lavishly and rushing to the door, "you are home."

TWENTY-TWO

o felt so much
better, she won-
dered why she'd
done without her
little rubber pal to begin with. Why had she wanted to get
pregnant? She had. She'd let him in unprotected on purpose. She'd just done it in that independent way she was
cultivating to impress the very man who was now with her
in the hospital, acting like a boyfriend. He was the first to
see her. His arms were full of flowers and gifts. She held
out her arm with the gold bracelet he'd just given her,
next to the plastic one from the hospital.

The nurse bustled in with a vase for the flowers and
smiled: she so liked to see that all too rare modern spectacle, the happy family, the father and daughter together
at the abortion.

"I really feel ready to go."

"Sam wants to keep you tonight, Ro. I'm staying in.
What would you like to do tomorrow?"

"Oh, Daddy, you always talk as if there were a whole
day you could spare me, when you really mean lunch or
twenty minutes or something."

"A whole day. I've cleared the decks. Well, almost. I have a meeting at the UN at eleven that I made them guarantee in writing would be over before lunch, and something at four."

"See? That leaves lunch."

"Where are we having lunch, then? And dinner?"

"Dinner?"

McDonald nodded. Ro's toes wiggled under the sheet. She looked adorable, childlike in the hospital room. Brown from the sun, his eyes, his shoulders. She was a real cutie pie. That French boy was the right one: St. Cyr, a count, fine manners — and not so much money that he'd ever go through with marriage to the movie star he was running through the tabloids with. Much as the boy's father deplored it publicly, that movie star was just what the son of the president of France should be seen with before serious courtship. That was McDonald's first choice. Lord Cove's son was his second choice. He was a fine specimen; maybe a little too pink and hairless, something like an eraser, at this stage of his development, but Englishmen age beautifully. They get craggy and long, distinguished by time, whereas Frenchmen shrink, curl, and begin to show the effects of wine and whores. You are what you eat, and the kippers and eggs of England produce craggy cliffs in which sea gulls and eagles could nest, while the meal of the Frenchman is, McDonald surmised from what they look like at seventy, pussy.

When her father left, Ro examined again with satisfaction the gold bracelet he'd brought her. He had never looked so much like a teen-age date as he had on this visit. People really have only one age all their lives. They are six, sixteen, or seventy from the cradle to the grave. Some babies are little old people, some are mad teen-age whoopers, and some are babies throughout their whole lives. At seventy they are still six years old, like Winston Churchill with the world for a toy box. Ro's father was forever a teen-ager. In fact, he was a much better one now at sixty than he had been at sixteen, Ro judged from the photographs she'd seen of the skinny, brainy-looking party in old photo albums.

Ro herself was born to be thirty-five. Doris must have been middle-aged all her life. Mummy was forever a débutante (now wilting, a corsage in the refrigerator). Dan was — Dan! Ro had forgotten about Dan all this time!

Where was he, she wondered. Gaping at paintings in Connecticut? Reading *Town and Country* and trying to figure out the mystery of upper-class life? Jogging?

Why had Ro wanted to get pregnant by him? It was deliberate. The first time, she'd seduced him in a chair. Sat astride him, put him in, and detonated him with Panofsky's *Early Netherlandish Painting* scrambling around for a hold on his chest until it was thrown, splayed to the floor with a Vermeer staring, shocked, at what the students were doing three hundred years down the line.

The car, the library — practically every time they'd done it had been initiated by Ro, full knowing there was no little closed rubber door between his billion ravenous visitors and her golden egg. Telling him in the mountains was deliberate, too. Ro had told Dan in the wilderness because she wanted him to think of it as part of nature, not something that could be eliminated with devices in a city. It was crazy. Ro tried to trace her motives. She wanted to understand what had brought her to this hospital room, these bracelets of identification and reward.

The flowers by her bed bloomed gorgeously, unwittingly, probably still thinking bees would come even when they sat in the florist's morgue, amputees still receiving sensations from missing roots in the real earth. Ro suddenly felt she was a cut flower, sitting in a gorgeous vase her father gave her, waiting, perhaps, for bees that had gone.

"Biology," she said aloud. It must have been biology, some synapse or gland responding to some primordial signal and galvanizing Ro's body to an action before her brain had reviewed it.

Anyway, it was all over now. Nausea was gone. The ambivalent response to an extant but shadowy future was resolved by making that future disappear into the fog, throwing it off the bridge so high, you couldn't hear the splash or scream.

Ro shook her head and riffled her toes. She stretched; making a fist with each hand, she pushed down past her crotch, under the blankets.

"Don't have intercourse for a couple of weeks, please," said the kind, scrubbed surgeon. She wondered how often he did it.

Ro turned on the televison set to chase away these personal thoughts. She made a face and felt something sour release at the back of her mouth and run down her throat. The first thing focusing on the damn television set was a Roto-Rooter commercial.

*

McDonald the knight wiped his longsword of infidel blood and replaced it in its scabbard. The battle was won. The maiden was saved from the dragon of pregnancy. Now she could have a real prince or, at the very least, the scion of an adequate industrialist.

"Stop at the corner, Dan," he said to the chauffeur. "I probably won't need you until tomorrow, but check in with Miss Laitch."

It must have been a stifled sneeze, but for a moment it sounded as if the chauffeur had giggled.

McDonald walked the half block to Vanilla's, glancing back to make sure he was unobserved (just as he had as an undergraduate before entering Skull and Bones).

On the age-rounded humps of the carpeted stairs of the fair maiden's tower, McDonald reflected how tough one had to be with life. He didn't like things like the business just concluded at the hospital, but men who couldn't roll up their sleeves and do dirty work were soon culled and discarded.

It was amazing how restless and ornery all the parts of a man's life become the minute they felt they were getting less than the attention they deserved. He had neglected Ro. He was ashamed to realize her graduation had slipped by him, along with her passage into womanhood. She was damn near Vanilla's age! What a blessing he felt about her coming to him with her woman's problem. She had needed his tough decision to crack through the prison abuilding around her. Marrying that ridiculous little Tarzan she'd canoed home with would have cost her years and him a million.

His elation moved on to consider another happy event. McDonald was more enthusiastic about his upcoming appointment to France than he let on to anyone. It was going to be the best part of his life so far. He would have his beloved daughter to school, advise, entertain, and introduce. This unpleasantness just disappearing into the Manhattan sewer system had brought her back to him, with an admonition to pay closer attention to her that McDonald graciously accepted. It could have been much worse. What if she had gotten married and brought her ridiculous husband home to live? Relief swept McDonald up Vanilla's stairs like a rising bubble.

Vanilla in Paris was another delight in store for the new ambassador. At the Comédie Française, at the races, at Fontleroy, and other weekends that called for dear, attractive company, they would be seen, admired, and envied. Vanilla had that wonderful edge of style that would grow only keener in Paris. He was so good for her. McDonald was pleased to imagine how, when he was dead and Vanilla was a beautiful sixty-year-old hostess at a dinner party in some great city of the world, what John Russell McDonald had brought into her life would color every corner of the room in which she sat. She would be toasting her grand lover of long ago as she raised her glass to her company. The spirit of her grand lover of long ago would flicker in the red depths of her glass, chuckle in the bouquets of flowers, glow in the paintings, and glitter in the crystal and silver. The Cézanne would be in that future's room (a picture he'd given her out of real passion, in the face of terrible consequences if it were ever known. If Jane ever found out he had not sold her mother's Cézanne, but, in fact, had bought it himself and given it to his mistress, his marriage and all that it brought him would end. It was the headiest thing McDonald had ever done, but Vanilla was the headiest experience he had ever felt). He would be with his dearest love then, less corporeally, but no less passionately than he was about to be right now. Walking up the last flight to Vanilla's landing, he did pause to hope she was in. He hadn't called. He was supposed to be in Connecticut. But he felt she had to be there, because he needed her now.

Finally, there was Jane's French incarnation to consider. McDonald's first thought was to get a house an hour out of Paris. Jane could decorate the place, see to the garden, have people out to praise her style and taste. It would be fun for her. McDonald would come out with the president and his wife, who, being in much the same circumstances with her husband as Jane, would be wonderful company for her. After all, if one had as European a marriage as McDonald, it certainly made sense to take it to Europe.

McDonald chuckled imperfectly because of the climb up Vanilla's stairs. He could see the entirety where others saw only parts. This had made him rich. Now it helped him improve the lot of every one of these women, Ro, Vanilla, and Jane. He had convinced them all, they had responded, and their lives had improved as a result. Even though he knew how much he was doing for Vanilla, how much his power, wisdom, and money were enriching, broadening, and flavoring her life, he got that silly feeling of helpless confusion as he opened the door to her apartment. He still felt like the lucky kid admitted to the treasure house of her sexual favors, as though she, not he, were the one who really knew what was going on in the world.

Voices, the thud of panic, and an instant sense that something was terribly wrong arrived in McDonald before he sorted out the spectacle before him and deduced its unhappy information. Vanilla held the sheets over her nakedness in a pointless, comical misapprehension that she was successfully keeping a secret. Steigen shouted,

"Oh, Jesus!" and ran for the bathroom. McDonald's first thought was how she had let that bastard Steigen play with all those gorgeous valves and gauges she now so demurely shrouded. When Steigen reappeared, McDonald rushed at him before he even considered what he was doing. He threw a punch with all of his strength, which only pulled him off balance as it hooked a whistling fish of air.

McDonald was down, now, on all fours, the beast at bay, in the pit, helpless, as the cruel natives danced around above, hurling insults, rocks, and soon the spears that would sting him with death.

"Are you all right?" Vanilla asked McDonald.

"Are you all right?" Steigen asked also.

"You better just go," Vanilla told the art dealer.

"I just want you to know this just happened, John — it just happened. We weren't like this — John," said Steigen, as his legs, filling and straightening the formerly limp trousers on the chair, reminded McDonald of what he'd done with Vanilla.

"You better go, Paul," said Vanilla, demurely. Steigen, tortured by the loss of his best client, plunged out into the cruel world. "It's true, John," said Vanilla in the same demure voice. "We weren't doing this. It just happened."

McDonald could see it didn't hurt Vanilla a bit, but Lord, how it hurt the woolly mammoth now a captive in the pit beneath her. It hurt him like a shark bite, a bull's horn, a hosing down with broken glass — it hurt so terribly, he fell on his side and pulled up his knees like a scared child.

TWENTY-THREE

This is your father, Dan," said Doris simply when the chauffeur entered the sitting room.

"Hey, man," said the chauffeur, extending his hand.

Dan rose and shook hands. The automatic gesture gave him a moment to consider what was taking place as emotions blitzed him. The chauffeur didn't say anything. He simply grinned. There wasn't a trace of doubt, guilt, or confusion in his manner. He shook hands with the son he'd deserted sixteen years before with the aplomb of a livestock judge facing the camera with the boy whose sow got the blue ribbon.

Dan knew it was true the minute Doris said it. There was no doubt this was his father's face, this grinning skin igloo with a puff of fuchsia smoke coming out the top. This middle-aged punker chauffeur was the banal incarnation of Dan's million dreams about his missing father. The chauffeur put his arm around Doris, who caved into it with a lover's familiarity. This couple stood grinning happily at their witness.

Dan's head rang as if it were the clapper of a great bronze bell. An earthquake suddenly began to shake the room, pitching things to the floor, opening cracks, shattering glass — no, it wasn't an earthquake; it was Dan quaking as tears suddenly spit out of his boiling eyes and awful cries rose through his throat.

"I'd cry, too," Doris said, beaming. "Would you like a drink, darling? I'm afraid alcohol is all I have in my little stash." She spoke flirtatiously.

Soon they were all sitting, sipping drinks, chatting inconsequentially, or so it seemed for a moment until Dan realized that, while it was true they were all sitting with legs crossed and glasses in their hands like people talking, no one was saying a word. All of a sudden the paternal travesty asked, "How's your ma?"

"Great," squeaked Dan. "Great."

"Yeah, I've been meaning to send something, but whenever I get close, some damn horse goes evil on me. It's karma. It's all karma. So. You look fine."

"Yeah. I'm great."

"Two Dan Novitskis!" observed Doris. "Two handsome men in my little apartment, where there hasn't even been one in just ever so long."

"She still into art?"

"Mom? Yeah. I am too. History of Art."

"What about spiritually?"

"What?"

"Where are you spiritually?"

"I don't know what you mean."

"That means you probably aren't anywhere, spiritually. But be peaceful. The patterns appearing just under the surface will come strong. Someday we'll all see the race happen right in the *Form*. The race on the track

will only be a replay of our vision. I've almost seen it
happen twice — the yeti, the snow leopard, the race seen
before it's touched by daylight."

Dan looked at him. It was so weird to imagine this
creature with his mother. He must have been different.
The chauffeur's suit was not a good fit. He looked like a
rented pallbearer. At first Dan thought this stranger-
father's socks were too short; then he discovered the
man's lurid bare shanks were sprouting sockless from
ankle-high boots that closed with a zipper. Without asking or even wanting to know, Dan believed this man had
done time.

"You two probably want to catch up," offered Doris.
"I'm going to have a bath and you just talk man talk."

It was the first time Dan ever wished Doris would not
leave the room. The father made more drinks and talked
more nonsense. Dan was calmer. The drubbing drinks
tenderized his brains. He wanted to laugh a little at this
thing who looked like something from Howard Pyle's
Book of Pirates. The coo-coo spiritual advice and ex-
con's paranoia continued to find expression.

"It's all fixed. This son of a bitch McDonald and the
rest have it all fixed up to come their way and that's why
it's so good we have this little break. Like Kali says — I
call her Kali." He grinned with a toss of his head that
caused his top knot to point toward Doris in the bathroom. "It's pure karma, this little break. She only told
me last night, and I didn't sleep. I sat in the lotus position
and faced the dawn, man — because this is what I been
waiting for. You marry the little princess, son. You are
my vision."

After a while Doris yodeled in the bathroom, and the
father staggered toward the sound. Dan sat in his chair,

disbelieving everything, refusing to hear the shouts and splashes of water sports accompanying the rush of humidity from the open bathroom door. When he couldn't avoid accepting the actuality of his situation, Dan bolted for the front door.

The two hours' wait for a train to Connecticut sobered and sickened Dan. The train was filthy and his head hurt, but the truth was even more filthy and more painful.

*

On the train, the soiled old plush seats shone like dirty bruises. The dust-glazed windows were more translucent than transparent. Litter scuttled over the floor of the screeching passenger car, but the commuters were fashionably dressed, oblivious of their grim surroundings, except for Dan, who found this bankrupt environment vividly appropriate to his mood.

The fancy living in spotless rooms, the rosy future, and the distant past all changed places. The future disappeared, replaced by a swiftly backtracking present that sucked memory and fantasy into its stains and tears as it rushed toward old pain and forgotten nightmares. That man was so bizarre and awful — what a father to find! Dan tried to remember his first impressions of the hateful lover of Doris. He'd seen him appear throughout his visit, and marked every time: the D'Artagnan bow, the pigtail, the occasional little cakewalk from around the limousine when he thought he was unseen. Dan had thought it was funny. That was when the show was free. After paying the terrible admission, he considered it the greatest rip-off of his life.

With a rush of shame, Dan remembered standing in McDonald's dressing room thinking that his own father might be standing that very moment in a similar facility — how ludicrous! He looked again at the congregation on the train, silently reading the service in financial newspapers, and thought he would have preferred any man on that train for a father than that cloudy, gaunt, post-hippy, so confident in his burned-out nonsense, philosophy, and hopeless career, who had just cavorted before Dan's eyes with that big, pale rose cauliflower, Doris.

At some point near the end of his trip, a bitter, rueful laugh forced its way up through a shame-crusted passage in Dan. He had been so sure all that grandeur was his! It takes only a moment to adjust to enormous improvement in circumstance, and bitter years to adjust to even slight declines. When it was better before, people refer to it the rest of their lives, like Russian dukes driving taxis. When things were worse before, the past disappears with wonderful rapidity.

TWENTY-FOUR

In regained Connecticut, Jane McDonald was playing tennis with a man Dan estimated to be somewhere around her own age. The game, with its self-enclosed purpose and expectations further enclosed by physical lines and even more finally enclosed in a black chain-link fence, made Dan feel as incommunicado as if he were watching a cage at a zoo. He felt like a man in a dream unable to shout the news that would save him. He even imagined imparting all he had to say in the brief pauses between points:

5–0	Hi.
30–0	Ro's had an abortion.
30–5	Could I borrow some money?
30–30	I can pay you back.
40–30	I'm going home.
Deuce	I love you.
Add in	But there's something you should know —

the chauffeur is my father.

Game, set, and match. Farewell, unseeded player!

The man playing tennis with Jane beamed like a car with headlights on no matter what happened. He had a mustache and a well-cared-for look, like a garden. Only when he saw Dan did he stop glowing a moment and look puzzled, as though music had unexpectedly stopped.

Jane followed her opponent's cloudless, Nordic eyes and found Dan. She waved, and her hair bounded lighter and higher. But in rhythm with the rest of her as she scurried to receive serve. For some reason, despite all the terrible events that had marched through Dan, he thought of nothing but how wonderful Jane McDonald looked in that dark square of tennis, like the unicorn in the tapestry.

The chauffeur's son looked enraptured at the lady of the house. Perhaps one day he would take a woman in a ditch, live in a hut on the castle grounds, and wait to watch the great lady ride by on a caparisoned palfrey. When it happened he would groan, return to his hovel, beat and mount the toothless hag who was his lot.

The grinning foil of Jane's tennis game shouted. He had an accent. Dan noticed stupidly that a ball had flown out of the tennis court and fallen at his feet. The accented man was shouting to him to throw it back over the fence. Dan entertained the notion that there might be a note on it from Jane: "4:00 P.M. in the garden behind the pool."

"Sanks," saluted the mustache man when Dan mortared the ball back into the tennis playpen.

Just the sight of her made Dan's pain bearable, even though she had nothing to do with the ugly events that had just trampled him. She swatted the ball the way Dan knew she would. Her rear domes rolled against each other as she scattered back and forth, whacking the yellow dot connecting her to the figure who caused a rising jealousy in battle-battered Dan, who felt as if he had just dragged home after passage clear across the frozen carnage of Napoleonic Russia.

Dan was pleased when the tan, problem-free-looking
European missed a shot. This creature's little groan of
disappointment would be a much greater sound if it
stemmed, instead of from a lost point, from Dan's peasant's scythe twisting in his belly, making him the first
victim of the revolution sweeping serfs from the fields
over the castle walls to loot the tyrants' greedy hoard,
with Dan saving only the great lady from the slaughter,
rape, and gorging of the blood-maddened churls.

"I thought you were in town," said Jane, presented as
a pattern of contiguous diamonds by the chain-link fence.
Would she pass the con a file to saw his way through the
iron bars separating them?

"Yeah, I was" was all Dan managed to say before she
returned to the percussion of a long rally with this jerk
whose awkwardness was made even more laughable by
little flourishes he had invented to cover his incompetence, the way vain bald men rake a covering for their
domes from some final hair source above the back of
their necks.

Dan couldn't leave the tennis match, even though he
should have been packing, loading his van, studying
maps, and calling home. ("But Dan, you are home," the
witch had said before the apparition came flapping in,
shrieking his misbegotten fatherhood like an imprecation.)

The unreality of the McDonald grandeur placidly surrounding Dan now made the discovery of his father
somewhat fantastic. But, in fact, the reason Dan knew
the horrible news was true was the utter banality with
which it struck him. Of course that was his father, that

long clown masquerading in modern disguises. The punker stuff had seemed so funny to Dan when he thought of it as something sneaked past John Russell McDonald. But when it arrived on his own doorstep, it seemed pathetic and affected, the refuge of a scoundrel.

Dan stayed in the synthetic time of the tennis game to delay his return to the real stuff, the river full of corpses and shrieks that would soon carry him away from the enchantment here. The foreign man had moved ahead of Jane in the match. Dan expected it; the macho bathos of this man's transparent, shallow soul required victory, even over a woman. Dan squinted at his glossy, selfish rival. *She couldn't possibly have ever let such a patent bungalow as this lay a finger on her,* he hoped.

The bastard finally won, not by skill or grace, but by brute strength. Dan's foot wanted to shoot forward like a speeding toy train across the grass and trip the son of a bitch as he passed, holding his racquets like Miss America's roses, pulling at his snowy headband.

"Dan, this is Nicki von Eltz," she said, sheened with perspiration, throbbing from exertion, her muscles collected by exercise. Couldn't Dan simply fly into Jane, like a bee disappearing into a lily?

"How do you do."

Looking at this Nicki von Eltz, Dan decided no creature of nature is more vain and smug than a forty-five-year-old man who has had enough things go his way to possess better toys, more hair, and less fat than his colleagues. This was the obvious case of this man grinning venomously at him now, rushing to dismiss Dan from the presence of his vile courtship of Dan's Faerie Queene.

Dan hung around, to Nicki's obvious annoyance. He sensed it didn't bother Jane a bit.

"What would you like, Jane?" asked the SS man.

"A very light Scotch and soda."

The Nazi's criminal fingers probed the ice bucket like a burglar in a jewel box, grinning all the while.

"Will you have something, Dan?" offered Jane.

"Sure, the same. That sounds good." Dan was pleased to sense Nicki's annoyance. Nicki jammed Dan's ice down the throat of a glass and slopped Scotch at it in noticeable contrast to the hairdresser's touch he had used in the preparation of Jane's highball.

The three of them sat in spidery garden furniture, tinkling their drinks and smiling. Nicki clearly wanted to be rid of Dan. He scowled at him with a quick jerk of his head, as if he were dismissing a waiter. Dan's buns only gripped more forcefully at the tasteful green webbing of his chair.

"Could I talk to you alone?" asked Dan to Nicki's dismay. When Jane assented, the obnoxious collection of conceit, arrogance, and all other known strains of the bacterium of pride rose and, with a phony grin, departed for the house.

"I take a shower," he said with an exhibitionist's fondle of his abdomen, a grip Dan just knew he wished to lower to his crotch.

Alone with her in the pretty green garden, the last thing Dan wanted to do was tell her what he must.

"Well, I've got to go home."

"Oh, why?"

"Ro just had — she just, well — she isn't pregnant anymore."

"Oh, my God, what happened?"

"She had it taken care of."

"Oh, Dan!"

Jane's comforting embrace unfortunately placed Dan in the same criminal class he had assigned to the recently departed Nicki. He could sense her whole anatomy from the parts touching him, like an anthropologist rebuilding a dinosaur from a single rib. He didn't move or speak until she took her arm back. He stared sadly at the grass, letting Jane think it had to do with noble regrets about Ro, when in fact it concerned his own guilt. Why shouldn't a woman have an abortion if her lover has fallen for her mother? It's what Dear Abby would advise. Of course, only Dan knew this nuance of Ro's case, and he certainly could never reveal it to this particularly sympathetic witness.

"The thing is, I'm completely broke, too. I've got some money in Boise."

"Don't worry about that."

"Hello out there." Nicki grinned from an upstairs window, his naked upper body hanging smugly out over his elbows. "You must come in, the water's fine." Jane gave him a smile and wave and he returned inside to, Dan imagined, play with himself.

TWENTY-FIVE

omen closed over like holes in the sand. The gaping orifice McDonald had entered to find spread around that alien cock was now demure, placid, as closed as Vanilla's mouth as she nursed the knight where he lay dismounted, pinned by his own armor to the cruel earth. She was so genuinely concerned for his agony, it seemed impossible she was its cause. She consoled and soothed him as if it were someone else who had betrayed him.

The drink he knocked back did nothing; bounced like an Indian's arrow off a Spanish breastplate. He glowered at her, sitting enthroned as she held his hand, cocked her head and smiled — encouraging the baby to stop crying.

"You bitched me, you whore," he said to her as he left. Halfway down the stairs, he remembered the Cézanne, but he couldn't bring himself to look at Vanilla again. He took a last step to a stair that wasn't there, almost twisting his ankle as he tilted awkwardly, a shudder slamming up his body. He could only pray he would never have to endure the sight of her again — faithless, rotten, immoral Vanilla.

McDonald took a cab to his office. Out the window the millions passed, looking as if they were all enduring the same awful pain. McDonald would not let it cripple him. He hadn't gotten so far above the pedestrians he watched by brooding over the antics of bitches. He sat up straighter in the cab.

As it had so often at bad moments, the panoply of McDonald's estate reassured him. Obsequious lesser men reacted to his passage through the office like primitive natives discreetly watching the shadow of an airplane rather than taking the chance of gazing directly upon it.

McDonald was furious to find himself agonizing over Vanilla at his desk, his battle station. Damn her. Why did he care so? It was just a bodily function — a better meal than other restaurants served, a deeper sleep, a more successful elimination. It was just a grunt and spasm — those weren't stars he had seen with her; they were just leftover light sparkling in the rods and cones of lidded eyeballs. Vanilla was just an exceptional physical satisfaction. So why was McDonald wasting fury and grief over finding her with that sleazy art dealer who had so often served McDonald in pimplike capacities, introducing him to girls, finding them jobs and apartments? Of course Steigen was a pimp and Vanilla was a whore. But these damnations produced a saddening satisfaction. McDonald saw his pulse was beating much too fast in the wrists above his white-knuckled fists.

The thing was to eliminate this problem by solving it. McDonald winced stoically and called Doris to come at once to the office.

When he told her everything, Doris was unable to stay seated or keep back her smile. She walked slowly and, in her own way, not unmajestically up and down before she answered her embarrassed employer. It was practically too good to be true. All that had tormented her had magically turned around to serve her.

Doris called a number that didn't answer. That pleased her. McDonald was growing impatient with Doris' antics. She smiled maddeningly before she spoke.

"There's no one at the apartment now, John. The chauffeur and I will go get the picture, and that's that."

She held out her hand for the keys.

"Honey, I don't know what I'd do without you," said McDonald, handing over the keys to Vanilla's apartment.

McDonald was greatly relieved. He resolved to give Doris ten thousand dollars extra when he let her go in the fall. Getting back the Cézanne lightened McDonald's grief considerably. It eliminated a potentially embarrassing revelation, and it served as some revenge for what Vanilla had done to him with those pretty legs wrapped around that son of — no, he would not think about it another minute.

After all, thinking in terms of family, today was one of great victory. Ro had been saved from a foolish error. He had been so touched by her at the hospital, noticing physical similarities, extending plans to help her over ground he'd traveled, feeling her poignant affection for him. He called her at the hospital.

*

"I'm really awfully bored, and I don't feel like spending another minute here," said Ro at the hospital.

They made plans to have some fun. McDonald was pleased to notice he had stopped thinking about that dreadful thing.

Sitting at the restaurant wasn't as comfortable as Ro

imagined. She felt she was sitting on a cold hole inside herself. Her father's clams weren't sights she wanted to see, so pink, with that cup of red goo in the middle. Ro took a solid quaff of wine and tried to elevate her thoughts from these moist, naked, baby gobbets he thrust into the red and raised to his mouth. It was like Grand Guignol all of a sudden, a spectacle to make her think back through the anesthesia to what had happened. Ro ordered asparagus and salad. This was a time for vegetarianism.

"I've been thinking a lot, Dad."

"What about, dear?"

"About Paris. There's a great course there for museum work."

"Really?"

"The whole thing sounds marvelous."

Daddy wasn't as ebullient as he'd been at the hospital. He'd flare up in lambent affection and smiles and then subside, looking hooded and beady-eyed around the restaurant, as if it were filled with spies. She seemed to get the happiest results by discussing Paris, but even that subject had some flaw that made him look all of a sudden as if he'd come on a bad clam.

He ordered another bottle of wine and got only madder as he drank it.

"I think the first thing is to get an apartment, Daddy. I don't want to live at the embassy."

"Rue de la Bruyère," he said roughly. "Thirty-something. It's all fixed up, on the Left Bank. Audrey Hepburn. You'll have a great time. Romantic as hell. Twenty minutes even if there's traffic. Martini; I'm having a goddamn martini."

Ro had never sat through anything like this with her

father. She began to think his strange dismay was caused by her abortion. She took a taste of his martini.

"May I have one too?" she asked. He was glad for the company. She wanted to forget the whole gooey immoral mess.

"You want to see something?" one waiter said to another some time later. "Be real careful and don't say nothing, OK? But take a look. The old guy there and the girl?"

"Yeah."

"He's the ambassador to England or France or something, and that's his daughter. Two bottles of wine and three martinis apiece."

"They're both crying."

"You better believe it. And I checked; it really is his daughter."

icki von Eltz's departure was made soon after Jane talked to him alone upstairs. Dan was bothered by the possibility that the German was undressed during the audience, even though he informed himself it was none of his business. The grin and little slap to Dan's shoulder before von Eltz descended into the soft fragrant leather of his Teutonic luxury car annoyed Dan. He obviously considered Dan no more than a little boy with a hurt thumb or an embarrassing digestive disorder.

The enormous monstrosity of Dan's paternity seemed to grow back in direct proportion to the shrinkage of von Eltz's car down the one-point perspective of the long driveway. That unexpected sporting diversion of watching Jane at tennis seemed Arcadian, a Fragonard that was gone, leaving Dan in the *Guernica* opened upon him by Doris' door. The Horrible Fact was back to fill him. The tennis game had been only a strange and unexpected parole from the shame box in which he again found himself.

Jane thought the boy's terrible mourning was over Ro.

She hated to see him in such a hurry to leave while he was still so sad and empty-handed.

"Can't you stay a while, Dan — talk to her?"

"No, I've really got to get going real soon. Right away. I'm real sorry about asking, but I'll send the money back as soon as I get home."

Dan was almost ashamed to look at her. What if she discovered who he really was? He wanted to hurry back past the meteor hole to the oblivion of Boise. Boise was one place he felt sure that awful man would never come. Suspense that the McDonald limousine with its horrific pilot would suddenly return up the driveway and open like a kernel of horror popcorn in front of this beautiful woman goaded Dan to rush and twitch.

Jane drove Dan into town to cash a check. He was relieved to be away from the site of the limousine's inevitable return. He considered how if he had enough money to get back to Boise even if the son of a bitch was waiting right in front of the door when he and Jane got back, he could run for his van and hit the road, leaving the monstrous pair of Doris and the chauffeur to say whatever they wanted to Jane and the rest of this family he would never ever see again.

That idiotic sensation of infatuation returned as Dan sat in the car with Jane. It caused him to bleat suddenly as a sigh vibrated some unexpectedly vulnerable vocal cords. Jane smiled sympathetically and patted his knee, thinking, no doubt, he was wailing over Ro. Ro was the one thing that suddenly meant nothing to Dan. The operation in New York had aborted his emotional ties to her. She seemed like a stranger in a distant city. The pat on his knee, however, caused the entire focus of Dan's being to rush to the site of its impact. Dan smiled bravely at

Jane. To his dismay, a tear ran down his cheek like a rip.

Jane stopped by the side of the road and held his cheeks in her palms, staring intensely at him, as sorry for him as she'd be over a fallen fledgling. The effect of her cupped palms against his face, like a pair of muscular gardenias, radiated straight through Dan's face into his brain, breaking down that organ's cautionary, civilizing facilities. He embraced her, squeezing her body with a sudden tremor before releasing her, turning away, and blushing the color of steak tartare.

Jane petted his soft, bubbly hair. She was confused. She had been pitying, maternal, and understanding when she reached for him, but what flowed back through her touch was responsive to none of those good-hearted offerings.

He looked back at her. It was suddenly clear. They kissed with a bolt of passion, and swarmed over each other in the contusing interior of the now steaming car.

"Wait, wait," she whispered urgently. Dan didn't dare even open his eyes, which he kept rammed into her thigh as it flexed to operate the car. She drove somewhere, forever. His stomach was as tight as if he were bench-pressing three hundred pounds. He squeezed everything, even his face, as he felt her leg pedal the controls.

Her hand began to model the back of his neck. That eased and calmed him. He sat back up, reached around her, holding her boldly and staring in wonder at her smile.

She was so elegant and beautiful, she didn't look or act undressed when she was. They were in a clearing in some woods to which she'd somehow navigated. He pulled off his clothes into knots and shook until they embraced. At some point he felt it hop inside her and they undulated to the Grand Symphony. When Dan came, he could only think he had just fucked the sun.

She laughed and lit a cigarette. They walked back to the car, whose doors were open the whole time like a bird protecting its young in the nearby bushes by pretending to be wounded. She was too beautiful. Dan kissed her.

Both grinned in suspenseful silence as the car eased back down the twin shining stripes it had made on the grass of the unused road.

"How'd you know about this place?" offered Dan from the thousand opening remarks he'd been sifting.

"I didn't. I just drove in. Sometimes things are there when you need them."

They both laughed. He came close to her again as they rolled through the bush.

"You're just like a girl," he said. She smiled. Her blue eyes glittered.

"Sit somewhere discreet, Dan," she said as they pulled out onto the hard surface of the real world.

Dan was exalted and shaken. Like Christopher Columbus, he had gone beyond where he was headed, even though he was only halfway there.

"Why do you say that word?"

"What word?"

"Chimney-boo or whatever it is?"

"Cimabue — Cimabue was the first great painter in the world whose name anybody knew."

"Cimabue."

"Right."

Jane glittered, tucked her head, and drove through the suburban landscape.

Columns made of stone by ancient Greeks in forms that celebrated their structural ancestors, the trees became wood again thousands of years later to adorn the colonial temples of private success in this stretch of southern New England. The motif was copied yet again by modern millionaires who liked the classy implication of a classical device. Columns were ancient man's victory over nature, his connection to the gods.

"At home they only use columns on banks," observed Dan to Jane. "Here they have those little ones around every door and sometimes big ones."

"New England," replied Jane. "Greek Revival, they call it."

"I know," said Dan. "History of Art."

"Oh, that's right."

"All this green and the columns and everything — this whole part of the country looks like the back of a five-dollar bill."

Jane laughed delightedly, as she had at dinner when he joked with her.

"Would you like to come out west with me?" asked Dan.

"What?"

"Fishing up in the mountains or something?"

"You're very sweet, but I think it might be a little awkward."

"Right."

Feeling a little like an idiot was becoming so familiar around Jane that Dan felt right at home. Asking her out west — how ridiculous! Was she supposed to ride in a van with a cooler full of beer and a lot of humid gear stinking in the back? Wake up, Dan; this was she, the Faerie Queene herself. Among other things, she was the wife of John Russell McDonald and the mother of Ro.

Jesus Christ. He should just tell her about the chauffeur and get the hell out of here.

"Tell me about it."

"What?"

"Fishing up in the mountains."

"Oh. Well, it's beautiful. Really beautiful. My uncle has a fishing camp and I've spent a lot of my whole life up there. I know it pretty well, where to find them. Did you ever fish?"

"In Sun Valley once, waiting for a divorce."

Dan's stare turned interrogative. "I didn't go through with it. You used to have to wait up there in Sun Valley to get a nice divorce. You could get sort of tacky divorces in places like Mexico or Reno, but the nice ones meant a little time in Sun Valley. Anyway, I did go fishing then."

"I think that's how my uncle got started. Guiding ladies."

"Did he teach you everything you know?"

"Yeah."

They laughed. But Dan felt bad, placed as he was by this conversation in a slightly tawdry corner.

"I just fish up there."

Jane's smile went from the tight line of wisecracking to something so soft and warm that Dan kissed it.

"The water's shiny black and you drop your fly on it. Then it rips open silver and the fish is right there, dancing with death," said Dan straight from his heart.

A chill went over Jane.

There was, Dan thanked God, no limousine at the house when they returned in softening, blurring evening. She left him, disappearing into her rooms to change for dinner. Dan was suddenly bereft of most of his identity.

He wasn't just a stranger there, but an enemy alien, a U-2 pilot burying his identification in a Russian forest. Part of him was fleeing the horrible identity grasping for him from the hairy arms of the chauffeur. Another part had been surgically removed in New York. He no longer held his office as fiancé of the daughter. Now with no Jane there, Dan was almost no one. The room in which he stood stared at him. Pictures whispered to chairs rumors he couldn't hear, but that he suspected concerned the dubiousness of his right to be there. The fierce Jackson Pollock painting said "Crasher," and the fireplace opened its mouth in surprise. The Modigliani tilted her head and looked with some sympathy at the miscreant.

Jane instinctively reached to cover her nudity when the door opened. Dan walked in with a strange formality. She put on the robe she had held over the face of her body.

"I'm going."

"Right now?"

"Right."

"We'll see each other again, Dan."

"We will?"

"In dreams, if nowhere else."

"Oh, right."

"But maybe somewhere else, too. Maybe I'll come out and see you in the mountains in a while."

"Really?"

"Yes. Will you show me how to fish and everything?"

Dan nodded. He believed her.

It was wonderful to start his van in the fading daylight with hope, to wave at her in the window of that incredible house, to be off.

Then, halfway down the driveway, Dan's van was

stopped, staring at the massive, stupid, indomitable grille of McDonald's limousine. He backed up. The limo pulled up next to him, stopping with a jolt. All its doors cracked.

The chauffeur, Doris, and Ro all got out. Only John Russell McDonald stayed inside, glowering.

TWENTY-SEVEN

Two galleons range alongside each other and with clumsy pointblank cannonade begin each other's total devastation.

The van and the limousine let loose all hell on one another. The stink of black powder and burning ship, the filthy smoke and screams of the maimed made a holocaust that drew Jane to pull back the delicate foam of her window curtain and look below. She saw that Ro, Doris, and a bizarre figure in black with a bald head and a feather or something were backing Dan across the lawn. Then McDonald emerged from the limousine to watch the figures on the lawn like a field commander on the heights peering through binoculars at the progress of his distant tanks.

Jane took a quick look in the mirror and, pleased by the excited glitter in her eyes, gave an adjusting pat to her hair and flew down the hall and stairs, out the door and toward the emergency.

"Look. Just leave us alone will you?" Ro ordered Doris and the chauffeur.

"Of course, dear. Come, darling," said Doris to the

freak backing beside her. Jane almost bumped into their retreat.

"Park the damn car, will you?" barked McDonald at the Halloween celebrant Doris was encircling with her arm. When he did, covering his purple pigtail with his hat, Jane recognized with a start that he was the chauffeur.

"Hi, Jane," said Doris with the same unnerving cheer with which she'd spoken at the pool.

"Aren't they adorable?" she added as Ro and Dan walked off across the lawn, Ro talking, Dan slumped. Ro looked like a coach escorting the relieved pitcher to the dugout.

"Jane," said McDonald sharply. Jane stepped toward him. He reached for her hand and then marched her back toward the house, saying nothing, pulling her in the first available door, the kitchen door, pointedly closing it on Doris, who promptly headed toward the garage, where the chauffeur was putting away the limousine.

"The goddamndest thing happened," he said.

"You sound so 'Right to Life' all of a sudden," replied Jane to McDonald's confusion.

"What?"

" 'The goddamndest thing' — doesn't that expression refer to Ro's abortion?"

"What the hell are you talking about?"

"Dan told me. You took her into town and talked her into an abortion right while the rest of us were working on her engagement party. You always were ahead of everyone, even when you're behind their backs."

"That's not the point at all, damn it. It's that crazy son of a bitch" — McDonald poked toward the garage — "that's the son of a bitch's father!"

"I'm not sure I follow the genealogy."

"That chauffeur is the boy's father. Doris knew all along."

Emergency produces odd choreography: discussions are held in bathrooms or basements, bodies lie in rooms designed for sitting or standing, meals are served in closets and attics, as victims, perpetrators, adulterers, cuckolds, and witnesses struggle for a grip on the suddenly reeling and wheeling ball of earth. McDonald had backed Jane into a canning pantry, off the kitchen, reeking of the old Labrador, Jack, who jumped to his feet, fell, and tried it again to serve as host to these strangely possessed visitors. Jack jumped and fell again when the pistol started going off down by the garage.

The beautiful young couple walking across the vast, impeccable lawn of the handsome estate in the summer gloaming would have served the purpose of any advertiser seeking to aura his product with high-class romance. It looked good, but they were discussing unhappy subjects.

"I didn't know until today!" said Dan.

"It doesn't matter."

"Right."

"Well, it doesn't matter, Dan. You're yourself."

"Yeah."

"I don't want you to leave like this."

"Why not?"

"I think we have a lot to talk about."

"I don't."

"Dan, you just have to accept the fact that I'm not going to be pushed into anything."

"I didn't push you anywhere."

"Well, don't just run off in the night like this."

"Why not?"

"Don't you want to get to the bottom of everything?"

"I am at the bottom of everything."

"Very funny."

"I don't want to stay here."

"Because of what?"

"Everything."

"Because he's your father? Dan, you are yourself."

"Yeah, you said that."

"Well, it's true."

"It's not true in your case though, is it?"

"What?" Ro stopped the stroll and tensed.

"Never mind."

"What do you mean by that?"

"Let's just say we have very different fathers, Ro."

"I admit that."

"And it turns out you were right to do what you did."

"What do you mean?"

"To have the abortion. I wish to hell my mother had."

Dan was crying, walking away, when he, too, like Ro, the Lab, and the McDonalds, jumped at the sound of pistol shots coming from the garage.

McDonald ordered people back with his arm. He was the baron, after all, of this estate. He trudged solitary toward the garage, smelling the gunsmoke as he got near. The rest of them followed at a respectful distance. McDonald considered the possibilities. Four shots: it could be murder, murder-suicide, double suicide, or perhaps just the suicide of a very bad shot. There was another report of the pistol, which made McDonald jump (he wished he hadn't, in front of onlookers).

The window above the garage was where the gunsmoke was coming from. McDonald stood still a minute looking up. Doris' head came through the window; then the chauffeur's made it a pair.

"Attention, everybody," said Doris, still waving her pistol. She said something to the chauffeur, who shook his head and took it out of the frame. She turned back to the crowd.

"We're getting married," said Doris. She waved her pistol and fired again, but the thing was empty.

"What the hell is this damn nuisance?" McDonald admired his own leonine roar, the baronial outrage he shot like a storm of arrows at the higher window.

"Dan, Dan, come up," urged Doris. Dan took one step toward Idaho, but McDonald grabbed his arm in a vibrating, enraged grip, as if by throwing Dan down he could make the outrageous disorder disappear. McDonald was surprised by the strong young arm in his hand. He didn't want to test its strength.

"I think you'd better go up there," he growled confidentially, "and tell those two to clear off this place immediately." McDonald turned and held his arms out, shooing Ro and Jane toward the house. But the manic Doris shouted something that stopped him.

"And thank you, John, for the painting — what a wedding present!"

Dan was halfway between the contestants, a tennis ball stopped in the air, wishing only to shoot out of the court and be lost in the brush.

"Dan, darling, come up," Doris urged. Dan moved with the stately step of the condemned up the scaffold stairs to the chauffeur's apartment. Doris was still leaning out the window, conversing with McDonald, as he entered.

"We both love it, John. We're both crazy about his

landscapes. Shall I bring it to the window and show Jane?" she teased. Then she waved as the McDonalds shrank toward the big house.

"Well, Dan, isn't this fun?" said Doris, with a shiver of delight. She held her hands toward a painting propped on a sofa in the gesture of a fisherman telling a fish story.

"Beer?" asked the chauffeur from his kitchen. The phone rang. It rang and rang, a signal that only made Doris shake her head and giggle.

Dan and Dan held bottles of beer and diverted their mutual embarrassment by staring at the picture on the sofa. The phone rings gave a disturbed rhythm to the conversation.

"Well, I'm going back to Boise."

"Oh stay, darling — come to the wedding. I'm going to be your mom."

"It's true." Dan senior grinned.

"That's great," chirped Dan.

"Yes, it's a Cézanne," said Doris. Dan looked closer. It was. It was hard to believe McDonald would just give a Cézanne to his secretary on her marriage. But then, the standards here were all on the fabulous side. Looking at the beautiful landscape between Doris and his father was disorientingly incongruous. Dan felt like a living book pinched between bookends emitting electric shock.

"Boy, that's great."

"That's John phoning — *to find out how we like it,*" said Doris, who began to hoot with laughter, which was joined in by the chauffeur as though they had tossed a grownup's secret over the little boy's head.

"I just have to get home or something," said Dan.

Doris and the chauffeur followed Dan downstairs to his van with surprisingly authentic parental departure protocol, urging him to drive safely, get plenty of rest, and beware of danger and scoundrels. No one emerged from the McDonald house to wave as he started down the driveway.

The van was moving forward, but Dan felt as if the wheels were turning the wrong way, the way they do on wagons in the movies.

How he craved the pedestrian peace of Boise and the safe, remote, peopleless beauty of the Rockies! But he felt as if he were already returning even as he fled. Next time, he would bring more shirts.

Dan forgot the cautionary bump in the driveway. The jolt caused him to jam his thumb. He winced and stuck it in his mouth as he pulled out onto the public road.

make the Soviets pay a high financial and political price for the invasion.

It was recognised that the more arms the US supplied the more guerrillas were likely to be killed. For some with longer memories, the roll call of guerrillas supported and then betrayed by the west in the fight against communism was already long, and included Vietnamese, Laotians, Albanians, Czechs, Poles and Ukrainians. But any reservations those in the administration may have had were swept away by a Congress that was determined to do whatever was necessary to repel the Soviet invaders. For the first – and perhaps the last – time in recent memory, Congress was actually the driving force behind a covert action programme. In any event, such reservations were only voiced during the dying months of the moralistic Carter administration. Once President Reagan took office at the beginning of 1981, the Afghan cause became a crusade against the 'Evil Empire'.

In January 1980, Brzezinski went to see President Anwar Sadat of Egypt and President Zia ul-Haq of Pakistan. Egypt was seen as a prime source of arms and the cooperation of Zia was essential if the arms were to reach the guerrillas. Carter tried to sweeten the pot for Zia by offering him $400m in aid, only months after US aid to Pakistan had been cut off when Carter became convinced that Pakistan was developing nuclear weapons. Zia, after some arm twisting, agreed that arms could travel through Pakistan – but he dismissed the aid offer as 'peanuts' and demanded more.[7]

In addition, the US contacted China and Saudi Arabia for help in the fight. Egypt, a Moslem country and staunch ally of the United States, agreed to support the training and arming of a guerrilla army to fight the Soviets, as did the Saudis. The Chinese were more reticent but joined the effort the following month. The support of Egypt and China was to prove critical to the war as both had vast stocks of Soviet-type arms: both countries either had old stocks from their time as allies of the Soviets or produced Soviet arms under licence using Soviet tools and dies. Supplying the Afghan guerrillas with Soviet arms made good sense as they would be compatible with any equipment they might capture from the enemy.

Two weeks before his death, to the surprise of both the Americans and the Soviets, Sadat confirmed his involvement in the covert arms supplies. In an interview with NBC News in September 1981 (which the Soviets later described as a 'political striptease'), he said: 'Let me reveal this secret. The first month that Afghan incident [the invasion] took place, the US contacted me here . . . the United States sent me airplanes and told me, "Please open your stores for us so that we can give the Afghans the armaments they need to fight," and I gave the armaments.'[8] The Saudi role was limited to financing the purchase of the weapons and providing a certain amount of humanitarian aid.

In 1980, US funding for the Afghan war was around $20m but by 1985 this had risen to $500m, to $650m in 1987 and a similar sum in 1988. Saudi Arabia, by funding the guerrillas to the tune of $525m, had paid in part for Airborne Warning and Control Systems aircraft supplied by the US.[9] There was already a fledgling guerrilla army in existence in Afghanistan which had been fighting against the Amin government since 1978. At the time of the invasion, the guerrillas opposing the Amin government may have numbered ten thousand, but these were fighting intermittently and in general were pursuing a policy of opposition to central government rather than any coordinated war effort. However, within two years of the invasion, over three million Afghans – a fifth of the total population – had fled the country, most of them settling in refugee camps in Pakistan with the balance going to Iran.

These refugees provided a vital recruiting base for the guerrillas whose numbers settled at between 90,000 and 120,000. Of these a third would be fit for combat at any one time, a third would be trekking to and from the combat zone and the remainder would be resting at base. These rebels were poorly armed and relied on fieldcraft that had remained unchanged for hundreds of years: ambushes and assassinations which took account of their unparalleled knowledge of the terrain. These tactics were to prove inadequate when matched against Soviet air power.

'The Afghan guerrillas were brave to the point of stupidity,' said one US intelligence source. 'They simply did not understand the meaning of fear and time and again would stand in front of a Soviet tank firing their machine guns, watching the bullets bounce off the armour and then look surprised when they got shot. It was brave but it got them nowhere.'[10]

It was one of the ironies of the Afghan war that the Soviets had begun it using massive force and smart tactics that worked well enough to secure Kabul and install a puppet regime. After that, control of the war appears to have passed into the hands of more conventional military men. For the first two years, the Soviet military employed methods that had served them well in World War II and which they had seen little reason to change. These also happened to suit Soviet doctrinal methods which allowed for little flexibility in the field and a rigid chain of command. The Soviets developed a number of strongly fortified positions based around the main cities and from these they launched periodic well-armed forays into the field. These were invariably led by tanks and supported by large numbers of infantry in armoured personnel carriers. The guerrillas, who could generally see them coming, were either long gone by the time the Soviets arrived at the target area or, more usually, had set up ambushes.

But as casualties mounted so the Soviets changed their approach, keeping the tanks in camp. Western intelligence noted Soviet tactics go through two distinct phases. The first began with mass movements of conventional ground forces supported by Hind helicopters circling at around 3,000 feet looking for targets of opportunity and backed by fighter bombers which carried out carpet bombing of villages, towns and supply routes. Later the Soviets brought in forward air controllers who acted as spotters for the fighters and provided advance information for helicopters, which were constantly on alert, ready to fly at a moment's notice.

For the first time ground troops, helicopters and fighters were integrated for combined operations. This new phase saw both troop carrying and attack helicopters using flying techniques known as nap of the earth which allowed them to fly close to the ground to strike swiftly and suddenly at known targets. This new tactic was something outside the experience of the guerrillas who had become used to fighting and then melting into the familiar terrain. Now, the Soviets were using the ground to their advantage, together with high flying reconnaissance aircraft to gather intelligence and to direct airborne forces.

The Soviets also established hundreds of small forts around the country designed to control the high ground and limit the movement of guerrillas along their traditional mountain paths. While the mujahedeen were able to lay siege to these forts for long periods they could be resupplied by air and proved difficult to attack successfully.

To channel the guerrillas into ground of their own choosing the Soviets expanded their scorched earth policy, ruthlessly destroying by bombing any villages that might be used as guerrilla bases. This policy had gradually narrowed the fighting options available to the guerrillas and they had made the classic mistake of retreating into a series of fixed camps along the border with Pakistan from where they would launch periodic raids which usually took the form of limited seiges using artillery and heavy machine guns. The new Soviet tactics were gradually depriving the mujahedeen of the three qualities essential to the successful prosecution of a guerrilla war: speed, deception and surprise.

By 1985, the Soviets were winning and something had to be done. While few believed they would actually be defeated, a growing body of opinion among western intelligence analysts believed that the mujahedeen might simply become a minor irritant to the Soviets and that eventually they would lose heart for a war that had cost them their country and very heavy loss of life.

The key to the war was air power and what was needed

was something that would neutralise it, to change the balance of power back in the direction of the guerrillas and allow them to make the Soviets bleed.

A Stinger in the Tail

Until 1985, there had been a marked reluctance by the US, on the advice of both the State Department and the Defence Department, or any other country to ship new weapons to the guerrillas. First there was a recognition that their poor training would make it difficult for them to use anything other than the most basic systems and second there was a fear that any new weapons would swiftly find their way to the black market and thence into the hands of the Soviets.

But fears of the war firmly turning in the Soviets' favour led to a change of policy, and the solution that the western governments supporting the guerrillas came up with was the ground to air missile. Since 1982 the guerrillas had some SA–7 Grail anti-aircraft missiles supplied by Egypt but, after some early successes, these were of limited use. The Grail is a heat-seeking missile and can be easily distracted by reflections hitting snow or heading for the sun instead of an aircraft's engines. Also, the Soviets quickly adopted the simplest of counter measures: a flare which baffled the missile's guidance system. Grail. Finally, the guerrillas were reluctant to use the missile as it left a distinctive white exhaust trail which gave any Soviet pilot clear directions to his next target.

In March 1986 Abdul Haq, a commander of the Islamic Party of Yunis Khalis, visited the British Prime Minister, Margaret Thatcher, in London. During that trip the British government agreed to supply a number of Blowpipe missiles to the Afghan guerrillas. The first batch of fifty missiles, shipped from the manufacturers, Short Brothers in Belfast, reached the guerrillas that summer. Each missile cost $21,000 and the launcher $94,000. The first batch was followed by a further three hundred which were sent via Pakistan in the summer of 1987.

But, as the British army had learned in the Falkland Islands war four years earlier, the Blowpipe is difficult to use and can prove unreliable in combat. The shoulder-fired weapon is guided to its target via a radio link and, after firing, the operator must simultaneously target the missile and track the target. This sounds difficult and indeed it actually takes a great deal of practice to perfect.

The guerrillas in Afghanistan had neither sufficient missiles nor the training to use them properly. In June 1987, when asked about the Blowpipe, Abdul Haq, already disenchanted, replied: 'Those who are using the Blowpipes do not praise them: we cannot even shoot down slow-moving helicopters. Anyway, we have received only very few systems.'[1]

A year before the first Blowpipes arrived, the US had received a request from President Zia that the mujahedeen be supplied with Stinger missiles from the US inventory. This missile was front line US equipment that had only begun to enter service with the American army three years before. The shoulder-fired missile can be carried and fired by one man, and its passive infra-red guidance system has inbuilt defence against a number of counter measures. It is also extremely simple to operate: the firer simply points the missile in the direction of the target and pulls the trigger.

But the CIA had four major concerns. First, they were nervous about expanding the war and worried the Soviets might be provoked into bringing the war deeper into Pakistan. This was essentially a political issue and while the Agency sent up warning signals, there were others such as Fred Ikle, the Under Secretary of Defence, Michael Pillsbury at the White House, and Democrat Representative Charles Wilson who saw the Afghan war as a crusade from which the US should not be diverted. They overruled the CIA political objections.

Second, Langley was concerned that if Stingers were handed to the guerrillas, the technology would inevitably reach the Soviets. They had already received manuals for the Stinger from a Greek spy but there was concern that a complete missile system would make copying the missile much easier. These fears proved justified as the Soviets managed to capture or buy forty Stingers.[2]

However, as an upgrade of Stinger was already under development, this risk was considered acceptable.

Third, there was a worry that the Stingers might fall into the hands of terrorists elsewhere. This was a real, but less quantifiable risk. In Zimbabwe, guerrillas had used SA-7 missiles to shoot down civilian airliners and both the PLO and the IRA now have SA-7 missiles. The PLO have already used a missile to try to shoot down a civilian airliner in Kenya, and the IRA have plans to attack British military aircraft using their missiles. The CIA felt that the addition of Stingers to their armoury, while a serious threat, was not enough to stop the shipment.

Fourth, the CIA were concerned that in the rush to supply the equipment, not enough thought had been given to training the guerrillas to use the missiles. Initially, this was seen by the fervent supporters of the supply of Stingers as simple foot-dragging by Langley and the objections were overruled.

After a year of haggling, supporters of the Stinger option in the State Department, the Pentagon and Congress ordered the deliveries to begin and the first cautious supplies of Stinger missiles began to arrive from the United States in September 1986.

The first batch of two hundred missiles was introduced in ones and twos. This slow delivery was another source of friction between the White House, Congress and the CIA who were once again accused of being reluctant partners in the operation. The missiles were distributed to a few selected guerrilla leaders who received a month's training from Pakistan army personnel at a base near Islamabad in Pakistan.

The first time the Stingers were used in Afghanistan they

hit nothing. This was a serious disappointment both to the Agency and to the political supporters of the guerrillas in America. This failure was particularly marked when compared with a similar delivery that had been made to Jonas Savimbi's UNITA guerrillas in Angola. There, the US-trained guerrillas had hit six of their first seven targets.

Immediately, the profile of the mission in Afghanistan changed. Ex-US special forces working directly for the CIA began training the mujahedeen to use the Stingers effectively. Second, there was a belated understanding that as a stand-alone weapons system, the Stinger is of little value. Instead, it has to be integrated into an air defence network that includes heavy machine guns, other missiles and well deployed ground forces.

For the CIA this represented a considerable challenge. Most of the fighters were unable to read and write and had no understanding of ground tactics, let alone the complexities of flight patterns and arcs of fire. The solution was a teaching aid that combined the latest in satellite imagery and three dimensional modelling that enabled the guerrillas to be taught the basics of air defence entirely visually. It was a brilliant and imaginative invention, the details of which remain highly classified and have become a model for tactical instruction to guerrilla forces around the world.[3]

At last, the missiles proved their worth near Jalalabad at the beginning of October when four helicopters were shot down on the same day in full view of the local townspeople. News of the weapon's prowess spread rapidly among the guerrillas and the Afghan population and the Stinger's reputation reached mythical proportions. Encouraged by the early success, the US increased its supply of weapons so that six hundred had arrived by the beginning of 1987 and were being widely distributed among the guerrillas.

The impact on the war was immediate. The Soviet and Afghan government forces were forced to abandon their tactics of flying low and circling with helicopters and fighters to provide constant air cover for the ground troops. 'The Soviets really had their eyes watering,' commented one western intelligence analyst. 'They couldn't use their helicopters as they had no real counter measures against the Stinger and their fighter bombers had to fly out of accurate bombing range. They became so nervous that even the helicopter aircrews were being issued with parachutes.'[4]

Both Pakistani and US intelligence sources were widely cited as claiming that the Stingers were shooting down around 1.3 to 1.4 Soviet and Afghan aircraft each day. This was initially true but the Soviets swiftly changed their tactics to keep out of range wherever possible. The true figures are that before the introduction of the Stinger, Soviet and Afghan air losses were around one a month from SA–7 missile and heavy machine-gun fire. After the Stinger was fully operating in 1987, those losses increased to around six a month. This was still a considerable improvement and sufficient to force the Soviets on the defensive.

A US army study after the Soviets had left showed that the guerrillas shot down 269 aircraft in 340 firings, scoring an average 79 per cent hits, an impressively high score.[5]

Even with the Stingers, it was still very unlikely that the mujahedeen would win the war but at least they were able to defend their main camps, and morale was sufficiently improved for them to once again start fighting their own version of a guerrilla war.

For the Soviets also, the Afghan war now appeared unwinnable, particularly after a campaign of terrorism and subversion inside Pakistan had failed to deter the Zia government from providing a safe haven for the guerrillas. For Soviet President Mikhail Gorbachev, the Afghan war was gaining the Soviets nothing and costing them a great deal economically and politically. He declared victory, which could not have fooled even the most gullible communist party member, and announced that he would be withdrawing all Soviet forces from Afghanistan.

Officially, the last Soviet forces left the country in March 1989. However, in October 1989, US intelligence asserted that Soviet military advisers had stayed behind to maintain the Scud missiles which have proved very effective against guerrilla camps around the country.

A report prepared for the State Department and the White House by US intelligence agencies said that 'all functions connected with the security, transportation, storage and launch of Scud missiles are handled by Soviet advisers' wearing Afghan uniforms. Afghan guards patrol the missile base at Darulam, six miles south of Kabul, but Afghan 'military personnel are not allowed within several hundred meters of this area.'[6]

The presence of these troops does not suggest that the Soviets wish to renew their commitment to the Afghan war. On the contrary, even hard-line military commanders in the Soviet Union have made clear in conversations with their western counterparts that they have no wish to once again become embroiled in a war they now know they cannot win.

Once the Soviets departed, the Afghans reverted to type. Without the hated Soviets to focus their united attention, the guerrillas had only the Afghan government as a target. This proved insufficient to unite the disparate groups who started to fight each other. At the same time, they changed their tactics from fighting a classic mobile war using their knowledge of the countryside. Instead, they laid siege to the major city of Jalalabad, which was expected to fall within days.

In fact, the guerrillas failed to take the town and suffered heavy losses over a period of weeks. It was an ignominious defeat that made the guerrilla movement even more introspective. The siege was very costly in weapons and that shortage combined with hoarding by each of the bands meant that there was insufficient equipment to prosecute the war.

In June 1989 both the CIA and Britain's SIS had resumed covert shipments of arms and other equipment to the mujahedeen. However, with the departure of the Soviets the importance of the Afghan war was diminished, not least because the true character of the Afghan guerrillas reappeared. There is now little political capital to be made from the conflict and it seems likely that support from the west will slowly wither away.

The west considered the departure of the Soviet troops a victory for the guerrillas and a triumph for western opposition to the invasion which had been consistently applied since the Soviets first invaded nearly ten years before. Certainly, the Afghan war was the first example in post World War II history where a guerrilla force supported by the west had succeeded in changing the policy of the Soviet Union.

For many in the Reagan administration, to whom the Afghan cause had become a holy crusade, the withdrawal of the Soviets was little short of a major victory. For the intelligence community, too, Afghanistan was a watershed. The covert arm of the CIA had been decimated by President Carter who believed covert warfare to be morally distasteful and generally politically unnecessary. He and his director of central intelligence, Admiral Stansfield Turner, had preferred to put their faith in passive measures such as satellites and signals interception. But in the dying months of his presidency he authorised the start of what would turn out to be the CIA's biggest and most successful covert operation.

But in the self-congratulation that followed the Soviet withdrawal, three key legacies of the war were generally overlooked: the impact on Soviet society and its armed forces, the arms market created by the war and the heroin and marijuana market that has grown in Pakistan and Afghanistan as a result of the war.

7

A Dreadful Legacy

The combat experience gained by the Russian armed forces in Afghanistan has made them the most experienced group of fighting men and women in the world today. Today, there are 80,000 Soviet officers alone who have seen combat in Afghanistan and they have evolved tactics that may be routine for NATO armies but are innovations for the Warsaw Pact forces.

NATO has always judged that the inflexibility of the Soviets and their rigid training methods will be to the allied advantage in war. But Afghanistan has now taught the Soviets that flexibility and individual initiative on the battlefield are essential – particularly when fighting a highly mobile enemy with better knowledge of the terrain.

'Since Afghanistan we have seen the Soviets making great efforts to make the stereotype training programmes more flexible,' said one NATO intelligence source. 'They are trying to give more authority to officers further down the chain of command but how much they will succeed remains to be seen. After all the American military bureaucracy absorbed the Vietnam experience as if nothing had happened.'[1]

Soviet pilots and ground force commanders, however, now have several years of actual combat, in which equipment and tactics have been tested. A whole generation of helicopter pilots, instead of merely going to the practice range once a week to fire dummy rounds, has become used to firing live missiles and cannon while under fire from a real enemy.

But the institutional memory of wars lasts at best for one generation. When the US invaded Grenada in 1982 only eight or nine men out of a full Ranger batallion had any combat experience. Wars are always fought by the young and most of the Soviet armed forces are conscripts. In five years, the majority of those who fought in Afghanistan will have rotated back to civilian life and only the regulars will be left to pass on their knowledge.

A secret study of the war conducted by the US army in the spring of 1989 had seven main conclusions:

The Soviets proved more flexible than expected in fighting the war. They were able to mix light and heavy aircraft for offensive missions; adapt Spetsnaz special forces to the tasks of light infantry operations; and use artillery in 'flexible and innovative ways'.

The Soviets used mines heavily, including some never seen before. Perhaps thirty million or more were used in the conflict.

Psychological warfare operations were vital to the guerrilla operations while the Soviets showed little understanding of the importance of hearts and minds in an insurgency war.

The Soviets proved unable to use artillery to attack targets of opportunity.

Their logistics system was inadequate.

When ambushed, the Soviets appeared unable to take the initiative and were often killed inside their vehicles.

The best fighters were the heli-borne Spetnaz special forces. The ordinary troops were poorly trained and fought badly.[2]

It is too early, in fact, to say what political impact the war has had on the Soviet military command. One of the tenets of the communist army (or any other army for that matter) is never to engage in an unwinnable war. There may now be a recognition that guerrilla wars fought in a purely military way can be unwinnable – particularly if the opposition is being sustained from across a friendly border. This is a lesson already learned by the United States and Britain, among others, and has discouraged foreign military intervention by both those nations. If the Soviets have understood the military lesson of Afghanistan, then their willingness to commit troops in a foreign country may have been reduced.

But in order to teach the Soviets the lesson that military intervention in the affairs of other countries does not appear useful, the western governments funding the mujahedeen have helped to underwrite the development of the largest illegal arms market in the history of the modern world.

In Washington, the mujahedeen were seen as a ragged band of fearless fighters, the few against the many, the poor peasant armed only with Second World War weapons fighting the might of the Soviet army. There was some truth in all these appealing images, but they served to gloss over other, less palatable truths. For centuries, the tribal chiefs in the North West Frontier province in Afghanistan and Pakistan had been a law unto themselves. Answerable to no one, they now encouraged a major arms smuggling industry to flourish alongside traditional agriculture and general commerce.

The sheer scale of the business generated by the aid to the guerrillas was extraordinary. In 1987 aid in cash and arms, including that from the US and Saudi Arabia, totalled more than $1 billion – fully half of the total exports on the west's 'grey' arms market. (The grey market is where exports are officially approved but not publicly acknowledged.)[3] If half of that in turn was siphoned off to the black market (where the profits margins are substantially larger) corrupt individuals in the Pakistan government, in the military, and among the mujahedeen would have made profits in excess of $250m.

Over the period of the war more than $1.5 billion in cash and arms was diverted from the guerrillas. In an area that connects the natural villainy of the Afghan with the Pakistan government, where corruption had been refined to an art form, it is hardly surprising that many have been seduced. The mixture of Pakistani corruption and the Afghan aptitude for making money by any means produced an industry which had little to do with a holy war against the infidel Soviet invaders and a great deal to do with profiteering.

To overcome the initial reluctance of the Pakistan government to get involved in the supply of weapons to the guerrillas, the US agreed that once the weapons reached Pakistan, responsibility for passing them to the mujahedeen would rest with the government of President Zia. Specifically, much of the arms trafficking was carried out by the Interservices Intelligence Bureau (ISI), military intelligence. According to western diplomats in Pakistan and to intelligence sources involved with the traffic, it was here that the corruption started. A case of 100 Kalashnikov AK–47 assault rifles might be delivered from Egypt by ship. In mint condition, at least a third of these weapons will be siphoned off by the military themselves, either to replace old stocks in their own armouries or to sell on the black market. This was not the case with high-technology American systems such as the Stinger missiles where delivery was carefully controlled.

Almost from the beginning of the war there was clear evidence of this kind of diversion. For example, by 1983 one of the seven main political movements had received a total of only 11,000 small arms, around 130 machine guns, 450 rocket-propelled grenade launchers and 30 mortars. More than 7,500 of the rifles were Lee-Enfields which were not being supplied by any of the covert operations but were widely held by the Pakistan army.[4]

Part of the siphoning off occurred in Peshawar where weapons destined for the guerrillas were handed over to the control of the Pakistan border regiments. A proportion of those handed over were then stolen and several more would be sold by the mujahedeen leaders themselves before they actually reached the fighters in the refugee camps or over the border.

Also, each local tribal leader required members of any other band going through his area to pay tribute, usually in the form of cash or weapons. After all, traditional business that had established recognised patterns over centuries should not be disturbed by the temporary inconvenience of a war.

As one American diplomat based in Karachi put it: 'If all

the Kalashnikovs that have been sent to the mujahedeen had actually reached the guerrillas, they would have about three guns each.'[5] Or, as one US intelligence officer said: 'For every hundred guns we were sending to the Afghans we were lucky if fifty reached them. And even those that got there were often sold off by the mujahedeen to make a quick buck. But there was nothing anybody could do about it. The cause was such that no one wanted to start lifting stones to find out what horrors might be underneath.'[6]

By the end of the war, the guerrillas had received or captured a bewildering array of weapons including 12.7mm and 14.5mm machine guns, the 7.62 PKM general purpose machine gun, RPG–7 85mm rocket launchers, 120mm mortars and a number of tanks and armoured personnel carriers. All of these have found their way on to the black market.

Peshawar itself offers the most visible sign of the benefits the war has brought to the community. Ten years ago this was a sleepy provincial town where the unwary traveller going the wrong way down a one way street would find the most dangerous obstacle in his path a donkey-driven taxi gently plodding down the road with its driver asleep. Today it is a thriving entrepot, with spies, black marketeers and mercenaries all jostling for a share of the considerable action. Leading guerrilla commanders live in the fashionable suburb of University Town, in luxury villas complete with the latest western gadgetry such as videos, microwaves and Mercedes limousines.

Holidays, too, have played their part in shaping war. One local journalist was astonished to find that an attack he had planned to watch on a local Afghan army base had been cancelled because the local mujahedeen commander was on holiday in Florida.

The town of Darra lies about twenty-five miles south of Peshawar near the border with Afghanistan, and arms have been manufactured there since 1897. Darra is in the 'tribal territories' where the Pakistan government has little influence. Afghan refugees are scattered throughout the area: towns like

Paracinar and Miran Shah, where Lawrence of Arabia was briefly stationed in the 1930s, house huge depots of black market weapons. Giant warehouses are stacked with cases of Kalashnikovs with Arabic markings, mortars, rocket launchers, and tons of ammunition in green metal boxes and wooden containers with American markings line the walls.

The craftsmen in the town specialise in making reproductions of every type of gun including the popular AK–47. But the town also sells the genuine article and AK–47s will change hands for between $500 and $1,000 each depending on the quantity required. At the same time the price of the .303 Lee-Enfield rifle, the standard Afghan weapon before the war, has slumped to around $50, two hundred per cent below the pre-war price.[7] The dealers will deliver the shipment anywhere in Pakistan, the usual destination being Karachi, the country's major port.

By the time the Stinger missiles arrived in Afghanistan in 1986, the whole black market system had become institutionalised and it was hardly surprising that a new opportunity to make money was taken up.

To date, although the Basque separatist movement ETA is known to have purchased arms on the Pakistan black market, there is no record of Stingers reaching terrorist groups. The Indian government believes that Sikh extremists in the Punjab have bought Stingers but they have not yet been used, and there have been unconfirmed reports of the IRA exploring the possibilities. But in any case, if they have not yet reached the terrorists, there certainly are large quantities of Stingers circulating on the black market. Intelligence sources estimate that of the 350 Blowpipe missiles supplied by Britain, 87 were diverted by the Pakistan authorities and an unknown number resold by the guerrillas to the black market. Of 800 Stingers, 200 were reportedly diverted to the black market or to Pakistan's own armoury.[8]

A far more serious diversion came to light in October 1987 when two Iranian gunboats were captured in the Persian Gulf after they had fired at US Navy helicopters. On board the patrol boats were parts from Stinger missiles and a battery used to power part of the missile system. The battery had a serial number which enabled the US authorities to trace it to a batch that had been delivered to the mujahedeen some months before.

Two different accounts of how the missiles reached the Iranians emerged. The first suggested that two commanders from the Hezbi Islami party of Younis Khalis, a militant Islamic guerrilla group, sold up to sixteen missiles in May 1987 to members of the Iranian Revolutionary Guard for up to $1m.[9] Khalis himself said that members of his group had come under attack when a five-truck convoy strayed into Iran. The Iranian border guards, he said, had mistaken them for Afghan government troops and opened fire. The Iranians captured two of the trucks while the other three managed to escape.[10]

General Alexei Lizichev, the head of the Soviet army and navy's chief political directorate, claimed that Soviet intelligence had firm information that 33 Stinger missiles had been sold by guerrillas to Iranian agents and 10 more were sold to Iranian drug smugglers. Each allegedly fetched around $300,000, roughly three times their usual market price.[11]

Although the US government publicly accepted Khalis's story, it is now privately recognised that his men did indeed sell the weapons and that the tale of an attack was simply a cover.

The Soviet journal *Pravda* responded to news of the Stingers being found in Iranian hands with an article criticising Washington: 'These are weapons whose spread might lead to unforeseen consequences. It is simply a miracle that the Stingers [and incidentally, the British Blowpipes as well] that are being supplied to the Dushmany [insurgents] have yet to turn up in the arsenals of other groups involved in international terrorism on air routes. As they say, don't dig a pit for someone else, lest you fall into it yourself.'[12]

Further evidence of the market in Stingers came when the American ambassador to the gulf state of Qatar attended a military parade in April 1988. He was astonished to see three Stinger missiles proudly on display. At that time, the Americans had refused to sell Stingers to Qatar and the assumption is the state had bought them on the black market.

After the Iran affair, attempts were made by the US to tighten up on the distribution of Stingers but without much success. This effort was also hampered by an explosion in Rawalpindi in April 1988 which killed one hundred people when an arms dump containing around $80m worth of arms destined for the guerrillas blew up. Some reports suggest that the dump exploded shortly before the Americans were due to carry out a detailed inventory of the stocks held there. In fact, the US now has no clear idea just how many missiles are floating around the black market. Estimates vary from less than 100 to more than 300.

At the beginning of March, 1989, the US administration made clear to the CIA that it wanted the Agency to try to recover as many of the missing missiles as possible. However, as no one knows where the missiles are or indeed how many of them are missing, it is unlikely that this CIA mission will be successful. As Representative Charles Wilson, who was instrumental in organising the first shipment of Stingers, puts it: 'Nothing is worth as much as a Stinger and the mujahedeen aren't stupid.'

Former US Defence Secretary Frank Carlucci puts it rather more succinctly: 'We'll never get them back, never.'[13]

Various attempts have been made by the US Congress to discover exactly how much cash and arms were siphoned off before they reached the fighters in Afghanistan. But these efforts were only ever half-hearted as Afghanistan was considered a popular cause and all agencies involved could simply refuse to cooperate. For example, in February 1987, Representative William Gray asked the General Accounting Office to investigate the covert operation following allegations that, between 1980 and 1984, 70 per cent of all aid had been siphoned off. However, the CIA refused to cooperate with the investigation and it died before it even began to hear evidence.

By contrast, the Reagan administration's support for the Nicaraguan Contras – a less popular cause – was under constant scrutiny by Congress.

A particularly striking example of the double standards applied by US Congressman is that of the Democratic Senator from Arizona, Dennis DeConcini, a member of the Senate Select Committee on Intelligence. In 1985 he picked up reports that the Administration might be planning to send Stingers to the Contras.[14]

'At the time there was going to be a vote on Contra aid, so we discussed the possibility of attaching to the Contra vote an amendment that would prohibit Stingers going to the Contras. In the short time that it took for us to almost literally discuss it and then go over to the floor, we had about four phone calls from the Administration asking us not to do it. First of all, an undersecretary called us, then I think it was Abrams that might have called him, then it was Admiral Poindexter and then finally the Senator said "Well, Mr Poindexter, if you are so interested in not having Stingers go to Central America, I would really like to discuss this with only one other person." And as we got to the floor the President called the Senator and said, "please do not introduce this bill."

The Senator and the President worked out a compromise that essentially kept the Stingers out of the hands of the Contras. By contrast, 'The Senator doesn't have any problems with the Stingers going to Angola or Afghanistan. In fact he supports those efforts.'

The Senator did argue for additional safeguards on Stingers and was one of a number of Congressmen who tried to prevent Stingers being distributed to friendly Gulf states worried about possible air strikes from Iran.

The diversion of cash and arms and the money generated by arms sales on the black market was not simply a matter of the Afghanistan war being prolonged and the lives of courageous guerrillas being lost unnecessarily. The loose controls on the traffic which were tacitly accepted by all western governments involved have helped fuel a growth in the illegal traffic of drugs from Afghanistan and Pakistan. This is a heavy price the west is only just beginning to pay for the war.

Growing the opium poppy and the marijuana plant in the North West Frontier province that straddles the border of Afghanistan and Pakistan has been a flourishing industry for centuries. Britain used to process the opium during the days of the Empire at the end of the last century, and sell it to the Chinese. In independent Pakistan it was legal to take opium until 1978 and there were government controlled shops selling to the addicts and the doctors alike.

The Afghan war gave a trade that was being attacked by an international US sponsored anti-drug drive a new lease of life. To communities that had seen their traditional trading patterns and way of life destroyed, growing a cash crop like opium became a vital alternative source of income. For the warlords who controlled the villagers, opium was also a useful cash resource with which to buy guns or influence. The result has been a production boom in the country. For example, in Pakistan where the US anti-drug drive had clearly begun to have some effect by the 1984/5 growing season, when only 45 tons of opium were produced, with the influx of refugees from Afghanistan and the loss of control in the frontier province, production tripled to 120 tons the next year.[15] By the end of 1987 that figure had risen to 160 tons and today it looks set to continue rising.

But the Pakistan production figures are insignificant when compared with the crop in Afghanistan. In 1984, Afghanistan produced around 150 metric tons of opium. By 1987 that figure had risen to more than 500 metric tons and in 1988 the figure may have been as high as 800 metric tons, the vast majority of which was exported.[16]

Again, the war is largely responsible for this increase. The Soviet policy of scorched earth and the depopulation of rural areas destroyed much of the country's traditional economic infrastructure. The people who remained in the country were forced to turn to agriculture that did not depend on complex irrigation systems, and so was less labour intensive. Many farmers started producing opium as a way to survive. At the same time, as the local currency collapsed, so barter became a more important part of everyday life with drugs as a common medium of exchange. While destroying traditional crops on the one hand, the Soviets actually bought forward in the opium market by paying farmers up front for that year's crop. They hoped this would gain them influence among the farming community and thus slowly reduce the influence the guerrillas had in the countryside. There is no real evidence that this proved a particularly useful strategy but it certainly contributed to the increase in opium production.

The opium poppy is cultivated in 27 of Afghanistan's 28 provinces but mainly grows in the eastern provinces bordering Pakistan including Kunar, Nangarhar, Paktia and Paktika, some provinces in the north such as Jouzjan, Kunduz, Takhar and Badghis and in the Helmund Valley in the south. Overall, around 13,500 hectares are cultivated with opium of which 10,000 are in the eastern provinces near Pakistan. Opium is now the primary crop in thirteen of the twenty-eight provinces.

To give an idea of the profits available from the trade, heroin is sold for around $3,000 a kilo already hidden in the chosen method of smuggling, be it a wooden ornament or a can of curry powder. In Britain, wholesalers sell heroin at around $2,000 for 30 grams with the street price doubling to $4,000 for 30 grams. The small pushers cut the drug to around 30–40 per cent of its strength and sell it at between $100-$200 a gram. Thus heroin that wholesales for around three dollars a gram in Peshawar retails for nearly $650 on the streets of London.[17]

Under General Zia, many senior military officers became involved in the drug trade to supplement their own meagre incomes – thus ironically attracting a better class of officer to the military. Military aircraft and army trucks were routinely used to transport the drugs from the North West Frontier to Karachi for shipment abroad. The profits generated for the military are immediately visible in their lifestyles even today: many live in the smartest suburbs such as Clifton in Islamabad where President Benazir Bhutto lives.

In January 1988, the Parliamentary Secretary of Defence told the National Assembly in Islamabad that officers found smuggling drugs were simply dismissed the service and did not face trial. Of ten army officers and one air force officer found guilty of drug smuggling offences, one was sentenced to nine months in jail, two escaped from army security, seven were dismissed the service after courts martial, and one faced proceedings in a civil court. The top drug barons are widely known to both the Pakistani leadership and to the western drug agents operating in the country. They include senior army generals and politicians.

The United States is involved in a big drug eradication programme in the country but the corruption is so endemic that it has met with little success. The effective element in the anti-drug programme is crop destruction, but western customs officers say that even here the drug barons manage to make a profit by burning poor quality opium and pocketing the cash compensation for doing so.

As one western customs agent put it: 'Corruption here is just about total. All the law enforcement agencies are so corrupt that I cannot see the situation ever changing. It extends to the customs, the police, the levies, the army, the airport security authorities, the port officials, the courts and the politicians. They are all working to get money through drugs. Occasionally they make big seizures but it does not mean anything. It's usually doing a favour for a competitor or the arrested smuggler or to impress the Americans so that they can get more money.'

The French, Dutch, Germans, Swedes, Australians, British, New Zealanders and Americans all have drug enforcement agents operating in Pakistan. They divide into two camps. The minority try to cooperate with the Pakistan authorities while the vast majority try instead to gather intelligence about planned shipments which is then passed to their colleagues abroad where there is at least some prospect of a successful arrest and subsequent trial.

Iran, too, has become directly involved in shipping drugs to the west. According to *The New York Times*, the small town of Robat near the borders of both Iran and Pakistan in the southwest of Afghanistan has undergone a minor boom. What was once a small village now boasts two butchers' shops, five bakeries and fifteen restaurants and its own electricity generating plant protected by guerrillas armed with anti-tank rockets, anti-aircraft guns and automatic rifles.[18]

In 1983, the US Drug Enforcement Agency was asked for the first time to report on what was known about the role of the guerrillas in the drugs business. The DEA reported that many of the Afghan guerrillas were using drugs to buy arms and pay their followers. After returning from a fact-finding trip to Pakistan in December 1983, David Melocik, a DEA official responsible for liaison with Congress, confirmed that the guerrillas were dealing in drugs. 'You can say the rebels make their money off the sale of opium. There's no doubt about it,' he said.[19] 'The rebels keep their cause going through the sale of opium,' he added. At that time the DEA estimated that 50 per cent of the heroin on American streets came from Afghanistan. American interests had become mutually incompatible because the administration wanted to fight drug trafficking but also to see the rebels win their war against the Soviets.

In consequence nothing of significance was done to interrupt the growth of the drug trade alongside the arms business. Instead, every effort was concentrated on giving the guerrillas everything they could need – and more – to fight and win the war. In 1983 Pakistan had 30,000 heroin addicts and today the government will acknowledge a figure of 700,000 while some believe the real figure may be closer to two million. One in ten of Karachi's eight million population are now addicts.[20]

The Golden Crescent of Afghanistan, Iran and Pakistan supplies nearly half the heroin marketed in the United States and Canada, 80 per cent of heroin sold in Europe and all the heroin available on the African continent. The Pakistan/ Afghan border is the site of the majority of the plants processing opium into heroin.

The most important processing factory, which was set up with the help of the American Mafia, is in the hills overlooking the new boom town of Robat, in Afghanistan just over the border from Pakistan. The factory is run by followers of Gulboddin Kekmatyar, leader of the Hezbi Islami mujahedeen group. The Hezbi Islami received the bulk of covert US aid despite their close ties with Iran and Islamic fundamentalism.[21]

Two other guerrilla groups, the Movement of the Islamic Revolution of Afghanistan (Harakat) and the Union of the Islamic Revolution of Afghanistan (Ittihad) are also heavily involved in the heroin traffic. Each of the groups exact tribute in kind for any drug caravan passing through their territory.

The leader of the Harakat group, Mowlavi Mohammad Nabi Mohammadi, defence minister in the interim Afghan government, has confirmed that his men are involved in the traffic. 'Our farmers are poor. They have to make a living and the opium poppy has traditionally been one of the crops.'[22]

If history is anything to go by, peace will bring to Afghanistan a period of unparalleled lawlessness, during which each of the well-armed and trained tribal leaders will fight not for control of Afghanistan (that has become a sideshow now that the hated Soviets have gone) but for a share of the growing and highly profitable arms and drugs business which is the long-term legacy of the war.

In the 1950s and 1960s, similarly, the CIA ran a series of covert operations in Burma, Laos and Thailand aimed at stopping communist expansion in the region. As a forerunner to the Afghan experience, the US became involved in an area that had cultivated the poppy for centuries and saw it as a useful cash crop. But while the local warlords were happy to support the American effort to repel the communists, they also saw a useful opportunity to make a great deal of money in the arms and drugs business. This ambition was helped by the involvement of some individual Americans who took an active part in the drug smuggling both to line their own pockets and to provide another source of income for the guerrillas.

When the Americans left South-East Asia they also left behind them an entrenched drug industry which is now known as the Golden Triangle and last year produced around the same amount of opium as the Golden Crescent. The drug trafficking is now virtually impossible to eradicate: the CIA-armed warlords have total control over vast tracts of the inhospitable countryside.

There is no doubt that the Soviet invasion of Afghanistan was an outrageous breach of international law and a danger-ous precedent that the west was right to condemn. It was also right for western countries led by the United States to provide cash and arms to the guerrillas to fight for the return of the country. But in the headlong rush to support a good cause, commonsense and natural caution were ignored, and massive quantities of arms and money were transferred to the guerrillas without any serious attempt to control the traffic.

There was really no logic to this, as the reputation of the Afghans has been consistent for centuries: they are a tough, courageous, ruthless and utterly untrustworthy race. Yet this seemed to have been forgotten not just in the immediate aftermath of the invasion but in the years until the Soviets left. The Afghan cause must have been the first really popular covert operation this century and as such no politician was prepared to stand up and sound a word of caution. Even though senior officials in the intelligence community sounded warnings to Congress, the White House and the Defence Department, the political momentum behind the cause was such that they were repeatedly dismissed.

This chaotic approach to covert warfare resulted in corrup-tion on an unrivalled scale – and may indeed have institution-alised corruption in the Pakistan armed forces (with the full knowledge of General Zia ul-Haq) where before there was simply occasional graft. At the same time, the growth of the illegal arms market not only ensured that many previously impoverished guerrilla leaders became very rich but also sophisticated weapons such as the Stinger missile could reach the hands of unfriendly government or terrorist groups.

But it is when the huge surplus of arms is combined with the growth in the drugs market that the future really begins to look bleak. As Afghanistan is divided up between the different guerrilla groups the result will be a number of fief-doms where gun law rules over a slave population producing drugs to satisfy the immensely profitable market that has developed since the Soviet invasion of Afghanistan.

The ultimate irony of this bleak picture is that the war that the west pursued, paid for and armed with such fervour was won. On February 15, 1989, the day the Soviets completed their withdrawal from Afghanistan, a small party was held for the CIA's Afghan Task Force which had run the covert war. As the CIA director, William Webster, pointed out to the one hundred people present, they could take credit for running 'one of the most successful operations in the country's history'.

The immediate post-withdrawal euphoria was understand-able, but it is unlikely that history will be quite so enthusi-astic. The legacy of that victory will be a new war in Afghanis-tan. Only this time the enemy won't be the Soviets but the Afghan people themselves. And this time they won't be called freedom fighters but drug traffickers and this time victory for the west may prove infinitely more difficult.

PART THREE: THE DEALER

8

This Gun For Hire

Just after lunch on Monday, October 7, 1985 four Palestinian terrorists were cleaning their weapons in cabin Number 82 on board the cruise liner *Achille Lauro*. Suddenly the door to their cabin opened and a passenger who had lost his way stepped into the room. The four men rushed the man, clubbed him aside and spread through the ship. One pair burst into the main dining room where 97 of the ship's passengers were sitting. The other 653 passengers had all got off earlier that day at the Egyptian port of Alexandria for a tour of the Pyramids. They were due to rejoin the ship that night in Port Said for the short journey to the next stop at Ashdod in Israel – where the terrorists in fact had originally planned to attack.

Firing their guns into the dining room ceiling, the two terrorists shouted in fractured English that the ship was now under their control. Meanwhile, the ship's captain, Gerardo de Rosa, alerted by his second officer, had rushed from his cabin to the bridge to be confronted by the other two terrorists, one of them the leader, Majed Molqi.[1]

The terrorists were members of the Palestine Liberation Front, a militant member of the Palestine Liberation Organisation. The leader of the PLF, Abu Abbas, was on the executive committee of the PLO and was therefore a senior figure in the organisation and a very close confidante of PLO Chairman, Yasser Arafat.

The four terrorists on the cruise liner travelling on Argentinian, Portuguese and Norwegian passports, had boarded the ship at her home port of Genoa. They had not mixed with the other passengers, and no one had suspected their real mission. Now they separated the passengers and crew into national groups, putting the Americans, two Austrians and a six-strong British dance troupe together on the ship's deck, next to some oil drums which they repeatedly threatened to ignite. All four were armed with pistols, machine guns and a plentiful supply of grenades. For the British and Americans forced to sit on deck the grenades proved particularly terrifying as the terrorists repeatedly pulled their pins and made as if to throw them into the nearby fuel drums, only to laugh, replace the pins and walk away.

The terrorists forced the captain to head for the Syrian port of Tartus from where they hoped to be able to negotiate the freedom of Palestinians held in Israeli jails. But Syria, worried about what Israel would do and the political repercussions, refused to allow the terrorists access to the port. In the negotiations that followed, the terrorists repeatedly threatened to begin killing the hostages. When this failed to move the Syrians, one of the hostages, Leon Klinghoffer, a 69-year-old American Jew, was taken aside from the rest of the passengers. Klinghoffer, confined to a wheelchair after two heart attacks, was in no position to resist the hijackers. They shot him, once in the head and once in the chest, and two of the ship's stewards were forced to dump his body overboard.

News of the hijacking was picked up in Washington at 7.00 am local time by the National Security Agency, which heard a distress call broadcast from the ship. The Terrorist Incident Working Group was brought together on that Monday morning to devise a response. It was agreed that two different units from the special forces would be sent to the region immediately. Delta Force, who would carry out any rescue mission on land, were despatched from Fort Bragg; and Seal Team 6, who would carry out a sea attack left from their base at Dam Neck, Virginia. Both forces were ready to go by 11.00 that morning.

In addition, a headquarters unit from the Joint Special

Operations Command was sent from Fort Bragg under the command of Brigadier General Carl Stiner. Incredibly for an operation that should have been light and flexible, the force eventually numbered nearly 500 men. The sheer size of the force meant that they weren't actually in the area, ready on Cyprus, until late Tuesday – a delay of thirty-six hours.

Even then, American plans to assault the ship were frustrated. Refused entry to Tartus, the terrorists had first planned to go to Cyprus. But they then received instructions from Abu Abbas to return to Port Said, where they arrived on Wednesday. The Seals planned to assault the ship that night but behind the Americans' back the Egyptian government had been secretly negotiating a peaceful end to the hijacking. Abu Abbas himself went out on a tug to the *Achille Lauro* taking with him the promise of a safe passage for the terrorists. At 4.30 that afternoon the terrorists left the ship, landed at Port Said, and disappeared.

Until the terrorists had vanished, no one knew that an American citizen had been brutally murdered during the hijacking. But the American Ambassador then soon learned of Leon Klinghoffer's death and in a decoded message to his embassy he ordered: 'You tell the [Egyptian] Foreign Ministry that we demand they prosecute those sons of bitches.'

The Egyptian government blandly told the Americans that they were too late; the terrorists had already left the country, for an unknown destination, probably Tunis. But the National Security Agency had in fact been listening to President Mubarak's telephone calls and knew that while the Egyptian government was telling the Americans the hijackers had already left, the Egyptian President was urging his aides to get the terrorists out of the country as quickly as possible. The NSA further discovered that the terrorists were hiding in a location near the Al Maza air base outside Cairo and the plan was for them to fly out the next morning, Friday, on board a commercial Egyptair 737.

This presented Washington with a new opportunity to capture the terrorists and bring them for trial in the US.

There are different accounts of who thought up the idea of intercepting the Egyptair plane once it had taken off, but certainly Lt-Col Oliver North is one of those who claimed credit for the scheme. What is certain is that North had been playing a key role in the *Achille Lauro* affair on the National Security Council as part of his general duties coordinating the counter terrorism effort.

According to North, he approached Admiral John Poindexter, the National Security Adviser, and reminded him of the incident in the Second World War when American fighters had intercepted the aircraft carrying Japanese Admiral Yamamoto and had shot it down. 'Why don't we intercept the terrorists' aircraft and force it down to a friendly air base?' North asked Poindexter. 'Then we can bring the terrorists back to America for trial.'

Poindexter was enthusiastic, as were Secretary of State George Shultz and President Reagan. The newly appointed Chairman of the Joint Chiefs of Staff, Admiral William Crowe also enthusiastically endorsed the plan. Defence Secretary Caspar Weinberger was less keen but by the time he was contacted during a trip to Canada the operation was already up and running.

Any plan to intercept the aircraft, however, depended on US intelligence agencies coming up with confirmation of not only when the terrorists left Egypt but the precise details of the aircraft, its identification and course. The problem was enormous. The intelligence assessment was that since the aircraft could fly from Egypt to Tunis, Malta, Cyprus, Lebanon, Syria, Iraq or Iran, very precise intelligence targeting was required by the National Security Agency.

Early on Thursday evening F–14 Tomcat fighters took off from the USS *Saratoga* and established a combat air patrol across the Mediterranean between Egypt and Tunisia. The NSA had supplied the tail number of the terrorists' aircraft as well as a garbled message that apparently read in part '707 on board the 737'. This made no sense until it was learned from other intelligence sources that Egypt had actually put men from their own anti-terrorist unit, Force 777, on board the aircraft to escort the terrorists out of the country. In fact, the presence of the 777 men had been predicted by US intelligence who had a very low opinion of the trustworthiness of the Egyptians. The Americans had set up and trained Force 777, but were quite prepared now to shoot them if that was necessary in order to capture the terrorists.

The F–14 fighters were guided by an E2-C Hawkeye radar aircraft from the *Saratoga*, which directed two of the fighters to a likely target. One of the pilots made a positive identification by shining a torch at the tail of the aircraft where its number was prominently displayed. After the plane was refused permission to land in Tunis and Tripoli it tried to turn back to Egypt. The F–14s prevented this, and then directed it to land at the US Air Force base at Sigonella in Sicily.

At the same time, men from the Seal team commanded by Stiner had left their staging post at the British RAF base at Akrotiri in Cyprus and were heading for Sigonella in two C–141 transports just behind the Egyptian aircraft. The Egyptian plane landed and rolled to a halt at the end of the runway. Immediately behind it came Stiner's men, who landed with their aircraft darkened. At the same time, some of the Seal team who had been left behind at the base prior to the planned assault on the *Achille Lauro* boarded trucks and drove rapidly down the runway to join the assault. Both groups of Americans surrounded the Egyptian aircraft.

The Italian ground force commander at the base was appalled at what he saw as an infringement of Italian sovereignty. He called out his own forces who surrounded the Americans. It was a very tense standoff that could easily have resulted in American forces opening fire on troops belonging to a NATO ally. In fact, the situation became so tense between the Americans and the Italians that a number of fist fights broke out, with the Italians coming off worse.

Fortunately however, the crisis was resolved by Italian Prime Minister Craxi, who promised to arrest the terrorists. (The Italians did arrest the four hijackers, tried them and sentenced them to long jail terms.) The US was also keen to get hold of Abbas, the man who had set up the hijacking in the first place, but here Craxi was less reassuring: apparently Abu Abbas and an official from the PLO's office were holed up in Cairo.

Then on Friday morning, an Egyptair flight took off with Abu Abbas and his PLO colleague on board. Shadowed by fighters from the Italian air force and Stiner in a US Navy Executive jet, the aircraft landed at a military base just outside Rome. But then, on Sunday morning the plane discreetly made the short hop to Rome's Leonardo da Vinci civilian airport where the two terrorists, reportedly disguised as Egyptian officers, boarded a Yugoslav airliner for Belgrade.

The Americans then tried to get Abbas extradited from Belgrade but before the legal efforts were complete, a business executive jet had landed at Belgrade airport, taken Abbas on board and flown him to Tunis.

In the aftermath of the *Achille Lauro* affair, investigations by the CIA and other intelligence agencies concentrated primarily on finding out from whom the terrorists had obtained the many weapons used in the attack. A second line of inquiry looked at who had supplied Abbas with his executive jet to leave Belgrade. The name that answered both questions was Monzer al-Kassar, the world's biggest dealer in illegal arms.

The following month, on Saturday, November 23, three terrorists travelling on false Tunisian and Moroccan passports boarded Egyptair Flight MS64 at Athens en route for Cairo. Shortly after take off, the leader of the gang, 22-year-old Omar Ali Marzouki, entered the cockpit and informed the captain that the aircraft was now under his control. In the main cabin, another of the terrorists was collecting passports from the passengers as a preliminary to separating Americans and Jews from the rest. Halfway down he approached Medhat Mustafa Kamil who drew a pistol and shot the terrorist dead. Kamil was a security guard and immediately came under heavy fire from the other terrorists. He was hit six times but survived. The other three security guards on the flight did nothing except place their pistols under their seats.

The shooting had pierced the cabin shell and caused instant depressurisation. The pilot rapidly descended and requested an emergency landing at Luqa airport in Malta. As soon as the aircraft landed, the terrorists demanded fuel to take them on to an undisclosed destination. The Maltese refused to supply the fuel so the terrorists shot two Americans and three Israelis. Three of the victims survived but the bodies of the other two thrown out on the tarmac prompted the Maltese to begin organising a rescue attempt.

Sensitive of their sovereignty and also closer to Libya (never a comfortable neighbour) than to the United States, the Maltese refused an offer of military assistance from the Americans. Instead they agreed that a team from the Egyptian Force 777 should attempt an assault on the aircraft.

The Egyptians made just about every mistake possible in the planning and execution of the assault. They had no idea where the terrorists were located in the aircraft as they had failed to interrogate passengers who had been released or to use surveillance devices; they had no equipment to stun and disorientate the terrorists for the first few vital seconds of the assault; and before the night attack the airport lights were turned off, which alerted the terrorists that an assault was imminent. Finally, for unexplained reasons Force 777 decided on a simultaneous assault through the side emergency exits, plus an attempt to enter the cabin by blowing a hole in the floor from the luggage compartment. In the event, the explosive charge used was so huge that the six seats immediately above the blast were ripped from their mountings and all six passengers were killed when the seats hit the cabin ceiling.

Incredibly, the incompetence was compounded when the Force 777 men threw smoke grenades into the aircraft. Passengers were unable to see the emergency exits and the Egyptian commandos were unable to see the terrorists. Those passengers who managed to grope their way to the exits were then mistaken for terrorists and came under fire from

Egyptian troops surrounding the plane. The aircraft was swiftly engulfed in flames and in the shambles fifty-seven passengers and one terrorist died.

Again, as part of the post-hijacking analysis by western intelligence agencies, attempts were made to identify the hijackers and to discover where they had obtained their arms. Although they called themselves members of 'Egypt's Revolution', a previously unknown terrorist group, it was subsequently learned the men were members of Abu Nidal's terrorist organisation. Nidal is the world's most dangerous terrorist and his men have been responsible for more brutal attacks than any other group. He is supported by Syria and Libya. US intelligence believes that, once again, the weapons for the Egyptair attack were supplied by Monzer al-Kassar.

In their efforts to counter terrorism, American agencies including the CIA and the DIA had built up extensive files on Monzer al-Kassar, dating back to the early 1970s. Their files had been augmented by others kept by Britain's intelligence services and those in France and Spain.

'We have absolutely no doubt that he is very bad news indeed,' says one intelligence source. 'Kassar has been dealing in guns and drugs for years and has got very rich in the process. Anyone investigating this man should be very careful.'[2]

Monzer al-Kassar was born in En Nebk, Syria, in 1946. His father was a former prime minister of Syria and ambassador to India. His cosmopolitan background has given him a gift for languages and he speaks Russian, Urdu, English and Arabic fluently. He uses six passports including those issued in Brazil, Syria and Argentina. His Syrian passport number 045785 lists his profession as 'merchant'. This bland description covers a variety of enterprises which include smuggling heroin and hashish on behalf of the PLO, supplying guns to different terrorist organisations and acting as the official arms salesman for Bulgaria and Poland.[3]

Al-Kassar first came to the attention of the British authorities in 1974 when he was convicted of conspiracy to supply cannabis oil. He was jailed and released in October 1975. He appears not to have learned from his experience because he immediately became involved in a complicated operation to smuggle drugs produced on land in the Beka'a Valley, under the control of the PLO. The Beka'a Valley lies between two ranges of mountains, the Jebel Liban and the Jebel esh Sharqi. To the north is the Syrian border and the large Syrian city of Homs. To the west is the Lebanese port of Tripoli. The Beka'a is a rich and fertile area, traditionally the garden of Lebanon. When the PLO made Lebanon their home they began intensive cultivation of hashish in the Beka'a. Al-Kassar helped the different PLO groups, including the Popular Front for the Liberation of Palestine and the Syrian-backed Saiqa, to distribute the drugs around the world.

At this time, al-Kassar formed a close friendship with Rifaat Assad, younger brother of President Assad of Syria. Rifaat was not only head of the Syrian secret service but also in charge of some of the security in the Beka'a Valley and, according to western drug enforcement and intelligence sources, received a considerable income from the drugs traffic. After Rifaat fell out with his brother in 1986 and no longer headed the Syrian secret service, he became a frequent visitor at al-Kassar's house in Spain. Rifaat's successor, General Ali Duba, remains a close friend of al-Kassar.[4]

The operation that al-Kassar set up worked like this: refrigerated lorries arrived in Lebanon where the drugs were loaded in false floors and walls. They were then driven north to Syria, through Turkey and Bulgaria to a staging post in the mountains at Pristina near Skopje. The drugs were then transferred to private cars which were driven through Europe to their ultimate destination. The British end of the operation was run by a friend of al-Kassar's, Henry Shaheen, an antique dealer from Andover in Hampshire. Shaheen was a British subject born of an Egyptian father and British mother, and had a long criminal record. Shaheen would steal cars in Britain, drive them to Yugoslavia and then use them to ship the drugs back to Britain.

The trucks that had originally transported the drugs from Lebanon would return for another cargo, stopping in Sofia in Bulgaria on the way and using the profits from the drugs business to purchase arms for shipment to the PLO. Al-Kassar profited from both ends of the deal by taking a cut from the drugs profits and acting as middleman for the arms transfers.

The traffic came to the notice of the US Drug Enforcement Agency in Salzburg in early 1976 and a major international operation was launched to bust the organisation. The result of this was the arrest in Britain of Shaheen and al-Kassar, who at that time was living in Sloane Square in London. At a trial in June 1977, Shaheen was sentenced to eleven years in jail. The jury acquitted al-Kassar on a charge of plotting to steal cars and failed to agree on two charges of conspiracy to contravene the 1971 Misuse of Drugs Act. However, he was convicted at a retrial in October 1977 and sentenced to two and a half years in jail. During this trial he admitted that his Syrian passport was forged and he claimed that he was wanted in Syria for desertion from the Syrian armed forces. This seems unlikely given his subsequent close relationship with the Syrian government.[5]

Tall, slim and good-looking, al-Kassar always charmingly protests his innocence of any involvement in any deals other than legitimate arms transfers. In an interview in June 1987, he denied he had ever been convicted of drugs charges in Britain. 'I spent several years in prison in England, not serving sentence, but in preventive detention. I was tried three times. In the first two I was declared innocent and in the third the jury was unable to reach a conclusion after several days of deliberation. The judge therefore instructed them to reach a decision, and they declared me "guilty of charges and guilty of one". The judge said "I have no choice but to convict you" but he gave me a sentence identical with the time I had already spent in detention. The charge was traffic in arms and drugs, but there were neither arms nor drugs.'[6]

On his release from jail, al-Kassar briefly went to Lebanon.

There he carried out his first operation with the terrorist Abu Abbas, kidnapping a Saudi businessman, Hosni Suleiman Scudian, and demanded a $5m ransom. But after the Saudi government applied pressure on President Assad in Syria who in turn let his displeasure be known to al-Kassar and Abbas, the victim was released. All the two men got for their trouble was $65,000 that Scudian had with him at the time of the kidnapping.

Shortly after this, al-Kassar shifted his headquarters from London to Spain's Costa Del Sol. He bought the luxurious Mifaldi Palace outside Marbella next to the Yiyhad Palace owned by King Fahd of Saudi Arabia. Accompanied by his wife Raghda and two daughters and surrounded by forty Filipino servants and ferried about by a fleet of cars including Rolls Royces and Mercedes, al-Kassar appeared the prosperous and successful businessman. He swiftly became a familiar figure at the local Andalusia Plaza Casino in Marbella where he would only play blackjack and insisted on sitting at his own table. To friends who went with him to the casino, he would proudly display a dog-eared cheque which he used to get chips. This was a not-so-subtle way of showing his friends what a skilful gambler he was – especially as he would play in only a twenty-minute burst before retrieving his cheque.

He had learned from his experience in England and was careful not to get directly involved in smuggling arms or drugs in Spain, although he became known locally as 'the Prince of Marbella and Darkness'. To the intelligence community who keep a close eye on him, he is known as Deadly Nightshade.

In the west, most of al-Kassar's arms dealing operations were run by a company called Alkastronic, based in Vienna. In the east, he had offices in Sofia in Bulgaria and Warsaw in Poland.

Over the next five years al-Kassar, with the help of his three brothers, consolidated his position as the most important supplier of illegal arms to terrorist organisations, including Abu Nidal, Abu Abbas, the Popular Front for the Liberation of Palestine (General Command) and the Democratic

Front for the Liberation of Palestine. He also became one of the principals involved in the trafficking of both heroin and hashish from the Middle East to Europe. According to the DEA, he has clear links with Lebanese drug traffickers, who are nearly all associated with the PLO; with members of the Italian underground criminal movement, the Camorra, based in Milan; with the Pied-Noir underworld in Marseille and with a Syrian/Lebanese gang in Madrid.[7]

At the same time, his credibility on the grey and black arms markets was becoming firmly established. In the 1960s and 70s, the Saudi Arabian middleman, Adnan Kashoggi, was perhaps the most well-known and influential arms broker, working on behalf of companies, government and other dealers. While much of the arms business involves the payment of bribes and other inducements to secure contracts and Khashoggi did his share, within the fairly elastic morality of the arms business Khashoggi was a legitimate operator. But the growth of terrorism and the isolation of a number of countries such as Iran led to the rise of a new breed of dealer who had no interest in legal niceties or in any moral principles, however elastic. This was the perfect opportunity for Monzer al-Kassar and he quickly became the single most important dealer on the underground arms market, specialising in arms produced in the eastern bloc.

Al-Kassar came to London for the final time in May 1983 to appear on behalf of the defence in the trial of John Berry who was charged with being in possession of electronic timers that could have been used to detonate bombs. In evidence to the court, al-Kassar claimed that he represented the South Yemeni government in arms deals with Poland and also claimed to have acted on behalf of the Syrian government. Although convicted, Berry jumped bail and fled to Spain where he was set up in a Marbella flat by al-Kassar.

After this the British government took a decision to bar al-Kassar from the country because of his known association with terrorism. When he arrived in England in his private jet in 1987 he was refused entry. This was the beginning of an effort by the Europeans to restrict the activities of al-Kassar, which was to lead to his expulsion from Spain.

In Hamburg, West Germany, Ephraim Alperm, an Israeli agent, was assassinated on September 13, 1983, possibly by Khamal Ghazoul, a member of the Palestine Liberation Front. Responsibility for the killing was claimed by a previously unknown group, Black September Sabra and Chatila, which the West German police believe was a cover name for terrorists from Abu Abbas's PLF. At the time, al-Kassar was thought to be orchestrating PLF activities in Europe, and the West Germans believe he may have played a part in the Alperm assassination. As a result of that attack and other intelligence made available to the West Germans by other western countries, al-Kassar is now banned from West Germany also.

In November 1984, Khamal Ghazoul attempted to assassinate a Lebanese secret agent living in Madrid, Elias Awad. Ghazoul was arrested and told police he had tried to kill the Libyan because he was one of those responsible for the massacre at the Sabra and Chatila refugee camps. In fact, Spanish police believe he was acting on behalf of the al-Kassar family. Awad himself told police that he was convinced the al-Kassars had told his assassin where he was staying. During interrogation, Ghazoul denied knowing al-Kassar. However, when he was released on a technicality, prior to fleeing to South Yemen, he immediately went to stay with Monzer al-Kassar.

In 1985, al-Kassar was accused of supplying a suitcase full of explosives to Mohammed El Jadoban for an attack on the Jewish Quarter in Paris. The British police claimed that al-Kassar obtained some of the explosives from his old friend John Berry in Spain. He was tried in absentia and sentenced to eight years in jail. That sentence remains in force but it did not stop the French government from approaching al-Kassar in 1986 to see if he could mediate with the kidnappers of four French journalists kidnapped in Beirut on March 8. According to the French newspaper *Liberation*, France paid the kidnappers from the Revolutionary Justice Organisation $2.3m for the release of two of the journalists, using al-Kassar as one of the intermediaries. The *Liberation* story was officially denied by French Premier Jacques Chirac.[8]

However, al-Kassar has admitted that he was contacted by a French 'Colonel Nicholas'. 'A gentleman called Monsieur Nicholas came to Spain and contacted me through friends. He said that through my connections in the Arab world I could be of assistance. I said it was too big a problem for me. He said that he had to travel to Lebanon and Syria but was afraid to do so. I said that he could accompany me when I travelled to Syria where I could guarantee his safety since it is a country where there is a government, law and order . . . I took him with me to Beirut, although warning that he did so at his own risk. In Beirut we separated for two hours, during which he carried out business the nature of which I do not know. When he came back he looked like someone who has achieved nothing. I myself obviously have no power to get anyone released in Lebanon.'[9]

This rather disingenuous account does not impress either British or American intelligence who are convinced both that the French did pay the ransom and that al-Kassar had a key role in the deal. Two of the hostages were released on June 20, 1986.

That same year, al-Kassar was involved in two other incidents which illustrate his close links with international terrorism and his passionate hatred of the Israelis. According to US intelligence, al-Kassar contacted a British arms dealer, Dave Tomkins, to get him to hire a couple to rent an apartment in Madrid. Once installed, the couple were instructed to tear out the kitchen fittings and dig up the floor. Under the concrete floor they found a large Samsonite briefcase with a combination code of 190. Inside the case were five packages which contained guns and ammunition including a Star .38 pistol and a short Browning automatic. The weapons had been deposited there by terrorists backed by Monzer al-Kassar and they had been arrested some months previously.

Monzer did not know if they had talked in jail so used cut outs to recover the weapons in case a police trap had been set.

While that operation was going on, al-Kassar was setting up a dummy arms company in Amsterdam which was the first step in a sting designed to draw an Israeli arms buying team to the city where they would be killed by a hit squad imported from Syria.

For the operation, al-Kassar teamed up with two arms merchants, Dave Tomkins and another European, Frank Conlon. Tomkins was a former mercenary who had fought in Angola in the mid–1970s. He turned to arms dealing and had gained an international reputation as a tough operator who would get a job done without asking too many questions. Monzer told Tomkins only that a lucrative arms deal was involved.

Frank Conlon is an Ulsterman, who now lives in both England and Miami. In his late forties, with light curly brown hair and a soft Irish accent, Conlon is a familiar and success-ful figure in the arms business. He knew al-Kassar well but was sufficiently nervous of him to have planted listening devices in his Marbella home so that he could find out if the Syrian was plotting behind his back.

Using the name of a company already in existence in Sierra Leone, a basement apartment was rented in Amsterdam in the company name. It was fully furnished complete with a large table with automatic weapons stored inside the centre support. The company then produced a list of weapons for sale that was passed to the Israelis. On the list was ammu-nition for T–62 tanks which al-Kassar knew the Israeli-backed Christians in Lebanon had captured from the Syrians. Ammunition was scarce and the bait was enough to draw the Israelis out into the open.

After some discussion, it was agreed that two Israeli dealers could come to Amsterdam for a meeting in the company flat. They would be met by a hit squad from the PFLP (GC) sent in from Syria.

What al-Kassar did not know is that Conlon was secretly working for Israeli intelligence and he had passed details of the operation back to his Mossad controller. The police in Amsterdam were alerted and the flat was raided before the Syrian hit squad arrived.

In June 1989, Monzer offered Tomkins £20,000 to kill Conlon, an offer which Tomkins refused. By September 1989, al-Kassar had raised the price on Conlon to £100,000. It is not yet clear if anyone has accepted the contract.[10]

In the United States, a great deal of work had been done in the preceding five years to produce better cooperation between all the different US law enforcement agencies and so ensure a free exchange of information and a common counter-terrorist policy. At the same time, cooperation between agencies such as the DIA in the United States and the Secret Intelligence Service in Britain had improved enormously. This improvement in information processing had generated a great deal of new material about terrorists, drugs and illegal cash and arms transfers. The one name that repeatedly cropped up in each country's computer database was Monzer al-Kassar. Beginning in 1985, the US had been applying pressure on the European countries to either arrest al-Kassar or expel him.

'This guy sat at the centre of an enormous arms, drugs and terrorist network and the Europeans were allowing him to operate openly on their turf,' commented one US intelligence official. 'We should at least have been making life difficult for the guy, make him sweat a little, keep him on the move and make him pay some kind of price.'[11]

The targeting of al-Kassar was given a high priority by the US intelligence community. It is all the more surprising then that Lt-Col Oliver North, the man who had played a key role in the capture of the terrorists who had hijacked the *Achille Lauro* and who was responsible for coordinating US counter terrorism policy, should turn to al-Kassar when he needed to buy black market arms.

For three years beginning in 1984, Oliver North was at the centre of an effort to sell arms to the Iranians in exchange for American hostages being held by Iranian backed terrorists in Lebanon. At the same time, North was helping to organise a cash and arms support network for the Contra guerrillas fighting against the Nicaraguan government – a network established in defiance of the US Congress which had put a ban on arms supplies to the Contras.

Over the three years, North and his colleagues generated $47m for the Contras, of which around $25m came from profits on the sale of arms to Iran. The cash was processed through a number of dummy companies and special bank accounts set up in Switzerland.[12]

Al-Kassar was first approached by the North network in June 1985 and was then paid $1m for arms that al-Kassar purchased from the Polish government arms manufacturing company, Cenzin. Those arms were shipped to a Caribbean island at the end of August and then passed on to the Contras.

That first successful mission encouraged the North team to try a second shipment the following year. Al-Kassar was again approached and asked if he could supply a shipment twice as large as the first, to include AK–47 assault rifles, three million rounds of 7.62mm ammunition and hand grenades. Immediately after al-Kassar had agreed, Albert Hakim, a North associate, bought a Panamanian registered freighter, the *Erria*, through a Panamanian shell company, Dolmy Business Inc. On June 20, al-Kassar was paid a deposit of $500,000 by another Panamanian shell company, Energy Resources International, which was owned by Stanford Technology, a US based company owned by Albert Hakim.

The *Erria* docked at the Polish port of Szczecin at the end of June, loaded 158 tons of arms and set sail on July 10. The ship arrived at the Portuguese port of Setubal south of Lisbon where it loaded another 200 tons of arms on July 18 which had been purchased from the Portuguese firm, Defex.

The *Erria* shipment then fell victim to funding difficulties. For two months the *Erria* stayed in Portugal with 'engine trouble', while North, Hakim and another colleague, retired Air Force General Richard Secord, tried to sell the arms on to the CIA. Ironically, one of the arguments used to persuade the CIA to buy the arms was that if they failed to do so, they would revert back to al-Kassar and might then find their way to international terrorists.

In August the CIA eventually agreed to buy the arms from Hakim for $2.2m and in September, the *Erria* travelled to the French port of Cherbourg and unloaded the arms on September 13. The guns and ammunition were then loaded on to another vessel, the *Iceland Saga*, which sailed for the US. On October 8, the guns were unloaded at the US army's Sunny Point munitions depot while the ammunition was offloaded at Wilmington.

In testimony to the Tower Commission investigating the Iran-Contra affair, Oliver North testified that he had been forced to install a $16,000 security system at his home because he feared assassination by Abu Nidal. A quiet word with his business associate, Monzer al-Kassar who in turn could have had a word with Abu Nidal would presumably have been a cheaper option.

The Iran-Contra affair was very embarrassing for the American government and for those involved in countering terrorism in the US administration. Since the election of President Reagan, the US had been making great efforts to persuade western governments to take a tough stand against terrorists. In particular, in every instance where the US had learned of governments negotiating ransom payments with terrorists or allowing terrorists to operate on their territory, there had been a series of demarches by US officials to make clear the US government's displeasure. The Iran-Contra affair revealed that senior US officials had been attempting to trade arms for hostages. Even more galling, US officials had been buying arms from a man who was recognised by every western intelligence agency as one of the key men responsible for keeping terrorists supplied with arms, those arms having been used to kill US citizens.

At the beginning of 1987, the US began to apply considerable pressure on governments in both east and west to try and isolate al-Kassar. There was a meeting in Paris of nine western countries where the focus was al-Kassar. It was decided then that the maximum pressure should be applied to all countries to keep him on the move. The Polish government agreed to restrict the activities of al-Kassar and at the beginning of July, the Spanish Secretary of State for Security issued an exclusion order banning him and his brother Haitham from entering the country.

Al-Kassar arrived at Madrid airport from Beirut on July 23. On board the aircraft with him and his brother was Izzeden Salman, the brother of the Syrian commander responsible for troops stationed in the Beka'a Valley. Waiting for him at his Marbella palace was his house guest Rifaat Assad. But immigration officials refused al-Kassar and his brother permission to enter the country and after spending the night in the international transit lounge, the two men left on a flight to Vienna.

Over the next year, Monzer al-Kassar spent time in Austria, Copenhagen, Sweden and his current home in Hungary. At each stop, US officials alerted the host government and applied sufficient pressure to force him to move on. Aside from Spain, the most important of these bases was Austria, where in 1983, Monzer and his brother Ghassan had set up a company called Alkastronik in the Zelinkagasse in Vienna. It was from these offices and his luxurious flat in the Kaasgrabengasse that al-Kassar consolidated his fortune.

Today, al-Kassar commutes between homes in Budapest, Kuwait and Damascus. He remains a key influence on the international arms market and is still involved with drugs. More recently, he has been supplying chemicals to the Colombian drug barons to help them process cocaine.

His underground network of terrorists remains in place in Spain. What is currently concerning western intelligence agencies is that that network might still be used for new terrorist outrages in Europe.[13]

The hounding of al-Kassar has been an interesting illustration of how much the counter-terrorist effort has changed in recent years. Fifteen years ago, the focus would have remained on the simple terrorist, the man who pulled the trigger or planted the bomb. Today, western intelligence agencies rightly spend more time on attacking the men behind the terrorists – the paymasters and the arms suppliers. The fact that al-Kassar has been forced out of Britain, Spain and Austria is a testament to the success of this new policy. But the fact that he is still able to call Hungary, Kuwait and Syria home shows the limitations of a more effective counter-terrorist strategy.

PART FOUR: THE DEAL

9

The History

On Tuesday, December 20, 1988, the British Secretary of State for Defence, George Younger, announced in the House of Commons that the contract for a new design of main battle tanks for the British army would be awarded to the British company, Vickers. Vickers were not awarded the full $2 billion contract for the 626 tanks ultimately required, but were only given a $162m contract for nine prototype tanks, for evaluation in September 1990, when they would be tested against their main competition, the Abrams made by an American company, General Dynamics, and the West German improved Leopard II.

This 'half-contract' was the result of a compromise carved out by the British cabinet as a way of trying to keep the tank industry in Britain while not risking too much taxpayers' money. The fact that Vickers received any contract at all was a surprise to all those involved in evaluating the technical information.

Most of the senior army commanders who used tanks believed that Britain should have bought the American Abrams; Sir Peter Levene, the chief of Defence Procurement, believed that Abrams represented less financial risk; even the Defence Secretary, George Younger, lobbied hard in cabinet for the Abrams. Yet the cabinet opted for the Vickers tanks.

The British tank contract is worth looking at in detail for two reasons. It explains why so much defence equipment fails to work properly when it enters service and why the Soviet

Union has been narrowing the quality gap between its own forces and NATO's. It is clear that military procurement decisions are too often driven not by military requirements but by political considerations.

Tanks operate at the leading edge of weapons technology. They have to be able to see farther and fire faster than the opposition, using a gun and ammunition that together have some prospect of penetrating the opponent's armour. The days of drawn-out tank battles with ranging shots and time for thought have long gone. If a British tank commander's first shot at an enemy tank doesn't destroy it then he himself will be destroyed.

To maintain that vital superiority, which is measured in seconds, requires not only superb training but also reliable equipment. Computers, lasers, night sights, and the gun's complicated loading and firing system all have to work on demand. And if a tank is taken by surprise then its armour has to be strong enough to resist the enemy's most powerful anti-tank weapon.

Since 1945 western tactical and strategic thinking has recognised that the tank remains the supreme tool for manoeuvre on the battlefield. Today, according to NATO, the Warsaw Pact has 51,500 main battle tanks while NATO has 16,424, making the tank the most important single conventional weapon in the armoury of either side.

The evolution of a new main battle tank for the British army went through a number of phases. In 1959, the first prototype of the Chieftain tank was produced by the Royal Armoured Research and Development Establishment at Chertsey in conjunction with the Royal Ordnance Factory in Leeds. The Chieftain gun barrels were produced by the Royal Ordnance in Nottingham.

Nine hundred Chieftains were eventually built for the British army and throughout their service life they were regularly updated with new equipment as the technology improved and the threat changed. For example, the 12.7mm ranging machine gun was replaced by a Barr and Stroud tank laser sight, then a Marconi improved Fire Control System was installed and finally, to give the Chieftain an effective night fighting capability, a Thermal Observation and Gunnery Sight (TOGS) was installed.

All these improvements gave the Chieftain a better theoretical capability, but it still remained very vulnerable. Each of the four-man crew worked inside a hot, noisy and desperately confined space. Going into battle in a Chieftain was like trying to pass an exam in applied mathematics while sitting inside a pressure cooker with a bongo band playing out of tune on the outside.

By the time the Chieftain gunner had run through all the movements required to bring his gun to bear and fire it, he would most probably have already suffered the first hit from an enemy round. That is always assuming that he had managed to get to the battle in the first place, propelled by his notoriously unreliable Leyland engine.

At the beginning of 1985, the army hoped that many of these problems had been solved with the introduction of the Challenger Tank, made by RARDE (Chertsey) and the Royal Ordnance factory at Leeds. Its mobility and greatly reduced maintenance workload were seen as two major advantages. But, as had been the case with the Chieftain, to get the Challenger into service compromises were made on the specification. For example, to meet the specification for handling a front attack by enemy armour without an unacceptable weight increase, protection was pared from other areas. Protection at the Challenger driver's feet is actually less today than it was in the Second World War, and protection for the belly of the tank is non-existent. Also, just as the Chieftain became a jungle of piecemeal, ill-coordinated equipment making it impossibly complex to operate, the same problems soon arose with Challenger.[1]

Responsibility for the initial design work on the Challenger fell to the Royal Armament Research and Development Establishment at Chertsey in Surrey and one of those involved in the project explains how it developed during a period of considerable financial stringency.[2]

'Several improvements were introduced into service through the introduction of "appliqué kits". Each new appliqué kit brought its own peculiar integration problems with it and the right hand side of the turret wall next to the gunner and commander became more and more complicated as "improvements" were introduced. At no time was finance available to sit down and restructure components and systems so as to alleviate the plumbing nightmare in the turret.'

But the Challenger was not all bad. Perhaps the most significant technological advance on the new tank was the adoption of British Chobham armour. In the past, tanks had relied on thick sheets of steel for protection but the better the protection, the heavier the tank and this affected range and speed. Chobham armour used a number of new composite materials that provided much better protection for less weight.

Unfortunately, by the time Challenger entered service another revolution in armour had taken place which put the advantage once again firmly with the Soviets.

In the late 1970s the Soviets began installing Explosive Reactive Armour (ERA) on their tanks. This system, which had been rejected by the US army, consists of a number of steel boxes, each about the size of a cigar box, bolted onto the side of a tank. When a missile or round hits the box, it explodes outwards and dissipates the force of the incoming charge. It is stunningly effective, and it makes many of the west's anti-tank systems ineffective.

Clearly something had to be done.

In 1986, it had already been decided that what Britain needed was a completely new tank that would have the best of the new technology and would stand a chance of actually being ahead of the pack for its first decade or so of service. But, to a medium-sized military power like Britain, the cost of developing a new tank within a short time-span is prohibitive if the job is to be done properly.

This situation led to the decision that planning should begin for a replacement to be ready around the year 2000, and in staff talks at colonel level with the West Germans it was found that they were of the same mind. They needed to replace their Leopard I tank but their MOD had been told by its minister that the next tank would not be funded unless it promised significant technological improvements.

Those involved were aware that the only really significant advances in prospect were in gun technology, and these were unlikely to be available until the turn of the century. So the British provisional timescale seemed to fit everyone: there was also a useful political spin-off in that the development of a common European tank had been a longstanding proclaimed goal of NATO.

Two teams were set up to try to draw up a common specification for the new tank, and after some discussion, agreement on a common way forward was reached and a paper was sent up the chain of command recommending project approval. The Director of the Royal Armoured Corps (DRAC), who advises the army on tank matters, made it clear that a joint venture was his preferred objective, and all those responsible for the budget agreed – with serious money not starting to be spent until the late 1990s.

The army entered 1987 confident that for the first time they were on course to build a tank in a collaborative programme to agreed international specifications. Then, in February 1987 Vickers Defence Systems entered the fray.

10

The Competition

In October 1986, Vickers had taken over the Royal Ordnance factory at Leeds that produced the Challenger. This gave Vickers a monopoly on tank production in Britain and they built a modern factory at Leeds at a cost of $25m, which was completed in December 1987. But the success of this essentially speculative venture was dependent on export orders or on a new order from the British army.

The last of the Challengers from the Leeds production line would be delivered at the end of 1989 and after that the company's order book for the factory would be virtually empty. Despite its show of optimism, the company had no real hopes of winning exports for Challenger. But the company knew that the government were considering buying a new main battle tank and that discussions were well advanced with the West Germans so, rather than face the prospect of shutting their Leeds factory, they decided on a preemptive strike by offering to build a brand new tank themselves for the British army.

They gave two briefings in the MoD main building in Whitehall in March and April 1987, both very professionally presented and concentrating on those areas where the company knew no final decisions had been made, such as gun performance and protection. The company proposed that they would supply a new tank called the Challenger 2 which would be a new tank using enhanced systems throughout, all controlled by a tidy, ergonomic turret and at the attractive price of £1.3m each. The first tank would be delivered around 1992.

These briefings were well received and there was an immediate acceptance among the senior officers present that the Vickers deal stood a real chance of succeeding.

But for the past two years there had been an important sideshow taking place that was to have a critical effect on Vickers' plans.

In 1985, Peter Levene was appointed as Chief of Defence Procurement in the MoD. In a revolutionary move he was brought in from industry, paid a salary several times that of senior civil servants and given a brief to reform. His target was the inefficient and expensive procurement system that frequently produced equipment that was late, over budget and that failed to work to specification.

Levene is a tough and intelligent man with a mind uncluttered by the entrenched traditions of the civil service in general and the Ministry of Defence in particular. From the moment he arrived in the MoD he had been appalled at the generally inefficient way that the MoD ran its procurement system and at the poor quality of equipment delivered by much of British industry. In the past industry had nearly always won contracts on a 'cost plus' basis which meant they bid one price (and usually only one company was invited to bid) and then that price rose depending on how difficult the company found the contract. For the defence industry it was, literally, a licence to print money, and companies grew fat on the profits.

Despite considerable opposition from the institutionalised structure inside the MoD and from the military, Levene forced through a number of sweeping reforms. The most important of these was that whenever possible contracts should be awarded only after competition, and on a fixed price with penalties for late delivery.

When the tank order arose, Levene had a perfect opportunity to prove that things really were different in the defence procurement business. From the moment that Vickers became involved, Levene was determined that such a prestigious contract should be awarded competitively, and let both the Americans and the Germans know that he would welcome tenders for the tank contract from them.

The potential prize was huge. If America's General Dynamics could win the British tank contract then Vickers would be out of the tank business and the American company would be perfectly positioned to provide a new NATO tank in the next century.

Vickers had hoped that an announcement of the tank order in their favour would be made in July 1988. But Levene's insistence on competition meant that the Vickers bid had to be extremely detailed, so that it was not until just before that date, at the end of June, that Vickers submitted its bid for the contract, offering the Challenger 2, an enhanced version of the existing Challenger with a new turret, improved armour and a new fire control and sighting system. The new Vickers tank would have a 120mm rifled gun.

In July 1988, General Dynamics submitted their first bid for an uprated version of the MIAI tank already in service with the US army. The new version would have better armour, an improved fire control system and a 120mm smoothbore gun.

Krauss Maffei submitted the Leopard II but this was not offered with a similar enhancement programme and was quickly ruled out, particularly because of the comparatively low quality of the armour.

For the Director of the Royal Armoured Corps and his staff at Bovington there were immediately three areas of concern: ergonomics, reliability and gun performance. The army were determined to avoid the cramped and complex working environment that they had experienced in both Challenger and Chieftain and wanted a turret that was simple to operate.

In the past, both reliability and gun performance had fallen foul of Britain's very conservative method of designing and buying military equipment. For years a great deal of British military equipment had been created by the MoD's own research and development organisations.

In the case of Challenger, considerable sums of money had already been spent on the Chieftain/Challenger Armament (CHARM) programme to develop a new L30 high pressure 120mm rifled gun to replace the current Challenger gun. That weapon was being developed by Royal Armament Research and Development Establishment at Fort Halsted and they clearly had a vested interest in seeing the project through.

Britain was the only country in NATO committed to a new generation of rifled guns. On the other hand, since the new L30 British guns could be fitted to existing Challengers and Chieftains, if Britain now opted for a smoothbore, it would be operating two different systems in parallel for a number of years with all the logistical problems that would involve.

Then, in June 1987 two official studies gave senior army officers accurate data clearly demonstrating that their existing guns were wildly inaccurate. The British guns were capable of hitting the target at 2,000 metres only one round in every four, an appalling statistic which virtually guaranteed a very short life indeed for all British tanks in war. Perhaps understandably the figures were initially greeted with disbelief in the MoD. However, the statistical base and analysis was sound and the figures were accepted as accurate by the end of 1988.

The next question facing the army was to what extent the proposed L30 replacement was going to suffer from the same weaknesses. At first, they had no idea what was causing the accuracy variations between shots. Then it was discovered that the quality control at the Royal Ordnance factory in Nottingham had been virtually non-existent.

Barrels had been heated up for various purposes, then left horizontal, supported at either end, to cool. The result was bent barrels which were then straightened when cold. This set up spurious stresses in the barrel which would affect the whiplash that occurs when the gun is fired.

The army then learned that in every other 120mm gun

factory in the world the barrels are heated when vertical in a special forge to prevent bending when cooling. The Nottingham factory had no such forge.

The army presented these findings to the L30 project manager who said that no work had been done to iron out the problems so he could not say that the L30 would be any different from the guns already in service. But he did say that quality control had improved and that the factory was using superior steel.

At this stage, the team responsible for developing the specification for the next tank circulated to brigadier level a requirement – known as a staff target – for an Anglo-German tank to enter service 'around the year 2000'. It laid down requirements which were far in excess of what were likely to be achieved by a Challenger successor.

Knowing what Challenger 2 was actually likely to be able to do, the team simply revised the staff target so that it could at least appear that the specification was achievable. Thus, by the time the competition actually got underway, the specification had been massaged so that Vickers were able to compete. If it had been left as originally written, there would only have been one competitor with any prospect of meeting it and that would have been General Dynamics' Abrams tank.

In the middle of the deliberations of the army men carrying out detailed comparisons between the Vickers and the General Dynamics tanks, details of a new Soviet tank known in the West as FST–1 were revealed. The new tank had composite armour and a formidable 135mm gun capable of comfortably penetrating any armour currently in service with NATO armies. In the US, information on the new tank appeared as the army there was seeking funding from Congress for its own tank upgrade and it did the job – $5 billion was authorised.

Armed with details of the FST–1 and future Soviet plans, the British army found that in virtually every area the Challenger 2 would be outperformed by the Abrams. They concluded that the future Abrams would enjoy 50 per cent better protection than that given by the improved Chobham armour on the Challenger, since the Abrams would have reactive armour panels. In addition, the requirement for protection from top attack that the Abrams satisfied had not in fact been written in, so neither Vickers nor the MoD had any real idea of its cost.

The L30 gun, when it entered service in the mid–1990s, would be able to penetrate the Soviet armour in service in 1989. But that performance was only equal to the 120mm smoothbore currently in service with American and German tanks and was certainly no match for the next generation of gun that was already being tested by the Americans.

The only aspect of the Challenger which was an improvement on the Abrams was in fuel consumption: the Challenger used three gallons a mile and the Abrams eleven gallons. This was a serious difference but General Dynamics claimed it would be cut in half by the improvement programme and the army considered that when set against the overall cost of the programme, the fuel costs were not significant.

In the spring of 1988, the army established that the reliability of their tanks was even worse than had been suspected. Reliability had been measured not on how often a tank broke down but on availability in any 24-hour period. The figures suggested that availability for Chieftain averaged 55 per cent and the more modern Challenger 52 per cent. As spares are more numerous for Chieftain its figures are better than Challenger even though Challenger breaks down marginally less often. Even these appalling figures are selective as they refer only to the engine of the vehicle.

Shortly after this another vested interest, the Royal Armament and Research Development Establishment at Chertsey, prepared a report which compared the West German Leopard II tank with the General Dynamics MIAI Abrams, and the Vickers Challenger 2. Although they had difficulty in obtaining comparative data, the report made gloomy reading.

On reliability, the report quoted the probabilities of completing a theoretical battlefield day. Chieftain achieved 50 per cent, Challenger 55 per cent, MIAI 75 per cent and Leopard

2.98 per cent, a figure which they discounted as being improbable. The American figures had been prepared from a detailed analysis of the 600 MIAI tanks in service compared with the British analysis of their 400 or so Challengers.

The study also revealed that the Abrams could travel 1,600 miles before its automatic gearbox broke down, while the Chieftain could manage just 550 miles. The trend was clear. The British tanks were significantly less reliable than the competition.

For the army and for the MoD procurement executive, the statistics raised some fundamental questions. How, they asked themselves, could they have any confidence that enough money, time and trialling would be spent to get the new British tank up to standard? At best, Vickers would be testing across less than a dozen specially built prototypes while the Americans would have a data base around 1,000 times larger.

To senior army officers, who had originally backed the British bid almost by reflex, the figures were damning and a growing number of generals were coming round to the unthinkable possibility that Britain should buy an American tank.

A major influence over senior army officers, however, was the view of the Chief of the General Staff, General Sir Nigel Bagnall. Known affectionately to his men as 'Ginge' because of his red hair, Bagnall was a talented – many would say brilliant – military thinker. In a peacetime army that had produced few real leaders with sound intellects at the very top, Bagnall was the exception. A powerful personality who had a sharp tongue with those he considered ill-prepared or ignorant, Ginge was surrounded by staff officers who hung on his every word. He had made it clear from the start that he favoured the Vickers tank, arguing that it was inconceivable that Britain should buy anything other than British. His strong support for the tank had a significant impact on any other officer's willingness to voice support for the Abrams.

Despite the evidence, therefore, by April 1988 the Staff Requirement was in circulation and the MoD's Equipment

Policy Committee had agreed the staff target, so that tacitly the Challenger 2 option was the favoured solution.

Suddenly, in about May, among Ministry of Defence officials there was a change of mind. Realising that the Treasury was going to give them the money for a new tank irrespective of which one they bought, the army seemed at last to appreciate just what risks they would be taking by opting for Challenger. The results of the various studies had been widely circulated and at every level from tank troop commanders up the chain of command, there was now one voice asking for the Abrams.

Peter Levene, too, was nervous about the contract going to Vickers. He was responsible to the Defence Secretary for meeting the army's specifications and was therefore keen to keep the contest open for as long as possible.

But the army's entry into the debate with a strong point of view had come too late. In the cabinet, Lord Young, the Secretary of State for Trade and Industry, was pushing the Challenger 2 solution, since it would secure Vickers' future, guaranteeing jobs in the depressed north of England. For Young the arguments were essentially political: a vote for Abrams meant his department would be attacked for betraying British industry. A vote for Vickers, on the other hand, could only win him the support both of Tory backbenchers and the Opposition. Young never understood the technical details of the project but that did not diminish his status as a powerful advocate for the Vickers cause.

Vickers Defence Systems, meanwhile, had decided to launch a risky but very well organised publicity campaign in defiance of MoD instructions for a complete publicity blackout.

11

The Decision

The Vickers campaign concentrated on three key areas: jobs, exports and chauvinsim. All three were carefully calculated to strike a chord with members of parliament and the press.

Beginning in September 1988, the chairman of Vickers, Sir Donald Plastow, invited selected journalists to the company headquarters overlooking the Thames. A charming, personable man, Plastow was always eloquent and convincing in selling the virtues of the Challenger. To each of his visitors he made the fair point that he had inherited some shoddy products when he took over the Royal Ordnance factory in Leeds and that the new company was being unreasonably blamed for the reputation of the old.

Vickers claimed that if the contract went to the Americans up to 10,000 jobs could be lost in Britain. But, in fact, General Dynamics had made clear to the government that they would build the Abrams under licence in the UK. There was, therefore, no serious threat to jobs.

Vickers further claimed that the company saw potential exports for the Challenger 2 that could be worth an initial $6 billion with at least double that value in spares, ammunition and other items. Kuwait was one of those countries where Vickers saw export potential, yet in the middle of their lobbying the Kuwaitis asked for bids for their tank contract and Vickers were not on the list of those invited to tender. (Yugoslavia eventually got the deal.)

In any event, the Ministry of Defence's own arms sales

organisation, DESO, disagreed with those figures. 'The real prospects for overseas sales were not as high as Vickers claimed,' said one official involved. 'We have no doubt that if Vickers produce a good tank then we shall sell some of them. But, just in case they don't, links were negotiated with General Dynamics so that we could sell the Abrams.' (The then head of DESO, Sir Colin Chandler, retired from the MoD in 1989. In January 1990 he took up his new post as Managing Director of Vickers Defense Systems.)

The Americans had in fact offered the UK a unique marketing agreement for third country sales, excluding Egypt where GD already had a contract, and Canada. If the UK won a contract, they would receive 100 per cent of the value of the deal, and even if GD won the contract, Britain would still get a percentage of the contract value.

But Vickers' final appeal was in many ways the most convincing: Britain had invented the tank and placing an order overseas was portrayed as selling part of the country's birthright.

Each of the arguments struck an emotional chord with the politicians. Over a hundred Tory MPs signed a House of Commons motion calling for the contract to go to Vickers. The Labour leader Neil Kinnock went to Leeds and in a passionate speech supported the Vickers bid. Inside the cabinet, Lord Young argued that it was vital for jobs and the UK industrial base that the tank contract go to Vickers.

These developments were viewed with some alarm by the army. There was a general fear that the argument was being won by Vickers without anyone being made aware of the real issues. The arrival in September of General Sir John Chapple as Chief of the General Staff in succession to Ginge Bagnall also influenced the argument. Chapple was not firmly committed to either view and was quite prepared to listen to the arguments. As a result, the senior officers felt free to express their serious reservations.

In October 1988, Major General Nick Ansell, the head of the Royal Armoured Corps, wrote to Major General Anthony

Mullens, the Assistant Chief of Defence Staff (Operational Requirement, Land), recommending the Abrams. Soon after, General Sir Brian Kenny, the Commander in Chief of the British Army on the Rhine also wrote to General Sir John Chapple, the Chief of the General Staff, in support of Abrams. In talks with Defence Secretary George Younger, both Sir John Chapple and the Deputy Chief of the Defence Staff (Systems), Admiral Sir Jeremy Black, supported Abrams.

For Peter Levene, the arguments remained almost entirely economic. He was charged with getting Britain the tank that represented the best value for money at the least risk and both he and others in the procurement executive felt that to achieve the stated goals Vickers would need to make quantum technical advances in armour, gun manufacture and fire control systems. General Dynamics had already spent $2.98 billion on research and development into the Abrams tank and were committed to spending a further $1.5 billion on developing the Mark 2 Abrams. The General Dynamics experts believed that a continuing research and development budget of $200 million a year was essential simply to keep pace with the changing threat. That was roughly equal to the total Vickers research and development commitment to the Challenger 2.

The MoD's Equipment Policy Committee met at the beginning of November to make a final recommendation. Although it is generally believed that they produced a balanced report that did not favour either side, in fact, the committee came down firmly in favour of Abrams. But when that recommendation reached ministers on the sixth floor of the MoD it caused alarm and, as one senior official puts it: 'The recommendation was massaged so that it appeared we had no strong views either way.'

For the next two weeks, Peter Levene was trying to improve on the best and final offers made by both Vickers and General Dynamics. He personally telephoned members of the General Dynamics board and forced them to improve their offer. By the beginning of December the prices both were offering were almost identical at around $1.6m a tank for 626 tanks with the first entering service in 1992.

On December 20, the cabinet met to make a final decision on the contract. Lord Young argued strongly that Vickers should be given the full contract while Younger argued that in view of the technical and economic risk a compromise was needed. The Prime Minister supported Younger and the cabinet decided to give Vickers $162m to build nine prototype tanks for testing over the next nineteen months. A number of strict milestones for the performance of the engine, armour, fire control system, gun and ammunition were spelled out. In autumn 1990, the army would do a complete evaluation of the progress to date and only then would the full contract be awarded. At the same time, General Dynamics would continue to develop its upgraded Abrams and be asked to submit its own proposals.

This was probably the best compromise that the army and the Abrams supporters inside the MoD could have hoped for. 'We bought quite a bit of time for the money,' said one official.

In October 1989, Vickers announced that they had successfully achieved the first milestone and had met eleven key technical and performance requirements. This was a significant advance for Vickers but their major problems still lie ahead.

The tank decision raises serious questions about the way Britain and other allied nations buy their defence equipment.

In comparison with the M1A1 Abrams Mark 2 the Vickers Challenger 2 came second in every single major test. In its armour, gun and engine performance the Vickers tank was significantly outperformed and in the opinion of every single one of the qualified tank experts judging between the two systems, the Abrams was the first choice. It was also the first choice of those in charge getting the best value for money for the taxpayer.

Yet the first round of the battle was won for Vickers by using arguments many of which were either wrong or misleading, and with the support of politicians who had no clear idea of the defence issues involved.

Individually, the European countries are too small to afford the massive research and development costs involved in producing a major new weapons system. Collaboration cuts those costs and exports can produce economies of scale that make the equipment affordable. Going it alone is a luxury that countries like Britain can no longer afford.

In Britain, the House of Commons Select Committee on Defence routinely produces reports that are critical of equipment purchased by the Ministry of Defence. The list of equipment that has been late or has failed to work properly is unhealthily long, and the waste of taxpayers' money runs into the billions. Perhaps Vickers will get it right. Perhaps the next British tank will out-perform the American Abrams and be good enough to defeat the best the Warsaw Pact has to offer. And perhaps not.

In the end, this competition, like hundreds of others that occur within NATO each year, was not simply about jobs and money. It was really about buying a weapon that British soldiers could fight in with some hope of defeating the enemy and surviving. If governments are to retain the confidence of the military and to expect them to fight their wars, politicians need to demonstrate both intelligence and courage. In the case of the British tank competition, both qualities were dangerously lacking.

12

The Deal of the Century

In a 1988 arms deal that was to be the biggest this century, it was ironic that the British negotiators flew to the Caribbean island of Bermuda on 4 July, America's Independence Day. The deal signed that weekend represented a watershed in the arms business: proof that the fortunes and influence of the United States had declined in the Middle East in favour of the British, with the Russians pushed firmly into third place in the world league table of arms exports and with the French, the traditional rivals of the British, denied any share at all of the spoils.

The summons to Bermuda had come earlier that week from His Royal Highness Prince Sultan bin Abdul Aziz, the second Deputy Prime Minister, Minister of Defence and Aviation, and Inspector General of the Saudi Arabian armed forces. Sultan is the world's longest serving defence minister. His fondness for good food and hawking, his small, greying goatee beard and jolly laugh make him the quintessential Arab: also he knows his business, and his love of negotiation makes him a formidable opponent.

He had been due in Britain that weekend but had torn some ligaments in his knee when he fell while attending a funeral in Saudi Arabia. After treatment, he had decided to convalesce in Bermuda, an island he had first visited with his brother the late King Faisal after the latter had undergone open heart surgery in the United States.

The British party included Sir Colin Chandler, the head of

Defence Export Services, the Ministry of Defence's own arms exporting agency, Air Vice Marshal Ron Stuart-Paul, the head of the Saudi armed forces project in the MoD, and John Weston, the director of British Aerospace in charge of the Saudi project. The three men checked in to the Bermuda Sheraton and the following day were chauffeured to a discreet white villa on the outskirts of the island's capital, Hamilton.

At the end of the villa's driveway, the car stopped alongside a red carpet that had been rolled out across the lawn leading to the front door, an obvious indication of the importance the Saudis attached to their visitors. As Colin Chandler got out of the car, the tall figure of Prince Sultan emerged from the villa and walked carefully down the carpet, supported by two walking sticks.

Over cups of the strong dark coffee favoured by Prince Sultan, the two sides finalised the arrangements for the supply of a range of defence equipment that over the next fifteen years will ensure Britain's position as the number two arms exporter in the world, after the United States, and the most influential arms exporter to the Middle East.

That weekend the Saudis signed a Memorandum of Understanding – the first stage before a formal contract – for the supply of a minimum $30 billion of arms from Britain. The deal, known as Al Yamamah, included Tornado fighters, Hawk jet trainers, the construction of two air bases, helicopters, missiles, mine counter-measure vessels and communications equipment for electronic warfare. As is increasingly common in arms deals today, the equipment would be paid for not in cash but in the Saudis' own major export, oil. Also, the British government agreed to promote joint ventures up to 25 per cent of the value of the British technical component of the contract. This means an initial target of around $3 billion of British investment in the kingdom. However, there is no timescale for the investment and British industry has proved reticent in the past about investing in a country which has no real record of being able to produce manufactured goods.[1]

The foundations of the 1988 deal were laid three years earlier. The Saudis were concerned that Islamic fundamentalism was on the rise in Iran and could well spread to Saudi Arabia where the workers in the eastern oilfields, bordering Iran, were sympathetic to the brand of Islam practised by Ayatollah Khomeini. At the same time, Saudi support for Iraq in its war with Iran made Saudi a likely target if Iran chose to expand the war. The aircraft in the Saudi inventory were either old or unsuitable to fight a defensive war against Iran. What the kingdom wanted was not simply fighters for air to air combat but aircraft that, if Saudi Arabia was provoked, could be used to penetrate Iran's defences and attack cities and military targets. In other words the Saudis wanted a deterrent that would keep the Islamic fanatics at bay.

By April 1985, the British learned through their intelligence network in the kingdom that the Saudis had given a letter of intent to the French government for the purchase of Mirage 2000 fighters. In a last minute lobbying effort, the British argued that the French aircraft were unsuitable and instead proposed that the Saudi air force buy the Tornado IDS, the ground attack version of the European fighter.

The Saudis had already approached the Americans, their traditional arms supplier, to ask if they would supply the F–15E, the US equivalent of the Tornado. Unfortunately for the US government, Israel saw any attempt by the Saudis to buy ground attack fighters as a potential threat and the influential American Jewish lobby swung into action to block the sale. Washington eventually replied that not only could the Saudis not have the F–15E but the US would supply no ground attack aircraft of any sort, nor any weapons for the F–15Cs already in the Saudi inventory that might be used for ground attack. The US also told the Saudis that they would place restrictions on where the aircraft could be based, thus ensuring they were well out of range of Israel (and also out of range of key parts of Iran as well). And finally, the Saudis were told to come back in two years when the political climate might have changed.

By contrast, Margaret Thatcher, the British Prime Minister, wrote personally to King Fahd, the Saudi ruler, in July 1985. She said that not only could the kingdom have the Tornados but they could base them where they wanted, they could take delivery immediately and they could have the weapons they needed. The Prime Minister seems to be highly regarded by many leaders of developing nations. 'She is seen as being powerful, decisive and conservative,' said one of the Saudi negotiating team. 'And then, of course, she is a woman and in the kind of society most of these people come from such power in a female is unusual so there is a certain curiosity value.'

Whenever Prince Sultan came to London on a private visit he made a point of dropping in at No 10 Downing Street for tea, which gave Mrs Thatcher an opportunity to cement the Anglo-Saudi relationship.

The intervention of the Prime Minister had a critical effect on these negotiations and has proved influential in others. She, unlike other western leaders, takes an entirely pragmatic view about the arms business, believing that arms exports – provided they are to a friendly power – are good for the balance of payments and can give Britain considerable influence in the world.

There were frantic negotiations between the British and the Saudis during the Paris Air Show that summer and, under the noses of their French hosts, the British stole the contract.

Britain had initially hoped for a contract for around twenty-four Tornadoes but to their astonishment, when the final documents were produced by the Saudis in September 1985, the contract was for seventy-two aircraft and a comprehensive fit of weapons plus the construction of new airfields. The whole package was worth around $10 billion, roughly three times what had been expected. The increase in the contract value was entirely due to the attitude of the American government. Their unhelpful response to the Saudi request played into the hands of the more aggressive marketing men from

Britain who were free from the interference of lobbyists and had the active support of the Prime Minister.

Between 1985 and 1988, the Saudis persisted with their requests to buy arms from the United States. Although some were supplied, between February 1986 and April 1988, five major deals were refused by Congress. These included 48 F–15 fighters, 1,600 Maverick missiles, 800 Stinger missiles, armour-piercing uranium ammunition, and ground equipment and maintenance equipment for airborne early warning aircraft. Each rejection hardened the Saudi view that any deal needing to be authorised by Congress was likely to fail, despite the protestations of friendship coming out of the White House.

As one Saudi official pointed out: 'We would prefer buying weapons from the USA. American technology is generally superior. But we are not going to pay billions of dollars to be insulted. We are not masochists.'[2]

This reticence by the US led to a steady decline in US arms sales to the kingdom. In 1979 sales reached a peak of $5.4 billion falling to $724,000 in 1986 and $636,000 in 1987.

Shortly after the last rejection by Congress in April 1988, the Saudis got in touch with the British Ministry of Defence suggesting that they would be interested in buying still more equipment. As usual, the British were completely accommodating. There was no question of preconditions or post conditions: the weapons the Saudis wanted would be supplied if the price they could afford would make a profit for the British arms manufacturers.

It is a measure of the difference between the US and British attitudes to the Saudi deal that the Israeli lobby in Washington was so successful. In Britain, Israel's lobbying arm, the British/Israel Public Affairs Centre, first heard of the deal five days after the Memorandum of Understanding had been signed in Bermuda. They were therefore denied any opportunity to influence the deal and the Israeli government was simply left to make the predictable criticisms.

Mr Yossi Ben-Aharon, a key aide of Israel's Prime Minister

Yitzhak Shamir, condemned Britain for supplying weapons to the Arabs while continuing a ban on exporting arms to Israel. 'We cannot discount the possibility that if we are faced with a multi-front confrontation with a number of Arab states, Saudi Arabia, at the worst moment, would hit the soft underbelly in the south, using the new arms it is acquiring from the British,' he said.[3]

Of course, for Israel to lobby against the US supplying the weapons simply ensures that Saudi will buy the arms it needs from a country that Tel Aviv is less able to influence. At the same time, to combat the new Saudi arms, Israel will have to enhance its own defences and this will mean an increased defence investment at a time when the country can ill afford it.

In any event, as is so often the case in arms deals, Israel's public posture was compromised by what she, too, had been doing behind the scenes. In July 1985, shortly after the US Congress rejected the sale of F–15 fighters and Lance ground based missiles to the Saudis after pressure from the Israeli lobby, Saudi turned not just to Israel but also to China for help. That month, the Saudi ambassador to Washington, Prince Bandar ibn Sultan, flew to Beijing and negotiated the purchase of up to 50 intermediate range CSS–2 missiles. Known to the Chinese as the Dong Feng 3, the 66-foot long missile is armed with a conventional warhead and has a range of 2,700 miles thus enabling the Saudis to hit any target in Israel, although their real target was Iran.

The Chinese and the Saudis fooled American intelligence about the existence of the missiles by including them in a cargo of Silkworm missiles for Iraq which were transshipped through the kingdom. Once the cargo reached Saudi – having been counted in by American intelligence – empty boxes were trucked to Iraq while the real missiles headed south to a new 'ammunition store' the Saudis claimed they were building in the desert south of Riyadh.

The missiles are capable of carrying nuclear warheads but had been specifically modified by the Chinese so that they can only be used with conventional warheads and these modifications were made with the help of Israeli technicians who for the past five years had been helping China modernise its armaments industry. So, while the Israeli lobby in the United States stopped the US selling Lance missiles with a range of 130 kilometers to the Saudis, Israelis working in China were helping the Chinese to modify missiles with a range of 2,700 kilometers for sale to the kingdom.[4]

Both the United States and Israel appear to have learned some lessons from the Chinese and British deals. The US hopes to sell the Saudis 315 main battle tanks, seven multi-launch rocket systems, air defence radars and armoured personnel carriers before the end of the decade. This time round the Bush administration has warned Congress that if the deals are stopped then the Saudis will simply go elsewhere, most probably to Britain. For its part, the Israeli lobby has privately met with Prince Sultan, the Saudi ambassador in America, to discuss future arms sales to the kingdom.

But, important as they were, the Saudi arms deals were not just about cash, oil and weapons. They were in many respects the culmination of changing patterns in the arms business that today have transformed the nature of the market. Technological advances in weapons have led to an enormous rise in the cost for any nation building up an armed force sufficient to deter anything other than a small local peasant rebellion. Emerging nations now demand not rejected stock from the superpowers' armouries but sophisticated weapons that have prestige as well as capability.

In the Saudi-British deal, for example, one of the sticking points had been the Saudi requirement that the British buy back twenty-four Lightning fighters first sold to the kingdom by the British in the 1960s. Prince Sultan insisted that these aircraft had an antique value and could be readily sold.

'Pass them on to Gadaffi in Libya,' he suggested to the British. 'He'll buy anything.' With bigger sums at stake, the British did indeed buy back the aircraft, for around $3m. They remain under protective canvas covers lined up on the runway at British Aerospace's airfield at Wharton where they will remain until they fall apart. Not even Gadaffi is interested in such vintage weaponry.

Over the years such curious requirements have become an integral part of many arms deals. For example, the British government has exchanged bananas for jet fighters (with Ecuador) and in one extraordinary case, Hawk jet trainers were sold to Finland and payment was made in part in Finlandia vodka and metal circular staircases. To sell off these goods the aircraft's manufacturers, Hawker Siddeley, persuaded a local department store, Bentall's in Kingston-on-Thames, to organise a 'Friendly Finland Fortnight' where both staircases and vodka could be picked up at bargain prices.

The fact that Saudi Arabia – a country that twenty years ago would only have been able to buy obsolete stock from the arms manufacturer's bottom drawer – is able to buy such modern weapons is a mark of how rapidly the market has changed. As the Saudi deal clearly showed, the amount of leverage that the supplier countries can now impose on the buying nations is much less. In many respects, power has now moved from the seller to the buyer. Hard bargains can be struck and barter is the common currency.

That change in the power structure has led to two distinct trends. Every weapon system designed today is made with exports in mind. Countries like Britain or France cannot afford to make weapons that are not going to sell to foreign countries – the research and development is simply too expensive. That in turn means that developing nations are getting weapons designed with them in mind, weapons that are designer killing machines, made for efficiency and cost effectiveness in their own environment.

That evolutionary process in weapons development went through a period of something close to revolutionary change in the 1980s. The world arms market was transformed with new manufacturers producing new, cheap, weapons, and the catalyst for this change in the arms business was the Iran-Iraq war.

PART FIVE: THE IRAN-IRAQ WAR

13

The Arms Bonanza

Like many of the great conflicts, the start of the Iran-Iraq war on September 22, 1980 was low key, an unlikely beginning to what was to become the biggest conventional war since World War II. President Saddam Hussein of Iraq had told his neighbours that he planned to teach the ambitious Ayatollah Khomeini a lesson by giving Iran a bloody nose. His troops advanced with the blessing of the moderate Arab states, all of whom feared the threat posed by the Khomeini brand of Islamic fundamentalism.

It is an old axiom of warfare never to attack a revolution, and Saddam Hussein found that the Iranians were a much tougher opposition than he had expected. Although the Iraqi forces seized large tracts of Iranian territory within the first two weeks, Hussein's offer then of a negotiated peace was turned down. Indeed, the Iranians drew on a seemingly inexhaustible supply of troops filled with revolutionary fervour, who rushed to the front and held off later Iraqi attacks.

Over the next eight years, the fortunes of the war changed between the sides, with both countries regularly proclaiming the start of another 'final offensive' which never quite materialised.

The tactics used in the war were reminiscent of those employed on the Somme in the First World War: trench warfare and soldiers in wave attacks which took no real advantage of the new weaponry available to both sides.

Inevitably, such a traditional approach to modern war

was enormously expensive both in arms and men. The exact number of casualties on both sides is difficult to obtain with any accuracy but western intelligence sources generally seem to agree on a total figure of around 500,000. To kill that many people, both sides spent around $500 billion, a substantial proportion of this on weapons, in what was the single largest bonanza for freelance arms dealers seen anywhere in the world at any time.

The war came at a time of declining export markets for arms and provided a useful outlet for companies and countries desperate to keep their flagging industries working. Although most countries in both west and east remained officially neutral in the war, a new underground network of dummy companies, shady dealers and willing shippers sprang up, often with the approval of governments.

In fact, there was an extraordinary feeding frenzy by the sharks of the arms business. Fifty countries sold arms to the protagonists in the war. Of those fifty, four countries sold only to Iraq, eighteen to Iran and twenty-eight, including France, China, Italy, South Africa, Britain, the United States and West Germany sold weapons to both sides.[1]

From the start of the war, most of Iran's purchases of arms were arranged through the Iranian Military Procurement Offices, also known as the Logistics Support Centre in the headquarters of the National Iranian Oil Company, based at 4 Victoria Street, London. The sixth-floor offices, next door to the British government's Department of Trade and Industry, housed between twenty and forty Iranians and a further 200 locally hired staff whose sole job was to find and buy arms.

On the face of it, this was a peculiar state of affairs, since the British government, along with most other western nations, had a ban on arms sales to Iran. In fact, the British made a clear decision to allow the offices to operate precisely because they were so centrally located. The British Security Service, commonly known as MI5, mounted a major intelligence operation against the centre and its employees. With the help of the intelligence monitoring centre at GCHQ in

Cheltenham, the Security Service was able to routinely listen to all telephone calls, intercept all telexes and facsimile messages and, using other systems, observe and listen to conversations between arms dealers and the Iranians.[2]

Despite such surveillance, the Iranians were occasionally able to circumvent the British watchers. In 1986, the then government-owned Royal Ordnance Factory in Bridgwater, Somerset, signed a contract with a Greek company to sell 2,362 kilograms of Tetryl, a detonating explosive. The contract was given an export license but the cargo, packed in twenty containers, was eventually diverted via Yugoslavia to Iran.[3]

The British government responded with justifiable anger. But, as with many other western countries, there was a strong element of hypocrisy in the British policy in the war. Officially neutral and with a ban of arms sales to either side, there was clearly a willingness to exploit the war if political criticism could be contained.

Two landing craft built by Yarrow shipyard were delivered to Iran in May 1985. The ships had originally been ordered by the Shah and were supposed to be used for disaster relief. The British maintained they had to fulfil the contract and had received reassurances from the Iranians that the vessels would not be used in the war. Of course, as the British might reasonably have guessed, once delivered, the ships were immediately taken over by the Iranian navy and used in the war.

In 1986, the British authorised the sale of six radar systems made by Plessey and worth $370m to Iran. Once again, the Iranians promised to use the equipment only for civilian purposes.[4]

The procurement office in London was closed in September 1987, following an Iranian attack on the British tanker *Gentle Breeze* in the Persian Gulf.

Until the closure of the offices, the British were able to build up a detailed picture of Iran's war effort by the nature of its arms purchases. This information was routinely shared with the United States and other western allies and enabled western countries to intercept a number of illegal arms deals.

The first deal attempted by the London buyers was illustrative of the problems they would face in the years to come. An Iranian expatriate, Behnam Nodjoumi, agreed to sell the Iranians 8,000 US TOW anti-tank missiles. The missiles did not exist and Iranian military officers sent to Belgium to inspect the cargo were kidnapped and made to send false messages back to London authorising the deal. Police arrested Nodjoumi just before the cash was due to be handed over. He was later sentenced to ten years in prison.[5]

The war did not simply encourage confidence men to sell weapons that did not exist. It was also an opportunity for governments to make huge legitimate profits. At the start of the war, Iran was almost entirely dependent on the west for arms. The United States had been the main supplier of arms to the Shah, with the result that the Iranian air force flew American aircraft and the army drove American tanks. Such a commitment to one source can bring advantages in purchasing discounts and ease of training but it also makes the country concerned dependent on a single source of spares. After the revolution Iran had to search the world for US-made equipment and steadily diversify its arms buying. All that meant paying a premium above the market price for every missile and shell.

Those premiums attracted every type of arms dealer to the Iranian honeypot: the underground dealers from the illegal arms market, governments who made no secret of their deals with the protagonists, and companies and governments which operated entirely in secret.

Even such nominally neutral countries as Sweden and Switzerland profited from the war. Iran bought two hundred Scandia trucks and large numbers of Boghammer fast patrol boats from Sweden. It also bought around four hundred RBS–70 laser-guided anti-aircraft missiles from the Bofors division of the Swedish arms company Nobel.

Switzerland sold Iran six Pontius PC–7 training aircraft in

August 1984 for $4m and helpfully included detailed plans for converting the aircraft from civilian to military use.[6]

The eagerness to feed at the trough made for some unlikely eating companions. Both China and North Vietnam, which had fought against each other, supplied weapons to Iran. In fact, for the first two years of the war, China supplied Iraq with around $3 billion of arms. Then, realising that Iran was prepared to pay higher prices for a wider range of goods, the Beijing government switched sides and began supplying fighters, small arms and missiles at the rate of around $1 billion a year to Iran.

For North Vietnam, which had captured billions of dollars worth of American arms in the fall of South Vietnam in 1975, the war opened up a new and highly profitable market. In the course of the war they supplied US M–48 tanks, M–113 armoured personnel carriers and millions of rounds of ammunition worth more than $1 billion.

Most countries were not as fortunate as North Vietnam in having a large stock of unwanted equipment. North Vietnam was also lucky in that there were no anxious congressmen, members of parliament or other elected officials to ask difficult questions about any arms deal. Even so, a remarkable number of countries managed to bypass their own regulations. A typical example began in November 1984, when a Lear jet landed at Tripoli airport. There were three passengers on board, Eric Schmidt, the Austrian Secretary of State, Peter Unterweger, the managing director of Noricum, the arms manufacturing subsidiary of the state-owned Voest-Alpine steel works, and the company's sales manager, Johann Eisenburger. They had arrived in Tripoli hoping to meet the Libyan defence minister and discuss the sale of artillery and ammunition.

Unterweger had been appointed head of Noricum in February with a brief to make the loss-making company profitable. Just before his appointment, a critical deal with India had gone sour. A contract had provisionally been agreed with the Indian government of Indira Gandhi for the sale of 350 cannons worth around $424m. After her assassination, her son Rajiv awarded the contract to a Swedish company, leaving Noricum with the armaments, many of which had been manufactured in advance. As Unterweger was later to explain, 'the situation at the Noricum plant in Liezen was simply catastrophic. The 1,200 workplaces were under threat and there were no big orders coming in.'[7]

The trip to Libya was just one of a series that had been made over the previous few months in a desperate effort to win new contracts. This time, the Noricum officials had the official stamp of approval of the Austrian Secretary of State, who hoped to meet the Libyan Defence Minister and persuade him to buy some Austrian artillery. In the event, the Austrian delegation waited for twenty-four hours and the Libyans never showed up. The following day, Schmidt flew back to Vienna while the Noricum men stayed behind, promising the Secretary of State they would set up a future meeting.

In fact, the men had a hidden agenda which had already been written for them by Monzer al-Kassar, the Syrian arms dealer. He had given the men an introduction to a senior Libyan general in the office of the secretary of the army. As soon as the Austrian Secretary of State flew out of Tripoli the Noricum officials met with the Libyan to discuss a much more lucrative deal: the sale of arms to Iran.

Under Austrian law, it is illegal to sell arms to a country at war and there was therefore an outright ban on all arms exports to Iran. Thus at the November meeting it was agreed that, if a deal was finalised, the Libyans would agree – for a fee – to sign any documentation setting out Tripoli as the destination for the weapons. In the arms business, all export deals require a document known as an End User Certificate, that spells out the type of weapon being exported and its destination. A fake end user certificate, if it is to work properly, requires the cooperation of a senior official in a foreign government, a man able to sign any forms and if necessary respond to a telephone call or telex message querying his government's involvement. In this case, the Austrians found a willing partner in the Libyan general.[8]

When the Austrians left Libya, they told their government that they had secured a deal to sell the Libyans 150 GHN–45 cannons with spares and ammunition. The deal was worth around $250m. In fact, with the help of al-Kassar, Noricum had actually done a deal with the Iranian government for the supply of 300 cannons. The Iranians were paying around 20 per cent more than the original Indian contractors for the same product.

Any export deal has to have government approval and it is difficult to believe that a deal of this size did not raise some serious questions in the Austrian government – not least because even a sale to Libya of such a volume would have a significant impact on the balance of power in the area. Peter Unterweger has refused to identify any people who may have authorised the deal. Investigations by the Austrian government suggest that, at the least, the then head of Voest, Dr Heribert Apfalter, authorised the deal.

To smooth the path of the cannons, Noricum, with the help of al-Kassar, forged the end user certificates, and set up two dummy companies – Flatstones in Liechtenstein and Convalor in Panama – to siphon off $56m in bribe money.

Noricum even agreed a performance bond with the Iranian government where they would be obliged to pay $66m if the contract was not completed. By the time the first details of the contract emerged at the end of 1986, the bond had reduced to $28.3m. However, even that left the Austrian government in the embarrassing position of being contractually obliged to pay the money on behalf of a state-owned company to the Iranian government for a contract that was against the law.

The first batch of guns was safely delivered to Tehran. Later that year, in a separate deal, a shipment of gun barrels was sent to Brazil. They got as far as Yugoslavia when Brazil failed to make the next payment due under the contract. Rather than bring the barrels back to Austria, Noricum simply made a new deal with Iran and the weapons were moved to Tehran under the original end user certificate in a deal worth $60m.

For Monzer al-Kassar, the Noricum deal was just one of many carried out during the course of the eight year Iran-Iraq war. Like many arms dealers, Monzer took no sides in the war, preferring to sell arms to any who would buy them. In 1985, for example, his company Alkastronic sold Bulgarian RPG-7 rocket launchers to Iran for $45m. The cargo was labelled 'technical equipment and agricultural machinery' with an African country named on the end user certificate.

But even without the aid of such professionals as al-Kassar, other countries managed to do deals with the Iranian government. An Italian firm sold 30,000 mines to Syria using a Spanish company in Barcelona to supply an end user certificate showing the arms were destined for Nigeria. After delivery to Damascus, the mines were passed on to Iran where they were used against Italian ships patrolling the Gulf as part of a European naval task force.[9]

The Swedish government sold Boghammer patrol boats which were used to attack western shipping, including US naval forces in the Gulf.

Perhaps the most interesting relationship that emerged out of the war was that between Israel and Iran. On the surface, the two nations had nothing in common: Iran's leader, the Ayatollah Khomeini had made no secret of his support for those who wished to see Israel destroyed and Israel had every reason to fear the rise of Islamic fundamentalism in Iran which might unite the Moslem nations against the Jewish state. In addition, Iran was supported in the war by Syria, Israel's most dangerous enemy. A victory for Iran could only harm Israel's interests by reinforcing the influence of Syria.

But Israel had been one of the Shah's major arms suppliers and had even planned the joint development of a surface-to-surface missile. When Khomeini took power in 1979, Israel's sales of $500m a year in arms were immediately cancelled. However, the seizing of the US embassy and the holding of American hostages meant that any prospect Iran had of getting spares and new weapons from the US disappeared. At the same time, Israel was concerned about the fate of an estimated 50,000 Jews living in Iran.

There then began a relationship of convenience that earned Israel foreign exchange, gave her influence over the fate of Iranian Jews, and also allowed Iran to keep its military machine operating.

In 1980, Israel supplied 250 spare tyres for F–4 fighter bombers, artillery shells, mortars, rifles and Chieftain tank spare parts. After pressure from the Carter administration these sales were stopped until after the release of the US hostages, when they quietly resumed. Israel quickly became one of Iran's most important allies in the war, supplying critical equipment such as Hawk surface-to-surface missiles, 360 tons of spare parts for US made tanks, and hundreds of tons of small arms and artillery ammunition.

Nearly all the equipment that Israel sold to Iran originated in the United States and was either directly imported or made under licence. In theory, Israel is supposed to ask permission before passing on such equipment to a third country. Permission would never have been granted in this case and so it was never sought. This was a risky business for Israel, which relies on the economic, political and military support of the United States for its survival.

Throughout the war Israel appears to have judged that the Iranians were unlikely to achieve a military victory. However, a victory of some kind by Iraq was conceivable. If that occurred, the status of President Saddam Hussein would rise considerably. Before the war Hussein had ambitions to make Iraq the most powerful nation in the region holding sway over neighbours like Saudi Arabia. If Iraq were to win the war, Israel feared that Hussein might feel confident enough to launch an attack against Israel. This policy decision ensured that Israel became one of Iran's most important suppliers – selling weapons worth around $800m every year. But this commitment to the unstable and unreliable Khomeini regime also led the Israelis to make some serious foreign policy mistakes. One of these led to the exposure of the biggest sting operation ever mounted by the US customs service and the other almost led to the resignation of Ronald Reagan as President of the United States.

14

The Brokers of Death

For two days Adnan Khashoggi, well-known Middle East fixer and arms dealer, hosted his own fiftieth birthday party. In part the occasion was a celebration that the overweight and unfit Saudi Arabian had reached such an age. But it was also an opportunity for one of the world's most flamboyant dealers to show off his wealth and status to the world.

The glamorous occasion also provided an opportunity for some of the guests to do a little business. One of the guests was Samuel Evans, a London-based lawyer who for years had represented Khashoggi in many of his business deals, although Evans had never helped with arms deals, the most lucrative Khashoggi ventures. Evans had made plenty of money on the back of Khashoggi's success and was eager for more. He had always only received fees – the crumbs from the middleman's table – and never the bribes and commissions that are the fixer's real path to riches.

Another guest was Nickos Minardos, a Greek-born actor in television soaps who lived in Beverly Hills. Minardos was an old acquaintance of Khashoggi's and with his tanned good looks and easy charm he brought a touch of male Hollywood glamour to the party. But, like Evans, he was tired of living on the edge of the fast-paced world of wealth and fame that he saw around him and he was conceited enough to believe that instead of being a bit player he could win a leading role.[1]

Evans and Minardos made an unlikely couple. The former, tall and slim with distinguished silver hair, lived in Chester

Square in London's West End with offices in nearby
Grosvenor Place. He came from a wealthy St Louis family
and was a well-known figure on the London social scene.
Minardos was simply a good-looking small-time actor with
ambition, the kind that Hollywood attracts and destroys by
the hundred.

It is hardly surprising, given the identity of their host, that
the two men should talk about the arms business and the
possibilities that were around on the market. The talk then
turned to the Iran-Iraq war and both men agreed that here
was a real potential bonanza, a chance of wealth for everybody if only they could work out a way to take advantage of
it.

Earlier that year Evans had been introduced to Cyrus
Hashemi, an Iranian who was the cousin of the speaker of
the Iranian parliament, Hashemi Rafsanjani. Apparently
exceptionally well-connected, Hashemi was an impressive
figure. He spoke fluent English, wore expensive suits and silk
shirts, and was comfortable in the world in which Evans
himself lived. Evans in turn introduced Hashemi to
Khashoggi and in June 1985 the three formed the World
Trade Group to sell arms and agricultural machinery to Iran
and to market oil.

Around the same time, Khashoggi met with another
Iranian exile, Manucher Ghorbanifar, who also promised
lucrative arms deals with Iran. Ghorbanifar was a former
informant for the Savak, the Shah's secret police, and since
the Khomeini revolution he had been living in exile in Paris.
He had established himself as a conduit for political information and business contacts with the new Iranian regime.
A jolly, highly plausible man, Ghorbanifar was in fact an old-
fashioned confidence trickster, a rogue who was trying to turn
the west's ignorance of Iran to his own advantage. He had
approached a number of western intelligence agencies in the
past with information, all of which had proved to be inaccurate – and in fact the CIA had put out a 'burn notice' on

him, meaning that he should be regarded as unreliable and ignored.[2]

Despite his shady background, Khashoggi, who was in some financial difficulties himself, was taken in by Ghorbanifar. Ignoring Hashemi, the two men went off on their own and tried to set up deals using the Israelis and Ghorbanifar's claims of influence with the Iranian regime. This was the start of what became the secret effort by a small group in the American government to ship arms to Iran in exchange for the release of US hostages held by Iranian-backed terrorists.

Forced to go it alone, Hashemi then approached Evans and told him that the Iranians had asked him to arrange for the purchase of a massive quantity of American-made arms including aircraft, helicopters, missiles and ammunition. The deal would be worth up to $2.5 billion and Evans would get a 10 per cent commission. He immediately agreed to try and find a supplier of the weapons.

In October, Evans met with Hermann Moll, an arms dealer acquaintance, at the exclusive Les Ambassadeurs club in London's Park Lane. The flashy club is popular with Arabs and businessmen and unlike other more select clubs, business is expected to be discussed and deals concluded over lunch. Moll was a German national who had made his home in London. By profession an advertising salesman, he had got into the arms business after he had started selling space for Jane's, the respected publishers of military reference books. His first deal had occurred only two years earlier, when he had sold 50,000 pairs of army boots to Saudi Arabia.

Like all arms dealers, Moll lived in a strange half world of fact and fantasy where the big deal is always the next one and where hope and optimism are unjustified by the success rate, which is generally very low.

Moll arranged a package that included 15 F4-E fighters from Egypt, 200 Sidewinder missiles, 30 M48 tanks, 140 engines for them and radars for the fighters. The total package was worth around $320m. Moll added 15 per cent commission which was divided so that Hashemi would get 5 per cent,

Evans 2 percent and Moll 8 per cent. Even so, this would leave Moll with $25m. 'Even I, who have a hard head for money, trembled slightly at the tempting prospect,' said Moll.[3]

At the same time, Evans had brought Nickos Minardos in on the deal. Minardos contacted two Israeli arms dealers, Guri Eisenberg and Israel Eisenberg. In January 1986, through their company Bazelet International Trading, the two Israelis offered a package of weapons which included 3,750 Tow anti-tank missiles worth $61,875,000, 18 F–4 fighters worth $360,000,000, and a final package worth $415,130,880 which included 5 C–130E Hercules aircraft, 2 Hawk missile batteries, 46 Skyhawk fighter bombers, 30 Sparrow guided missiles, 200 tyres and tubes for F4 fighters, 200 Sidewinder air-to-air missiles, 200 Maverick laser guided bombs, 600 surface-to-air Chapparel missiles, flare dispensers and radar equipment.

The Eisenbergs guaranteed to supply valid end user certificates which would allow the goods to be exported from Israel, and on January 23, they told Evans that the weapons would have certificates showing the destination of the arms as Turkey. Several Turkish government officials at that time were doing a lucrative business in forged certificates.

Minardos also got in touch with a retired Israeli army general, Avraham Bar-Am, who worked with an American living in Israel, William Northrop. Bar-Am was a well-known figure in Israel. He had been cited for bravery in both the 1967 and 1973 Arab-Israeli wars and was still in the army reserve with an advisory position on the Northern Army Command.

Through their Liechtenstein-based company, Dergo Establishment, Northrop and Bar-Am offered to sell to the Iranians via Evans an arms package worth $343m which included 50 long range artillery howitzers, 1 Cobra helicopter engine, 5,000 Tow missiles, 13 F5 aircraft, 4 Huey helicopter engines and 2 Turboprop engines for C130 Hercules transport aircraft.

Both the Eisenbergs and General Bar-Am were offering for

sale weapons which were almost entirely of American origin. In a country as small as Israel the arms business is watched closely by the government and treated as an important contributor to the national economy. It is inconceivable that a deal on this scale could have taken place without the official sanction of the Israeli government. That they were prepared to do such a deal in defiance not only of their own agreements not to transfer such weapons to foreign countries without US approval but also to do so in defiance of an American arms embargo against Iran is a measure of Israeli confidence that they could weather any US criticism.

Throughout the discussions with Hashemi all the arms dealers had found it difficult to pin him down about money. The normal process in such deals is that the buyer's bank telexes the seller's bank to confirm that funds are available. Hashemi had an account at the Chemical Bank in New York and, while bank officials had confirmed over the telephone that money was available, they had so far refused to put such confirmation in writing. In separate conversations at the beginning of April, Hashemi promised that if the several dealers, including Evans and Moll, would fly to New York, he would provide both cash and letters of credit as a sign of good faith.

Hermann Moll was the first to arrive in New York, on British Airways flight 179 on April 22. He was met at John F Kennedy airport by a man who introduced himself as Hashemi's driver, and was escorted to a smart Mercedes 500 SEL limousine.

The driver dropped Moll off at the Beekman Tower Hotel where a suite had been reserved for him on the fourteenth floor. After a quick gin and tonic Moll was summoned by telephone to Hashemi's suite on the floor below. Over drinks the two men finalised the terms of the deal and Moll made clear that he would arrange end user certificates for the arms and, if necessary, deliver them to Iran himself. The two men agreed to meet again the following morning.

Moll went to the hotel cocktail bar at the top of the building for a nightcap. He now takes up the story: 'They know how to serve drinks here, anyway, I thought, as I took my first sip of the stiff gin and tonic, in a tall glass crammed with ice and a large slice of lemon. Looking back over the meeting with Hashemi I was fairly satisfied. It was true I had not yet actually laid hands on any money but it wasn't conceivable, surely, that he would bring me all this way if he didn't mean business. And he had seemed quite interested in the additional items I had proposed to him. There could be a great deal of money indeed in our quiet friend Cyrus Hashemi . . .

'My train of thought was interrupted by a disturbance behind me, a jumble of rapid footsteps that I couldn't instantly identify. Before I could turn round I felt something cold on the back of my neck. My instant reaction was that a waiter must have spilled a drink on me but in less than a second I realised that what I felt was metal being pressed hard against my flesh.

' "Don't make any move, US Federal Customs. Mr Hermann Moll, you are under arrest."

'Twelve customs agents surrounded me, six of them pointing revolvers at my face . . . I recognised one of my assailants. He was the young man who had met me two hours earlier at JFK airport.'[4]

Nickos Minardos was next to stop off in New York to sort out his problems with Hashemi. He, too, was met at the airport by the helpful chauffeur who had greeted Moll. Minardos met with Hashemi and was then chauffeured to the Vista Hotel in the World Trade Center. On the way the car made a diversion to the underground car park at the US Customs House where he, too, was arrested.

Meanwhile, Evans, the Eisenbergs, Northrop and Bar-Am had been warned by Israeli intelligence not to go to the US and instead it was agreed that the whole group would meet outside US jurisdiction, in the British colony of Bermuda.

When Evans and the Israelis arrived on the island on a flight from London, they were surprised to find themselves refused entry and ordered back onto the aircraft, which was continuing on to the United States. All the men refused to reboard the aircraft and were then arrested for illegal entry into the island.

That day, the US government applied for their extradition and five weeks later they joined Hermann Moll in jail in New York awaiting trial. In all, warrants were issued for the arrest of seventeen people who were accused of illegally exporting arms worth more than $2 billion to Iran and with conspiring to issue false end user certificates.

Immediately after the arrests, the Commissioner of Customs, William von Raab, held a press conference at which he said: 'You've probably heard of the merchants of death. Well, these people are the brokers of death. They would have operated a terrorist flea market selling everything from conventional weapons to some of the most sophisticated weapons in the world. The Iranians would have used these weapons to make war against their neighbours or to spread international terror against the free west. Without a doubt, the bloody hands of international terrorists would have been on the trigger of the TOW missiles, really an ideal weapon for this dirty business.'[5]

The whole team had been the victim of the most successful undercover operation run by the US Customs Service as part of Operation Staunch, set up in 1983 and designed to stop the flow of arms to Iran.

From the start, Cyrus Hashemi had been working as an undercover agent for the US customs. Cyrus and his older brother Djamshid and younger brother Reza first came to the attention of the American government at the time of the hostage crisis in 1979 when they offered their help to the CIA in negotiating with the Iranian government. But the brothers operated a company in Manhattan and so the CIA checked with the FBI who decided to bug their New York office. These bugs turned up evidence that even then the Hashemis were involved in smuggling arms to Iran.

When it eventually came to arrest the brothers in 1984,

only Djamshid was in the US, staying with his wife and family in a Virginia suburb of Washington, DC. To lure the other brothers to America, the customs service used exactly the same technique that was to work so well two years later. An undercover agent managed to persuade Reza to fly on business from London to Bermuda where he would be arrested and deported to London via New York. In the event, Reza flew via New York on his own initiative and was arrested at the airport.

Cyrus Hashemi himself was due to fly to New York from London on Concorde that week but cancelled his reservation at the last minute, after he received a telephone call from the office of the New York District Attorney, Rudolph Giuliani. Exactly what kind of deal was done has never been revealed but Hashemi was clearly offered a reduction in any sentence he might receive on the arms smuggling charges provided he cooperate in the later sting against Evans and the Israelis.

At every stage of the operation, Hashemi was monitored by undercover customs agents and all his telephone calls were recorded and meetings secretly videotaped. The customs even opened a false bank account in the name of Galaxy, Hashemi's company. This account was supposed to have $1 billion in it, placed there by the Iranian government to buy arms. In fact, it never had more than $100 and Chemical Bank officials agreed to lie about the balance if inquiries were made.

It was without doubt one of the Customs Service's most successful operations and all involved were confident of getting convictions on every count. But then things began to go badly wrong.

On Wednesday July 16, Hashemi collapsed at his London office with an apparent heart attack. He was taken to the nearby Cromwell Hospital where, after tests, he was moved to the neurological unit. Bone marrow tests indicated that he was suffering from leukaemia. Treatment began immediately but he died on July 21. The post mortem specified that death had been caused by acute myeloblastic leukaemia, an extremely rare form of the disease.

Three months before his death Hashemi had a thorough physical examination and was pronounced fit. He was a regular tennis player and jogger and at forty-seven, there was no reason to suppose he was ill.

Hashemi's brother, Djamshid, was convinced that his brother was murdered to prevent him giving evidence at the trial. 'My brother trod on too many toes,' he said. 'I passed on to him a warning from the Middle East that he would one day have to pay for what he had done, but he laughed it off. I believe my brother was murdered. I will pursue the killers and bring them to justice even if it takes the rest of my life.'[6]

The murder theory is certainly attractive. Some of those under indictment weave a complicated conspiracy story, claiming that Hashemi was actually murdered by the US customs after he had fallen out with them. A more likely possibility is that some of his arms dealing associates decided to kill him for betraying them. However, there is no evidence at all to support either theory. Scotland Yard investigated all the evidence, including that supplied by the Cromwell Hospital and the doctor who carried out the post mortem, and concluded that Hashemi had indeed died from the official cause, leukaemia.

But whether he had died from natural causes or not, the death of their star witness had left the district attorney in New York with a serious hole in his case. Worse was to come.

At the beginning of November 1986 the covert dealings of members of the US administration with Khomeini were exposed, the arms and intelligence on Iraq that had been supplied in the vain hope that the Iranians would advance the freeing of American hostages being held in Lebanon.

Back on Sunday May 25 1986, just over a month after key figures in the Hashemi arms smuggling operation had been arrested, an unmarked Israeli cargo plane began its final approach into Tehran airport. On board were 208 boxes of spare parts for Hawk ground-to-air missiles. Also on board were the former US National Security Adviser, Robert McFarlane, Lt-Col North, his boss Howard Treicher and

George Cave, a former CIA station chief in Tehran and a fluent Farsi speaker. Also with the party was Amiran Nir, an Israeli adviser on terrorism. North took along a chocolate cake from a Tel Aviv kosher bakery with a key on top to symbolise the opening of a new era in Iranian-American relations, and a pair of antique pistols.

The flight was the culmination of more than a year's negotiation with the Iranians. The American officials had become convinced that moderate factions in Iran could be persuaded to deal with America and to that end tons of weapons had been supplied by the Israelis and the US. In exchange for the arms, North, McFarlane and his replacement at the NSC Admiral John Poindexter hoped that the Iranians would use their influence to secure the release of American hostages being held by Iranian terrorists in Lebanon.

In fact, like the rest of the operation, the Tehran visit was a failure. The Americans had been suckered into a long running confidence trick by Manucher Ghorbanifar, the same man who had wooed Khashoggi away from Hashemi and Evans the year before. Ghorbanifar had seduced the Americans with grand promises of his ability to influence the Iranian government. The Israelis, who repeatedly assured the Americans about Ghorbanifar's credentials, saw the possibility both of making money and of bringing America closer to Iran at the expense of their almost equally feared enemy, Iraq.

The CIA, who had rather more experience in the covert world than North or McFarlane, were less convinced, and to check his bona fides, they gave Ghorbanifar a lie detector test in January 1986 while the deals were underway. The only question he answered truthfully was his own name. The polygraph indicated deception on all other questions – such as whether he was under the control of the Iranian government, whether he knew in advance that no American hostages would be released as a result of any deal with the US, whether he cooperated with Iranian officials to deceive the United States and whether he acted independently to deceive the US.

Inevitably, the operation was a disaster and exposed America's ban on arms sales to Iran as a fraud. In addition, their counter-terrorist policy, which was underpinned by the basic philosophy of not negotiating with terrorists, was in tatters.

Samuel Evans and his associates had always maintained that they believed they would be selling arms to Iran with the covert but official approval of the United States government. It had been a flimsy defence, given the evidence of the videotapes and the wiretaps. But now that the American government had been exposed doing exactly what the New York District Attorney had charged them with, their defence was immeasurably strengthened. It would be very difficult for the prosecution to argue that arms sales to Iran were against US policy when administration officials had been party to such sales.

The accused Israelis probably had the best defence of all. While they had been setting up their deal, probably with the knowledge of their government but without the approval of the US, their own government had been acting with the US to send arms to Iran. It was an impossible muddle which no jury would be able to understand.

The New York District Attorney recognised the changed circumstances of the case and all the defendants were released on bail, and then allowed to travel abroad in February 1987. Since that time there have been tentative approaches to Adnan Khashoggi to see if he would testify against the accused. But as Samuel Evans is still his lawyer, this seems unlikely. In any event, his knowledge of the deal is minimal.

It looks as if all the seventeen accused will never be brought to trial. The key witness is dead, the Iran-Contra scandal has reduced the US government's appetite to confront anything to do with Iran and, perhaps most importantly, the Iran-Iraq war is over.

15

Out of the Ashes – A New Contender

Before the Iran-Iraq war began, political and military theorists had often argued that a conflagration between two oil producing countries in the Middle East could mark the beginning of World War Three. A reduction in oil output would lead to huge price rises while the superpowers, anxious to secure their own energy sources and looking for power and influence in the region, would inevitably get involved. In fact, the war came at a time when the industrial nations were conserving energy after the shock of the oil price rises in the mid–1970s. So, the price of oil actually fell and the international markets barely seemed to notice the decline in output from the two protagonists.

It had also been expected that a war between two such well-armed nations using some of the most sophisticated equipment available in the world today would demonstrate for the first time the chilling effects of modern weapons. In fact, the reverse was the case. This was not a fast war with both sides employing air power, tanks and artillery to produce combined arms assaults and flexible manoeuvre warfare. Instead, neither side used its technological capabilities to the full.

The Iranian air capability was limited from the early days of the war by a lack of equipment but the Iraqis had no such difficulties and could have used their vastly superior air power

Monzer al-Kassar, the world's biggest illegal arms dealer who has sold weapons to both terrorists and to Colonel Oliver North. Expelled from Spain, he now lives in Damascus and Budapest from where he masterminds an international drugs and arms empire

This unassuming factory under construction is in fact a chemical weapons plant being built at Rabta in Libya. Western companies helped build the plant and even exposure of Colonel Gadaffi's plans has done little to halt work

Soviet AKMS assault rifles, American pistols and traditional bolt action rifles are prized items of this Pakistani arms dealer's inventory – part of the arms business resulting from the Afghan war

Stinger missiles were the single key weapon that turned the tide of the war in Afghanistan. Many of the missiles supplied by the CIA have been lost

Drug barons have exploited the war in Afghanistan, and heroin – most of it exported to the USA – is now the principal source of income for many guerrilla leaders

French customs officers boarded the cargo ship *Eksund* in November 1987 and discovered arms destined for the IRA, courtesy of Colonel Gadaffi of Libya – the largest such shipment ever

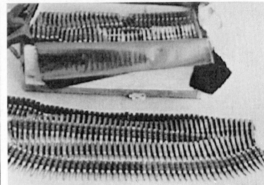

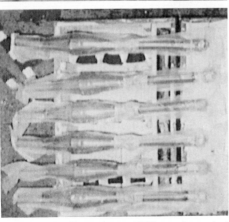

On board the *Eksund* were 150 tons of arms including (a) Soviet rocket-propelled grenade launchers, (b) ammunition, (c) rockets for Soviet Mark 7 surface to air missiles and (c) AK-47 assault rifles. The haul came as a complete surprise to Western intelligence

The secret nuclear research establishment at Dimona in the Negev Desert (*top*) where Israel secretly developed nuclear weapons in a specially built underground bunker known as Machon 2 (*bottom*). These pictures helped confirm Israel for the first time as a nuclear power

Mordechai Vanunu (*right*), the 31-year-old technician who betrayed Israel's nuclear secrets to the London *Sunday Times*. He worked on Israel's nuclear programme for ten years and his revelations led to an Israeli intelligence operation using an agent known as Cheryl (*below*) to seduce him and lure him to Rome. He was then kidnapped and taken to Israel, tried and jailed

In March 1988 Iraqi jets bombed a Kurdish village using cyanide gas. This father and son were among the victims of an attack which clearly illustrated the dangers of chemical weapons proliferation

Three IRA terrorists planning to explode a massive bomb in Gibraltar were shot dead on the island by the SAS on March 6, 1988. The shootings prevented a major terrorist outrage, but even so the SAS (*below*: three of the team) were accused of murdering the terrorists. The inquest into the shootings later found that their actions were justified

Two days after the Gibraltar shootings Spanish police discovered in a Marbella car park an 141-pound Semtex bomb, guns, ammunition, false passports and timing devices hidden by the terrorists

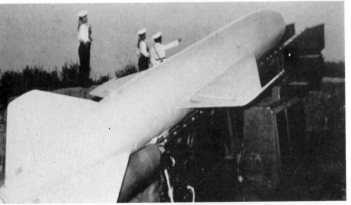

Above: In October 1987 the Soviet Union invited Western observers to witness the destruction of chemical weapons at Shikhany. All the weapons shown were from the Second World War. Western intelligence believes that the Soviet Union is currently manufacturing new chemical weapons

Silkworm missiles were shipped by China to Iran and showed developing countries the value of ballistic missiles. Armed with chemical or nerve agents, these missiles are as powerful as some nuclear weapons to control the skies and thus control the war. For reasons that remain unexplained, Saddam Hussein refused to commit his air force to the conflict, a strategic error that cost his nation dearly in cash and lives.

Neither the United States nor the Soviet Union showed any inclination to get involved in the war. It is true that the US, which before the war had branded Iraq as pro-Soviet and a nation supporting terrorism, became closer to the Hussein regime. In 1982, the US removed Iraq from the list of those countries which supported terrorism and in 1984 full diplomatic relations were restored. This shift in Iraqi loyalties away from the Soviet Union was a major coup for the US. The Soviet Union, for its part, continued to talk to both sides but did little to determine the course of the war.

The absence of heightened world tension because of the war in part accounted for the lack of urgency with which the superpowers and other bodies such as the United Nations looked for a solution. Everyone seemed almost content to let both sides go on killing each other just so long as the war did not spill over into other countries.

This parochial view has had an extraordinary effect on the world arms market. The Iran-Iraq war was such an enormous consumer of arms that it brought to the market new nations that were able to develop indigenous arms industries on the back of the conflict. Countries such as Brazil, North Korea and South Africa, pygmies in the international arms business at the start of the war, were among the giants by the end.

From 1984–88, arms exports by the US to the Third World fell from $4,905m to $3,490m. During the same period, China's exports increased from $1,207 to $2,011m, Brazil's from $271m to $338m and North Korea's from $36m to $109m.[1]

These new suppliers, aided by some of the more traditional arms exporters, had a major impact on the global arms trade. According to the Stockholm International Peace Research Institute, deliveries of major weapons to countries around the Persian Gulf have accounted for 30 per cent of all arms sold to the Third World in the period 1984–88, rising to 48 per cent for the Middle East as a region.[2]

In 1988, SIPRI listed seventeen major arms deals that had occurred on the grey or black markets over the previous seven years. Although this was only a small fraction of the real figure, it is worth noting that sixteen of them listed Iran as the destination for the arms. As the report discloses: 'China and North Korea continue to sell large quantities of major weapons to Iran. In addition to the notorious Silkworm anti-ship missiles, China supplies the bulk of Iran's military equipment. North Korea has supplied large quantities as well and is widely thought to be the source of mines used by Iran against merchant vessels in 1987. A French government report issued in September 1987 revealed that Paris permitted secret sales of artillery shells to Iran in order to help a failing company. Portugal and Spain do nothing to stop large exports of munitions to Iran. Argentina also began to support Iran in 1987 with a $31m munitions deal'.[3]

With a ceasefire in place, there will remain a significant market while both sides replenish their stocks. But in the longer term, for those countries like Brazil that have come to depend on arms exports for a significant amount of their foreign earnings, the end of hostilities might represent quite literally an end to their own developing economies.

The reality, of course, is that such exporters will instead simply look for new markets, either in the Middle East or elsewhere in the Third World. The competition in such markets used to be governed by the vague semblance of a code of national interest. In other words, if the United States or the Soviet Union wanted to sell some military equipment, they would only do so if there was some political advantage to the deal. At the same time, worried about the leaking of military secrets, they could be guaranteed not to pass on their latest equipment.

The countries newly arrived to the arms business have no such code, however loosely it may be defined. South Africa, for example, is happy to find customers anywhere in the world; North Korea has no scruples, and Brazil with a massive foreign debt cannot afford to have any.

Such a large number of unscrupulous arms manufacturers searching for new markets must result in a new development in the arms business. Since NATO and the Warsaw Pact are moving out of the arms race, Third World countries, previously denied access to modern weaponry, will now be able to buy sophisticated arms at very competitive prices, and this could have a profound effect on their economies and political stability. Encouraged to buy arms they do not need and cannot afford, their external debt will increase. In turn, this will have an adverse effect on internal policies.

At the same time, conventional disarmament will lead to two new factors affecting the arms business. First, those countries committed to cutting their conventional forces will try to sell their surplus stocks. Second, arms manufacturers will have to find new outlets away from their traditional markets.

Countries buy arms either because they see a need to have weapons to deter their neighbours or because they have expansionist ambitions. Even those leaders who simply buy weapons as symbols of power may be tempted to translate symbolism into action. As tension between the major powers declines, it is certain that the nature of warfare, too, will change. Future dangers lie not in a conflict in Central Europe between NATO and the Warsaw Pact but in Africa, Central America or the Far East, where for the first time a large number of countries will have the equipment to wage war in the modern way, with massive firepower.

It is ironic that the war which has fuelled this new trade in arms is the best illustration that such weapons are worse than useless in the hands of those who do not understand how to use them. Neither Iran or Iraq used their weapons to best advantage and on most occasions behaved with about as much military expertise as a child playing with a new toy tank.

To be used effectively, modern weapons have to be employed in combination. Air power supports the ground forces, artillery supports the tanks and the troops on the ground are backed up by mortars, tanks and counter battery fire. In the whole of the war, neither side appeared to have a coherent strategy. Even when the Iranians launched one of their many 'ultimate offensives' they did so with men rather than machines, with raw courage rather than well-placed artillery barrages.

The longer the war went on, the weaker Iran became. With their already faltering military decimated by casualties and purges, the Iranian armed forces gradually ground to a halt. But although a victory for the Iranians eventually became inconceivable, the Iraqis were finding even the status quo expensive in men and money. Peace, even to two such egocentric and irrational men as Saddam Hussein and the Ayatollah Khomeini, was the only solution.

The Iran-Iraq war gives some force to the moral argument that developed nations should not sell sophisticated weapons to the underdeveloped world. However, that argument is now academic as the future of the arms business is no longer in the hands of a few major powers. There is little that can be done now to prevent the expansion of the arms market; sanctions cannot be imposed to prevent countries buying arms or manufacturers prevented from selling weapons. Anyway, countries like Brazil and South Africa economically have no choice.

Ironically, one of the countries that will be competing for arms exports will be Iran. When the war began in 1980, Iran manufactured virtually no arms. But in the eight years of the war, with new weapons, ammunition and spares hard to come by, Iran rapidly developed its own industry. Government leaders in Tehran claim that the country now manufactures its own small arms, ammunition, mortars, artillery and a wide range of missiles. The only product not yet produced by the Iranians is a fighter aircraft. While claims of self-sufficiency, given the level of Iranian buying on the black market, are certainly exaggerated, there is hard evidence that their arms industry is producing a wide range of weapons.

At a military exhibition in Tehran in October 1988, the Iranians displayed an armoured personnel carrier, a remotely piloted vehicle, and a range of surface-to-surface rockets of a previously unknown type. Just how well these systems work is not known but, like the Israelis and the South Africans, the Iranians have had plenty of opportunity to test them under battlefield conditions.[4]

The first indication that Iran intends to aggressively market its own products came in January 1989, when an Iranian delegation attended the Security and the Army Exhibition in Libreville, Gabon. A sixty-three strong delegation headed by the Iranian Defence Minister Mohammad Hossin Jalali arrived at the exhibition, bringing a wide range of their products, including small arms and rockets. Each visitor to the Iranian stand on the second floor of the exhibition centre received a bag of pistachio nuts and a ten-rial coin with the inscription 'Oh Moslems, Unite! Unite!'[5]

The Iranians will need to produce more than nuts and encouraging mottoes if they are to compete seriously in the arms market. But one thing eight years of war has given the Iranians is an unparalleled knowledge of the illegal arms market – they know more shady dealers, have more dummy companies and have better contacts than any other nation. This knowledge will stand them in good stead in the years to come.

16

The Bomb in the Basement

Israel's possession of a nuclear armoury – or at least the ability to assemble one within days, or even hours – has been widely accepted by Arab leaders, western (and no doubt Soviet) intelligence agencies and armchair strategists since the middle 1960s. It is not credible that a nation so beleaguered, so vulnerable, so single-minded and so scientifically adept should have neglected to equip itself with some weapon of last-ditch deterrence and ultimate resort.

But despite many clues and telltale events down the years, the proposition has never been definitively proved. The most that any Israeli government has been willing to say on the subject, from David Ben-Gurion to the present administration of Yitzhak Shamir, is that Israel will not be the first to introduce such weapons into the Middle East.

As with most commitments to a policy of no-first-use, the precise meaning of the assurance remains wrapped in deliberate ambiguity to ensure that potential enemies are never absolutely certain of their intentions and capabilities in time of war. What is certain is Israel's deep and long-sustained interest in nuclear matters.

In 1948, while the newborn State of Israel was still busy winning the first of its wars for survival against its Arab neighbours, the Israeli Defence Ministry (IDM) set up a Research & Planning Branch and despatched a team of geologists into the Negev desert in search of workable uranium deposits among the region's extensive potash beds. The fol-

lowing year, 1949, a team of promising students was encouraged to enroll in appropriate university departments in Switzerland, Holland, Britain and the United States, with a view to
specialising in the booming new discipline of atomic physics.

That same year, a nuclear research and development
department was established in the Weizmann Institute at
Rehovoth, named after the country's first president, Chaim
Weizmann, who was himself a scientist of international repute.

These initial investments quickly paid off. In the early
1950s the Rehovoth group not only discovered large reserves
of low-grade, but perfectly mineable uranium in the arid
wastes south of Sidon and Beersheba, but also made important advances in the economic production of heavy water, one
of the key materials required for the construction of atomic
reactors. This, as well as being useful in itself, provided valuable know-how to trade with the several other nations at
that time determinedly seeking ways to sidestep Washington's
jealously guarded nuclear monopoly.

The most important of these was France, whose talented
but mainly left-leaning scientists had been systematically
banned from the American Manhattan Project and reduced
to a minor supporting role, no nearer to the bomb than the
far side of the Canadian frontier.

Back in July 1944, before the Hiroshima and Nagasaki
explosions, the Free French leader, General Charles de Gaulle
had decided that a revival of atomic research must be a prime
post-war priority when he came to power. But in the cold-
war atmosphere of 1950, the first head of the French Commis-
sariat à l'Energie Atomique (CEA), Frederic Joliot, had been
forced to resign on account of his communist leanings. Conveniently for Israel, however, his replacement, Francis Perrin,
just happened to be an old and close friend of Dr Ernst
Bergmann, and Bergmann had just been appointed (on the
recommendation of Albert Einstein) as first director of the
Weizmann Institute's nuclear programme. A balding chain-
smoker and workaholic, Bergmann was a visionary who gave
a firm direction to Israel's scientific investigations. For the

next four years, he gathered round him the best brains of Israel and Jews from abroad who had a background in the sciences. 'There are those who say,' he wrote, 'that it is possible to purchase everything that we need, including knowledge and experience, from abroad. This attitude worries me. I am convinced . . . that the State of Israel needs a defence research programme of its own so that we shall never again be as lambs led to the slaughter.'[1]

According to Francis Perrin, the US gave France access to some of the information gained during the Manhattan Project on the strict understanding that it was not passed to a third country. But, 'We considered we could give the secrets to Israel, provided they kept it to themselves,' said Perrin.[2]

Perrin maintained that the Israeli plant at Dimona only had the capacity to produce one atomic bomb a year, which would have been sufficient for Israel's purpose as he understood it. 'We thought the Israeli bomb was [aimed] against the Americans, not to launch it against America but to say "if you don't want to help us in a critical situation, we will require you to help us, otherwise we will use our nuclear bombs." '

Two years after Bergmann's appointment, Prime Minister David Ben-Gurion's government secretly established the Israel Atomic Energy Commission (IAEC) and put it under the control of the Defence Ministry, whose deputy director-general at that time was the rising young Israeli technocrat, Shimon Peres.

Born Shimon Persky, at Vishneva, in Poland, in 1923, the future Israeli prime minister had first won his leadership spurs with the clandestine Haganah organisation, during the Zionist struggle against the British mandate authorities. During 1943 he spent a month in Beersheba jail after being picked up for map-making in a forbidden area, and took his *nom de guerre*, Peres, from the desert eagles he watched at that time soaring over the Negev. But the boyish adventurer had long since matured into a skilled administrator and polished international diplomat.

By 1952 he was already a familiar figure in Paris, where he had developed a web of high-level military and political contacts, and was ideally placed to get early details of French nuclear ambitions, and the key moves that were being made towards their achievement.

That summer work started on France's first plutonium-producing reactor, a 42 megawatt pile of Marcoule, capable of producing 10kg of the metal in a year; and St Gobain, the big glass and chemicals firm, had been asked to prepare preliminary studies for the plutonium extraction plant which was needed as the next, and crucial, step towards producing a bomb.

Franco-Israeli relations grew steadily warmer. In 1953 the two countries signed their first nuclear cooperation agreement (though it was only publicly announced the following year) and as a quid pro quo the CEA bought, unseen, the Weizmann process for heavy water preparation without the use of electricity. This was immediately successful and helped build up a valuable reserve of mutual respect between the scientists of the two countries. Peres, the architect of the deal, moved up to director-general of defence.

Soon after, in 1954, Tel Aviv belatedly admitted to the existence of the IAEC and its military connections, but few people at the time attached any particular significance to this. The Laniel government in France fell, to be replaced by one even more sympathetic to Israel, headed by Pierre Mendes-France. St Gobain successfully brought in its pilot plutonium plant at Fontenay-aux-Roses, and in November the details of the collaboration pact, and the heavy water deliveries, were jointly revealed by the French foreign minister, Jules Moch, at a UN disarmament conference in New York, and by his Israeli opposite number, Moshe Sharett, in the Knesset.

In May 1955, after a year of bitter cabinet in-fighting and against the opposition of at least one-third of the scientists in the CEA, France finally opted to build its own independent nuclear arsenal, known as the Force de Frappe. The necessary funds were committed from the defence budget and France embarked on construction of a full-scale plutonium separation facility at Marcoule.

Meanwhile President Eisenhower's Atoms for Peace programme – a rather belated attempt by the US to halt proliferation by sharing the non-military part of its closely guarded nuclear technology – was extended to Israel. Washington authorised construction of a tiny, 5 megawatt 'swimming pool' reactor at Nahal Soreq, conveniently close to the Weizmann laboratories, and between 1956 and 1960 arranged for some fifty-six Israeli scientists to receive training at the US Atomic Energy Research centres in the Argonne National Laboratory and at Oak Ridge.

The year of Suez, 1956, began with yet another French election and again the result – a government headed by Guy Mollet, with Maurice Bourges-Manoury at the arms ministry, and Abel Thomas as his very sympathetic *directeur de cabinet* – was very much to Israel's advantage. According to Pierre Pean, the French journalist who has written by far the most detailed reconstruction of the Franco-Israeli nuclear collaboration, it was that summer that the nuclear relationship between the two countries really took off.[3]

When the Egyptian president, Colonel Nasser, announced his intention of nationalising the Suez Canal on July 26, France and Israel had already agreed on a massive arms deal that included fighters, tanks and small arms. Peres, with Ben-Gurion's full support, wanted to expand the relationship and asked the French to supply a 1,000 kilowatt atomic reactor. At first the French had ridiculed the idea but then Peres suggested that Israel could, under certain circumstances, support French military action against Nasser. The French correctly took the nuclear deal to be the quid pro quo for Israeli support for the Suez invasion.

Circumstances then played into the hands of Peres. The British began talking of postponing the Suez operation for two months to give diplomacy another chance, while the Americans were talking of a long-term covert operation to topple Nasser. Peres saw that if he volunteered Israel's help, his country could replace Britain as France's ally in the venture, in which case France would accede to anything Israel wanted. His judgement proved right.

On September 17, four men sat down to dinner at the residence of Jacob Tsur, the Israeli ambassador: Peres, his top nuclear expert, Ernst Bergmann, and the leading figures in CEA, the now thoroughly militarised French atomic agency, high commissioner Francis Perrin and administrator-general Pierre Guillaumat.

The men discussed in detail possible nuclear cooperation between France and Israel. The designs discussed over the coffee and cognac at that dinner were the essential blueprints of Israel's first reactor.

On September 20, Peres cabled Ben-Gurion with the details of the French offer and Israel's possible role in the Suez campaign. Ben-Gurion's reply was enthusiastic: 'Congratulations! I am very proud of the agreement on the other matter [the atomic reactor]. As to the three options on timing, the partnership [with France] is most to our liking. If they act at their convenience, we will back them to the best of our ability.'[4]

Work started almost immediately. Before the end of September, two senior CEA men, Bertrand Goldschmidt and Jules Horowitz, had been given the task of preparing the initial plans. But by October 10, when Peres and Abel Thomas, at the arms ministry, sat down to sign the formal agreement, the parameters had already changed.

Suez was going badly, and Israel's future security, always fragile, began to look extremely bleak. It was probably at this point that the reactor site, which was originally intended to be at Richon-le-Zion, near the Weizmann Centre, was shifted to the depths of the Negev; and that was only the first of many fundamental alterations as the treaty (finally settled in 1957, and still unpublished) evolved into its final form.

According to the journalist Pean, the crucial breakthrough came on November 7, the day after the allies, under intense international pressure, accepted a humiliating ceasefire, and started to withdraw from Suez.

Peres and Golda Meir, then Israel's foreign minister, had flown in the previous midnight and conducted three hours of urgent talks with senior French ministers and officials, including Bourges-Manoury and Thomas. Continued Israeli occupation of the Sinai, which their tanks had so dramatically captured, was now clearly, in the long-term, untenable, and their most urgent object was to seek French support in the difficult negotiations that obviously lay ahead.

But they also found time to discuss the future of the nuclear project, and in the morning an anguished Guy Mollet recognised the urgency of their concern. '*Je leur dois la bombe. Je leur dois la bombe*,' (I owe them the bomb, I owe them the bomb) he is alleged to have told his inner circle of advisers that morning; a groan interpreted by one aide present as meaning, 'We had let them down. We had to give them some counterweight for the sake of their security. It was vital.'

Certainly there was an element of guilt in the relationship but there was also a feeling that Israel had fought well in Suez and now deserved support as a strong ally and not simply as an underdog. For the next year Peres shuttled between Israel and Paris and the arms relationship became so close that Israeli officials were given offices in the French defence ministry, a move reciprocated by the Israelis.

At the beginning of 1957, Peres decided that a 1,000 megawatt reactor was not sufficiently ambitious and instead asked the French for a 24,000 megawatt. After some difficulty – France was going through a period of political instability – the deal was agreed. The best guess at the final contents of the 1957 agreement is that it probably covered three main areas: (1) the building of the Dimona reactor; (2) the development of a plutonium extraction plant; (3) joint work, with the Dassault aviation company, on the Jericho missile, whose 260km range would be sufficient to bring Cairo within hitting distance. There may also have been a clause giving Israel access to the data from France's planned weapons tests when they started, in the Sahara, in the early 1970s.

Among the handful of high-fliers that made up Israel's nuclear establishment, the news of the Paris accord were not greeted with universal enthusiasm. In fact it generated intense controversy, as a result of which no fewer than six of the seven members of the IAEC resigned, leaving only Ernst Bergmann, who was always close to the defence ministry, to hold the fort. But as loyal citizens, they kept their doubts strictly to themselves, and have never publicly discussed the reasons for their abrupt departure.

The return of Charles de Gaulle to power on June 1, 1958, changed the face of post-war France. It ended a long period of weak government, economic setbacks and imperial illusions; and it heralded a drastic rethinking of policy, everywhere from the constitution to the conduct of foreign affairs. In the end it led to almost total severance of the Franco-Israeli military link – but that was still almost a decade into the future. In the meantime, the covert and unacknowledged building of Dimona proceeded apace.

From 1958 to 1960, hundreds of tons of material, fabricated and assembled all over France, travelled by road, train, and ship to Israel. At least 500 French scientists, engineers, workers and officials were in the know (plus their wives, children, employers, mistresses, secretaries, etc.) but although the American Central Intelligence Agency had begun to smell a rat, there was no public leak.

The reactor core, carefully labelled and documented as a sea-water desalination plant destined for Latin America, left one quiet weekend from Saint-Nazaire. In the summer of 1960, several tons of heavy-water were collected from Saclay one Saturday morning by three CEA mini-vans, trans-shipped to larger lorries in the underground car park at CEA's Paris headquarters in the Rue de la Université, and driven from there to a quiet corner of the military airport at Le Bourget, where they were loaded into a Nord 2500 military transport, stopping briefly in Sicily, and then arriving at an

Israeli military airstrip in the Negev. Almost certainly the heavy water came from Norway, which should under the terms of the Franco-Norwegian supply contract have been informed of any onward despatch. But, as with all other aspects of the arrangements, no word of the operation was divulged.

In February 1959, the St Gobain team successfully produced its first ingot of weapons-grade plutonium, using spent fuel-rods from the first of the Marcoule reactors (now increased to three). Just under a year later France exploded a fission device and established itself as the fourth of the world's independent nuclear powers.

But it was at this point that de Gaulle, fresh from liquidating most of France's African empire and successfully inaugurating the Fifth Republic, turned his mind to Israel. In May, his foreign minister, Couve de Murville summoned the Israeli ambassador, Walter Eytan, and dropped a bombshell. France, he stated, had decided, after all, that it would not supply uranium to fuel the Negev reactor, unless and until the whole project was made public and put under international supervision.

Peres, now promoted from the defence bureaucracy to deputy-minister, wrote in his diary on May 16: 'Disturbing news from France'. The French wanted the existence of the Dimona reactor to be made public, to be subject to international supervision and, until these two demands were met, all shipments of uranium would cease.

This was bad news for the Israelis who had relied on the secrecy of the project to keep the Arabs from entering a new and even more terrifying arms race. The Israelis were still several years from making a nuclear bomb and wanted the project kept secure until they had the bombs in place. Despite one nasty moment when the pilot of a light plane in which Peres and his son were travelling from Eilat to Tel Aviv drifted off course and almost landed in Jordan, with all the Dimona documents on board, the project had remained firmly under wraps.

But now there seemed little hope of keeping the lid on – unless some way could be found to stall, and persuade de Gaulle to change his mind.

In June, Peres went to Paris to hear from Guillaumat what had gone wrong ('It's the number of Frenchmen employed at Dimona – about 2,500 at the peak, if wives and families are included. Their contract says they are being sent "to a warm climate and desert conditions" and it's not difficult to figure out where that is'). Then, a week later, Ben-Gurion followed, to talk directly to the President.[5]

Over dinner, de Gaulle asked sotto voce: 'Tell me frankly, just what do you need an atomic reactor for?' De Gaulle extracted a promise from Ben-Gurion that he would not develop a bomb and the French President promised to reconsider his position.

The lull did not last long. In August, Couve summoned Eytan again and told him that if Israel made no move to go public, all French contribution to the reactor-building would cease. Peres spelled out to Ben-Gurion what he saw as the only real alternatives – to drop the project and claim its $130m cost in compensation, or insist, whatever the difficulties, that the contract be carried out. He himself inclined to the second choice, and in November returned to Paris for what he knew, according to his diary, would be 'delicate, almost hopeless' negotiations.[6]

Against all the odds, though, he succeeded. He persuaded Couve to agree that Israel itself would complete the construction, while France continued to supply the equipment and dropped her demand for international control. The only remaining stipulation was that Ben-Gurion must still make a public statement about the reactor, and describe its proposed research objectives. That was reluctantly accepted. But on December 9, 1960, before Ben-Gurion had a chance to oblige, a major crisis blew up.

The Americans (possibly following up on Egyptian intelligence reports) suddenly woke up to the fact that something significant was happening at Dimona when a U2 spy plane took pictures of the strange group of structures which was starting to spring up in the Negev. Ben-Gurion's initial attempt to pass it off as a 'textile works' (and then to revive the 'desalination plant' idea) quickly backfired, and soon Washington officials were talking openly about the likelihood of an Israeli atom bomb within five years.

France came under bitter attack, accused of supplying a replica of the plant that had just produced its own highly controversial A-weapons, and Nasser, almost incoherent with fury, threatened to mobilise four million men to invade and demolish Dimona.

Back in Jerusalem on December 20, Peres briefed his aides and officials on the Dimona project. He warned them that over the next few days it was likely that the prime minister would be making a statement about the project. He told them that:

1. The Dimona reactor, like its small, inadequate sister at Nahal Soreq (now on stream) was only for research purposes.

2. Dimona, contrary to rumour, was a long-range programme designed for the development of the Negev.

3. It existed purely for peaceful purposes.

4. No country in the world is subject to international supervision, and those who suggest that Israel should be the first are the same people who advocate the internationalisation of Jerusalem.[7]

The next day, Ben-Gurion duly admitted to the Knesset that a reactor was being built, but denied it was anything to do with producing a bomb.

As part of his briefings on current international issues, the incoming US President John F Kennedy was told by the CIA that it looked to them as if Israel was working towards producing a nuclear bomb. On January 3, 1961, the US Ambassador to Israel, Ogden Reid, demanded answers – before midnight – to five questions: (a) what was Israel planning to do with the plutonium produced by the reactor; (b) would she permit impartial inspection; (c) would she allow visits from the International Atomic Energy Authority (set up with fifty-four members, including Britain and the two nuclear superpowers, in 1958) or some other friendly body; (d) were there any additional reactor-building plans; (e) could she declare unreservedly that she had no intention of building atomic weapons.

Ben-Gurion and Golda Meir, deeply affronted, agreed to let the time of the ultimatum pass. When they did finally answer they evaded the plutonium query, rejected hostile states 'meddling in our business', accepted some visits 'but not yet', denied any further reactor plans, and declared once more that there would be no nuclear weapons.

Those were the events as the news-reading public saw them, but behind various closed doors, there were other, more significant developments. The most important of these, in practical terms, was the freezing of work on the plutonium-separation plant which was being built alongside the reactor by a forty-strong team of St Gobain men, fresh from their technological triumphs at Marcoule.

At the end of December 1960, all but a tiny, skeleton group of them were recalled to Paris, and all work on this key element in the project ceased for more than two years. It was this decision which allowed de Gaulle to boast later in his memoirs, that 'we halted the aid for initiating construction near Beersheba of a facility for transforming uranium into plutonium from which, one bright day, atomic bombs could emerge'. But that claim was either disingenuous or misinformed.

On January 6, 1961, there was a closed-door session of the US Senate Foreign Relations Committee, the proceedings of which were only de-classified in the 1980s. The following exchange neatly demonstrates the gulf which regularly divides what official Washington wishes to believe about Israel's more belligerent activities, and what the more sceptical suspect.

Secretary of State Christian Herter: 'There has been something of a flurry in connection with the nuclear reactor in Israel . . . Certainly we had never been told about it . . . but the present statements of the Israeli government are that this is still experimental, leading to a power reactor . . .'

Senator Bourke Hickenlooper: '. . . I think the Israelis have just lied to us like horse thieves on this thing. They have completely distorted, misrepresented and falsified the facts . . .'

The Egyptian leader, Colonel Nasser, adhered firmly to the Hickenlooper camp. Later that spring he convened the Council of the Arab League with the primary objective of mounting a pre-emptive strike against Israel – ostensibly to block plans to divert the Jordan waters, but also with a view to subverting her nascent nuclear potential. But by the time he was ready to move, in 1967, it was almost certainly already too late.

Bowing to American pressure, in 1961, the Israelis finally agreed to an inspection tour by US atomic scientists. But this was very carefully orchestrated so that the visitors never got anything but a most superficial idea of what was going on. Inside the control room at Dimona the Israelis had constructed a range of dummy gauges which successfully convinced the Americans that the reactor was entirely for peace purposes. When the scientists returned to their hotel room, agents from the Israeli secret service broke into their rooms and photographed their notes of the visit to reassure themselves there were no lingering doubts.

But American intelligence agencies continued to have serious doubts about the Israeli programme, doubts that were reflected inside Israel's own political and scientific community. At a time when the country did not have sufficient money to buy wheat to feed the people nor machinery to build a strong industrial base, the expensive nuclear programme was a serious drain on resources.

By the time Peres visited Washington once more in April 1963, the Americans were firmly convinced that Israel was indeed intending to manufacture nuclear weapons. Peres came to Washington hoping to buy American Hawk missiles to counter similar missiles recently sold to Egypt by the Soviet Union. But the Hawk was nuclear capable and therefore it was made clear to Peres that any deal would be tied to US demands for regular inspections of the Dimona site.

At an informal dinner party shortly after his arrival, Peres found himself sitting next to Senator Stuart Symington who told him: 'Don't be a bunch of fools. Don't stop [making atomic weapons]. And don't listen to the administration. Do whatever you think best.'[8]

At first, his meeting with President Kennedy was not so encouraging. After some preliminary sparring about the missiles, Kennedy asked Peres: 'On this subject of the missiles, the danger is that there's no point in having missiles unless you place non-conventional warheads on them. Don't you agree that the warheads are more dangerous than the missiles?'

Peres: 'Let me say that a missile with a conventional warhead is very different from a bomb released from a plane. The main feature of the missile is that it is unmanned. It sows terror and enhances the sense of power of those who employ it, because there are no effective means of defence against it.'

Kennedy: 'That's true. But as you know, the atomic warheads are more dangerous than the missiles.'

Peres: 'The missiles exist already, while the atomic warheads won't be around for a long time, if at all.'

Kennedy: 'You know that we follow with great interest every indication that an atomic capability is being developed in the region. It would create a very perilous situation. That's why we have been diligent about keeping an eye on your effort in the atomic field. What can you tell me about that?'

Peres: 'I can tell you forthrightly that we will not introduce atomic weapons into the region. We certainly won't be the first to do so. We have no interest in that.'

This statement became the standard Israeli response to any questions in the future about the nuclear programme. In fact, of course, as every intelligence analyst, politician and nuclear scientist well knows, it takes a matter of hours at most to bring the already manufactured components for a nuclear device together. Nonetheless, over the years Israel has successfully hidden behind this misleading statement. The meeting with Kennedy concluded like many others in the future: Israel received its Hawk missiles.

To the outsider, the behaviour of Kennedy and his government seems little short of irresponsible. They had firm information from their own intelligence services that Israel was embarked on a nuclear programme, yet at no time did Kennedy firmly confront the Israelis with the evidence. Instead, he simply accepted the bland denials at face value. The Israelis read the American acceptance of their promises as a tacit approval for the nuclear programme.

Levi Eshkol, who came to power in 1963, was opposed to the development of the nuclear bomb and he was supported by his chief of staff Yitzchak Rabin and General Yighal Allon, who was then serving as a cabinet minister. Among the military, too, there was considerable disagreement over the best way to defend the territory against the growing military might of the Arabs. The more conservative generals like Allon believed in conventional defences arguing that the Arab world would be permanently divided and no match for the superior Israeli technology and training.

But General Moshe Dayan, then Chief of Staff of the Israeli Defence Forces, argued that the Arab nations were oil rich and would one day be able to afford the most sophisticated western weapons. Israel, on the other hand, would never be able to afford a Middle East arms race and, if a united Arab army were ever to attack Israel, she needed an ultimate weapon of last resort – a nuclear bomb.

By the end of the year, the Dimona reactor was running with a requirement of twenty-four tons of uranium a year, initially made up of ten tons of indigenous production, ten tons from South Africa and the remainder from France. Under their secret agreement, France was supposed to process the plutonium that resulted from the nuclear reaction at Dimona and return the enriched uranium back to Israel. It was this enriched uranium that would be used to make bombs. But France was no longer a guaranteed supplier, as the Israeli programme continued to cause concern. With their usual foresight, however, Israel had a solution to this problem already in hand.

Some time in 1956, there was a meeting between Berg-mann, Peres and Isser Harel, then head of the Mossad. The discussion centred around the various methods available for obtaining enriched uranium by covert means. Bergmann believed that the Dimona reactor would not be fully oper-ational for at least six years so there was plenty of time to put an operation in place. The decision was taken to exploit the then very weak regulatory system in place in the United States to siphon off enriched uranium and ship it to Israel.[9]

To achieve this goal (and incidentally to train a number of Israeli scientists in the latest American nuclear technology), the Israelis recruited Dr Zelman Shapiro, a research chemist who had been closely involved with the Manhattan Project and was very well connected in the growing nuclear industry.

In 1957, Shapiro formed the Nuclear Materials and Equip-ment Corporation (NUMEC) based in Apollo, Pennsylvania, with cash which the CIA believes was supplied by the Israelis.

At this time, the nuclear industry was in its infancy and little had been done to regulate those companies involved in the business. Using his personal contacts, Shapiro was able to bid for government contracts to process uranium and to produce fuel for reactors and the space programme. For exam-ple, Admiral Hyman Rickover, the father of the navy's nuclear programme, gave him his division's valuable con-tracts. With that kind of official approval, Shapiro gathered a healthy list of international clients.

At the same time, NUMEC agreed with Israel that the company would serve as a 'technical consultant and training and procurement agency.' This relationship worked so well that a separate company, Israeli Isotopes and Radiation Enterprises (ISORAD), was formed, owned jointly by NUMEC and the Israeli government. According to NUMEC's financial statements, ISORAD was specifically designed to develop methods of preserving fruit through irradiation. In reality, it provided a pipeline for uranium and other nuclear technology that led straight to Dimona.

By the beginning of the 1960s, US concern about NUMEC surfaced at two levels. First, inspectors for the Atomic Energy Commission felt that the safeguards imposed by Shapiro were totally inadequate. In particular, Shapiro was doing things to disguise the amount of uranium passing through his plant. Although specifically prohibited from doing so by his government contracts, Shapiro was mixing enriched with ordinary uranium so that keeping track of a particular contract was virtually impossible. As the regulatory system depended almost entirely on a careful process of weighing-in exact amounts of uranium at the start of the production line and weighing-out an exact amount at the end, sloppy processing meant that the AEC could keep no real check on the product.

While NUMEC was ignoring warnings from the AEC, US intelligence agencies were becoming increasingly concerned at what they saw as Israel's clear attempt to develop an independent nuclear industry with the potential to make nuclear weapons. A major effort had been launched to try to discover where Israel was getting all its information and although the finger clearly pointed at France, the AEC's reports of sloppy bookkeeping at NUMEC led the FBI to take a closer look in Apollo, Pennsylvania also.

What they found was that Baruch Cinai, an Israeli metallurgist, and Ephraim Lahav, the scientific attaché at the Israeli embassy in Washington, were regular visitors at the plant where they had access to classified documents that detailed the current state of parts of America's nuclear programme. Shapiro was also a frequent visitor to Israel.

Shapiro was warned to improve his records and to control the flow of foreigners – particularly Israelis – going through the NUMEC plant. These warnings were ignored. Then in April 1965, AEC inspectors learned from Shapiro that 130 pounds of uranium, enough to make at least six atomic bombs, were missing. The AEC demanded an explanation and Shapiro told them the material had merely been buried in the two huge waste pits at the factory designed to hold all the contaminated by-products from the plant. Both pits were dug up and the contents analysed. Negligible amounts of uranium were found.

AEC investigators then tried to go back over NUMEC's records to track the missing uranium and discovered that records for twenty-six of the thirty-two contracts that had been awarded to NUMEC were incomplete.

Over the next three years a number of investigations were carried out by the FBI and the AEC into NUMEC. Shapiro's telephone was tapped and it was learned he used a scrambler for many of his conversations. The code proved impossible to crack. He was followed and seen to have secret meetings with Israeli officials.

Despite all this circumstantial evidence, Shapiro continued to win government contracts and in 1967, Shapiro sold NUMEC. In a final accounting, the AEC believed that 572 pounds of enriched uranium had disappeared and the CIA believed that at least 200 pounds of that had ended up in Israel.

If Israel now had enough uranium to make nuclear weapons, the country still lacked a substantial supply of basic uranium to feed the Dimona plant. In 1968 most of the industrialised and Third World countries had signed the nuclear Non-Proliferation Treaty (NPT). The signatories agreed to do nothing that would help other countries develop nuclear weapons. It was a fine start to establishing an international regulatory process, but unfortunately the countries most likely to develop a nuclear capability – Israel, India, Pakistan, South Africa, Argentina and Brazil – had refused to sign. Even so, it was now much more difficult for Israel, or any other country, to overtly get the materials required for developing a nuclear capability.

Israeli intelligence has played a central role all along in helping Israel develop its nuclear weapons and in preventing others from doing so. Now, once again, it fell to the Mossad to find some uranium to fuel Dimona.

The first clue that the west had to the solution that Mossad came up with occurred by a complete accident. In the early 1970s, the Israeli government had authorised an aggressive policy of assassination against terrorists known to have targeted Israelis. In particular, the hit squad tracked down all those who had been involved with the assassination of Israeli athletes at the 1972 Munich Olympics. The man who had organised that attack was Ali Hassan Salameh, a key figure in a terrorist group called Black September. (He was also for many years an important informant for the American CIA.) The Mossad tracked Salameh to Norway and a squad was sent to kill him. Unfortunately, they had identified the wrong man and gunned down an innocent Moroccan waiter.

One of the hit squad, Dan Aerbel, was captured and under interrogation he told the Norwegians that he had once owned a steamship, the *Scheersberg A*, which had carried uranium to Israel. Of little interest to his Norwegian questioners, the confession was of great interest to other European intelligence agencies. Under further questioning, Aerbel revealed for the first time how Israel had smuggled more than two hundred tons of uranium from Europe to Israel, enough to keep Dimona operating for many years.[10]

In 1965, the Israelis had contacted a former Nazi fighter pilot called Hubert Schulzen who owned a small chemical company called Asmara Chemie in Wiesbaden. Asmara had begun making soaps and dyes, but with the arrival of nuclear and chemical weapons in Europe he had switched to making cleansers and decontamination creams and had won several lucrative contracts with the US army. Asmara was a small, prosperous firm with a steady and growing income.

Schulzen had been shot down during the Second World War and suffered serious head injuries. Although the wounds had healed he suffered recurring pain and in 1965 went to hospital for an operation. Immediately after the operation he was approached by an Israeli furniture manufacturer who dangled the carrot of future contracts and invited him to Israel for part of his convalescence. He enjoyed his stay and made a number of good friends, some of whom were fronting for Mossad.

Within three years the Israelis had replaced the US army as Schulzen's largest customers and the business was bringing in record profits. Then the Israelis came to Schulzen with the deal of a lifetime. Would he, they asked, act as the middleman in buying two hundred tons of uranium oxide for shipping to Israel? Schulzen agreed immediately. It is not known just how much incentive the Israelis offered but the uranium alone cost $2.4m and was worth many times more than that to the Israelis.

In March 1968, Asmara approached a Belgian company, the Société General des Minéraux which possessed large stocks of uranium: these had been shipped from their mines in Zaire shortly before that country gained its independence.

Although they were keen to sell, SGM had never heard of Asmara and they were under certain obligations to ensure that the uranium was going to a good home. The European Commission had established a regulatory organisation called Eurotom which was designed to control the flow of nuclear materials, including uranium. Eurotom had no real powers of enforcement however, and it relied on the honesty of all the European countries and the companies involved for it to work effectively. The Mossad had recognised its weaknesses and set out to exploit them.

SGM's checks on Asmara showed it to be a reputable company and a check with a Swiss bank showed that the purchase money for the uranium was already in place, waiting to be handed over. Schulzen also reassuringly explained that the uranium was needed as his company was expanding into the petrochemical industry and needed the uranium as a catalyst.

Before uranium can be used as a catalyst, it has to be processed and Schulzen told SGM that an Italian company SAICA, based in Milan, had agreed to carry out the work.

To get the uranium to the company, Asmara proposed to SGM that it would be shipped by sea from Belgium to Italy. Technically this was a breach of EEC rules as the uranium would be outside EEC waters and therefore required a special export licence. In fact under Eurotom's regulations a licence is deemed to have been granted if the organisation raises no objections within a specific period, which is what happened in this case.

The Mossad used a Turkish front man, Burham Yarisal, to buy a suitable ship, the *Scheersberg A*, for $250,000 in cash. Registered under a Liberian flag of convenience nominally owned by Dan Aerbel, and crewed by Mossad agents, the ship sailed from Rotterdam on Sunday November 17 for Genoa with the two hundred tons of uranium in the hold. It never arrived.

Somewhere in the eastern Mediterranean the *Scheersberg A* rendezvoused with an Israeli merchantman guarded by gunboats from the Israeli navy. There the uranium was transferred in barrels with the word 'Plumbat' stencilled on the side.

It was more than six months before the alarm bells began to ring at Eurotom and even then they were so muted that few people heard them. Desultory enquiries were made at Asmara and at the Italian company SAICA. Both simply refused to answer and no officials ever took the trouble to visit either of them to question them in detail. If they had done so, they would have found that Asmara was a small concern with no capacity to store even a fraction of the two hundred tons of uranium it had purchased, and SAICA was a varnish factory with no capacity for carrying out the chemical processing of the uranium.

Neither the EEC nor Eurotom ever bothered to investigate the matter properly, preferring instead to forget the whole problem. To have launched a massive investigation would have exposed the nuclear safeguards for the sham that the Israelis had realised them to be. Instead the organisation chose to cover up the affair. If it had not been for the accidental capture of the Mossad agent in Norway, it might well have never been revealed.

With both enriched uranium and now a plentiful supply of ordinary fuel for the nuclear reactor, Israel had all the raw materials both to be self-sufficient in nuclear power and to manufacture her own nuclear weapons.

All the indications suggested to the western intelligence community that Israel was determined to make a nuclear weapon and might already have done so. But, like so much intelligence analysis, these conclusions were imperfect. Although the CIA and the DIA believed that Israel was now a nuclear power, they had no real confirmation.

For Israel this situation seemed perfect. By keeping the bomb in her basement, Israel could continue to claim that she would never be the first to introduce nuclear weapons into the Middle East. But there would always be sufficient doubt in the minds of her Arab enemies to prevent them pushing Israel to the brink. For some reason, however, this message did not get through.

In October 1973, the Egyptians launched a brilliantly planned surprise attack across the Suez Canal, catching Israel completely unprepared. Although the Israelis managed to hold on to the Suez front they were also being hard pressed by the Syrians in the Golan Heights. Then a counter attack in Suez failed disastrously. At 10pm on October 8, the Israeli commander on the northern front, Major General Yitzhak Hofi (later to head the Mossad) told General Elazar, the Chief of Staff: 'I am not sure we can hold out much longer.' This message was relayed to the Defence Minister, Moshe Dayan, who, at five minutes past midnight went to Prime Minister Golda Meir and told her: 'This is the end of the Third Temple.' (The first two temples in Jerusalem were destroyed by invading Babylonians and Romans.) He then asked permission from Meir to make ready Israel's nuclear weapons. The components for thirteen 20-kiloton bombs, each equivalent to the strength of the device dropped on Hiroshima, were taken from their secret underground store in the

Negev and rushed to a nearby airfield. There they were put together and put on Phantom and Kfir fighters. However, in the time it had taken for the order to be issued and the bombs to reach the waiting aircraft – some four hours – the tide of battle had turned in the Israelis' favour. The bombs were dismantled and nuclear war in the Middle East had been postponed.

Aside from the story itself, the interesting thing about that account is that it was leaked by the Israelis themselves to *Time* magazine who published it on April 12, 1976, three years after the event.

Clearly, the Israelis were concerned that their policy of keeping the bomb in the basement had not delivered a clear enough message to their Arab neighbours. So, by releasing the information, the message was being written in clear terms. But for those cynical government officials in Washington, London and Bonn who pore over every piece of intelligence that comes out of Tel Aviv or Jerusalem with a distrust bordering on the paranoid, even the *Time* article was not sufficient proof. It was possible, they argued, that Israel was merely leaking the story as a way of bringing the mythical bomb out of the basement. There were those in Israeli military circles who had been arguing that if the Arabs believed Israel had nuclear weapons, and it was made clear they would be used if Israel was attacked, then spending on conventional defence could be reduced.

It took another eleven years for even the most sceptical to be convinced. This time proof came not from sophisticated satellites, an intelligence coup or via some complicated Israeli plot. Israel's nuclear programme was laid bare by one man who had worked inside Dimona, who had a guilty conscience about his work, and who wanted to tell his story to the world. That man's name was Mordechai Vanunu and the story he had to tell would horrify even Israel's closest allies in the United States.

The Vanunu Revelations

Like so many of the best stories, the definitive account of Israel's nuclear programme came about entirely by chance. On August 26, 1987, the correspondent for *The Sunday Times* in Madrid bumped into another journalist he had met a few times previously, a Columbian named Oscar Guerrero. The two talked briefly and Guerrero claimed that he had a major story about the Israeli nuclear programme which he was about to sell to an American magazine. [1]

The Sunday Times correspondent persuaded Guerrero to offer it to *The Sunday Times* first. Jon Swain, one of the newspaper's most experienced journalists, flew from Paris to Madrid that night. What he was shown there was not impressive.

Guerrero produced some blurred colour photographs of what he claimed were 'glove boxes' (sealed units used to handle toxic substances) and some exterior shots of what looked like a large building surrounded by desert. Finally, there were shots of what Guerrero claimed was the bomb itself. To Swain, who had little knowledge of nuclear physics or the characteristics of a nuclear bomb, the evidence was unimpressive. So was the man.

Guerrero was an unstable combination of boasting and ignorance. He said his source for the photographs was 'the scientist who designed the bomb' and that there were many more pictures available. He claimed to have met the scientist in Tel Aviv and to have organised his escape to Sydney, Australia, where he was now in hiding. But when pressed he actually knew only the most superficial details about Israel's nuclear programme and clearly had not heard the full story from his source.

There were also some suspicions about his credibility as a journalist. Admittedly he carried a collection of photographs showing himself with various international figures, including Lech Walesa of Solidarity, Israeli leader Shimon Peres, Gerd Heidemann, one of the organisers of the Hitler Diary fraud, and PLO leader Issam Sartawi, who was assassinated in 1983, just after being interviewed by Guerrero. But despite such an apparent pedigree as an international reporter, he showed very little grasp of current affairs or politics.

However, the photographs did not seem to be fakes so he was flown to London for further questioning. The pictures were examined by an expert in nuclear engineering and although he too was not certain, there remained sufficient doubt to make the project worth further investigation.

A member of *The Sunday Times* Insight team, Peter Hounam, who had trained as a physicist, flew to Sydney with Guerrero to meet the 'scientist'.

On August 30, Hounam met with an extremely nervous Mordechai Vanunu – a man who in fact made no claims to have designed Israel's nuclear bomb. Instead, with hands shaking, chain smoking cigarettes and speaking in broken English, he detailed his fairly humble career as a technician working for the Israeli Atomic Energy Commission.

A Moroccan Jew who had emigrated to Israel, left his adopted homeland for Australia and then become a born-again Christian, he appeared at least spiritually confused. And although he claimed to be telling his story because his conscience was troubled by Israel's nuclear programme, it was more than a year since he had left Israel. In fact it was pure chance that he was telling his story at all. Vanunu and Guerrero had met when the latter came to his church in Sydney to do some painting and decorating. Guerrero 'the international journalist', who had photographs showing him with famous people, had been sent to the church as part of the work party organised and paid for by the Sydney unemployment office.

The two men evidently talked during the painting. Then, one day when Guerrero was working on the church roof, he fell fifty feet to the ground, bouncing off an outhouse on the way down. He was fortunate to survive the experience with only a bruised back but he spent some time in hospital recovering. During this period, Vanunu visited his friend and it was then that the two agreed that Guerrero should head for Europe and try to sell the Israeli's extraordinary story.

Vanunu claimed to have been working on plutonium production in Dimona and, to back up his claim that he knew what had been going on inside the plant, he produced a collection of slides which he claimed he had taken one evening when there were few people on duty.

These slides were projected onto the wall of Hounam's hotel bedroom at the Sydney Hilton and, unlike those first produced by Guerrero, they were a revelation. Each slide appeared to show new and extraordinary details of the nuclear plant: control panels of different plutonium production processes with flow diagrams above them showing how each process worked; shots of lathes inside glove boxes which could be used to machine plutonium; and shot after shot of the plant itself, both inside and out.

Vanunu claimed to have learned of the existence of a room inside the nuclear plant that was used for shows demonstrating the progress being made on *Operation Hump*, as the nuclear programme was called, to important visiting Israeli politicians and military officers. The room included detailed floor plans of the complex and models of the different stages of bomb production and even mock-ups of the bombs themselves.

Vanunu had noticed that the senior technician in charge of the room always left his key on top of his locker, so it was a simple matter for the young technician to borrow the key and gain access to the room during a shift change when the corridors were quiet.

He had managed to smuggle his Pentax camera into the plant, hidden under his university books in a holdall. Searches of workers were always cursory but if the camera had been found Vanunu had an explanation ready: 'I would have told them that I had forgotten it was there. I deliberately left the film out so as not to arouse suspicions. All they would have done would be to take it off me and hang it on a hook so I could collect it on the way out. I took in the film in the same way a few days later. The real risk was bringing the film out, they could have developed it, but I was not discovered. I had worked there a long time, many of the guards were my friends. There was trust between us.'

Two pictures in particular showed a lithium deuteride shield, used in the construction of the hydrogen bomb, a weapon capable of yielding the explosive force of half a million tons of TNT. If Israel had actually produced such a weapon then her nuclear capability was far in excess of anything western intelligence agencies had estimated even in their most pessimistic assessments.

The information was sent back to London and checked with scientists working in Britain's nuclear programme at Aldermarston, and with other independent experts, including Frank Barnaby, the former head of the Stockholm International Peace Research Institute and a world authority on nuclear weapons. All those who saw the information believed that it was genuine.

From the outset, however, there was concern that Guerrero and Vanunu could be part of an elaborate plot by Israeli intelligence to get *The Sunday Times* to publish the story of Israel's nuclear programme. *The Sunday Times* had been unpopular with the Israeli government since it published a story in the 1970s about Israeli torture of Palestinian prisoners. If this were a hoax, it would be a perfect method for the Israelis to pay off old scores.

There was a risk that Vanunu and Guerrero were themselves just hoaxers, out to make money from *The Sunday Times*. Four years earlier *The Sunday Times* had been the victim of one of the most successful newspaper hoaxes of all time, the selling of the diaries allegedly written by Adolf Hitler which turned out to be forgeries. One of the main characters in the fraud was a collector of Nazi memorabilia named Gerd Heidemann, one of the very men whose picture had been taken alongside Guerrero.

Finally, the reputation of the Mossad and the Israeli security system in general suggested it was most unlikely that security measures were really so lax. Of all countries in the world, Israel was arguably the most concerned with security, and yet for months Vanunu was apparently able to roam around the nuclear plant taking photographs almost at will. Security checks had to have been negligible, which seemed very out of character for Israel.

Hounam took photographs of Vanunu which were sent to England. Another journalist then took them to Israel and, using a list of friends provided by Vanunu, set about checking on his background.

This stage of the investigation, coupled with what Vanunu had already revealed, helped piece together his background and early career. But, as part of their checking of Vanunu's background, the newspaper interviewed a woman friend of Vanunu's in Tel Aviv and, unknown to them, she had close contacts with Mossad. She alerted them to *The Sunday Times* investigation, and a secret operation was immediately launched to find Vanunu and stop him talking.

Mordechai Vanunu, known to his friends as Mordy, was born on October 13, 1954, in the old Moroccan city of Marrakech. His mother and father, who ran a small shop, had stayed on after the first major wave of Moroccan Jews, including one of his grandfathers and most of his aunts, uncles and cousins, left for Israel in 1952. Vanunu therefore started his education in a French/Arabic speaking school.

By early 1963, when he was eight and his other grandfather had died, anti-Israel feeling began to harden in Morocco and his parents reluctantly decided to leave. After a nightmarish sea journey from Casablanca to Marseilles, and a month in a French refugee camp, they finally arrived in Haifa on June 13, and from there were despatched, without much ceremony or option, to the remote southern town of Beersheba in the middle of the Negev desert.

It was in December of that year, thirty miles away across the arid landscape, that Israel's hush-hush new Dimona nuclear reactor went critical. But the almost-unpublicised event made little impact on an immigrant family busy trying to put down fresh roots. Young Mordy, after adjusting himself to the austere conditions, started to improve his Hebrew, sharpen up his mathematical talents, and prepare for life as an Israeli citizen.

At eighteen, like tens of thousands of other teenagers, he went off to do his three years' military service, which in his case included the 1973 October War. In 1974, as a trained sapper, he was on the far side of the Golan Heights, blowing up army installations before that territory was handed back to the Syrians. Soon after, he returned to civilian status and started to think about his future career.

In 1975, he decided to enrol at Ramat Aviv university, in Tel Aviv, to study physics, but a year later, after failing two important exams, he gave up and returned home to Beersheba in search of a job. It was there, by chance, that he ran into a friend of his younger brother, Meir, who happened to work at KMG, the acronym for Kirya le-Mehekar Gariny, the Negev Nuclear Research Centre, which is the body responsible for running the whole Dimona complex.

Hearing that they were recruiting additional staff and paying good money, Vanunu decided to apply. He filled in an application form at the KMG offices, which were then on the third floor of a building near the main Beersheba bus station, and was interviewed by a girl who he later discovered worked in the KMG security office. She grilled him to discover if he had a drug problem, criminal record or doubtful political associations, and a month later he was notified he had been accepted for training.

His first ten weeks were spent on a crash course in chemistry, physics, mathematics and English, held in the town of Dimona, ten miles away and the place where most of the 2,700 scientists, technicians and office staff lived. He found that two of the other forty-four candidates had been in the same class as his brother Meir at high school in Beersheba and most came from nearby towns. At the end of January 1976, they all took an exam, which everyone passed. Six of the group were rejected however, and Vanunu assumed, but was not officially told, that this was on security grounds.

Early in February, the survivors had their first look inside the KMG perimeter. They travelled in one of the distinctive blue-and-white Volvo coaches which transport the Dimona workforce. Nine miles down the highway to the Dead Sea they turned right down a side road and stopped at the first of two army check-points. The second, three miles further on, marked the entry to the main compound, which was additionally protected by an electrified fence and an extensive area of sand, meticulously raked by tractor and regularly examined to make sure that no unauthorised feet had tried to cross. Once inside, the new intake were required to sign the Israeli equivalent of the Official Secrets Act, forbidding disclosure of security-sensitive information under penalty of a prison term of up to fifteen years. They were also made to promise not to visit any Communist or Arab country for at least five years after leaving the service of the centre. During this session, Vanunu was issued with his pass number, 9657–8, and subjected to a series of health checks.

He and his classmates then embarked on a further two-month course, covering nuclear physics and chemistry, radio-activity, technical English, chemical engineering, and the rudiments of first-aid and fire drill. The lessons now took place in one of six classrooms at a small school on the site. After another examination in April, the group, now thinned out by a few academic failures, split up into two groups of fourteen. Half became radioactivity checkers, and the rest, including Vanunu, started preparing themselves to be process controllers.

His induction period at the centre lasted nine months. At last, on November 2, 1976, he was placed on the KMG payroll – the same month that thirteen US senators on a fact-finding tour of Israel were flatly refused entry to the Dimona complex. A year later, when Vanunu was working in the plutonium plant, he found a newspaper cutting which some-one had thoughtfully pinned up. It quoted the official com-ment made to these senators, that Israel had never produced any weapons-related material.

Vanunu was one of six allocated to Machon 2, the plu-tonium separation unit. Four others went to Machon 4, deal-ing with high-level radioactive waste. And a further four went to Machon 8, the central laboratory, primarily concerned with purity-testing and experimental development of new pro-cesses. Machon 2, with its two floors above ground and five more buried deep in the dusty desert scrubland, was one of the most complex constructions on the Dimona site. Its multifold activities, which ranged from heavy water improvement to the manufacture of bomb components, were then divided among units numbered from 10 to 92 (though quite a few were non-operational) and the new staff intake were given ten weeks to familiarise themselves.

Vanunu was given a special Machon 2 pass number, 320, his own locker (No.3), and told that he must always use the bathroom No.14. He was also introduced for the first time to Machon 2's chief engineer, who informed the new intake that they would each be required to specialise by learning the intricacies of two units particularly well.

Vanunu and two others were assigned to Units 11 and 92 (stripping the aluminum casing from spent fuel rods and repurifying the heavy water) with Units 31, 33, 36, and 24 (mainly concerned with plutonium) as their second subject. They later discovered that one man had died in unit 36 in 1969 when some alcohol exploded during cleaning. A week later, Vanunu was surprised to be called up for a month's reserve duty with his army unit but when the nature of his job was explained, he was quickly released.

Within seven days he was back in Machon 2, where he learned that, after passing his final tests, he would be working on the night shift from 11.30pm to 8.00am. After satisfying a three-man examination board comprising an independent engineer, one of the Dimona lecturers and a specialist in handling radioactive materials, he was appointed to a full-time post. On August 7, 1977, he reported for his first full day's work, his salary rising from $300 a month to $500.

About 250 people were bussed into Machon 2 each day and Vanunu was put on duty in the main control room, about twenty-five feet underground. His job, keeping the uranium and heavy water processes in operation, was fairly straight-forward, with most of the activity concentrated on the first and last two-hour periods of a thirty-hour cycle. 'It was a bit like bread-baking,' he said. 'During the cooking little effort is required beyond checking that nothing goes wrong.'

His main task, apart from reporting any faults that showed up on the control panels, was to change the oxygen-supply bottles, which until 1980 had to be done by hand. Vanunu was not tied to the control room during these quiet periods. He could spend time in the canteen, take a shower, or visit friends in other sections. But he was not allowed outside: the people in each Machon were encouraged to see themselves as a self-contained community with minimal contact elsewhere on the site.

In March 1978 Vanunu moved to units 12–30 which were concerned with uranium separation. He had learned this process on his own initiative during the training period, and now found the work quite easy. Everything proceeded automatically, round the clock, and merely required the regular preparation of routine reports. The main concern was to preserve every drop of chemical called TBP (tri-butyl phosphite) which the Israelis apparently found very hard to obtain. It had to be accounted for constantly and if any went missing, supervisors were called immediately to track it down.

In August 1979, Vanunu switched again, this time to Machon 4, where the most dangerous of Dimona's radioactive waste was treated. There was a suggestion at that time that Machon 2 and Machon 4 should be amalgamated, but this ran into stubborn resistance from the workers involved. The waste-disposal men refused to cooperate, either in teaching their own skills or learning the production techniques needed for plutonium, so the idea foundered.

Each of the different jobs that Vanunu had were repetitive and boring and he was left with time on his hands. In November 1979, he signed on for a part-time course at Ben-Gurion University in Beersheba. At first he intended studying engineering, and then, after a week, changed over to economics and Greek philosophy. This decision was eventually to have a big impact on Vanunu's outlook on his work.

But at first he was happy simply learning the different processes and getting a broader knowledge of the workings of Dimona. He took a short holiday and then returned to Machon 2, where he found that technicians and engineers were installing a brand-new unit, No.95, producing Lithium–6. This is a highly volatile metal which Vanunu knew, even from his very incomplete studies, was a key ingredient in advanced nuclear weapons.

His fears were confirmed one day, when he asked a supervisor what it could be used for. He was told, laconically: 'the hydrogen bomb'.

It took a year to install the extra process. There was a permanent staff of about three engineers, backed up by a cohort of technicians, and it was the end of 1980 before unit 95 finally came on line. As far as Vanunu was able to observe, it was the first important development at Dimona that was designed, built and installed entirely by Israeli scientists.

All the earlier equipment in Machon 2 was essentially French, and several senior supervisors had recalled, in the course of casual chats, how they had worked with the French engineers who had set up the plant in the early 1960s.

By now Vanunu had been promoted to a higher salary scale and was being employed on a wider variety of jobs and shifts. He also qualified for the privilege of being paid extra money for a car. On August 4, 1980, he set off for a long holiday in Europe using his saved-up leave allowance. It was the first time he had ever left his adopted country since arriving from Morocco. He returned to Dimona to find Unit 95 being tested. The work, which he shared with five other technicians, working on split shifts round the clock, took up the whole of that year. Now, when he again asked the senior engineers what Lithium–6 was used for, they said they did not know: 'It was made clear that our job was to produce Lithium–6 and not ask questions.'

By 1982, Vanunu was aiming for a full university degree in philosophy and geography, and getting more deeply involved in spare-time university politics. When the Israelis invaded Lebanon in Operation Peace for Galilee that year, Vanunu, like many other young Israelis, became seriously disillusioned about the direction his adopted country was taking. He went on demonstrations supporting various Palestinian causes and became increasingly vocal in his criticisms. For the first time, at the age of thirty, he contemplated leaving KMG and rejecting all it stood for.

When he finally left Israel for a new life in Australia on January 19, 1986, Vanunu took with him his photographs from Dimona. At this stage he had no clear idea of what he planned to do with them and he certainly had no idea either of their worth or their political significance.

On September 11, Vanunu was flown back to England by *The Sunday Times* so that he could meet with nuclear experts and have his story checked. The closer he was questioned the more convincing was the remarkable information that he revealed. The experts accepted not only that Israel had developed a nuclear capability but also that the plant had produced enough raw materials to make between 100 and 200 nuclear weapons.

Typical of the expert reaction was that of Frank Barnaby: 'I have had an opportunity to meet Mr Vanunu on a number of occasions and discussed in detail all the processes used in Machon 2, the building in which plutonium, Lithium–6 and tritium were made. As a nuclear physicist, it was clear to me that details he gave were scientifically accurate and clearly showed that he had not only worked on these processes but knew the details of the techniques. The flow rates through the plant, which he quotes, exactly confirm the quantities of plutonium that were being made.

'The total of thirty kilograms a year was a great surprise to me as it means that the Dimona reactor is very much larger – perhaps six or more times larger – than the size that is often officially quoted. One reason to change our assessment of Israel's nuclear policy after hearing his testimony, which seems to me to be totally convincing, is the sheer size of its nuclear arsenal.

'With a production rate of about thirty kilograms of plutonium a year, Israel could produce seven nuclear weapons a year. Israel could now have a total of well over a hundred weapons. This means that Israel is not the pygmy nuclear-weapon power we thought but a nuclear power of a status approaching that of China (which has about 300 nuclear weapons), France (about 500 nuclear weapons) and the UK (about 700 nuclear weapons). The USA and the USSR are, of course, in a class of their own; each has about 25,000 nuclear weapons.

'Another reason for now changing our assessment of Israel's nuclear status is its production of tritium and lithium-hydrides. Until now, the general assumption had been that, if Israel has produced nuclear weapons, they are so-called "first generation" nuclear weapons, based on the Nagasaki design. The crucial material in such a weapon is plutonium. The acquisition by Israel of lithium-deuteride implies that it has become a thermonuclear-weapon power – a manufacturer of hydrogen bombs – confirming its status in the same nuclear club as China, France and the UK.

'The evidence of *The Sunday Times*'s discoveries is that Israel has the ability to turn out weapons with a yield of 200–250 kilotons, equivalent in size to the latest ICBM missiles deployed by the United States and four or five times bigger than the Chevaline missiles now installed in Britain's Polaris submarine fleet. Israel has shown that a small developing country can become a thermonuclear power with virtually no help from others.'

Satisfied that the story was accurate, *The Sunday Times* prepared to put the allegations officially to the Israeli embassy in London. For the Israelis, the last few weeks had been difficult. Mossad lacked the vital intelligence that would tell them exactly where Vanunu was, although they had guessed by now that he was in England. During the checking process, official British government sources had been used to gain access to nuclear experts familiar with current technology, but relations between Israeli intelligence and the British Secret Intelligence Service or even with the Security Service are frosty at the best of times. About the only information that is shared relates to terrorism – and even that, when it originates in Jerusalem, is treated with great caution in London. So, on this occasion, Mossad didn't even bother to ask for help, knowing they would receive none.

For the Israelis, the issue was a simple one. Vanunu was a traitor. He should be prevented from talking and if possible brought back to Israel to pay for his crime.

18

Swallowing a Spy

The Mossad psychologists assessed Vanunu perfectly. They saw him as an immature, sexually inexperienced, rather naive man, ideal for a 'swallow' operation, the oldest trick in the spies' handbook. This means sending in an attractive and experienced female agent to seduce the target.

The woman Israeli intelligence chose to entrap Vanunu was 27-year-old Cheryl Bentov who had been born Cheryl Hanin in Orlando, Florida. During her junior year at Edgewater High School, she went to work on a kibbutz. Like many other receptive 17-year-olds, she was very impressed by Israel. She emigrated there and settled on a kibbutz at Hephzibah where she met and married an Israeli, Olfer Bentov, in March 1985.

To many, the adult Cheryl made a rather obvious Mata Hari. Plump, with dyed blonde hair, full red lips and heavily made up, she fitted less the role of the international spy and more of a cheap date. But, to Vanunu, tired of being cooped up in London hotels and watched by *The Sunday Times* reporters, she represented the freedom he wanted and the sex he had never had.

On Tuesday, September 23, the Israeli embassy in London was contacted by *The Sunday Times* reporters for comment about the Vanunu story. The query would not have come as a surprise to the Israelis. Eleven days before, Vanunu was walking down Regent Street in London's West End when he bumped into Yoram Bazak, a friend from Israel. Over coffee

the two got into an argument about Israel's nuclear programme and Vanunu hinted that he might be going to tell
what he knew. His friend replied: 'Although you are my
friend, I would find a way to take you back to Israel and put
you in jail.' If the Israelis did not know already that Vanunu
was in England, this chance meeting gave them the intelligence they needed.

But finding Vanunu's actual location was not easy. His
hotel was changed regularly and he was not registered in his
own name. Immediately after the visit by the reporters to the
Israeli Embassy, a mysterious two-man camera crew turned
up at *The Sunday Times'* headquarters in Wapping near Tower
Bridge. This crew was photographed by security cameras at
the plant, but despite intensive checks, it has been impossible
to identify them. The assumption is they were Mossad agents
on a reconnaissance mission.

The next day, Wednesday, September 24, the Israeli
Embassy commented on the Vanunu story: 'It is not the first
time that stories of this kind have appeared in the press. They
have no basis whatsoever in reality and hence any further
comment is superfluous.'

That evening Vanunu was walking in Leicester Square
when he spotted an attractive blonde girl. Vanunu's brother,
Meir, then explains what happened: 'For the first time in his
life, he plucked up the courage and made an approach. She
appeared to be shy but agreed to go for a coffee. During the
following days in London, she refused to sleep with him
but said she would feel comfortable doing so in a different
environment – not a hotel. At first she wanted him to go to
America with her (her family came from Florida) but he
refused. Then she suggested her sister's house in Rome. She
bought the air tickets and he promised to repay her.'

For the role of seductress, Cheryl Bentov had adopted a
new identity, that of her sister-in-law Cynthia Ann (Cindy)
Hanin of Spyglass Cove, Longwood, Orlando, Florida. Cindy
had married Cheryl's brother, Randy, on November 2, 1986.

Cheryl even told Vanunu that she was a 'make-up artist' which was close enough to Cindy's job of assistant beautician.

To the innocent Vanunu, Cheryl appeared as an unsophisticated girl who, like him, was alone in a foreign country and needing friendship. Denying him sex only made him all the more enthusiastic. Bored, with nothing to do but read English grammar books bought specially for him or go to films, he no doubt spun fantasies around Cheryl and the wonderful time they would have once they got to her sister's house in Rome.

On Monday, September 29, his infatuation with Cindy became known to *The Sunday Times*. He was repeatedly warned that he would be at risk if he travelled and while he clearly recognised the danger, his passion for Cheryl overcame all caution.

Shortly after 11.00 am on Tuesday September 30, Vanunu checked out of his hotel and disappeared.

By this time, Vanunu's information had been examined by nine different scientists, both in Britain and the United States, and in every case it proved to be accurate. That Sunday, October 5, *The Sunday Times* published the full story of Israel's nuclear programme.

But Vanunu's whereabouts remained a mystery. Over the next few weeks fragmentary reports emerged from Israel that Vanunu was in jail, had been charged and would be tried for unspecified crimes against the state. The first real clue to what had happened to him came on December 21 as he was being taken to court by prison van. He pressed the palm of his hand against the van window. On it he had written: 'Vanunu M, was hijacked, in Rome ITL, 30.9.86, 2100, came in Rome by BA fly 504'. This carefully written message was enough to prise open the Mossad operation to kidnap the man they considered a traitor.

After checking out of his hotel, Vanunu had gone to Heathrow airport with Cheryl who was travelling under the name of Miss C Hanin. They checked onto British Airways flight

504 to Rome and sat in business class seats 6E and 6F. Vanunu's brother Meir then takes up the story:

'Outside the airport, she hailed what he thought was a cab which took them to a house in a built-up area, probably in Rome itself. As they entered the house, Cindy [Cheryl] disappeared and two men and a woman grabbed Vanunu and stuck a hypodermic in his arm.

'He does not know how long he was out, maybe a day or longer. He drifted in and out of consciousness and remembers men discussing his murder. He came round in a windowless room in a ship. For several days he was kept there by two men. He was terrified, expecting to be killed at any moment. Occasionally he was drugged but by what he never knew – maybe his food. The men spoke only in English but with an Israeli accent and never questioned him about what he had done. He was not ill-treated. Eventually, a week after his capture, he arrived back in Israel and a copy of *The Sunday Times* was thrust under his nose. "See what you have done," they said.'

What Vanunu had done was to expose the full extent of Israel's nuclear programme. Much of the story had already seeped out over the years for anyone with the patience to piece the strands together, but never before had there been a convincing eyewitness account. Not even the western intelligence agencies, which had taken a close interest in the project for so long, had managed to get the fine detail that Vanunu presented to the world.

Vanunu was tried for treason after spending nearly 18 months in solitary confinement. He was sentenced to 18 years imprisonment in May 1988. To underline the official Israeli outrage at Vanunu's behaviour, he is being kept in spartan conditions in the high security jail at Ashkelon on the Mediterranean coast, where only his family and lawyer are allowed to make brief occasional visits.

Arab governments reacted with predictable outrage to the Vanunu revelations, but their protests were surprisingly muted. There was no serious attempt at coordinating a concerted response through the United Nations, for example. To most Arab leaders, who already viewed Israel as capable of any perfidy, the Vanunu revelations merely confirmed their worst suspicions.

It is difficult to gauge the long-term effect of Vanunu's tale. The important Arab countries are already embarked on their own escalatory programmes to produce either nuclear weapons, ballistic missiles, or chemical and biological weapons. The fact that Israel is actually confirmed as possessing nuclear weapons will do little to any of these projects.

The most interesting effect may be on Israel itself. For more than twenty years, the Israeli government has kept the bomb firmly in the basement. It still does. But as the economy has slowly disintegrated under the pressure of sustaining such a small country on what is, in effect, a permanent war footing, there have been repeated internal political attempts to bring the bomb out of the basement. This would allow the Israelis to threaten to use their nuclear weapons as a first line defence rather than as a weapon of last resort. And if that deterrent were believed – and the Arabs have plenty of first-hand experience that Israel keeps its promises – then resources currently devoted to conventional weapons could be diverted to more peaceful projects.

The Islamic Bomb

Shortly before he was hanged in April 1979, the former Prime Minister of Pakistan, Zulfiqar Ali Bhutto, smuggled a 200-page document out from his prison cell. The handwritten document was his political last will and testament and included a telling passage relating to Pakistan's capability to develop nuclear weapons.

'We know that Israel and South Africa have full nuclear capability,' he wrote. 'The Christian, Jewish and Hindu civilisations have this capability. The communist powers also possess it. Only the Islamic civilisation is without it. But that position is about to change.'

These were prophetic words from the man who was truly the father of the Pakistan bomb. In December 1972, Bhutto had called a meeting of the fifty top Pakistani scientists in the grounds of an old colonial mansion in the town of Multan, close to the border with India and far away from prying eyes. At that meeting it was agreed that Pakistan would use all her efforts to develop a nuclear weapons capability. Some of the scientists present even suggested that Pakistan could develop a nuclear weapon within three years.[1]

This was wildly over-optimistic, but at the time Pakistan had already received a Candu nuclear reactor from the Canadians which produced electricity for Karachi and they had plans to buy a plutonium reprocessing plant from the French.

Pakistan would have liked to develop an atom bomb using plutonium refined to 'weapons grade', the enrichment plant they bought from France in 1975, but it would be subject to international inspection. Instead, Bhutto opted for an enriched uranium based hydrogen bomb which would use Pakistan's own reserves of natural uranium, and an enrichment plant made entirely from goods and technology smuggled from the west. Therefore a totally covert operation was set up which has run continuously, if in different guises, ever since.

Although Bhutto had made a firm commitment to develop nuclear weapons, the technology was not as easy to find as he had thought. But in May 1974, Pakistan's traditional enemy India had tested her own nuclear device. Butto had always made clear that once India acquired a bomb then Pakistan would have to get one too. Some years before he had said: 'If India builds the bomb, we will eat grass or leaves, even go hungry, but we will get one of our own.'[2] This was no idle boast and the Pakistan government now used all the considerable ingenuity available to it to achieve that goal.

The key figure in this plot was a young Pakistani scientist, Dr Abdel Qader Khan. Born in Bhopal in 1936, Khan was educated in Europe and in 1972 was employed in Holland at a company called FDO which specialised in research into metallurgy, particularly as it applied to nuclear power. Then he moved to the Almelo Institute, a joint venture by Britain, West Germany and the Netherlands. The Institute was developing new methods of enriching uranium using a centrifuge. This technology was secret and access to the research was restricted. But Khan was married to a Dutch-speaking South African with a British passport, and in the small scientific community, where work rather than spying was the focus, he became completely accepted.

When Dr Khan returned to Pakistan at the end of 1975, he took with him comprehensive notes and photographs of the new uranium enrichment method and these were immediately put to use at a new plant being developed at Kahuta. In absentia Kahn was sentenced in 1985 to four years in jail by a Dutch court for stealing confidential papers. Two years later that verdict was overturned on a legal technicality because Pakistan had refused to serve Khan with the court summons and instead he was put on a list of undesirable aliens by the Dutch government.

But, like all good spies, Khan had recruited agents of his own, and when he left Europe a network was in place that would continue to supply Pakistan with information and equipment for the next fifteen years. One of the key figures was Henk Slebos, a Dutch engineer whom Khan had first met at university. Through his consultancy firm, Alkmeer, Slebos legally supplied Pakistan with 10,000 steel balls used in centrifuges. Then, in 1983, he sent to Pakistan a cargo of wide-band oscilloscopes. This was illegal, and in 1985 he was sentenced to a year in jail, later reduced to a six-month suspended sentence, and fined $6,800. This does not seem to have acted as a disincentive as, during 1985 and 1986 alone, Slebos received $312,000 paid into a West German bank account by the Pakistani embassy in Bonn. On Christmas Eve 1988, Kahn was stopped by police near the southern Dutch city of Bergen op Zoom. The car was being driven by Slebos who at the time was being watched by Dutch security police. Although he was carrying forged identity papers, Khan was recognised and put on the next plane to Pakistan.

With the designs and technology in place, all that was needed now were the raw materials. Here, too, Pakistan was able to exploit the poor security relating to all nuclear materials. A cover organisation was set up, the Special Works Organisation of the Ordnance Service of the Government of Pakistan, based in Rawalpindi. The equipment was actually bought using a series of dummy companies based in Britain, Amsterdam and Germany. Many of the companies made only a single order, resold the equipment to Pakistan, and then went out of business.

The network of dummy businesses, the millions being ploughed into the nuclear programme, and the statements made by Bhutto all contributed to a sense in the US intelligence community that Pakistan was well on the way to developing its own nuclear weapons. While the American government might not have been willing to do much about it, Congress was determined to curb Pakistan. In 1976, and 1977, the Symington-Glenn Amendments to the Foreign Assistance Act were passed to outlaw US assistance to any nation that receives unsafeguarded nuclear technology, or detonators, or that transfers a nuclear device. The 1978 Nuclear Non-Proliferation Act further tightened the existing restrictions on firms wanting to export materials that could be used to make a nuclear bomb.

After detecting repeated violations of the Symington-Glenn Amendments, President Carter cut off all aid to Pakistan in 1979. At the time, there was a debate within the State Department and the intelligence community that was to be repeated many times over the next decade. Some argued that aid acted as a useful lever and that if it were cut off the US government would have no means of pressuring Pakistan to change its nuclear plans. But the realists knew then, as they do now, that the best America could hope for was delay, never cancellation.

Shortly after US aid was cut off the Soviets invaded Afghanistan and Pakistan became a vital ally to the US in its support for the mujahedeen guerrillas and their fight against the Soviet invaders. Aid was restored in 1981 after Congress had hastily agreed a six-year waiver of the Symington-Glenn Amendments. As a sop to those critics of the aid programme, the Reagan administration warned Pakistan that her nuclear programme was endangering the aid.

In 1985, a Pakistani national, Nazir Ahmed Vaid, was caught trying to smuggle krytrons, which are special high speed electrical switches used in detonating nuclear weapons, out of the USA. The case caused outrage in Congress and resulted in the passing of a new amendment to the 1985 Symington-Glenn Amendments to the Foreign Assistance Act. The amendment stated that 'no assistance may be provided to any non-nuclear-weapon state that exports illegally, or attempts to export illegally, from the United States any materials which would "contribute significantly" to that country's bomb making capability.' For an aid cutoff to occur, the President would have to decide that the illegal exports were to be used for the manufacture of nuclear weapons. The amendment applied not just to foreign governments but to any individual 'who is an agent of, or is otherwise acting on behalf of or in the interests of' a foreign government.

Nevertheless the Pakistan nuclear weapons programme continued uninterrupted: the government of General Zia recognised that the US would never cut off aid to Pakistan and jeopardise their ability to support the mujahedeen. In June 1986, the Soviets warned Pakistan that they would not tolerate her developing nuclear weapons. This provoked the US to warn the Soviets to keep out of Pakistan's affairs. Washington had taken on the role of protector of Pakistan's nuclear programme.

On November 5, 1987, Arshad Pervez, a Pakistan-born Canadian citizen representing a company called AP Enterprises, contacted the Carpenter Steel Corporation of Reading, Pennsylvania. He wished to order 50,000 pounds of maraging 350 steel which he claimed would be 'remelted' and used in Pakistan.

Maraging steel is a particularly strong alloy made from nickel, cobalt and molybdenum. It is used in the manufacture of centrifuges for a uranium enrichment plant, and enriched uranium is the essential ingredient for one type of nuclear weapon. Pervez's claim that the steel would be 'remelted' was clearly nonsense as such a process would introduce impurities into the steel which would render it virtually useless.[3]

Two years earlier, Carpenter Steel had been approached at their London office by an official from the Pakistani embassy, Abdul Jamil. Describing himself as the 'procurement manager', Jamil claimed the steel would be used in a Pakistani gun factory to build components for an air-to-air missile. He even guaranteed that the steel would not be used in the Pakistan nuclear facility. Even so, Carpenter Steel made it clear that they would require an export licence from the US

Department of Commerce and at that stage the embassy abandoned the deal. They then seem to have decided on a more clandestine approach, using Pervez.

Believing that the steel might still be used in Pakistan's uranium enrichment plant at Kahuta, Carpenter immediately notified the US customs of this second approach.

On the instructions of the customs, Albert Tomley, Carpenter's general manager for international marketing, forwarded a quote of $256,000 for the steel to the headquarters of AP Enterprises in Toronto. Pervez then agreed to meet with Carpenter officials in Toronto to discuss the sale in more detail.

On November 9, Tomley flew to Toronto with an undercover US customs agent, John New, and, accompanied by an undercover Canadian agent, they met with Pervez. The Pakistani told the meeting that his client was a 'Mr Inam' of the Multinational Corporation in Lahore. 'Mr Inam' later turned out to be retired army Brigadier General, Inam al Haq. As part of his international network, al Haq had established a special company, Aluelex Systems Ltd, in the Isle of Man, a tax haven in the Irish Sea between Ireland and Britain.

Initially, Pervez claimed the destination of the steel was the Pakistan equivalent of the National Aeronautics Aero Space Administration (NASA). He then claimed the steel was going to a research project sponsored by Karachi University's research programme. Pervez asked the customs agent to help get an export licence for the steel. When John New told Pervez that such exports would be prohibited because the US government believed the steel was destined for Pakistan's nuclear facility, Pervez said he would be prepared to offer a bribe of $5,000 to the appropriate Commerce licencing officer.

Over the next few days, Pervez became worried that his bribe was too generous and suggested to New that he pay no more than $3,000. On January 13, Pervez came to the Sheraton Hotel in Philadelphia where he met with US Customs undercover agent Frank Rovello, who was pretending to be a Department of Commerce licence officer. Pervez handed over $1,000 as an initial bribe with the promise of a further $2,000 when the licence came through.

Ten days later, Pervez flew to Reading, Pennsylvania, for a tour of the Carpenter plant. During the stroll around the production area, Tomley said he had serious reservations about the order. Tomley pointed out that Pervez had said that the steel was going to be used in 'turbines and compressors' and at various times had claimed four other different uses for the steel. But in Tomley's experience Pervez would require thousands of tons of steel if they were to be used in the manufacture of turbines, far more than had been ordered. Forcing the issue, Tomley said to Pervez: 'The material is going to be used in a gas centrifuge enrichment plant to make nuclear weapons. Isn't that true?' Pervez nodded.

Despite this, in February Pervez sent Tomley a letter of credit and two certificates, one from the general manager of Multinations Inc and the other from the Pakistan Council of Scientific and Industrial Research, stating that the steel was indeed going to be used in turbines and compressors.

To maintain the fiction, a fake licence was then issued. But, even with his apparent certainty now of getting the goods, Perez continued looking for a cheaper source for the steel. At around the same time as Carpenter was first approached, another specialist steel company, Teledyne Vasco of Latrobe, Pennsylvania, had received an inquiry for maraging steel. This call came from one M I Fareed, representing a firm called Burkin Trade Links of Regent Street in London, but once the connection had been made, Fareed said all communications should be handled by BTL's Canadian office in Willowdale, Ontario, the same location as Pervez's front company, AP Enterprises.

Fareed also claimed that the steel would be used for turbines and compressors, but asked Teledyne Vasco to fake the exact nature of the steel by describing it as 'special tool alloy'. The company refused to do this and the deal died.

But five months later, armed with his valuable export

licence, Pervez tried another variation of the scam. Teledyne were contacted again, this time by an Aktar Syed, apparently representing the Canadian company, Hespeler Craft Industries. Syed told Teledyne that he had a valid export licence, which simply needed the supplier's name changed from Carpenter to Teledyne. The licence would turn out to be the fake document supplied by the undercover customs agents, but the deal failed earlier, when Teledyne were not prepared to undercut Carpenter's price.

At a meeting with the customs agent at the Hilton Hotel in Toronto on June 9, Pervez expanded his shopping list. He asked the undercover man where he could buy some beryllium. He wanted bars of the element which had to be 98 per cent pure and each bar had to be 7.6 centimetres by 7.6 centimetres by 68.4 centimetres. Scientists making a thermonuclear bomb surround the fissile material with beryllium, which acts as a neutron reflector and reduces the critical mass. There are no real civilian applications for the element.

The customs agent told Pervez that the export of such a sensitive item was strictly controlled, and also that its only possible destination could be Pakistan's uranium enrichment facility at Kahuta. Agent New now takes up the story: 'Pervez became nervous, laughed, denied that the steel was going to Kahuta, said he didn't know where it was going, but then, at the end of the meeting, told me laughingly that the "Kahuta client is ready".'

On July 14, US authorities arrested Pervez as he arrived at a meeting in Philadelphia to sign the contracts for the delivery of the steel. When the Royal Canadian Mounted Police raided his home near Ottawa they found more than a hundred letters and cables relating to the planned deal.

Pervez was eventually convicted of conspiracy, attempted exportation of beryllium and making false statements to the government and was sentenced to five years in jail.

The evidence was clear enough. Pakistan had been trying to obtain materials that could only be used in the manufacture of nuclear weapons.

The case could hardly have come at a worse time for the Pakistan government. In late 1987, the US Congress was scheduled to review special legislation covering foreign aid to Pakistan. Already, there had been many breaches of existing US legislation and repeatedly Pakistan had managed to argue that each one was a special case.

On February 16, 1987, the US ambassador to Pakistan, Dean Hinton, made a speech in which he appeared to confirm his government's belief that Pakistan was trying to develop a nuclear weapon. 'While Pakistan has publicly demonstrated a commitment to regional non-proliferation, I must add in all candour that there are developments in Pakistan's nuclear programme which we see as inconsistent with a purely peaceful programme. Indication that Pakistan may be seeking a weapons capability generate tension and uncertainty.'[4]

The following month, Dr Abdel Qader Khan confirmed for the first time what most western governments had suspected for many years: Pakistan did indeed have the bomb.

'They told us that Pakistan could never produce the bomb and they doubted my capabilities, but they now know we have done it. Nobody can undo Pakistan or take us for granted. We are here to stay and let it be clear that we shall use the bomb if our existence is threatened. America knows it. What the CIA has been saying about our possessing the bomb is correct and so is the speculation of some foreign newspapers.'[5]

Khan claimed that the uranium enrichment plant at Kahuta was capable of producing uranium enriched to 90 per cent, sufficient to make nuclear weapons. 'It was difficult, particularly when America and other western countries had stopped selling anything which could be used in manufacturing the bomb. Embargoes were put even on such small things as magnets and maraging steel, but we purchased whatever we wanted before western countries got wind of it.

'Having said that, I can tell you that the western world never talks about its own hectic and persistent efforts to sell everything to us. When we bought inverters from Emerson, England, we found them to be less efficient than we wanted them to be. We asked Emerson to improve upon the parameters and suggested the method. At that period we received many letters and telexes, and people chased us with figures and details of equipment they had sold to Almelo, Capenhurst etc. They literally begged us to buy their equipment.'

Khan had made his statements in an interview with a prominent Indian journalist, Kuldip Nayar, and as soon as it was published he denied the interview had taken place and claimed his comments were faked. Then Mushahid Hussain, a leading Pakistani journalist and editor of *The Muslim*, said he had been present during the interview. The following day Hussain's telephone was cut off and his own newspaper later printed a statement saying that Khan's comments had been fabricated, forcing Hussain to resign.

Of course, there was nothing particularly new in what Khan had said. All his statements did was confirm publicly what western intelligence agencies had been telling their governments privately for many years.

Despite the concern of the US ambassador in Pakistan, the admissions of the Pakistanis themselves and the apparent constraints of legislation, the US government responded to the Pervez smuggling case with a verbal two-step that when examined carefully meant nothing.

Speaking before the subcommittee on Asian and Pacific Affairs in the House of Representatives on July 22, 1987, Richard Murphy, the Assistant Secretary for Near Eastern and South Asian Affairs said that new approaches had been made to the Pakistan government.

'The Pakistan government, beginning in 1985, has provided unequivocal assurances, both in public and in private that it would not engage in illegal procurement activities in the United States. In the wake of the arrest of Mr Pervez, we have expressed our deep concern and have sought an explanation from the Pakistan government of what it may know of this matter. We have called attention to earlier statements that we would not tolerate violation of our laws and made clear that actions inconsistent with the assurances we have been given would inevitably have serious consequences for our relationship. We have also informed Pakistan that this case reinforces our concerns about Pakistan's nuclear programme and increases the need for steps to demonstrate that Pakistan's nuclear programme is "peaceful". The Pakistan government has denied any knowledge of or connection with this case and has offered its full cooperation in our investigation, including a commitment to take action against any individuals found to be violating Pakistani policy or laws.'

In fact, Pakistan did nothing to cooperate with the US investigation into the affair. The Pakistan government claimed a warrant had been issued for the arrest of Major General Inam al Haq, but he remains free.

Despite such obvious breaches of existing US legislation, a new six-year aid package to Pakistan worth $4.02 billion was passed by Congress in July 1987. The aid was the third largest – after Israel and Egypt – given by the United States and, on the available evidence, was in clear breach of the law.

President Zia had played a smart game of bluff when he told the American administration that any linking of the aid package with the nuclear programme would threaten his government's support for the Afghan guerrillas. In fact, this was an empty threat as Zia depended totally on the aid package to prop up his country's ailing economy. If the US had refused the aid, Zia would either have had to go to the Soviet Union for help – hardly likely, given that country's support for Afghanistan – or approach Saudi Arabia. There too he would have been unlikely to find a sympathetic ear, especially as the US could use its considerable influence to pressure Riyadh. It seems likely that without the US aid, Zia would be signing his own death warrant. Yet, his bluff was never called and the Reagan administration quietly submitted.

On December 17, 1987, President Reagan wrote to Congress that based 'on the evidence available and on the statutory standard, I have concluded that Pakistan does not possess a nuclear explosive device.

'The proposed United States assistance programme for Pakistan remains extremely important in reducing the risk that Pakistan will develop and ultimately possess such a device. I am convinced that our security relationship and assistance programme are the most effective means available to us for dissuading Pakistan from acquiring nuclear explosive devices.'[6]

Around the time the President was writing that letter, two Frankfurt based West German companies were covertly supplying Pakistan with a complete plant for the separation and enrichment of tritium – which can be used to enhance the effectiveness of an atomic bomb. Delivery of the equipment was organised by the Pakistani embassies in France and West Germany, in defiance of West Germany's export laws.

Throughout 1988, western intelligence agencies received regular reports about the involvement of West German companies in the export of nuclear materials to Pakistan. In part this was because the Americans and the British were tracking Libyan efforts to develop a chemical capability, helped by equipment smuggled from West Germany. By the year's end, more than seventy West German firms had been identified as being possibly involved in smuggling nuclear related equipment or technology to Pakistan.

In November 1988 in his annual report to Congress on the state of Pakistan's nuclear programme, the departing President Reagan wrote that 'as Pakistan's nuclear capabilities grow, and if evidence about its activities continue to accumulate, this process of annual certification will require the President to reach judgments about the status of Pakistani nuclear activities that may be difficult or impossible to make with any degree of certainty.' In other words, the administration was publicly accepting that Pakistan had a programme to make a nuclear bomb and the only remaining issue was how far that programme had gone. In his letter Reagan was careful to distinguish between the possession of a nuclear bomb and the development of a nuclear capability. The standard 'is whether Pakistan possesses a nuclear explosive device, not whether Pakistan is attempting to develop or has developed various relevant capabilities.'

But however little the US wanted to accommodate Pakistan's nuclear ambitions, it was becoming increasingly difficult for the President to continue certifying the country as nuclear free. In his letter the President warned that the US remained 'extremely troubled' by Pakistan's nuclear programme.

At the end of 1988, President Zia was killed in a plane crash, ending his military dictatorship. In the democratic elections which followed, Benazir Bhutto, the daughter of President Zulfiqar Bhutto, the father of the Pakistan bomb, was elected president. She claims that Pakistan's nuclear programme is solely for peaceful purposes – a claim identical to that made publicly on many occasions by her father. During a visit to Washington in June 1989, Bhutto told a joint session of the US Congress that Pakistan neither possesses nor plans to build a nuclear bomb. 'We will not provoke a nuclear arms race in the subcontinent. That is our policy.'

It may be that Benazir Bhutto is speaking the truth and she may wish to abandon her country's development of nuclear weapons, but it is not clear just how much freedom she has from the military who allowed her to take power.

In Pakistan, it is the military that control the politicians. It is they who see the clear benefits to them of nuclear weapons when faced with the superior military might of India. It is most unlikely that the military will allow Bhutto to abandon the nuclear programme, even if she should wish to do so.

On October 5, 1989, President George Bush wrote to Congress that 'Pakistan does not now possess a nuclear explosive device.' But the President added that 'Pakistan has continued its efforts to develop its unsafeguarded nuclear programme.'[7]

In other words, efforts by the United States to persuade the Pakistan government to stop its nuclear programme had failed once again. Even so, the President was not prepared to risk compromising the US aid package to the country by publicly damning the nuclear programme. It seems that until

Pakistan actually explodes a nuclear device, the US will fail to act with conviction. By then, of course, it will be too late.

When Pakistan does finally demonstrate to the world that she has joined the nuclear club, there will be the predictable cries of outrage from western governments. But Pakistan's nuclear programme has been known to those same western governments for the past fifteen years and aside from diplomatic rhetoric, little has been done to force the Pakistanis to stop their work on nuclear weapons. On the contrary, countries like West Germany and France have turned a blind eye as companies transfer knowledge and equipment to Pakistan.

Clearly, the laws preventing the transfer of nuclear technology are woefully inadequate, so much so that a single spy network established by one man in Holland in the early 1970s is still operating today. This means that when developing countries want to acquire technology they can, and those companies that wish to break the law to meet the demand can do so knowing that the chances of being caught are very small and the penalties insignificant.

Another lesson from the Pakistan experience is that the major powers actually have two agendas: one is the highly laudable one of preventing the spread of nuclear technology. The second is less laudable and recognises that political realities dictate the manner in which the first policy is implemented. In Pakistan's case, the need to support the mujahedeen in Afghanistan became for the United States a more important policy requirement than the accurate monitoring of Pakistan's nuclear programme.

It is easy to say that the west should do more to stop the proliferation of nuclear weapons, but difficult to come up with real solutions. Countries like West Germany could use existing legislation to severely penalise companies that break the export laws, and enforcement agencies could begin to treat high technology smuggling as something more than petty theft or a misdemeanour. But, even if that were to happen and there was to be a new-found political will, the technology is already available in the developing countries themselves for nuclear weapons to be readily available to a significant number of new nations by the end of this century.

PART SEVEN: CHEMICAL WARFARE

20

A Higher Form of Killing

There is disagreement among historians as to when chemical weapons were first used. Certainly, as far back as 2000 BC, the Indian epic tale Ramayana tells of the use of 'Sammahon-astra', projectiles which gave off a substance that produced stupor or hypnosis.[1] In 600 BC, Solon, the legist of the Athen-ians, contaminated the River Pleisthenes with helleborus, a plant that can be poisonous if ingested. The defenders of the town of Kirrha then contracted violent diarrhoea from drinking the water and were unable to fight.[2]

What is clear is that from the moment man started to wage war, the weapons he used were not simply those of direct fire, whether they be clubs or guns. Instead, he looked for ways to incapacitate his enemy at the minimum risk to himself. This was a sensible method of fighting as it reduced the risk to his own side while maximising the damage to his enemy. Certainly, there was no particular moral opprobrium attached to the use of such weapons: the British army wanted to use chemical weapons in the Crimean war but lacked a proper delivery system; and in the American Civil War when the north used crude biological weapons to poison southern water, both sides accepted the tactic as perfectly legitimate.

Although there was some concern in the nineteenth century about the use of chemical weapons, and even an early attempt at a treaty banning their use (The Hague Gas Declaration of 1899), it was not until some time after the First World War that a worldwide revulsion grew up against their use.

On April 22, 1915, the Germans dispersed 168 tons of chlorine gas against the French salient at Ypres. The gas billowed in great white clouds over the trenches and caused terror among the French troops who swiftly deserted their posts and fled to the rear, leaving a five-mile-long gap in the allied lines. But the Germans appear to have been as surprised as the French, and failed to take advantage of their opportunity – in part because they had not brought enough troops up to the front to advance over such a wide area.

From then on, both sides used chemical warfare extensively on all fronts causing 1.3m casualties of which 92,000 were fatal. Exact casualty figures are, in fact, very imprecise but a detailed record was kept by the Americans for both 1917 and 1918 and these show that of the casualties only 1.9 per cent were killed by chemical weapons while 23.3 per cent were killed by all other weapons – and this at a time when about half of all the ammunition fired had a chemical fill.

It is the memory of those dead and wounded from the First World War that appears to have scarred the generations that followed. A distinction seems to have been drawn between general conventional warfare, which is portrayed as clean and even honourable, and chemical warfare which is seen as dirty and definitely dishonourable. Of course, to anyone who studies warfare such a distinction is ridiculous and in fact at variance with reality. In a conventional war, non-chemical munitions are frequently indiscriminate in their application, causing large numbers of military and civilian casualties as well as the large scale destruction of property. Chemical weapons, on the other hand, can be used with some precision either to kill or incapacitate an enemy group and cause no damage to property at all. In the words of the pioneer of nerve gas development, Professor Fritz Haber, 'It is a higher form of killing.' If the object of warfare is to achieve political and economic advantage, then chemical weapons are the right tool: used properly they destroy the enemy army and leave the economic infrastructure intact for the conquerors to exploit.

As one NATO intelligence source puts it: 'We are prisoners

of our own prejudices. Which is worse, killing people with a few whiffs of gas or tearing them to pieces with jagged bits of hot metal?'[3]

Despite the faulty logic, there has been consistent political resistance against the use of chemical weapons. This resulted in 1925 in the Geneva Protocol, in which 118 countries agreed to ban the use of chemical weapons. Even so, the Italians used chemicals in Ethiopia in the late 1930s and Japan used them against the Chinese during the same period.

The Second World War provided the first lesson in the importance of chemical and biological weapons as a deterrent. In just the same way as nuclear weapons in the armouries of east and west act today as a deterrent against first use, so in 1939 did a series of misunderstandings create the same effect.

In 1936, two German scientists published a paper on work they had been doing on insecticides which had produced as a by-product a nerve agent called Tabun. This paper was read by British intelligence who became convinced that the Germans had a nerve agent and were prepared to use it. At the same time, two British scientists working in Edinburgh were doing their own research into insecticides and they in turn published their paper. No one in Britain realised the potential of their work for the production of chemical weapons, but German intelligence read the paper and immediately concluded that Britain, too, had developed a chemical capability.

After the outbreak of war, the British believed that Germany would use chemicals and a gas mask was issued to every British citizen as a precaution. After about a year it was learned that the filters on all the gas masks were ineffective and so an additional attachment was issued which was fixed on to the existing respirator. The Germans noticed this and concluded it was a filter for a new – and presumably very powerful – chemical weapon.

In fact, neither the Axis nor the Allied powers deployed chemicals at all throughout the war. The Germans did not use them because they believed the British would retaliate with their own new weapons while the British did not use their old-fashioned mustard gas because they thought the Germans would use their new nerve agents.

At the time of the German blitz on London, it was Winston Churchill who, against the advice of his service chiefs, was most enthusiastic about using chemical weapons. He recommended them because he felt they might be militarily effective and his views were not hampered by sentiment, as this memo of July 6, 1940, shows.

'I want you to think very seriously over this question of using poison gas. I would not use it unless it could be shown a) it was life or death for us, or b) that it would shorten the war by a year.

'It is absurd to consider morality on this topic when everybody used it in the last war without a word of complaint from the moralists or the Church. On the other hand, in the last war the bombing of open cities was regarded as forbidden. Now everybody does it as a matter of course. It is simply a question of fashion changing as she does between long and short skirts for women.

'I want a cold-blooded calculation made as to how it would pay us to use poison gas, by which I mean principally mustard. We will want to gain more ground in Normandy so as not to be cooped up in a small area. We could probably deliver twenty tons to their one and for the sake of their one they would bring their bomber aircraft into the area against our superiority, thus paying a heavy toll.

'Why have the Germans not used it? Not certainly out of moral scruples or affection for us. They have not used it because it does not pay them . . . The only reason they have not used it against us is that they fear the retaliation. What is to their detriment is to our advantage.

'Although one sees how unpleasant it is to receive poison gas attacks, from which nearly everyone recovers, it is useless to protest that an equal amount of HE will not inflict greater cruelties and sufferings on troops or civilians. One really must not be bound within silly conventions of the mind whether they be those that ruled in the last war or those in reverse which rule in this . . . I quite agree it may be several weeks or even months before I shall ask you to drench Germany with poison gas, and if we do it, let us do it one hundred per cent. In the meanwhile, I want the matter studied in cold blood by sensible people and not by that particular set of psalm-singing uniformed defeatists which one runs across now here now there.'[4]

In fact, the chiefs of staff continued to oppose the idea because they considered chemicals militarily inefficient and they worried about the German ability to retaliate in kind. Churchill reluctantly agreed to delay the use of chemical or biological weapons until the war situation got worse. In fact, the situation continued to improve and so Churchill never ordered his weapons of last resort to be used.

However, at one stage during the war, allied intelligence learned that the Germans were planning to use chemicals on the Russians. Churchill sent a warning to the Germans that if they did so the British would bomb German cities with gas. As the Germans already believed that Britain had developed new chemical weapons, the warning acted as a sufficient deterrent and chemicals were not used by the Germans on the Russian front.

Although considerable work has since been done to make chemical weapons more effective, the basic products have remained the same as those developed before the Second World War. In order to understand the range of material now available, it is worthwhile setting down just exactly what is meant by chemical weapons.

Chemical agents are divided into three different categories: lethal agents which are designed to kill; damaging agents which are made to cause short or long-term damage to humans but also can kill; and incapacitants which have only a temporary mental or physical effect.

The first anyone would know they were under attack by a lethal agent such as nerve gas would be a sudden tightening of the chest. There would be no greenish-yellow mist as described by those fighting in the trenches in World War I – modern gases tend to have no odour and no colour. Almost immediately the victims would be wheezing, vomiting and losing control of their bodily functions. Within minutes they would be having convulsions as the gas attacked the central nervous system, and moments later they would be dead.

Non-persistent nerve agents tend to be airborne and last minutes or hours. They can be delivered by aircraft or shell and are generally inhaled through the mouth or nose or absorbed through the eye.

Persistent chemicals can last hours or days and generally appear in the form of droplets and will be delivered by aircraft as a fine spray or 'rain'. They enter the body through any of the orifices or through the skin, and an infected person can frequently pass on the chemical to another through skin contact.

Nerve agents such as Tabun, Sarin and Soman are lethal and interfere with the nervous system and disrupt breathing and muscle coordination. Blood agents are also lethal and prevent the body tissues using oxygen in the blood. This type is popular with the Soviet armed forces and is developed as hydrogen cyanide. As one British officer serving in Germany puts it: 'We would find it very inhibiting. Two or three breaths and it's curtains.'[5] Choking agents are lethal too, and attack the breathing passages and the lungs and are normally non-persistent. Toxins are chemical compounds which can be either lethal or incapacitating. Damaging agents such as mustard gas are blister agents and cause severe inflammation and then blistering of the skin. Incapacitating agents temporarily disable anyone exposed to them with the effects lasting hours or even days.

In the civil war in Yemen in 1963–67, the Egyptians used phosgene supplied by the Russians to attack Royalist strongholds. The phosgene, which has the attractive smell of new mown hay, worked well, enabling the Egyptians to destroy the Royalist headquarters when attacks by bombs and rockets had failed. It also had the important psychological side effect of undermining the morale of the population.

Perhaps the most well publicised use of chemicals occurred during America's involvement in the Vietnam war. During 1967 and 1968 there was widespread spraying of a number of chemical defoliants including a product known as Agent Orange, so called after the orange drums in which it was stored. Under a project known as Ranch Hand vast tracts of Vietnam where Vietcong were believed to live were sprayed. Agent Orange caused plants and trees to grow at a rate which their systems could not bear and they would explode and die. The chemical contained dioxin which is known to produce a wide range of illnesses in laboratory animals and, possibly, in humans. There was a widespread belief among Vietnam veterans that exposure to Agent Orange had led to a much higher than average degree of sickness both in those who served in Vietnam and in their children.

By 1985, 249,000 Vietnam veterans and their families had made court claims for damages relating to exposure to Agent Orange. That figure included 64,000 claims for veterans' children who had been born with birth defects. The veterans sued seven chemical companies for damages and in 1986 received a record $180 million as an out-of-court settlement. However, none of that money has been disbursed as so far it has proved impossible to prove conclusively a link between any illness in humans and exposure to Agent Orange. To the frustration of the veterans, who remain convinced that they and their families have suffered, a number of studies commissioned by the US government has not even produced clear evidence that anyone exposed to the chemical has suffered at all.

If the Americans had run into problems in Vietnam, these were relatively minor compared with the information which was picked up by US intelligence in 1979. For some years, the US had been convinced that a Soviet factory on the outskirts of Sverdlovsk, 850 miles east of Moscow, was being used for the development of a new generation of biological weapons. Satellites had photographed Military Cantonment 19 (also known as the Microbiology and Virology Institute) and interpreters at the Defence Intelligence Agency outside Washington DC were convinced that the ventilation system, animal pens, smoke stacks, refrigeration facilities and extremely tight security including two layers of high wire fence bore all the hallmarks of a biological warfare facility.[6]

Then in May 1979, US intelligence received the first, fragmentary reports of an explosion at the site and a leak of poison gas from the factory which was killing hundreds of people not only in the factory but in nearby plants and in the communities downwind of the factory. The Americans believed that up to 22lbs of anthrax spores had been released into the air in an invisible cloud, contaminating an area three miles downwind of the factory in southwest Sverdlovsk. US intelligence learned that the Soviets had tried to contain the incident by a widespread immunisation programme with an anthrax vaccine which proved largely ineffective. For three months, medical teams were in the city monitoring the fall-out and follow-up studies were conducted that autumn.

Each of the people who inhaled the spores became ill the same day with symptoms similar to influenza and later pneumonia. All the victims died within a few days. American estimates put the death toll at between 1,000–2,000 while British analysts place the figure in the high hundreds.

The Soviets responded by denying that any leak had taken place. They admitted that a few people had died, but from intestinal anthrax which had been contracted through eating contaminated meat bought on the black market.

According to the Soviets, the outbreak was caused because some cattle had been fed with infected fodder and some of these cattle had been slaughtered and sold on the black market. Only sixty-six people had died, and over a number of weeks, not days as alleged by US intelligence.

'It was clear to us that infectious meat was the cause,' said Dr Pyotr Burgasov, a Soviet deputy minister of health who had visited the scene immediately after the outbreak. Local authorities had set up roadblocks and conducted house to house searches for suspect meat, killed three hundred stray dogs and burned thirty contaminated buildings to contain the outbreak. He claimed it was 'impossible' that any spores had leaked from the research facility in the town.[7]

Despite such denials, western governments remain firmly convinced that there was a leak of anthrax spores, not least because the symptoms exhibited by the victims were different from those likely if they had been infected with intestinal anthrax as the Soviets claimed. British scientists were perfectly satisfied that the Soviets had had an anthrax leak. In 1941, Britain had developed its own biological weapon to counter a possible German attack. They used anthrax spores which were tested on tethered sheep on the island of Gruinard off northwest Scotland. The sheep died and the island was uninhabitable for the next forty-seven years.

For many years the Soviets categorically denied that the Sverdlovsk plant was anything to do with chemical or biological warfare. However, under an addition to the 1972 Biological and Toxin convention agreed in 1987, the Soviets were obliged to list plants that had special facilities for handling such weapons. One of the plants listed was Military Cantonment 19.

Similar verification difficulties arose over American allegations in 1981 that Soviet-backed forces operating in Southeast Asia had been using chemical weapons against anti-communist forces. The US had picked up a number of reports from Hmong tribesmen in Laos and Cambodian anti-communist guerrillas fighting against Vietnamese Cambodian forces of aircraft and helicopters spraying a fine yellowish rain. Victims complained of vomiting, bleeding, blistering and severe skin lesions.[8]

From the roofs of local buildings the US obtained leaf and other samples which were covered in yellow spots. When analysed some of those samples were found to contain minute quantities of tricothecene toxins which US scientists believed could have produced the symptoms described.

The US charged that the Soviets were in breach of the Biological and Toxin Weapons Convention of 1972 which had been signed by the Soviet Union and 112 other countries. The US State Department charged that 'Soviet maintenance of an offensive biological warfare programme and capability, as well as their involvement in the production and transfer of toxins to surrogates in Southeast Asia, are in violation of the convention.'[9]

But other scientists were more sceptical and in January 1982, the British Chemical Defence Establishment at Porton Down discovered that all the samples contained very high levels of pollen. This was confirmed by other scientists, leading some to believe that the yellow rain was in fact caused by wild honeybees flying in very large numbers and excreting in vast yellow clouds. Bizarre as that theory may be, it remains the most logical explanation of the phenomenon, if one accepts that the Soviets had not in fact supplied some unknown new toxin to the Vietnamese and Cambodians.

The Yellow Rain allegations became an article of faith for many in the Reagan administration. The President and many of his supporters had come to government with a firm conviction that the Soviets were lying cheats in every area of arms control. The Yellow Rain evidence, such as it was, could be cited as clear proof of Soviet perfidy.

Chemical and biological weapons have become a focus for propaganda in east and west. Both sides claim the other has considerable offensive capability and much political capital is made of the apparent unwillingness of either side to negotiate a comprehensive treaty banning their manufacture and use. At present, the overwhelming weight of available evidence suggests that the Soviets have far greater stockpiles of chemical and biological weapons than the west and are better trained in the use of such weapons for offensive purposes.

According to the US Defence Intelligence Agency, the Soviet Union captured two German nerve agent production plants after the Second World War, dismantled them and shipped them to the Soviet Union. One of these plants is still operational in Volgograd. Those two plants formed the basis of the Soviet chemical and biological warfare industry. Since then, there has been a steady expansion of the industry so that today there are seventeen major sites involved in the production of these weapons. These are the Byelorussian Research Institute for Epidemiology and Microbiology at Minsk, the All Union Research Institute for Molecular Biology at Novosibirsk, Oblast (the largest centre with some 2,000 employees), Irkutsk Anti-plague Scientific Research Institute of Siberia and the Far East at Irkutsk, the Micro-biology and Virology Institute at Sverdlovsk, the Scientific Research Institute of Sanitation at Zagorsk, and in Moscow the D I Ivanovsky Institute for Virology, N F Gamaleya Institute for Epidemiology and Microbiology, the Moscow Research Institute for Viral Preparations and the Scientific Research Institute for Poliomyelitis and Viral Encephalitis. Six other sites at Omutninsk, Aksu, Pokrov, Berdsk, Penza and Kurgan are suspected of being involved with research and a significant amount of testing is done on Vozrozhdeniya Island in the Aral Sea and at Shikhany two hundred miles south of Moscow.[10]

Testing and deployment of chemical weapons is easily observed by satellite and other intelligence gathering systems. To discover if a chemical weapon is effective, it is necessary to try out the delivery system in different conditions of wind, rain, sun or snow, and observe for how long the substance remains active. To do this the Soviets (and the Americans) construct circular or rectangular grids which are surrounded by poles with sensitive measuring devices on them to detect the chemicals as they are carried on the air. While the con-struction of the testing facilities is thus easily observed, many biological weapons are affected by sunlight and are therefore tested at night. Thus it has not been easy for western intelli-gence to discover exactly what kind of weapons the Soviets have developed.

If such weapons are to work, the troops have to be regularly trained in their use. Unlike NATO forces, the Soviets and their Warsaw Pact allies receive regular training in chemical warfare. Directed by the Headquarters Chemical Troops in the Ministry of Defence, the chemical warfare organisation is headed by a three-star general and includes 45,000 officers and men in the ground forces alone with a further 55,000 available for call-up in time of tension or war.

These troops are regularly exercised and have been observed taking a strongly offensive role against imagined NATO forces. For example, in the Warsaw Pact exercises in Czechoslovakia in 1984 codenamed Druzhba, chemical attacks were simulated against NATO anti-tank defences. Each Soviet regiment has a chemical warfare battalion which is trained to go ahead of the troops either decontaminating sections of the front or marking safe areas by firing flags from inside a chemical-proof vehicle.

The Soviets currently have 30,000 decontamination vehicles in service, including the TMS–65 which consists of an aircraft turbojet engine mounted on a Ural–375 truck chassis, and sprays out a special solution to wash down contaminated vehicles. TMS–65s normally work in pairs with one on either side of the road. The operator directs the jet's powerful exhaust onto a contaminated vehicle and then injects a special mixture into the exhaust which is sprayed over the vehicle. Using this method, a tank can be cleaned in under a minute. The Warsaw Pact also have a range of systems for cleaning contaminated land and for washing down soldiers who have operated in a polluted area. By contrast, 'NATO forces have only one large-scale decontamination unit and that is a bucket,' according to one NATO official.[11]

Each Russian soldier, like his NATO counterpart, is issued with a protective suit and respirator, but also a decontamination kit. Significantly, the kit contains antidotes to both Soman and hydrogen cyanide, neither of which the west possesses. This is cited by western intelligence as evidence that the Soviets expect to use their chemicals. Indeed, some Soviet troops train using diluted lethal agents so that they become used to operating in a chemically poisoned environment.

In their war in Afghanistan, the Soviets tried out new biological weapons. These were never used as a major part of their counter-guerrilla army but were deployed simply to gain experience in their tactical use and their effect. One weapon used was lethal, and caused the dead body to turn black and putrefy in hours rather than the more normal days or weeks.

But in war, using chemical weapons simply on the battlefield would be very inefficient. In time of tension leading to war and immediately after the outbreak of hostilities, the intention of the Soviet forces would be to create maximum disruption in the military chain of command and demoralised chaos among the civilians. To that end, Spetsnaz commandos, the Soviet special forces, have received training in chemical and biological warfare. Allied intelligence believes that one of Spetsnaz's tasks would be to release chemical weapons deep behind the enemy front line, in Washington and London, for example, to create the maximum possible disruption.

In the mid–1980s the allies became seriously concerned at what they saw as an improved Soviet chemical capability and possibly a change in their strategic thinking that might indicate a greater willingness to use chemical weapons. The British asked the military's own intelligence arm, the Defence Intelligence Service, to brief the chiefs of staff on Soviet capability, intentions and the likelihood of use of chemical and biological weapons. To the surprise of the service chiefs the DIS briefing was short on hard facts and information about Soviet intentions and it emerged that, despite all the propaganda about Soviet chemical capability, there was very little information available. The service chiefs then went outside the intelligence community to an army expert on Soviet strategy, Brigadier John Hemsley, and asked him to undertake a similar study. He had already been looking at the problem for his own interest and he produced two reports, one that contained a small amount of classified information relating to weapons capabilities and was given to the military only, and a second report that was based entirely on unclassified material and was later published as a book by the Royal United Services Institute.

Publication of the book shortly after Hemsley left the army in 1987 caused considerable controversy inside the Ministry of Defence. The DIS were angered that a study had been completed by an outsider and further that it contained more information than they had themselves. There was also concern that the author named a long list of people who had given assistance in the research for the book, and their names made up a comprehensive list of intelligence officers working in the area of chemical weapons. Although the book had been cleared by the Ministry of Defence, DIS complained to the Special Branch that Hemsley might have breached the Official Secrets Act. He was visited by men from the Special Branch, warned that he might be prosecuted, and a number of his papers were taken away for further study. In fact, as the book had been prepared using documents that were already in the public domain and were unclassified, there were no grounds for prosecution and the matter was dropped. But the incident is interesting for two reasons. First, it illustrates how scarce hard intelligence is about the intentions of the Soviet military in relation to chemical weapons. Second, the reaction provoked by Hemsley's book suggests that its conclusions are uncomfortably accurate.[12]

Hemsley is in no doubt that without the deterrence of a credible NATO retaliatory capability, the Soviets plan to use chemical and biological weapons offensively. 'It is probable that the USSR would apply general strategic principles in any use of CBW against the United Kingdom with the aim of creating maximum problems for the population, initially through political blackmail and then by causing dislocation to public services such as rail and port facilities, communications and power. This would have the effect of grinding society to a halt by paralysing the system. The USSR has shown great interest in the use of hallucinogens and other anti-personnel agents against civil populations, therefore we may expect to see a very selective and clinical employment of CBW using the latest technology in this area, particularly psychochemical agents to cause civilian panic. The lack of destruction to the national infrastructure and the non-lethal nature of the CB agents involved would greatly reduce the risk of any nuclear retaliation.

'The key issue in appreciating the threat at this level is understanding the Soviet strategic concept for the employment of CBW. They view CB weapons in this context as weapons of psychological persuasion and are well aware of the total lack of any credible CBW civil defensive measures or precautions, not just in the United Kingdom but across the whole of NATO. At the moment, the Prime Minister does not have the ability to refute a Soviet threat to mount a CB attack on the United Kingdom in the event of United States reinforcement to Europe using British facilities. Both the Alliance and the Warsaw Pact know very well that a small scale and selective, non-lethal CB attack would not invite a nuclear response.'[13]

Fear of such an attack means that all allied troops would immediately put on their own chemical protection suits (Noddy suits) at the start of a war. These suits do give effective protection against the current Soviet stocks of chemical and biological weapons, but at a very heavy price in comfort and mobility.

'Wearing the Noddy suits is like going into battle with one hand tied behind our backs. Even such a simple task as aiming a rifle becomes much more difficult, while loading a 60lb shell becomes an enormous task. They are acutely uncomfortable and after a short time, the soldier suffers from dehydration and has water in his boots,' commented one NATO official.[14]

Even the Soviets recognise this problem. In their own studies, which are supported by similar findings in the west, they learned that performance reduces by as much as 50 per cent after six hours wearing a suit. They have produced a table setting out the maximum length of time a soldier should spend in a Noddy suit at various temperatures. If the temperature is about 86 degrees Fahrenheit then time in a suit should not exceed twenty minutes, while below 59 degrees a soldier can last as long as three hours. If these times are exceeded, performance will suffer and eventually the soldier will collapse from heat exhaustion.

The reality is that no soldier will be able to wear a suit for as short a time as twenty minutes and most will have to wear them for several hours and possibly even as long as a day. This would mean a serious degradation in the fighting ability of the force wearing the suits. This must act as a real encouragement for either side to launch a pre-emptive strike by chemical troops.

It is in part this fear of a surprise attack that has encouraged the west to continue developing its own chemical weapons. Even so, the United States is the only NATO nation still to manufacture chemical and biological weapons while Britain continues research to upgrade the defensive systems supplied to its troops.

In the United States, chemical weapons are produced at the Rocky Mountain Arsenal in Colorado, the Pine Bluff Arsenal in Arkansas, the Newport Army Ammunition Plant in Indiana, Muscle Shoals, Alabama and Aberdeen, Maryland. The weapons are stored at Umatilla, Oregon; Tooele Utah; Pueblo, Colorado; Newport Army Ammunition Plant, Indiana; Pine Bluff Arsenal, Arkansas; Anniston, Alabama; Lexington Blue Grass, Kentucky; Johnston Island in the Pacific and Aberdeen, Maryland.

Biological research takes place at the Centre for Infectious Diseases, at the Centres for Disease Control, Atlanta; National Cancer Institute, Frederick Cancer Research Facility, Frederick, Maryland; National Institutes of Public Health Service, Bethesda, Maryland; Plum Island Animal Disease Centre, New York; US Army Medical Research Institute of Infectious Diseases, Fort Detrick, Frederick, Maryland; Government Services Division, the Salk Institute, Swiftwater, Pennsylvania. Another eighteen sites are involved in further biological defence research but they are not directly involved in handling the more sensitive toxins.[15]

The exact size of the US chemical arsenal has not been revealed although it is likely to be in excess of 50,000 tons. These weapons are nearly all very old, as President Nixon ordered the ending of chemical weapons production in 1969. According to the Pentagon, 90 per cent of their chemical weapon stocks are too unstable to use and they will be destroyed at their storage sites once construction of special facilities has been completed in 1997.

This unilateral decision has not been matched by the Soviets, who continues to manufacture new weapons. The result is an ever widening gap in capabilities between NATO and the Warsaw Pact. In 1985, President Reagan persuaded Congress (after considerable pressure from the British government) to authorise the resumption of chemical weapons production, this time for a new binary weapon which will be safer than previous systems. The binary weapons, which began production in 1987, are essentially two different parts of a shell which when apart are completely harmless. But when the two parts are joined and the chemicals inside mix together, they form a deadly weapon.

The new binary weapon will be used in artillery shells, rockets (most probably the Multiple Launch Rocket System) and will be able to be delivered by aircraft, via a Bigeye bomb, deep behind the enemy lines. The US is developing both simple non-persistent chemicals and more sophisticated nerve agents. However, under West German law, it is illegal to store chemical weapons on their territory so all the new systems will have to remain on the US mainland. In the event of war, the stocks will have to be taken out of storage, the two parts of the system flown separately to Europe, joined together and deployed. This time-consuming exercise will be of little use against a surprise attack.

It is an interesting footnote that when east and west sit down to talk about binary weapons, each is in fact talking about a completely different thing. To the Americans binary means a single weapon that comes in two parts. To the Soviets binary means two weapons in one delivery system: a psychochemical agent and a nerve agent mixed together, for example.

Both sides now appear to have reasons for trying to eliminate chemical and biological weapons. The west is nervous of the huge Soviet stockpiles and their proven capability in using the weapons in battle. For their part, the Soviets are concerned about the relatively recent US production of new binary weapons. Neither side wants to have the spectre of chemical weapons hovering over a modern battlefield where their use would seriously restrict any ability to fight a conventional war.

In 1972, the Convention on the Prohibition of the Development, Production and Stockpiling of Bacteriological (Biological) and Toxin weapons and on their Destruction was signed by 111 countries. They agreed that they 'will never develop, produce, stockpile or otherwise acquire or retain microbial or other biological agents or toxins of types and in quantities that have no justification for prophylactic, protective or other peaceful purposes, or weapons, equipment or means of delivery designed to use such agents or toxins for hostile purposes or in armed conflict.'

The United States had already unilaterally stopped production of biological weapons in 1969 and destroyed all its stocks. But there were no verification provisions attached to this agreement, and in fact it is verification that has proved to be the major stumbling block in all subsequent negotiations to ban all CBW systems. 'The difficulty is that we need to be able to inspect all their production and storage facilities both known and suspected and they want to do the same,' explained one NATO intelligence source. 'There are two major problems with this. First, these weapons can be easily made using a normal factory that makes medicines one day and weapons the next. Second, the chemical companies are very concerned that the Soviets will simply use any treaty for industrial espionage. We will give them inspection rights, they will challenge a perfectly innocent plant, come in, see how some new chemical is made and head off to produce their own version. That is just giving them a licence to spy.'[16]

Verification problems brought about the collapse in 1980 of four-year-old talks designed to ban chemical weapons. Then in 1982, the forty-nation Committee on Disarmament began meeting in Geneva under the auspices of the United Nations to try to negotiate a global, verifiable ban on chemical weapons. Those discussions too have failed to make much progress because of the difficulties over verification.

In 1987, however, the same year that the US began its production of a new generation of chemical weapons, there were signs of movement on the Soviet side. They announced that they had ceased all production of chemical weapons and agreed to name their most sensitive units working on CBW and those plants that were under the control of the Ministry of Defence. They named eleven laboratories controlled by state bodies such as the Ministry of Health and four at Kirov, Sverdlosk, Aralask and Zagorsk controlled by the Ministry of Defence. This was by no means a complete list but it was the first admission by the Soviets that they had any such facilities at all.

That same year, the Soviets invited diplomats, scientists and journalists from the west to visit the chemical warfare facility at Shikhany. During the tour the Soviets admitted to possessing 50,000 tons of chemical weapons that could be delivered by forty-five different systems including missiles, bombs and aerial sprays. Designed to reassure the west of their new openness, the visit had the opposite effect. Western intelligence believes the Soviet chemical stockpile is between 300,000 and 400,000 tons or at least six times the figure admitted. This figure (a crude total) is obtained by adding up the known production capacity of various plants, the known storage capacity and the known wastage.

A second problem with the inspection visit was that all the weapons displayed by the Soviets dated back to the Second World War. 'Everything we saw was in either the German or Russian stocks either before, during or just after World War II,' said one western scientist. 'You have to view that in the context of all other aspects of the Russian armed forces. Everywhere else they have developed new equipment, often making very large technological leaps. Even if we did not have other hard information, it would be completely illogical and out of character to expect them to have made absolutely no progress at all in the past forty-five years.'[17]

But the commander of the Soviet Chemical Troops, Lieutenant General Stanislav Petrov, insists that the creation of the Soviet chemical arsenal was entirely in response to America's work in the area. 'Soviet chemical weapons are a deterrent. The Soviet Union has taken the political decision on the need to eliminate weapons of mass destruction, including chemical, by the year 2000. We believe this problem can be solved only provided a convention on a full chemical ban under effective international control is concluded. However, the Soviet Union did not wait for such a convention to be signed and stopped the production of chemical weapons, announcing also that it will start to eliminate chemical stockpiles at a facility specially built for the purpose near the city of Chapayevsk,' he said.[18]

The west has always found it difficult to gauge the truth of Soviet statements. But judging by their actions the Soviet leadership appear more willing to deploy and use chemical weapons than their western counterparts. During serious riots in the Soviet Republic of Georgia on April 9, 1989, Soviet troops were deployed to disperse the demonstrators. Troops armed with sharpened shovels and clubs and supported by tanks moved against 10,000 demonstrators in the region's capital Tbilisi. At least twenty civilians were killed and more than 700 treated in hospital.

It later emerged that the troops had also used both tear gas and a poison gas made from a chemical called chloroacetophenone, which was last used in the First World War. Initial statements by the Soviet Interior Ministry and army officials claimed that only tear gas had been used. Then, the

Communist party leader in Georgia, Givi Gumbaridze, said that, 'It has been established that tear gas was used and a second type of gas was also used. There are cases of poisoning and some people died.'

For western intelligence agencies and strategists, the Georgia riots were seen as particularly significant. The way they were dealt with graphically demonstrated how much a part of Soviet military thinking is the use of chemical weapons. This was underlined during demonstrations against the government in Romania in December 1989. Agents of the secret police, the Securitate, poisoned the drinking water of the town of Sibin. Large numbers of local people were infected by the chemical agent Sarin, which causes illness and, if untreated, death. It would be inconceivable for government troops of any western nation to use deadly chemical weapons in putting down anti-government demonstrations. To western military tacticians, therefore, the need for an effective chemical weapons treaty had been firmly underlined.

At the end of September 1989 President George Bush proposed that the United States and the Soviet Union cut their chemical stockpiles by 80 per cent within ten years. The next day, the Soviet Foreign Minister, Eduard Shevardnadze, in a hastily revised speech called for the abolition of all chemical stockpiles held by both superpowers. It is unclear just how much of this leap-frogging arms control diplomacy is serious. In a little noticed clause in Bush's speech, he called for the 80 per cent reduction 'if the Soviet Union joins us in cutting chemical weapons to an equal level, and we agree on inspection to verify that stockpiles are destroyed.' As neither side can agree on how big each other's stockpile is or the terms of any verification process, these were two significant caveats which are likely to block real progress for some time.

But while the United States and the Soviet Union go through yet another of their complex manoeuvres that are the precursors to a new arms control treaty, other nations have been busy developing their own chemical capability. It is here and not with the superpowers that the real danger lies. It is also here that the real problems emerge with any treaty banning the use of chemical and biological weapons. If past performance is anything to go by, these treaties will not work and western nations will ignore agreements not to help developing nations produce their own chemical capability. The result will be proliferation of a cheap and devastating weapon, one that many believe will be the weapon of choice for many countries in the next century.

Winds of Death

Chemical weapons are the nuclear bombs of the Third World: they are cheap, militarily effective and demonstrate an industrial sophistication and political will that some countries believe provides them with international credibility.

In stark contrast to the generally responsible view all developed countries take towards nuclear proliferation – no country has developed a nuclear capability in the past ten years – their laissez-faire attitude toward chemical weapons has allowed them to spread around the world at great speed. Precise figures are hard to come by, but analysts generally accept that, outside NATO and the Warsaw Pact, twelve countries probably have a chemical capability. These are Burma, China, Egypt, Ethiopia, Iran, Iraq, Israel, North Korea, South Korea, Syria, Taiwan, and Vietnam. A further eighteen countries have been trying to obtain chemical weapons and may have succeeded. These include Afghanistan, Angola, Argentina, Chad, Chile, Cuba, El Salvador, Guatemala, India, Indonesia, Laos, Mozambique, Nicaragua, Pakistan, Peru, the Philippines, South Africa and Thailand.[1]

Much has been made by western propagandists about the role of the Soviet Union in supplying chemical weapons to allies around the world. In fact, the Soviets have been generally responsible and cautious in their approach to chemical proliferation, with only Egypt, Ethiopia, Libya, Syria and Vietnam receiving limited stocks direct from Moscow. The remaining nations have all acquired their capability from western companies who either did not know or, more probably, did not care, what the supplies they were providing would be used for.

The United States has led the western world in drawing attention to the proliferation of chemical weapons. But allegations about Yellow Rain in South Asia harmed US credibility and western countries have since been reluctant to support US allegations of Soviet use of chemicals in Afghanistan, or of Libyan attempts to develop its own chemical manufacturing plant.

But even where the evidence was absolutely clear and there was a willingness to take action, western nations have often found themselves impotent.

Iraq invaded Iran on September 22, 1980, initiating what President Saddam Hussein of Iraq had promised his allies would be a successful war, lasting no more than a few days. He quickly realised that the Iranians were unwilling to surrender so easily. That same year, therefore, President Hussein began his quest for chemical weapons. Using the Iraqi state-owned Enterprise for Pesticide Production as a front, he began buying vast quantities of chemicals in Europe and the United States. The most important of these chemicals was thiodiglycol, which can be used in photographic developing, electroplating, print and the manufacture of inks. It is also a key component in mustard gas.

In 1983, Phillips Petroleum in Tessenderio, Belgium, received an order for 500 tons of thiodiglycol from the Iraqis. The order was met and the containers shipped to a specially built factory complex at Samarra north of Baghdad. There the thiodiglycol was used to make the mustard gas that would be used against both Iranians and members of Iraq's Kurdish minority over the next five years. There is no doubt that Phillips had no idea this product was going to be used for the manufacture of mustard gas. They must have been well aware, of course, that there was always that possibility, but at the time there were no restrictions on the export of such chemicals and no obligation on companies to report their planned export or destination.

For five years, the Iranian government alleged that Iraq was making widespread use of chemical weapons on the battlefield, a charge which Iraq repeatedly denied. Western intelligence agencies, however, had no doubt that Iraq was using chemicals and warnings were sent to a number of companies, including Phillips, that the state's Enterprise for Pesticide Production was a front for the Iraqi military. But such matters were mostly part of the confusing propaganda war between Iran and Iraq and were not taken very seriously by the public at large. That changed in March 1988.

Reporters were taken to see the remains of a village called Halabja in Northeastern Iraq. At the beginning of March, the Kurdish town with a population of 60,000 had been captured by Iranian troops. A week later Iraqi aircraft flew over the town and dropped a lethal cocktail of chemical and nerve agents on the enemy and on their own people alike.

One eye witness described the scene afterwards: 'Bodies lie in the dirt streets or sprawled in rooms and courtyards of the deserted villas, preserved at the moment of death in a modern version of the disaster that struck Pompeii.

'A father died in the dust trying to protect his child from the white clouds of cyanide vapour. A mother lies cradling her baby alongside a minibus that lies sideways across the road, hit while trying to flee. Yards away, a mother, father and daughter lie side by side. In a cellar a family crouches together. Shoes and clothes are scattered outside the houses. Carcasses of cows lie still tethered to gateposts.'[2]

Descriptions of the scene, along with US-intercepted Iraqi military communications, provided incontrovertible evidence that Iraq had developed its own chemical capability and indeed had used it. The US and other countries condemned the Iraqis and called for them to cease using such weapons. Around 5,000 people had died in the attack, a minute proportion of the million or so who had died in the war as a whole, yet worldwide condemnation of the chemical death roll was greater than any criticism of the other, far greater, casualties brought about by conventional means in the previous few months of the war.)

There was condemnation in the United Nations also, although, as usual, the organisation was unwilling to blame anyone and instead called on both sides to cease using chemical weapons. United States criticism of Iraq, furthermore, was tempered by political realities, since condemnation could drive Iraq towards the Soviets. So, while the US condemned the Iraqi use of chemicals, calls for economic sanctions were resisted.

Such western impotence must have acted as an incentive to President Hussein. Thirty-five miles southeast of Baghdad on the banks of the River Tigris lies the town of Salman Pak. According to Iraqi officials it is a summer resort popular with newlyweds and Baghdad residents wanting to get away from the oppressive humidity of the nation's capital. To western intelligence and to the Israelis, Salman Pak is also where the Iraqis have constructed a vast factory, including underground storage facilities hardened against bombing attacks, that is designed for the production of biological weapons.[3] So far, the factory has not gone into production but the US believes that Iraq has obtained cultures of Tularaemia, known as rabbit fever, which will be used to produce its own germ warfare agent.

Recognition in the west that chemical weapons are too easy for developing nations to manufacture has led to the setting up of a new ad hoc organisation to try to monitor the supply of suitable raw materials. In March 1985, the US Secretary of State, George Shultz, called for new efforts to try and curb the spread of chemical weapons. The Australian Department of Foreign Affairs then took the initiative in inviting a number of industrialised nations to a meeting at the Australian embassy in Paris in June 1985. The first meeting had representatives from Australia, Canada, Japan, New Zealand, the United States and the ten member nations of the European Community. The Australian Group, as it has become known, meets every six months, generally in Paris, and has managed to draw up a list of chemicals that are commonly used in the manufacture of weapons.[4]

By September 1987, the Australian Group had expanded to include Norway, Portugal, Spain, Switzerland and the European Commission. They identified eight chemicals that now require export licences from member states and a further thirty were placed on a watch list that members hoped would give early warning of a country's intention to develop chemical weapons. This schedule has been circulated to chemical companies with a request that they monitor the export of listed items and notify their host government when an order is placed.

The Australian Group is an excellent initiative. But problems of verification plague its chances of success. Governments can enforce a ban on the export of the eight key chemicals in the same way they can impose a ban on the export of a rifle or mortar. But export controls on conventional weapons have proved only partially successful and the same is true of chemical products. Also, conventional weapons are easily identifiable as such (a mortar is hardly likely to be used for shooting pheasants) while chemical uses are much more difficult to define.

This convenient ambiguity allows unprincipled companies and governments to ignore any recommended list. Without clear sanctions it is virtually impossible to police any form of chemical weapons control system and even then, if the price offered is high enough, a determined nation or group will still be able to get what they want.

Clear evidence for the failings of the existing measures of control came to light at the beginning of 1989. It is a revealing example, because the villain of the piece is also the country that every civilised nation agrees is a danger to world peace. That country is Libya.

The Genie is Out of the Bottle

When Ronald Reagan was sworn in as President of the United States in 1981, he inherited an America weakened by a series of foreign policy mistakes that had undermined its image abroad. In particular, the Soviet invasion of Afghanistan and the holding of American hostages by Iranian militants in Tehran were cited as evidence of America's impotence. This may have been unfair on President Jimmy Carter, but Reagan's conservative supporters were determined that they would make America strong again. Terrorism was an early and highly visible target.

To Reagan, it was incomprehensible that foreign zealots should murder innocent Americans abroad, often for causes that he did not understand. The President saw the American people largely as he saw himself, a nation trying to do their best for everyone in a troubled world. He frequently remarked to his aides that he thought Colonel Muammar Gadaffi was a madman, and his aides in their turn frequently remarked to him that Gadaffi was behind most of the terrorist attacks against Americans, even though there was no hard evidence to support such a contention.

It took four years for the Reagan administration to organise its counter terrorism policy and seriously move on Gadaffi, who was the easiest and most visible target available.

Despite a great deal of searching by US intelligence agencies, it was difficult to find firm evidence of Gadaffi's involvement in world terrorism. The Central Intelligence Agency analysts – who despite their hard-line reputation, tend to want facts to back up their prejudices – produced report after report that failed to lay the blame squarely at Gadaffi's door. Then, in April 1986, electronic intercepts made by the British and passed on to the Americans apparently proved Libyan complicity in the bombing of the La Belle discotheque in West Berlin where one American serviceman was killed and 230 were wounded. There have been repeated allegations that it was the Syrians and not the Libyans who carried out the Berlin attack. But a complete review by the CIA, DIA, the Israelis and British intelligence say that there is no evidence whatsoever to support this argument.

'If we had one single little molehill pointing to the Syrians, you could be certain we would make a mountain out of it,' said one US intelligence source. 'The united conclusion of all those who have investigated is that the Libyans were responsible.'[1]

The evidence was strong enough for Reagan to authorise a punitive raid on Libya. Later that month, the US launched Operation El Dorado Canyon which involved bombers setting off from US bases in Britain, joining others from the US Sixth Fleet in the Mediterranean and bombing targets in Tripoli and along Libya's coast.

The mission was a great public relations success in the US, but it seems to have done little to curb Gadaffi's enthusiasm for terrorism as a weapon of war: since the raid, he has stepped up his involvement with the IRA, increased his support for Middle East terrorists like Abu Nidal, and has intensified the revolutionary rhetoric, which is always an indication of how his mind is working.

What was more significant about the US commitment to stop Gadaffi was that, beginning in 1985, Libya was subjected to a most impressive US intelligence-gathering operation. The US organised regular flights by TR–1 surveillance aircraft from Mildenhall in Britain. These aircraft would overfly

Libya, photographing military installations and civilian targets of interest. At the same time satellites routinely listened to local and international conversations on both the military and civilian wavebands. Britain, too, played its part. The knowledge that Gadaffi had resumed supplies of modern arms to the IRA after a gap of several years led both the Secret Intelligence Service, also known as MI6, and GCHQ to mount an intensive operation against Libya. From its huge listening post in Cyprus, GCHQ was able to listen to thousands of conversations in Libya. Even the most classified Libyan codes are regularly broken by the British and any information gathered by GCHQ is shared with the Americans in its entirety.

Aside from terrorism, western countries were concerned that Gadaffi might also be involved in nuclear proliferation and chemical warfare. For at least ten years he had been helping to fund Pakistan's covert attempts to develop a nuclear bomb. A close watch suggested that Libya was providing funding but little else. Chemical weapons were a different matter.

In 1985 Libyan forces had invaded the central African country of Chad. In part Gadaffi was keen on simple territorial expansion, the building of a Libyan empire in Africa. But he also wanted to capture the mineral-rich Aozou strip, and exploit its wealth. His invasion was bitterly contested by local forces, with the aid of an enormous and largely unnoticed covert operation by the CIA. This operation was successful and the Libyan forces retreated after suffering heavy losses. But what made even this small war interesting to the intelligence analysts was that the Libyans made extensive use of poison gas.

In early 1986, during the Chad invasion, Libya had sprayed poison gas from a plane. Although, fortunately, the wind was blowing in the wrong direction and none of the agent landed on Chadian forces, this told the US that Libya had chemical weapons – and it was later learned they had been obtained from Iran in exchange for Soviet-made mines.[2]

The US shipped 2,000 gas masks to the Chadians and initiated a major intelligence collection effort, so that by the end of 1986 analysts from the CIA, DIA, NSA and the NSC all agreed that Libya possessed poison gas and was trying to manufacture further supplies of its own. It is rare for intelligence assessments written with contributions from different agencies to present a unanimous view – almost invariably there are dissenting footnotes as each agency attempts to put its individual stamp on the finished product. Six months later, the British and the Americans, working completely independently, picked up clear signs that Libya was well on its way to making its own chemical manufacturing facility, with Gadaffi buying in western technical expertise to develop his chemical plant.

For the British the prospect of Gadaffi making new chemical weapons and passing them on to the IRA was very worrying. The Americans, too, feared that they might become targets for Gadaffi-sponsored terrorists armed with chemical weapons. Even so, for the next two-and-a-half years many western governments, including those of Japan, West Germany, France and Italy, deliberately ignored the clear information for simple financial gain – one of the best illustrations of just how irresponsible governments can be when faced with the need to do more than mouth platitudes about arms proliferation.

In particular, British agents tracked the shipment of special steels and chemicals from both West Germany and Italy to Libya. These details were passed to the Americans who put the intelligence together with their own from Japan.

One of the key men in the Libyan scheme was Dr Ihsan Barbouti, a 61-year-old Iraqi architect who had drawn up many of the original plans for the complex at Rabta, thirty-five miles southwest of Tripoli. Barbouti claimed that he had been approached by the Libyans to design a complex to be used as a training centre for university-educated Libyans to gain experience in manufacturing industries currently dominated by westerners. Barbouti acted as middleman on all aspects of the project until June 1987, taking a 7.5 per cent commission on everything from steel bars to window glass. Also, one of his companies, Ihsan Barbouti International (IBI) Engineering, set up in 1985 in Frankfurt, reported a turnover of $180m in two years with a staff of only two. Barbouti categorically denies that he knew anything about Libya's plans to make chemical weapons at the plant.

The actual plans for the plant were drawn up by a subsidiary of the West German Salzgitter steel company, which is owned by the government. But, as one American official put it, 'the spider in the middle of the web' was a West German chemical firm, Imhausen-Chemie, which became involved with the Libya project in 1985 at a time when it was having problems meeting its bills.[3]

Imhausen commissioned the plans from Salzgitter at a cost of $3m. The designers were under the impression they were drawing up plans for a pharmaceutical factory in Hong Kong. Raw materials for the plant's construction and chemicals for the weapons themselves were shipped by Imhausen to a Hamburg firm, Pen-Tsao-Materia-Medica which had been set up by Imhausen founder, Dr Jurgen Hippenstiel-Imhausen. Pen-Tsao in turn was supposed to ship the goods to their subsidiary in Kowloon for a large chemical project in Hong Kong. In fact the goods were shipped by two Belgian firms, Cross Link and JG Trading, direct to the Libyan port of Tripoli. Pen-Tsao also shipped some of the basic ingredients necessary to make chemical weapons to Libya via Singapore and Hong Kong, in a deliberate attempt to disguise their ultimate destination.

Construction at the site was done by 700 workers brought from Thailand and employed by a Thai firm called Supachok.

The factory eventually spread over several acres, and included a metalworks plant built by the Japan Steel Works. The metalworking factory was commissioned from the Japanese company in 1985 and for the next three years they had officials regularly at the site. According to US State Department sources, the Japanese were easily identified by photo-reconnaissance because they marched to work each day. When the Japanese company was approached about the deal, they claimed the plant was part of a desalination complex to take the salt out of sea water. This excuse was greeted with some scepticism as the nearest sea is sixty miles away from the plant. By the end of 1988, the Japanese-built plant was producing nerve gas bomb casings at a rate of ten a day.

The specialised machinery to make the bomb casings and the actual steel used were both supplied by West German firms, and their shipment to Libya was closely monitored by British intelligence. It was the delivery of these special steels that helped convince the Americans and the British that Gadaffi was developing chemical weapons and not, as he variously claimed, 'perfumes' or 'medicines'.

For a year both Britain and America applied pressure on those countries whose firms were involved in helping Libya build the plant. Only the Japanese were persuaded to provide some assistance. They did not go so far as actually to withdraw from the contract, but they did provide some valuable intelligence to the US. Even this small crumb was only offered after the US threatened to expose the Japanese governments involvement to Congress at a time when import quotas against Japanese goods were being discussed. So the Japanese response had little to do with morality and everything to do with economic expediency.

In the summer of 1988, US intelligence picked up signs of a leak of toxic chemicals from the plant. Analysis was made of this leak and confirmed that the plant was designed for weapons production. If it were completed, the US believed it would become the largest chemical weapons factory in the Third World, capable of producing between 22,000 and 84,000 lbs of mustard gas and nerve agents every day.

The West German government was first alerted in May 1988 that West German companies were implicated in the Libyan scheme. They were told not only about the chemical plant but also that a West German firm, Intec, had supplied equipment that would allow Libya to convert its transport

planes to deliver chemical bombs. The West German govern-
ment promised to look into the matter but did nothing.
Despite repeated official and unofficial prompting, neither the
West German government nor any other implicated European
country took any action: indeed, the West Germans continued
to deny their involvement. Then, in November 1988, when
Chancellor Helmut Kohl visited Washington, both President
Reagan and Secretary of State George Shultz brought up the
matter of the Libyan plant. Immediately on his return to
Bonn, Kohl ordered an investigation but nothing was
established.

In Washington there was considerable frustration. By the
end of 1988, US intelligence was convinced that the factory
would be in full production in April. Recent overflights by
reconnaissance aircraft had established that the factory had
been surrounded by anti-aircraft batteries – defences that
would be hardly necessary if, as Gadaffi claimed, the factory
was being built entirely for civilian purposes.

These were the dying days of the Reagan administration
and for some of those in office, the arrival of President Bush
would be the end of an era that had produced many victories
for the right. However, despite a great deal of effort, their one
major failure was that Gadaffi was still in power in Libya. In
fact, not only was he in power but he was about to finish the
development of a plant capable of producing a new and
deadly weapon which it was feared the Colonel would very
probably supply to terrorist groups around the world – all
courtesy of the West Germans.

As a final gesture, some members of the intelligence community decided to leak the details of the plant to embarrass
the newly elected President Bush and force him to focus
attention on Gadaffi. At the time of the leaks, which had the
required effect, the precise intelligence was uncertain and the
US was embarrassed by the lack of detail available to back
up the allegations. As a result of a later investigation into the
leaks, a number of key intelligence personnel were purged.[4]

At the same time as first details of the plant were leaked,

other leaks from the Pentagon suggested that the US was considering a military strike against the plant, possibly using submarine-launched cruise missiles. In fact, this was deliberate disinformation as a military attack had never been seriously considered.

Coincidentally, at the end of the first week in January, a meeting of 140 nations had been scheduled in Paris to discuss improvements to the 1925 Geneva Protocol banning the use of chemical weapons. Libya planned to attend the conference and the US hoped that a timely leak would not only be a serious embarrassment to Gadaffi but also might provoke a reaction from the other delegates.

News of the allegations began to leak out at the end of December 1988. Both Libya and the countries that had supplied material for the plant predictably denied any involvement in chemical weapons manufacture. The Libyans claimed the plant was being made to manufacture medicines and the supplier countries, led by West Germany, publicly denied the American charges, stating that they had already been investigated and found to be unjustified.

Despite the massive publicity, the delegates meeting in Paris failed to agree any new restrictions on exports and produced instead a bland statement reaffirming their commitment to restricting the spread of nuclear weapons, coupled with a hope that the United Nations might do something about the problem.

But the publicity did provoke some reaction in West Germany, which had been the main target of the US charges. The government finally admitted that some companies might have been involved in the Libyan plant and in February, German customs confiscated more than 200 tons of chemicals destined for Libya that might have been used to make weapons.

This helpful attitude did not last long. By the beginning of March 1989, only two months later, the Thai workers who had been withdrawn at the end of 1988 were back at the site and both West German and Japanese firms were shipping raw materials to Rabta. US administration officials now believe that, short of launching a military strike against the plant, there is little they can do to prevent it going into full production.

It is not clear just how many of the companies involved knew what the Libyans were planning. Some companies, such as De Dietrich in France, which shipped glass-lined cauldrons to Libya, their clients did not adequately investigate what products were to be used for. Other companies did ask and were told lies, while the remainder knew from the start what was intended and deliberately set out to mislead their own governments. It has been very difficult for governments in any country to prosecute any of those involved. This difficulty exactly highlights a more general problem with the manufacture of chemical weapons: too many of the raw materials used have another purpose. A chemical needed for making medicines can just as easily be used for making chemical weapons, and a filtration plant or a steel works can also have a second purpose.

Libya is the most recent example of flagrant abuse by companies and governments in the west, turning a blind eye to the proliferation of chemical weapons in a complete abrogation of their duty under the 1925 Geneva Protocol. Unfortunately, new weapons are now being developed that will give leaders like Gadaffi or the terrorist groups he supports the power to hold the world to ransom or to destroy cities and even nations at will.

23

The Ultimate Weapon

On the evening of September 7, 1978, Georgi Markov, a
Bulgarian emigré playwright and author working for the
BBC's overseas service in London, was on his way home from
work. As he was walking over Waterloo Bridge, he passed a
bus queue and, as if by accident, a man waiting for his bus
fell against him pushing the tip of his umbrella into the back
of his right thigh. Turning, Markov saw the man bending
to retrieve his umbrella while mumbling an apology for his
clumsiness. Markov recounted the incident to a friend that
evening but thought little enough of it not to mention it to
his wife, Annabel, when he finally returned home.

In the early hours of the following morning he woke to find
that his temperature had risen to over 100 degrees. He turned
to his wife and said: 'I have a horrible feeling that this may
be connected with something which happened yesterday.' He
was taken to hospital, lapsed into a coma and two days later
he was dead.[1]

Doctors examined the minute puncture mark on the back
of his thigh and during the autopsy a tiny metal pellet was
removed from the wound. Under microscopic examination it
was seen that the pellet had four tiny holes which doctors
assumed had been filled with poison.

By an extraordinary coincidence, another Bulgarian exile
living in Paris, Vladimir Kostov, had been taken ill by a fever
a few days earlier, but had recovered. When he heard of
Markov's death he recalled that he too had felt a sharp pain,

but in his back, shortly before he became ill. He was x-rayed and doctors found a small pellet identical to that found in Markov's thigh and were able to treat him in time to save his life. On this occasion, there was a minute residue of poison left and British scientists working at Porton Down were able to identify it as Ricin, a particularly deadly poison derived from the castor oil plant.[2]

Such poisons, toxins and viruses are exceptionally deadly. A minute amount (0.077 of an ounce) of tularaemia bacteria, the source of rabbit fever, can produce a cloud 325 feet high, covering six-tenths of a mile, which could infect thousands of people. Or one gram of typhoid culture dropped into a public water supply could theoretically cause damage equal to 40 pounds of cyanide.[3]

Police investigating the Markov murder believe he was killed by a member of the Bulgarian secret police who had a tiny gun concealed in the tip of his umbrella. When the trigger on the gun was depressed, the platinum ball was fired out of the umbrella tip by gas pressure and injected into Markov's thigh.

Two things were interesting about the Markov assassination. The first was that the Bulgarians were prepared to attack and kill dissidents in foreign countries. But of much more interest was the method. The use of Ricin was the first hard intelligence the west had received that the Soviets and their allies were working on refinements to earlier chemical and biological warfare agents. Today, those early developments have bred a new kind of weapon, a weapon that allied intelligence services believe could transform the battlefields of tomorrow.

In the past, the difficulty with using toxins such as Ricin was that they were impossible to collect in sufficient quantities for use in war. Cobra venom, for example, is perfect for the isolated assassination using specially coated darts or bullets, but it would be impossible to breed enough cobras to produce sufficient venom to wipe out a regiment of troops in battle.

In 1972, the Convention on the Prohibition of the Development, Production, and Stockpiling of Bacteriological Weapons was signed. The treaty was an important first step in limiting the spread of biological weapons. But, as in all such treaties, significant compromises were made which left it fatally flawed.

The convention allowed for the possession of defensive systems but set no guidelines on when defensive becomes offensive. The convention also allows for no system of verification, so that each signatory has to rely on the word of others, and no arms control agreement can afford to assume the integrity of the signatories. As has been seen with agreements such as the Strategic Arms Limitation Treaty or the Anti-Ballistic Missile agreement, interpretation is subjective, frequently controversial and requires constant monitoring if all parties are to retain any confidence in their validity. Furthermore, bacteriological weapons are impossible to monitor effectively using normal satellites, radar or electronic detection systems, so a formal verification process is particularly necessary.

Even when breaches of the convention are discovered, complaints have to be made to the UN Security Council, a body not known for its robust approach to international problems. Also, the two superpowers have the right of veto over any proposed action by the Council which virtually ensures its impotence. Even if action were decided, the convention has no provisions for punishment or enforcement of penalties.

In any case, the same year that the convention was signed a scientific breakthrough was achieved that made it virtually obsolete. In November 1972, two California scientists, Herbert Boyer and Stanley Cohen, pioneered experiments that allowed the cloning of genes. The process, which has already revolutionised whole areas of science, is also changing the nature of warfare.

Each organism carries with it certain hereditary information which is passed on from generation to generation through its genes. Each gene contains a complex chemical called deoxyribonucleic acid or DNA which holds the information. A full complement of DNA – the entire genetic blueprint – is present in every cell of every living organism and directs each cell's activities. When a cell divides, it creates an exact replica of itself, including its DNA, and the DNA code that controls the process is virtually the same for all organisms – from viruses to human beings.[4]

What the two scientists achieved was to isolate the gene, cut out the DNA, and then reproduce it. The significance of this development is enormous. The genes in wheat that produce a strong, hardy and productive crop can now be reproduced in a factory – as can the genes to produce the perfect cow. Medicines in very short supply, such as insulin, can now be artificially manufactured both cheaply and with zero defects. The potential of the DNA breakthrough is only beginning to be realised but it will certainly transform much of society.

While there are many welcome benefits from such genetic engineering, there is also concern that such scientific manipulation will be used to design animals and crops, and even people, to be without fault, and this concern has led to restrictions on the type of work that can be done. But while genetic engineering (with controls) can thus be seen as a positive development, it can also become the ultimate weapon of war.

At its simplest the purpose of war is to gain political or territorial advantage at minimum cost. The methods used to achieve these aims have changed little since the gun replaced the bow and arrow as the preferred weapon. Certainly weapons are more powerful – firing further and faster, causing greater damage to property and people. But one of the ironies of modern warfare is that the firepower is such that one of the main aims of warfare – territorial advantage – may now be not worth the effort: the devastation caused by conventional weapons will very probably ensure that the economic infrastructure of a defeated nation will be destroyed along with much of its working population.

To break out of this warfighting impasse, a general would therefore like to have at his disposal a weapon that would cause no damage to property, would incapacitate rather than kill the enemy soldiers, would do no lasting damage to the civilian population, and would also have no effect on the attacking forces.

Early experiments in the 1950s and 1960s had shown the kind of effect weapons designed to disturb the performance of soldiers and civilians could have. In the United States in a secret programme, a number of soldiers and civilians were given experimental drugs without their knowledge. These resulted in an almost total breakdown of normal responses. British army personnel today are shown a film demonstrating the effects of these psychochemical agents, often derivatives of LSD or mescaline, when being trained at the army's Nuclear, Biological and Chemical Warfare School at Winterbourne Gunner near Salisbury. In one film, a squad of American soldiers are shown being trained in the field. Half of them have been drugged and the film shows how they swiftly become undisciplined and disorganised. But the film also clearly demonstrates the unreliability of such drugs as half the drugged soldiers become very lethargic while others become hyperactive. For example, one soldier tries to chop down a nearby tree with his spade.

Another film shows a cat in a cage which is given a small dose of a psychochemical drug. A mouse is then put into the cage and the cat, totally disorientated, perceives the mouse as a potent threat. Terrified, it retreats into a corner of the cage and then, in a macabre variation of a Tom and Jerry cartoon, as the mouse moves warily forward, the cat tries desperately to claw its way out of the trap.

As weapons, such drugs clearly have possibilities but they are both expensive to produce and unreliable in their effects. Serious work on perfecting a psychochemical weapon was therefore virtually abandoned until developments in genetic engineering created the possibility of scientifically creating a precise and inexpensive chemical that would produce perfect results every time.

In theory, genetic engineering allows the scientist to isolate particular toxins, to refine aspects of them to make them 'live' for very specific periods, and to design with absolute precision their effects on their human targets. For example, using such designer agents, the Soviets could explode a shell upwind of a regiment of infantry on the central front in Germany. Anyone affected by the wind-born toxin would begin to weep uncontrollably and be unable to fight. Or the toxin could instead make the forces rebellious and unwilling to follow orders. Such toxins are known as 'discipline breakers' and are considered a weapon currently available to the Soviet armed forces.

Of course, they need not be so benign. Designer agents could kill more people, faster and with less collateral damage than anything available in the recent past. Three scenarios should suffice to demonstrate the versatility of such a weapon.

Four days before the outbreak of war in Europe, Spetsnaz forces release canisters of gas in three cities in Denmark. The gas contains a genetically designed agent that causes severe vomiting in one target group and uncontrollable diarrhoea in another. The illnesses are such that the men, women and children affected are unable to go to work or school and normal life is totally disrupted. A message is passed to the government that the illnesses will wear off in precisely 72 hours and there will be no long-term side effects. But, the Soviets warn the government, if war breaks out and they mobilise their forces, other gas canisters already in place will be detonated and the population infected with lethal nerve agents for which the Danish government has no antidote. In those circumstances, would Denmark go to war?

In the first days of war, it is vital that American reinforcements arrive in Europe by air and by sea. Many European ports will be mined either by submarines or by merchant ships before hostilities begin. The mines can remain on the bottom of the harbour until activated by a radio signal. Instead of being loaded with explosives, they could be loaded with nerve agents and, this time, the weapon would be deadly and all dock workers, both civilian and military, would die.

In Britain there are seven power stations that are vital to

the national grid. Without them, Britain's industrial capacity grinds to a halt. It is a simple matter to fire a number of cruise missiles loaded with delayed action bomblets. The missiles would be fired at the power stations, drop their loads in an air burst over each of the targets with the bomblets timed to go off at different times over the next four days. First, this would overwhelm the national bomb disposal capability. Second, the nerve agents released by the bomblets would incapacitate – but not kill – all the power workers and shut down the power stations. This would be sufficient to cripple the British economy, seriously damage morale and undermine Britain's ability to fight. But, given that no one would be killed by such an attack, it would not be sufficient to provoke the British government into launching a retaliatory nuclear strike against the Soviets.

It is clear to western intelligence that the Soviets' chemical and biological weapons are not simply of tactical value, but of strategic importance in deciding the course of the war. This is strongly denied by the Soviets.

Hard evidence of these new weapons is difficult to come by because the intelligence is so sensitive. All one British scientist familiar with the Soviet technology will say is that 'There is considerable circumstantial evidence of a new generation of weapons based on designer agents.'[5]

The United States Defence Intelligence Agency is more specific. 'The Soviets now recognise the potential of modern biotechnology and genetic engineering – particularly since the Soviet Union has a greater need for advancements in agriculture and public health than the west. As such, the Soviets made the development of a biotechnological industry a top priority in 1974 and reaffirmed their commitment in 1981. Since that time, they have made remarkable progress in developing their biotechnological capabilities.

'Unfortunately, these same technologies are being used by the Ministry of Defence to develop new and more effective BW agents. With this biotechnological capability, naturally occurring microorganisms can be made more virulent, antibiotic-resistant, and manipulated to render current US vaccines ineffective. Such developments would greatly complicate our ability to detect and identify BW agents, and to operate in areas contaminated by the Soviets with such biological agents.[6]

Privately, US intelligence sources maintain that since the mid–1970s there has been a change in the targeting priorities of eastern bloc agents attempting to steal western technology. Before then there was a total concentration on gathering technology (such as the design of submarine propellers or the new guidance system for a missile) that had very specific military applications. But for the past ten years both the KGB and the GRU have devoted considerable resources to getting information about western developments in the field of genetic engineering. Of course, such information does have clear civilian applications. But what is also known is that the sensitivity of the military applications of genetic engineering is such that even the KGB are not privy to much of the information. Recent defectors have confirmed both the fact of the work and that details are so closely held.

Both the United States and Great Britain are spending millions of dollars each year trying to develop antidotes to these new weapons. Vaccines are being developed and a wide range of new chemical protection equipment is also being designed as it is thought that few, if any, of the protective suits currently in service will defeat the new toxins.

Currently there are no conventions, treaties or other agreements that address the threat posed by genetically engineered weapons. And, if history is anything to go by, any new convention or treaty will have to be a significant improvement on everything that has gone before. All previous attempts to limit the spread of chemical and biological weapons have failed, in part because the technology and the raw materials are so readily available, and exactly the same problems arise with genetically engineered weapons. They are cheap, and very difficult to detect. Potentially far more devastating than nuclear weapons, in the next century and perhaps before, designer agents will be the weapon of choice for ambitious countries like Libya and terrorists like Abu Nidal.

Such a vision may seem unnecessarily alarmist. In the past terrorists have proved to be extraordinarily conservative given their generally revolutionary ideals. Groups that began in the 1960s still use the same weapons and employ similar tactics today as then. The AK–47 assault rifle remains the preferred weapon – indeed it has become something of a revolutionary badge – and despite significant technological advances in whole families of weapons, terrorists still prefer the ordinary bomb detonated by a simple timing device. There has been no serious use of product contamination as a weapon, despite the clear vulnerability of modern societies to such economic blackmail, and, despite the apocalyptic predictions of a number of commentators, terrorists have not developed or stolen a nuclear weapon even though the technology is widely available.

But the whole nature of warfare is changing. As the superpowers make peace and begin to withdraw from the arms race, aspirant Third World countries will continue to have political and economic ambitions that can only be satisfied by the threat or use of arms. And, unlike nuclear power, genetic engineering can be redirected from peaceful purposes to the waging of war in a tiny step well within reach of many developing countries. For scientists working in this field, designer agents produce a new vision of the apocalypse more terrible than anything produced by the spectre of nuclear weapons. Unless steps are taken in the very near future to control the development of such weapons there is a real danger of that vision becoming reality. In the past, such controls in every area of weapons proliferation have never been completely successful. This time, the world cannot afford a non-proliferation initiative that fails.

PART EIGHT: BALLISTIC MISSILES

24

The Rubbery Crud Conspiracy

Since the signing of the Camp David peace treaty between Israel and Egypt on March 26, 1979, the United States has come to see Egypt as one of its most important allies in the Middle East.

Under the Camp David accords, America agreed to supply the government of President Sadat with $2 billion in aircraft, tanks and other weapons, along with $750m in economic aid. Since then, despite the assassination of Sadat and the chaotic state of the Egyptian economy, the United States and Egypt have grown steadily closer.

Egypt currently receives $2.3 billion in military and economic aid each year from the US. America has vast stocks of weapons and other supplies prepositioned in Egypt in case Washington decides to intervene militarily in the region. Exercises to test America's ability to deploy troops rapidly to the area are held regularly. During the Afghan war, Egypt was used as a covert conduit for much of the CIA arms to the guerrillas fighting the Soviet forces. Such involvement in clandestine activities on behalf of the US could be seen as an accolade from the intelligence community: Cairo not only thinks in the right way politically but also can be trusted.

The final seal was placed on the Egyptian-American strategic relationship on March 23, 1988 when US Defence Secretary Frank Carlucci and Egyptian Defence Minister Field

Marshal Abdul-Halim Abu Ghazala signed a new cooperative arms agreement. This ten-year Memorandum of Understanding gave Egypt special status as a strategic ally alongside Israel, Australia and Sweden. The agreement allowed Egypt access to American defence equipment and gave Egypt equal status with Israel and America's NATO allies.

After the signing ceremony, Abu Ghazala, considered the second most powerful man in Egypt after President Hosni Mubarak, returned to the Vista Hotel to meet with an old friend, Abdelkader Helmy. An Egyptian-born US citizen, Helmy had flown in for the meeting from his home in El Dorado Hills, California. The meeting was not to celebrate the new era of trust that had just begun between the United States and Egypt. Instead, the Egyptian defence minister wanted a progress report on a secret project to smuggle high technology defence equipment from America to Egypt.[1]

According to Helmy, the minister complained that the project was progressing too slowly and that in future all further shipments of material to Egypt should be coordinated with Colonel Abdel Monem Hamza, a military attaché at the Washington embassy. In fact, Hamza shortly afterwards became ill and his role was taken over by Rear Admiral Abdel Rahim El Gohary from the Egyptian Procurement office in Washington, and his assistant Colonel Mohamed Abdalla Mohamed.

The operation, which had the approval of the Egyptian government, involved breaking several of America's laws designed to prevent the illegal export of sensitive defence equipment and the illegal laundering of money — hardly the action of a close and trusted ally.

The scheme began around 1982 when Egypt, Argentina and Iraq decided to cooperate on the joint development of a new ballistic missile known by the Argentinians as Condor 2. The Condor 2 would have a two-stage rocket, a range of at least 1,000 kilometers and would carry a payload of 500kg, in the form of a nuclear, chemical, biological or conventional warhead.

Argentina had already developed a Condor 1 rocket with a range of around sixty miles and so had demonstrated a knowledge of the technology involved. The Egyptians had done some work on guidance systems and the Iraqis had the cash. All three countries perceived a strategic need for such a rocket: Iraq could attack deep into Iran and would not be dependent on future supplies from the Soviet Union or China; Egypt would have a system to match the Jericho missile being developed by Israel; and Argentina would gain considerable status in Latin America as well as having a weapon with which it could directly threaten the Falkland Islands, which it still hoped to get back from the British.

If any of those countries managed to manufacture and deploy a ballistic missile system, it would have a serious effect on the strategic balance and undoubtedly encourage neighbouring countries to acquire their own system or upgrade their existing capabilities.

To buy the equipment necessary, a network of companies was set up, mostly based in the Swiss canton of Zug. The most important of these companies was Consen, which also had offices in Monte Carlo. Other companies included Desintek and Condor Projetke based near Zurich. All had personnel recruited from the West German company Messerschmidt-Bolkow-Blohm (MBB), which had been heavily involved in the Condor 1 project.[2]

Although MBB deny their involvement in the Condor 2 project, a wholly owned subsidiary company, Transtechnica, has analysed results of test firings of the rocket's motors in Argentina and Egypt.

Iraq had constructed a vast missile testing centre called Saad 16 near Mosul in Northern Iraq. The complex includes a supersonic wind tunnel and ramps for testing rocket motors. The contract for constructing the complex was led by the Saad General Establishment (SGE), which works on construction projects for Iraq's State Organisation for Technical Industries. SGE employed as prime contractor the Gildemeister company of Dusseldorf which in turn bought equipment from a wide range of industrial companies. These included US corporations such as Tektronix of Beaverton, Oregon, who make computer graphics terminals and measuring instruments; Scientific-Atlanta of Atlanta who make telecommunications and satellite ground station equipment and Hewlett Packard who make computers. According to Hewlett Packard, electronic equipment was supplied to MBB which listed the SGE as the end user but described it as 'an institute for higher learning'.[3]

In fact, in the early eighties these exports were sent to Germany and on to Iraq perfectly legally. Then in April 1987, seven nations (the US, Canada, France, the UK, Italy, Japan and West Germany) signed the Missile Technology Control Regime to curb exports of equipment that might be used to develop missiles or chemical and biological weapons.

Under the control regime the signatories agreed not to export 'complete rocket systems (including ballistic missile systems, space launch vehicles and sounding rockets) and unmanned air vehicle systems (including cruise missile systems, target drones and reconnaissance drones).' Also not to be exported were individual rocket stages, re-entry vehicles designed for non-weapons payloads, some solid or liquid fuel rocket engines, some types of guidance sets, and arming, fusing and firing mechanisms.[4]

Behind all the formal language there was also an informal agreement to share intelligence about any efforts being made by Third World countries to gain access to such technology. Even countries that were not signatories to the agreement, such as Switzerland, have since helped provide information to the seven member nations.

One result of that shared intelligence was that on March 18, 1988, the US customs received information that a California based Aerospace scientist, Abdelkader Helmy, might be one of the links in a chain of people in the US secretly involved in the Condor project.

Helmy was an Egyptian but had become a naturalised American citizen in October 1987. He worked at the Aerojet

General Corporation in Rancho Cordova, California, where he was cleared to handle material classified Secret. Helmy was the chief scientist working on the research and development of a new shell for a 120mm gun.

In March, the customs watched Helmy meet with another Egyptian and ship two boxes to an address they discovered was that of the Egyptian military attaché in Washington. Suspicious, they began to tap Helmy's home and office phone. If Helmy had any kind of experience he would not have made the series of elementary mistakes that marked his career as spy over the next three months. Despite being under almost continuous surveillance, he made no effort to check for a tail. He talked freely on the telephone and he met publicly with others involved in the smuggling plot. But, most importantly, he forgot the first rule of intelligence work: never write anything down, but if you must, either keep it secure or destroy it. What Helmy did was to make notes to himself as he went along and then scrunch them up and throw them in the wastepaper basket by his desk.

From the start of their investigation, the customs made an arrangement with the refuse collection men that Helmy's trash would be put to one side for the customs to go through at their leisure. Each week revealed a new haul of incriminating documents, many of then carefully written in Helmy's own hand.

The first investigation of his rubbish revealed two pages of handwritten notes describing how to work with a material called carbon-carbon, which is an exceptionally tough, heat-resistant material with a low radar signature that is used in the manufacture of rocket nose cones, rocket nozzles and heat shields on re-entry vehicles. All exports of carbon-carbon require an export licence.

Further examination of the rubbish outside Helmy's house revealed drawings showing how a rocket nose cone could be constructed from carbon-carbon.

Helmy then purchased a fax machine and set up a dummy company called Science and Technology Applications which was registered to his home address. From listening to his telephone calls and searching once more through the trash, the customs agents discovered the indentity of Helmy's bank accounts at the Cameron Park branch of World Savings and Loans. The bank records showed that since December 15, 1987, $1,030,000 had been transferred from IFAT corporation in Zug. Some of the money had been used to buy carbon composite material including missile nose cones from two California companies.

Eventually, enough documents were pulled from Helmy's rubbish for customs to approach his boss at Aerojet, who identified the documents as 'a complete package to build or upgrade a tactical missile system'.

Helmy and two assistants were working to a shopping list sent to them by the Egyptian, Colonel Hussam Yossef, who was based in Austria. As the flow of requests from Yossef increased until eventually he was demanding thirty tons of different materials, Helmy had difficulty coping.

Most of the American companies he approached via his dummy company agreed to sell him the material with no questions asked. They had no particular reason to be suspicious in any case, as the goods were being sent to an apparently legitimate California-based company and there was no suggestion they would be exported.

Helmy's main assistant in the operation was Jim Huffman, a friend who worked as a marketing representative for an aerospace company in Lexington, Ohio. The two men would talk regularly to discuss progress. In one intercepted call on May 27, Huffman told Helmy that 'We took all the markings off the barrels and boxes,' of chemicals for making rocket fuel. 'The seven drums of plasticiser were listed as fatty acid of animal oil . . . the one drum of EPON was listed as plastic material . . . the Nordel rubber was listed as synthetic rubber or rubbery crud.'

The customs intercepted this shipment and opened the various drums to take samples. The rubbery crud was found to be di-ethyl-hexyl-azolate, a binder used in making solid rocket fuel.

The Condor project had been closely watched not just by the Americans but also by Israeli intelligence. In the past, when Egypt has attempted to develop its own missile capability, the Israelis have not hesitated to take action. In 1962 when the Israelis discovered that the Egyptians, then led by President Nasser, were building rockets that could be targeted at Israel, they acted immediately. The scientists working on the project had mostly been recruited from West Germany, and Mossad, the Israeli intelligence organisation, began a campaign of intimidation against them, which included kidnappings, threats and the posting of letter bombs. The campaign worked and the key scientists left Egypt.

In this latest case, the threat to Israel was potentially as serious. If Condor 2 succeeded, both Iraq, a deadly enemy, and Egypt, a friend today but possibly an enemy again tomorrow, would have the means to attack Israel with ballistic missiles against which she had no real defence.

At 3.00am on May 27 an empty Peugeot car parked in the street in Grasse in southern France was blown to pieces by a remotely detonated bomb. The car belonged to Ekkehard Schrotz, general manager of Consen, the Zug-based company coordinating the purchases for the Condor project.

An anonymous call to the Agence France Presse news agency claimed that a previously unknown pro-Iranian terrorist group, The Guardians of Islam, was responsible for the attack as a warning to Schrotz to stop his work for the Iraqi regime. But western intelligence services believe that the attack had all the hallmarks of Israeli intelligence and some believe that more such attacks are on the way unless the project is stopped.

The Egyptians also seem to have concluded that the Israelis were responsible. In a telephone call to Helmy on June 3, Yossef said that 'certain people tried to do away with us. They put something in a company car and it exploded. We suspect the ones next to us because the way the operation was executed by remote control indicates that the country next to us is the culprit.'

The Egyptian defence minister was initially linked to the conspiracy when two telephone taps recorded conversations between Helmy, his controller in Austria, Colonel Yossef, and the minister's liaison in Washington, Rear-Admiral El Gohary.

On June 1, Helmy telephoned Washington and learned that the admiral was having difficulty coping with the volume of material being shipped to Washington for trans-shipment to Cairo. Helmy reminded the admiral that 'when he, the minister, was here during the month before last,' there were discussions about 'things that are controlled and cannot be exported.' Helmy then brought up the forthcoming delivery of the rubbery crud. 'Both items were banned from being exported and we acquired them through our own ways or channels and you know that very well.'

When the admiral complained that 'I didn't expect to receive material that weighed six or seven tons from you,' Helmy replied: 'I understand that, he, the minister, wants the cargo shipped no matter what, that is what we were told and you will arrange for the shipment on the airplane that . . . usually leaves for Cairo.'

The admiral remained a reluctant participant in the operation and Helmy then called Yussef in Austria to try to get some pressure applied from Cairo. He apparently succeeded because two days later Yussef called to say that he had telephoned the admiral: 'I told him: "I'm calling you from the ministry in order to deliver you a message from our father and from our grandfather, who was at your end earlier regarding Dr Abdelkader . . ."' Investigators believe that the reference to 'our father . . . and our grandfather' referred to the Egyptian defence minister.

The pressure appears to have worked because the admiral himself came up with a suggestion for shipping the vast quantities of goods back to Egypt. In future, he told Helmy, he should make special wooden boxes that should be clearly labelled 'Personal Items of the Air Force Club'. They would then be shipped on the regular Egyptian Air Force C–130 flight from Washington to Cairo.

The customs decided to move in. On June 24 as a box labelled Personal Items Air Force Club, which in fact contained 430 pounds of carbon fibre for rocket nose cones, was about to be loaded onto an Egyptian Air Force C–130 at Baltimore-Washington airport, customs men arrested three key members of the smuggling ring. Helmy, his wife Albia and Huffman were charged with exporting materials without a licence and with money laundering. The Egyptian diplomats claimed diplomatic immunity and left the country two days after the arrest.

The customs service had completed a successful operation and the break up of the ring provided the US administration with the perfect opportunity to apply pressure on their close and trusted ally, Egypt, to drop the project.

In fact, before the arrests had even taken place, the diplomatic horse-trading had begun. The State Department, fearing the case might damage US-Egyptian relations, applied pressure on the customs service to drop the name of the Defence Minister, Admiral Abu Ghazala, from the records submitted to the Sacramento court. The customs refused the request claiming that if they did so, their case could be seriously undermined.

But under pressure from the State Department, customs service did omit all references to the involvement of Field Marshal Abu Ghazala. Privately, however, the State Department made plain to President Hosni Mubarak their unhappiness over the affair. The Egyptian government promised to cooperate with the US in their investigations but, in fact, nothing of importance was done and none of those involved was punished. Nearly a year later Abu Ghazala was moved from the Defence Ministry to become Presidential Assistant, a considerable demotion. However, this move was unconnected with the exposure of the spy ring.

The United States has treated the smuggling operation as a temporary aberration by a still trusted ally. Only five months after the arrest of Helmy and his associates, the US defence secretary met once again with Egyptian Abu Ghazala and President Hosni Mubarak in Cairo. In a meeting that was described as 'very friendly', Carlucci signed an agreement to allow the Egyptians to produce M1A1 Abrams tanks, the most sophisticated in the US arsenal.

This apparently relaxed US approach to the Egyptian spying directly contradicts their expressed concern about the proliferation of ballistic missiles. The United States has made a significant contribution to the MTCR, which was specifically set up to try to stop the spread of such missiles. In a speech delivered in October 1988, the US Secretary of State George Shultz warned against the proliferation of such missiles. 'The worst nightmare of all would be the eventual combination of ballistic missiles and chemical weapons in the hands of governments with terrorist histories.'[5]

This was not just idle talk. According to SIPRI at least twenty-two developing countries have active ballistic missile programmes while seventeen have actually deployed such missiles. What is particularly alarming about these figures is that every single nation that has a chemical and biological weapons programme has also embarked on a ballistic missile programme. It is clear that developing countries have recognised that ballistic missiles and chemical weapons are a far cheaper option than trying to buy or develop nuclear weapons.

It is one of the strange misconceptions of modern warfare that ballistic missiles are acceptable and a legitimate part of conventional warfare, while nuclear weapons are altogether more dangerous. This is nonsense. Mere possession of a ballistic missile gives the owner a dangerous deal of flexibility.

'All you have to do is unscrew the top, pour in the chemical, make one or two adjustments to stop it slopping around and you have a chemical weapon,' explained one western intelligence source. 'Then the ballistic missile introduces near certainty into your ability to hit a target. It is much more reliable than a bomber and many countries have no defence of any kind against such a system. All you hear is a double bang as it goes through the sound barrier and that is the first warning of its imminent arrival.'[6]

If Libya or Iraq were to launch a ballistic missile, armed with even a relatively ineffective chemical, against Istanbul, Rome or, more likely, Tel Aviv, then thousands of lives would be lost. This kind of weapon is all the more devastating because none of the likely targets have any form of defence against such weapons and would receive at best about five minutes warning.

The technology needed to manufacture ballistic missiles is difficult to acquire and many of the materials can only be purchased from the industrialised west. It is also very expensive – Argentina's contribution to the Condor 2 project is costing her more than $1.5 billion – which should act as a deterrent to some countries.

But countries such as China and Iraq are determined to do anything possible to acquire the necessary technology. In 1989, China was touring major arms shows with a cardboard cut-out of a new ballistic missile. Western intelligence believes that Beijing is actually looking for finance to help develop such a missile and judging by past performance, the Chinese will not care where the cash comes from.

There are only two ways that the proliferation of ballistic missiles can be halted. The first is the introduction of a tough international agreement that severely penalises companies which break the law by supplying equipment that can be used in such programmes. Too often in the past companies have shown little interest in the ultimate destination of the products they sell and even when they know goods are going to countries like Libya, there are always willing sellers.

Second, the industrialised nations who control the supply of raw materials must be prepared to penalise countries that flagrantly breach laws to smuggle or steal the technology they need. If a country like Egypt can lie and spy against its closest western ally and be rewarded with a deal to produce tanks under licence, why should any country care about breaking another's laws?

PART NINE: CONCLUSION

25

Towards a New Arms Race

An era in the relations between the United States and the Soviet Union is drawing to a close. Since the Russian Revolution in 1917 which brought the communists to power in Moscow, there has been conflict between the two great countries. This was a confrontation bred by ideological differences, a confrontation in which both sides detected aggression and an apparent wish to dominate the world both politically and economically, and the formation of NATO and the Warsaw Pact as military blocs after 1945 formalised the arrival of what became known as the Cold War.

This constant level of tension helped establish an arms race of unprecedented proportions, led by the Soviets and Americans and supported by their respective allies. Today, Europe is the most militarised piece of territory that the world has ever seen. And in the course of that militarisation whole families of weapons have been designed that are more powerful, more precise and kill more people than ever before. At the highest level there are enough nuclear missiles to wipe out the population of the world several times over, and at the bottom end there is enough conventional artillery to destroy Europe's industrial base in a matter of days.

For every weapon that entered the Warsaw Pact or NATO inventories, a gun or missile left those inventories and was sold to other countries in Africa, Asia or Central and South America. The arms race in the industrialised nations thus created a second arms race in the developing world.

There seemed no end to this senseless cycle until a confluence of events led by the arrival of Mikhail Gorbachev as President of the Soviet Union. For the first time since the Revolution, the Soviets had a leader who understood the modern world and was willing to take on those within the Soviet Union who challenged his perceptions. Gorbachev inherited a communist system in the Soviet Union that was morally and economically bankrupt.

The United States of the 1980s, too, had problems: a spiralling budget deficit and a political climate of opinion that was no longer prepared to tolerate the large increases in the defence budget that had been an annual feature of the first Reagan Presidency. Budget difficulties were also experienced by other NATO allies who had their own problems convincing their electorates that the Warsaw Pact countries, led by the Soviets, were really the aggressive stereotypes they had been led to believe.

With both sides at least prepared to talk about compromise, deals were at last possible. The first positive result was the 1987 agreement to withdraw all intermediate nuclear forces from Europe. This meant that the Soviets would withdraw 1,752 missiles and the US 859 missiles with a range of 500 to 5,500 kilometers. Those withdrawals are now taking place and mark the first step in reversing what has been a continuous forty-year military build-up in Europe.

Discussions are now underway to reduce conventional forces in Europe, to cut strategic forces and, after years of inaction, to seek a treaty curbing the use and deployment of chemical weapons. Such is the current momentum behind political change that Soviet and American leaders are vying with each other to produce the most attractive disarmament package. Both the US and the Soviet Union recognise that their people, who have seen the first glimpse of a peaceful future for their children, want to see more of it, and sooner rather than later. But aside from the propaganda war, the next decade could see a genuine restructuring of the international order, a Soviet Union that really has a defensive defence policy, and a reduction in defence spending among all nations.

With these real and potential changes, there have been other significant improvements. Under a different agreement designed to reduce tension, it is now routine for nations to be allowed to inspect each other's military exercises. This may sound a small step but for many military officers on both sides such inspections will be the first time they have actually met their potential enemy on the ground. In one particularly striking example of this in 1988, Warsaw Pact and NATO officers attending a British exercise in Scotland spent one memorable evening exchanging gossip and war stories.

All these changes should be viewed with healthy scepticism. Gorbachev could be ousted tomorrow. Or the unpredictable could happen and the Soviets and Americans could confront each other over a modern Cuban missile crisis. So the west should not lower its guard, but if the present trends continue, the next decade could see a transformation in the fortunes of war and peace.

The moves to reduce conventional forces in Europe look likely to continue although it is too early to say what the final outcome of these changes will be. What does seem certain is that the old order of NATO and the Warsaw Pact facing each other to fight a war on the central plains of Europe is finished. As the nature of the threat changes, so does the composition of the armed forces and the industries that serve them. Some opportunists maintain that forces in east and west may be cut by between 20 and 40 per cent by the end of this century. That will mean significant cuts in all types of equipment. Some of these cuts will be stipulated in treaties which means that to comply, all signatories will have to destroy large quantities of equipment. But many cuts are likely to be unilateral and rather than destroying tanks, aircraft and missiles, nations will try to sell the ordnance to other countries.

At the same time, industry, which has come to rely on a steady income from supplying national armouries with the latest high technology in weaponry, will attempt to reduce the affects of a declining traditional market.

The outlets for existing stocks and any spare production capacity lie in the third world where there is still a strong appetite for new and second-hand weapons. It seems certain that the competition to sell arms to developing nations will drive down prices and further fuel the new arms race.

But these changes in the arms race have been matched by major shifts in the nature of the race itself. What these shifts suggest is that the world is on the edge of a new and potentially more destructive arms race where increasingly destructive wars will be fought not between the superpowers but at a lower level of conflict.

Conflict can generally be viewed as an escalatory process where terrorists operate at the lowest end, rising through guerrilla warfare, conventional wars and finally to a war involving nuclear weapons.

It has been generally accepted in east and west that the future of warfare lies not in confrontations between the great massed armies of the superpowers and their allies. Instead most future wars will be conducted at a lower level by guerrilla forces or by the armies of developing nations in conflict with each other.

The numbers of these conflicts taking place in any one year have increased steadily from around three in 1945 to a fairly constant number of between thirty-five and forty today. In those wars to date, between three and five million people have died and perhaps three times that number have been wounded.

Furthermore, modern military technology, which becomes increasingly accessible, has made today's battlefield far bloodier than at any other time in man's history. In Afghanistan more than a million Afghans were killed by the Soviets and between three and five million became refugees in the ten-year war. In the Iran-Iraq war, around 500,000 died and 600,000 were wounded in eight years of conflict.

Understanding just how these wars came about and how

they could be fought at such cost for so long is fundamental to learning what can be done to change things in the future. The lessons that are to be drawn, not just from those conflicts but from other developments in the research and development of weapons, are a clear warning for the future. Too little thought has been given to preventing the proliferation of weapons below the nuclear threshold. The result of that has been the spread of weapons of massive destructive power.

At the lowest end of the spectrum, terrorists – despite their apparently revolutionary fervour – have invariably proved to be very conservative tactical and strategic thinkers. There is no real evidence of any great new ideas coming from terrorist organisations and despite some forty years or so of struggle it is difficult to find a terrorist organisation that has succeeded in its aims.

But those groups that have survived have done so because they have developed to become very professional organis-ations. The IRA is a good case in point. Twenty years ago it was unable to muster more than a few rusty weapons to defend the Catholic community. Today it has enough arms, courtesy of Colonel Gadaffi in Libya, to keep a small army going into the next century.

The IRA have understood the uses and value of technology. They have developed very sophisticated methods of using explosives, involving the most modern detonators that are proving difficult for the British to combat effectively. They are well-trained and also have a patient and effective intelligence gathering system. They have done all this not by spending vast amounts of money – their budget has been fairly static for some years – but by making use of new technology.

It was technology, too, that turned the tide in favour of the mujahedeen in Afghanistan. Without the Stinger ground-to-air missiles supplied by the Americans, the Soviet withdrawal would have been very unlikely. The Soviet withdrawal has been claimed as a great victory for a tough western policy aimed at making the Soviets pay for their 1979 invasion of the country. In those strict terms, the policy certainly was a success. But it seems that the west will be paying a very high price for its success in Afghanistan.

A badly managed covert operation saw corruption develop in Pakistan and Afghanistan on a scale unprecedented even in covert intelligence operations. Cash and arms were siphoned off so that tons of weapons, including Stinger missiles, are now on the black market. At the same time, the cash and arms have helped fuel an explosion in the growing and harvesting of opium and the smuggling of heroin from the region, most of which goes to the United States. The disciplining of covert operations like that in Afghanistan can only be achieved if the political leadership cares enough to institute effective controls. In Afghanistan such controls were lacking.

In the Iran-Iraq war, on the other hand, virtually every western country sold arms to one side or the other and many sold to both while pretending to impose a ban on such sales. Even where apparently illegal activity was detected, governments repeatedly turned a blind eye until the deals were made public by the media. Such behaviour not only helped prolong the war but ensured a transfer of modern technology to Iran that has now allowed it to develop its own arms industry.

But the most significant legacy of that war is the opportunity it gave fledgling arms manufacturing nations to get established. During the war, they had a steady market for their weapons and now that both sides are re-arming they have a further market to exploit. Because of the war countries like Brazil, North Korea, China and South Africa have become major players in the arms business.

Of course, none of these wars would have been possible without the aid of superpowers and their allies who either supplied the weapons and cash to fuel the wars directly, or allowed the arms transfers to take place.

The arms business used to be considered a disreputable and amoral one. It was argued that killing machines should not be sold and that they should be manufactured only for defensive purposes. It was also argued that most developing nations could not afford the weapons they were being offered and arms dealers were therefore encouraging such countries to increase their debt. These arguments are still heard occasionally but now most governments that have weapons to sell, do so. Driven by the need to produce exports, foreign exchange and a healthy domestic industry in Britain, for example, Prime Minister Margaret Thatcher has personally intervened in two of the country's largest arms deals – with Saudi Arabia and Malaysia – to ensure that Britain won the contract.

Of course, there will always be back-street dealers, techno-mercenaries who are uninterested in the consequences of what they do and only care about the profit. What is different about today is that governments and reputable companies are willing to join in and sell anything to almost anyone. Given the worldwide condemnation of Colonel Gadaffi in Libya and his proven sponsorship of terrorism, it is depressing that western companies, led by West Germany, helped him establish a plant to build chemical weapons. It is also depressing that America, knowing of Pakistan's attempts to develop a nuclear weapon, did nothing effective to stop them.

But if the developed nations show insufficient restraint, the newcomers to the business show none at all. Brazil, with one of the highest debts in the world, needs to sell arms to survive. South Africa needs to sell arms to support its ailing economy and is already isolated from the world community. Today, both these nations make some of the finest missiles, guns and support equipment in the world and will happily sell any of it anywhere, to anyone.

Not only is the arms business more diverse and the weapons it produces more powerful, but new weapons of mass destruction are on the horizon that will make even the most insignificant dictator a real power in the world.

Chemical and biological weapons are now cheap to make and available to most developing countries. But this is only the beginning. The full potential of genetically engineered weapons is not yet understood. So far only the Soviets are thought to have made the designer weapons available by this method. If western intelligence reports are accurate, then the world will see for the first time a weapon of enormous destructive power that can be applied with absolute precision to have very specific effects – the ultimate weapon. The technology for this is becoming widely available also. It is only a matter of time before Libya, Iraq or South Africa decide that, for them too, this is the weapon of choice.

In the past, developing nations have argued that if the major powers are allowed to possess nuclear weapons then they should be allowed their own, affordable weapons of equal destructive power. This has always been a specious argument. The transfer of war technology of whatever kind should be strictly controlled. Some controls, such as the Non-Proliferation Treaty and various export restrictions on arms and technology imposed by individual countries, already exist. But even in countries like the United States, which has pioneered many of the arms control measures, there appears to be a lack of serious political will to enforce such measures. Even when illegal activities are discovered, if action against them is politically inconvenient, then nothing is done. Thus Pakistan and Israel have continued to develop a nuclear capability while receiving substantial US aid, and Egypt has organised the smuggling of restricted technology from the US and has been rewarded for its efforts with new and better weaponry.

The United States and Europe, which together possess much of the technology wanted by the developing world, will continue to be a market place for the covert buying of arms, and for the smuggling of arms and technology. It is here that a control regime has to start and it is here that such a regime has to be effectively enforced.

Unless new and effective enforcement regimes are introduced, armies in west and east will be faced with large Third World forces of almost equal firepower. Recent wars in Afghanistan, Angola and Lebanon have already demonstrated this growth in military capability where small forces can defeat much larger armies. This matters because since the end of World War II, it is the unmatched strength of the few major military powers that has kept the ambitions of smaller nations in check. Wholesale proliferation of new weapons of frightening power will reduce that influence, with serious consequences for the world.

Notes

CHAPTER 1

1. The best account of the raid comes in J Bowyer Bell, *The IRA*, revised edition, The Academy Press, Dublin, 1979, pp. 258–260. Two other books are useful for a history of the IRA: Kevin Kelley, *The Longest War, Northern Ireland and the IRA*, Brandon Books, 1982; and Patrick Bishop and Eamonn Mallie, *The Provisional IRA*, Corgi, London, 1988. Of the three, the Bishop and Mallie book is the most impartial and reliable.

CHAPTER 2

1. A good account of Gadaffi's rise to power can be found in John Wright's, *Libya a Modern History*, Croom Helm, London, 1982.
2. Quoted in John Wright, *Libya*, op. cit., p. 174.
3. Details on the *Claudia* and its mission come from *The Times*, March 30, 1973; *Observer*, June 11, 1973; *Sunday Telegraph* April 1, 1973; and intelligence sources.
4. Bishop and Mallie, *The Provisional IRA*, op. cit., p. 246.

CHAPTER 3

1. A great deal has been written about the *Eksund*. The most accurate account appeared in *The Listener* on March 3, 1988, pp. 4–5. All the main British and Irish newspapers reported the background to the story, some accurately, others less so. I have drawn in part on all these accounts. I have also spoken to people involved in the search for the Libyan arms, and the analysis of the information is obtained from interrogating the crew. There are still gaps in the story but I hope this is the most accurate and detailed account.
2. Interview with British intelligence sources, July 1989.

CHAPTER 4

1. Frank Doherty, *Sigint used by Anti-State Forces: A Case Study of Provisional IRA Operations, in War and Order*, Junction Books, London, 1983, pp. 117–123. This gives one of the best open source accounts of IRA Sigint activity.
2. The most detailed account of the extraordinary career of Patrick Ryan appeared in the London *Daily News* on June 25, 1987. This material was prepared with the help of the former commander of the anti-terrorist squad Bill (Posh Bill) Hucklesby. The extremely detailed account, which was part of a series, revealed not only what was known by the British about Ryan but also how they knew it. The report caused fury in the intelligence and police community and there was consideration given to prosecuting Hucklesby under the Prevention of Terrorism Act.

Other details of Ryan's career come from intelligence sources and other newspaper accounts which are specifically cited in the text.
3. In an interview with the author, August 1988.
4. Information supplied by security forces in July 1988.

CHAPTER 5

1. Unless otherwise specified, the material for this chapter comes from interviews conducted by the author in London and Washington. The invasion is covered in more detail in the author's book *Secret Armies*. Additional interviews were carried out with western intelligence sources during 1988 and early 1989.
2. Quoted in Thomas T Hammond, *Red Flag Over Afghanistan*, Westview Press, Bouklder, 1984, p. 120.
3. Jimmy Carter, *Keeping Faith*, Bantam Books, New York, 1983, p. 472.
4. Zbigniew Brzezinski, *Power and Principle*, Farrar, Straus and Giroux, New York, 1985, p. 429.
6. ibid, p. 122.
7. Hammond, *Afghanistan*, op. cit., p. 218.
8. Hammond, *Afghanistan*, op. cit., p. 158; Jay Peterzell, *Reagan's Secret Wars*, Center for National Security Studies, Washington DC, 1984, p. 9.
9. Radek Sikorski, *Moscow's Afghan War: Soviet Motives and Western Interest*, Institute for European Defence and Strategic Studies, London, 1987, p. 56.
10. Interview, Washington, September 1989.

CHAPTER 6

1. *Military Technology*, June 1987, p. 91.
2. *Wall Street Journal*, February 16, 1988.
3. Details on this were supplied to the author in September 1989 by western

intelligence sources familiar with the project. As the system is still in use, details have been kept vague.

4. Interview with NATO intelligence source July 1988.

5. *Washington Post*, July 5, 1989.

6. *New York Times*, October 10, 1989.

CHAPTER 7

1. Interview May 1989.

2. *Washington Post*, July 5, 1989.

3. SIPRI in their *1988 Yearbook for World Armaments and Disarmament* produce a figure for the grey market but none for the black market which is much higher.

4. John Prados, *Presidents' Secret Wars*, William Morrow, New York, 1986, p. 362.

5. Interview, December 1988.

6. Interview in Washington, July 1988.

7. An excellent article on the conflict which touched on the arms business appeared in *The New Yorker*, April 11, 1988, pp. 44–86.

8. *Armed Forces Journal*, September 1987, pp. 36–40.

9. *The Sunday Times*, September 20, 1987.

10. *Washington Post*, October 20, 1987; *Washington Times*, October 13, 1987.

11. *The Times*, May 26, 1988.

12. *Pravda*, October 13, 1987, p. 5.

13. *The Times*, March 12, 1989.

14. Details of the Senator's views were supplied in briefings by his staff.

15. Report of the International Narcotics Control Board for 1986, Vienna, p. 19.

16. International Narcotics Control Strategy Report, Mid-Year Update, September, 1987, United States Department of State, Bureau of International Narcotics Matters, p. 204.

17. Unless otherwise specified information on the drugs business comes from western drug enforcement agents working in Pakistan who were interviewed in autumn, 1988.

18. *New York Times*, June 18, 1986.

19. United Press Wire service report, December 15, 1983.

20. *The Sunday Times*, November 27, 1988.

21. *The Times*, September 25, 1989.

22. ibid.

CHAPTER 8

1. The most detailed and accurate account of the *Achille Lauro* affair is in *Best Laid Plans* by David Martin and John Walcott, Harper and Row, New York, 1988, pp. 235–257. See also *Secret Armies* by James Adams, Hutchin-

son, London, 1988, pp. 274–279. There was also extensive newspaper coverage at the time.

2. Where possible, I have cited overt sources on al-Kassar's activities. However, a fair amount of the information comes from classified sources and will not be footnoted. Interviews were conducted in Washington, London, Paris and Madrid in 1988 and 1989.

3. *Readers Digest*, August 1986, pp. 49–55; *Le Point*, November 23, 1987.

4. This source of the PLO's income is discussed in James Adams' *The Financing of Terror*, New English Library, London, 1986. See also *Wall Street Journal*, April 3, 1984.

5. The most detailed account of the trial appeared in *The Guardian*, June 4, 1977.

6. Tiempo, June 9, 1987.

7. Tiempo, June 9, 1987.

8. The Associated Press reported the Liberation story on December 12, 1986.

9. Tiempo op. cit.

10. Details of this operation and its results come from US intelligence sources.

11. Repeated to the author in an interview in Washington, December 1988.

12. Three detailed accounts of the al-Kassar involvement with the North network appear in *The Los Angeles Times*, July 17, 1987 and December 31, 1987 and *Newsday*, April 19, 1987. Other information comes from Congressional investigators who looked into the Iran-Contra affair and US intelligence sources.

13. US intelligence sources, October 1989.

CHAPTER 9

1 Much of the material for this chapter came from a series of interviews conducted by the author during 1988 and 1989. All of these interviews were conducted on a 'background' basis. In other words, I agreed to keep the identity of my sources a secret. As some of the matters discussed are sensitive, I have not provided footnotes except where the information comes from either a non-UK or a published source.

2. Interview, February 1988.

CHAPTER 12

1. Unless otherwise specified, information on the Saudi deal comes from a number of sources familiar with the deal in the United Kingdom, Saudi Arabia and the United States. They were interviewed between July 1988 and March 1989.

2. Jane's *Defence Weekly*, July 23, 1988, p. 122.

3. *Daily Telegraph*, July 11, 1988.

4. *Washington Post* March 29, 1988; *Los Angeles Times*, May 4, 1988; Jane's *Defence Weekly*, April 2, 1988, p. 627.

CHAPTER 13

1. Anthony Cordesman, *Arms Transfers and the Iran-Iraq War*, unpublished copy, August 4, 1987, p. 14.
2. Details come from those involved who were interviewed in 1988 and 1989.
3. *The Times*, September 24, 1987.
4. *Business Week*, December 29, 1986, p. 46.
5. *Wall Street Journal*, January 30, 1987 and numerous newspaper reports of the trial.
6. Anthony Cordesman, *Arms to Iran: The Impact of US and other Arms Sales on the Iran-Iraq War*, American-Arab Affairs, spring 1987, pp. 13–29.
7. *The Guardian*, January 27, 1988.
8. Information on the Austrian arms deal comes from Wochenpresse, March 4, 1988; *Basta*, January 29, 1988 and US government sources.
9. *Washington Post*, September 8, 1987.

CHAPTER 14

1. Details of the Hashemi affair come from court records, numerous press accounts and a book written by one of the participants, Hermann Moll (with Michael Leapman) entitled *Broker of Death*, Macmillan, London, 1988.
2. Ben Bradlee, Jnr., *Guts and Glory, The Rise and Fall of Oliver North*, Grafton Books, London, 1988, p. 306.
3. *Broker of Death*, op. cit., p. 84.
4. *Broker of Death*, op. cit., p. 8.
5. *Washington Post*, 27 November, 1986.
6. *The Observer*, August 30, 1986.

CHAPTER 15

1. *SIPRI Yearbook 1989*, op. cit., p. 198.
2. *SIPRI Yearbook 1989*, Oxford University Press, 1989, p. 196.
3. *SIPRI Yearbook 1988*, Stockholm International Peace Research Institute, Stockholm, 1988, p. 190–191.
4. Jane's *Defence Weekly*, 19 November, 1988, p. 1252.
5. *Armed Forces Journal International*, March 1989, p. 58.

CHAPTER 16

1. Shimon Peres, *From These Men*, Weidenfeld and Nicolson, London, 1979, p. 132.

2. *The Sunday Times*, October 1987.

3. Pierre Pean, *Les Deux Bombes*, Fayard, Paris, 1982.

4. Matti Golan, *Shimon Peres, A Biography*, Weidenfeld and Nicolson, London, 1982, p. 49.

5. Matti Golan, *Shimon Peres*, op. cit., p. 94.

6. Golan, op. cit., p. 96.

7. Golan, op. cit., p. 97.

8. Golan, op. cit., p. 116.

9. The best sources on the NUMEC case are: David Burnham, 'The case of the missing uranium', *Atlantic*, April 1979, pp. 78–82; John J. Fialka, 'How Israel Got the Bomb', *Washington Monthly*, January 1979, pp. 50–7; Howard Kohn and Barbara Newman, 'How Israel Got the Nuclear Bomb', *Rolling Stone*, 1 December 1977, pp. 38–40; *New York Times*, 6 November 1973, p. 3; *Washington Star*, 6 November, 1977, p. A1; Peter Pringle and James Spigelman, *The Nuclear Barons*, Michael Joseph, London, 1982, pp. 293–8.

10. The definitive account of this operation comes in *The Plumbat Affair*, by Elaine Davenport, Paul Eddy and Peter Gilman, Futura, London, 1978. Also James Adams, *The Unnatural Alliance*, Quartet, London, 1984, pp. 157–161; Howard M Sachar, *A History of Israel*, Volume II, Oxford University Press, Oxford, 1987, pp. 124–125; Steve Weissman and Herbert Krosney, *The Islamic Bomb*, Times Books, New York, pp. 127–128.

CHAPTER 17

1. The information in this chapter comes from files gathered by *The Sunday Times* in the course of its investigation into the Vanunu story. I am particularly grateful to Peter Hounam, the reporter largely responsible for the investigation, and to Peter Wilsher who put together much of the published material.

CHAPTER 19

1. Steve Weissman and Herbert Krosney, *The Islamic Bomb*, Times Books, 1981, pp. 43–44.

2. Peter Pringle and James Spigelman, *The Nuclear Barons*, New York, Holt Rinehart and Winston, 1981, p. 388.

3. The most detailed account of this case comes in the Congressional Record, July 14, 1987; see also Congressional Record, July 31, 1987; *Boston Globe*, August 2, 1987; *Philadelphia Inquirer*, February 11, 1988. Various Congressional aides familiar with the Pervez case and the Pakistan nuclear programme were also very helpful.

4. Department of State incoming telegram, February 1987.

5. *The Observer*, March 1, 1987.

6. *Washington Post*, January 15, 1988.

7. *New York Times*, October 12, 1989; *Washington Post*, October 12, 1989; Jane's *Defence Weekly*, October 21, 1989, p. 845.

CHAPTER 20

1. Evelyn le Chene, *Chemical and Biological Warfare – Threat of the Future*. The Mackenzie Institute, Toronto, 1989, p. 9.
2. John Hemsley, *The Soviet Biochemical Threat to NATO*, Macmillan, London 1987, pp. 66–67.
3. In a briefing to the author, August 1987.
4. Robert Harris and Jeremy Paxman, *A Higher Form of Killing*, Hill and Wang, New York, 1982, pp. 127–129.
5. Interview with the author, summer 1988.
6. Information on the Sverdlovsk leak comes from interviews conducted by the author with the intelligence sources in London, April 1989; Defence Intelligence Agency, Soviet Biological Warfare Threat, DIA, 1986, pp. 4–5; Edward M. Spiers, *Chemical Warfare*, Macmillan, London, 1986, pp. 184–185; Harris and Paxman, *A Higher Form of Killing*, op. cit. pp. 220–221.
7. *Washington Post*, April 13, 1988.
8. There have been numerous articles on the Yellow Rain controversy. The US government case is well argued in two reports presented to Congress in March and November 1982, the first by then Secretary of State Alexander Haig and the second by his successor, George Shultz. The opposite view was presented in *Foreign Policy* of autumn, 1987, p. 100. Numerous press articles appeared on the subject with the *Wall Street Journal* generally taking the government line and the *Washington Post* opposing.
9. Chemical Warfare in South East Asia and Afghanistan, US Department of State Special Report No. 98, March 22, 1982.
10. Soviet Chemical Weapons Threat, Defence Intelligence Agency, 1985; Poison on the Wind, *The Christian Science Monitor*, January 2–6, 1989.
11. In an interview with the author in Germany, August 1985.
12. John Hemsley, *The Soviet Biochemical Threat to NATO: The Neglected Issue*, Royal United Services Institute, Macmillan Press, London, 1987.
13. ibid. p. 60.
14. To the author in Germany, August 1985.
15. Poison on the Wind, *Christian Science Monitor*, op. cit.
16. Interview with the author, April 1989.
17. Interview with the author, April 1989.
18. Novosti Press Agency, April 6, 1989.

CHAPTER 21

1. Elisa D Harris, Chemical Weapons Proliferation in the Developing World, *Brassey's Defence Yearbook*, Brassey's, London, 1989, pp. 67–88.
2. *Washington Times*, March 23, 1988.

3. ABC World News Tonight, January 17, 1989; *Washington Post*, January 19, 1989; *Washington Times*, January 19, 1989 and British and US intelligence sources.

4. Elisa Harris, Chemical Weapons op. cit., p. 79.

CHAPTER 22

1. A number of interviews with western intelligence agencies were conducted over the past two years. The most recent, in the wake of the intelligence review, took place in Washington in September 1989.

2. *New York Times*, 24 December, 1987.

3. *New York Times*, 31 December, 1988.

4. Intelligence sources, interviewed in London and Washington, August and September 1989.

CHAPTER 23

1. Georgi Markov, *The Truth That Killed*, with a Foreword by Annabel Markov, Weidenfeld and Nicolson, London, 1983, p. ix.

2. Harris and Paxman, *A Higher Form of Killing*, op. cit., pp. 197–198.

3. *Christian Science Monitor*, August 2, 1989.

4. Charles Piller and Keith Yamamoto, *Gene Wars*, Beech Tree Books, William Morrow, New York, 1988, p. 17.

5. Harris and Paxman, *A Higher Form of Killing*, op. cit., p. 189.

6. Interview with the author, March 1989.

CHAPTER 24

1. Details of the smuggling operation come from documents supplied by the United States District Court, Eastern District, Sacramento. In addition, the case has been reported in the *Washington Post*, June 25, 1988, August 20, 1988, November 1, 1988; UPI, October 26, 1988; Associated Press, October 25, 1988; and the *New York Times*, September 4, 1988. In addition, the BBC's *Panorama* programme broadcast a report entitled 'The Condor Conspiracy' on April 10, 1989. The author also received briefings on the project from western intelligence sources in May 1989.

2. *Defence*, May 1989, p. 305–306.

3. *Washington Post*, May 3, 1989.

4. Jane's *Defence Weekly*, April 22, 1989, p. 696.

5. Associated Press, October 29, 1988.

6. Interview, April 1989.

Glossary

AEC	Atomic Energy Commission
CE	Chemical Energy
COMSEC	Communications Security
DESO	Defence Export Services Organisation
DRAC	Director of the Royal Armoured Corps
ERA	Explosive Reactive Armour
FST	Follow-on Soviet Tank
HE	High Explosive
IAEC	Israel Atomic Energy Commission
ICBM	Inter-Continental Ballistic Missile
ICSS	Improved Computer Sighting System
IDM	Israeli Defence Ministry
IED	Improvised Explosive Device
INLA	Irish National Liberation Army
IRA	Irish Republican Army
ISI	Interservices Intelligence Bureau
JCS	Joint Chiefs of Staff
KE	Kinetic Energy
MGO	Master General of the Ordnance
MOD	Ministry of Defence
MTCR	Missile Technology Control Regime
NATO	North Atlantic Treaty Organisation
NORTHAG	Northern Army Group
NPT	Non Proliferation Treaty
NUMEC	Nuclear Materials and Equipment Corporation
OIRA	Official Irish Republican Army
PIRA	Provisional Irish Republican Army
PLF	Palestine Liberation Front
PLO	Palestine Liberation Organisation
RARDE	Royal Armaments and Research Development Establishment

REME	Royal Electrical and Mechanical Engineers
RPG	Rocket Propelled Grenade
RUC	Royal Ulster Constabulary
SAM	Surface to Air Missile
SIGINT	Signals Intelligence
SIPRI	Stockholm International Peace Research Institute
UN	United Nations
UNITA	Uniao Nacional para a Independencia Total de Angola
VHF	Very High Frequency

Bibliography

ADAMS, James, Tony Bambridge and Robin Morgan, *Ambush*, Pan, London, 1989.

ADAMS, James, *The Financing of Terror*, Simon and Schuster, New York, 1986.

Secret Armies, Hutchinson, London, 1987.

The Unnatural Alliance, Quartet, London, 1984.

AGA KHAN, Sadrundin, ed., *Nuclear War, Nuclear Proliferation and their Consequences*, Oxford University Press, Oxford, 1986.

BARNABY, Frank, *The Invisible Bomb*, I. B. Taurus, London, 1989.

BEIT-HALLAHMI, Benjamin, *The Israeli Connection*, Pantheon, New York, 1987.

BERTRAM, Christopher, ed., *Arms Control and Military Force*, International Institute for Strategic Studies, London, 1980.

BISHOP, Patrick and Eamonn Mallie, *The Provisional IRA*, Corgi, London, 1988.

BLEDOWSKA, Celina, ed., *War and Order*, Junction Books, London, 1983.

BOARDMAN, Robert and James F. Keeley, eds., *Nuclear Exports and World Politics*, Macmillan, London, 1983.

BELL, J Bowyer, *The IRA*, Academy Press, Dublin, 1979.

BRADLEE, Ben, Jr., *Guts and Glory*, Grafton, London, 1988.

BROGAN, Patrick, *World Conflicts*, Bloomsbury, London, 1989.

BRZEZINSKI, Zbigniew, *Power and Principle*, Farrar, Straus and Giroux, New York, 1985.

BRZOSKA, Michael and Thomas Ohlson, *Arms Transfers to the Third World, 1971–1985*, Stockholm International Peace Research Institute and Oxford University Press, 1987.

CARTER, Jimmy, *Keeping Faith*, Bantam, New York, 1982.

LE CHENE, Evelyn, *Chemical and Biological Warfare – Threat of the Future*, The Mackenzie Institute, Toronto, 1989.

COCHRAN, Thomas B., William M. Arkin, Robert S. Norris, Milton M. Hoenig, *Nuclear Weapons Databook*, Volume II, US Nuclear Warhead Production, Ballinger, Cambridge, Mass., 1987.

COLLIER, Basil, *Arms and the Men*, Hamish Hamilton, London, 1980.

DAVENPORT, Elaine, Paul Eddy and Peter Gillman, *The Plumbat Affair*, Andre Deutsch, London, 1978.

FOLTZ, William J., and Henry S. Bienen, *Arms and the African*, Yale University Press, New Haven, Conn., 1985.

FORD, Gerald R., *A Time to Heal*, W. H. Allen, London, 1979.

HAMMOND, Thomas T., *Red Flag Over Afghanistan*, Westview Press, Boulder Co., 1984.

HARRIS, Robert and Jeremy Paxman, *A Higher Form of Killing*, Hill and Wang, New York, 1982.

HEMSLEY, John, *The Soviet Bio-Chemical Threat to NATO*, Macmillan, London, 1989.

HOLDREN, John and Joseph Rotblat, eds., *Strategic Defences and The Future of The Arms Race*, Macmillan, London, 1987.

HIRO, Dilip, *The Longest War*, Grafton Books, London, 1989.

JASANI, Bhupendra, ed., *Outer Space*, Stockholm International Peace Research Institute, Stockholm, 1982.

KARAS, Thomas, *The New High Ground*, Simon and Schuster, New York, 1983.

KARSH, Efraim, ed., *The Iran/Iraq War Impact and Implications*, Macmillan, London, 1989.

KLASS, Rosanne, ed., *Afghanistan, The Great Game Revisited*, Freedom House, London, 1989.

KOZYREV, Andrei, *The Arms Trade; A New Level of Danger*, Progress Publishers, Moscow, 1985.

KELLY, Kevin, *The Longest War*, Brandon, Dingle, Co. Kerry, 1982.

KENNEY, Martin, *Biotechnology*, The University-Industrial Complex, Yale University Press, New Haven, 1986.

LONG, Franklin A, Donald Hafner and Jeffrey Boutwell, eds., *Weapons in Space*, Norton, New York, 1986.

MARTIN, David C, and John Walcott, *Best Laid Plans*, Harper and Row, New York, 1988.

MCINTOSH, Malcolm, *Arms Across the Pacific*, Pinter Publishers, London, 1987.

MOLL, Hermann, with Michael Leapman, *Broker of Death*, Macmillan, London, 1988.

MOODIE, Michael, *The Dreadful Fury*, Praeger, New York, 1989.

MORRIS, Charles R., *Iron Destinies*, Lost Opportunities, Harper and Row, New York, 1988.

MURPHY, Sean, Alistair Hay and Steven Rose, *No Fire No Thunder*, Pluto Press, London, 1984.

NEWHOUSE, John, *The Nuclear Age*, Michael Joseph, London, 1989.

NEWMAN, Stephanie G., *Military Assistance in Recent Wars*, Praeger, New York, 1986.

OHLSON, Thomas, *Arms Transfer Limitations and Third World Security*, Oxford University Press, Oxford, 1988.

PIERRE, Andrew J., *The Global Politics of Arms Sales*, Princeton University Press, Princeton N.J., 1982.

PILLER, Charles and Keith R. Yamamoto, *Gene Wars*, William Morrow, New York, 1988.

PRINGLE, Peter, and James Spigelman, *The Nuclear Barons*, Michael Joseph, London, 1982.

STEVEN, Stewart, *The Spymasters of Israel*, Ballantine, New York, 1980.

SACHER, Howard M., *A History of Israel*, Alfred A. Knopf, New York, 1981.
A History of Israel, Volume II, Oxford University Press, Oxford, 1987.

SCHMIDT, Christian, ed., *The Economics of Military Expenditures*, Macmillan, London, 1987.

SHAKER, Steven M., and Alan R. Wise, *War Without Men*, Pergamon/Brassey, London, 1988.

SHEEHAN, Michael and James Wyllie, *Pocket Guide to Defence*, The Economist, London, 1986.

SIKORSKI, Radek, *Dust of the Saints*, Chatto and Windus, London, 1989.

SPIERS, Edward M., *Chemical Warfare*, Macmillan, 1986.
Chemical Weaponry, Macmillan, 1989.

STOCKHOLM International Peace Research Institute, *Yearbooks 1980–1989*, Oxford University Press, Oxford.

THOMAS, Andy, *Effects of Chemical Warfare: A Selective Review and Bibliography of British State Papers*, Sipri, 1985.

WEISSMAN, Steve and Herbert Krosny, *The Islamic Bomb*, Times Books, New York, 1981.

WRIGHT, John, *Libya, A Modern History*, Croom Helm, London, 1982.

WYLLIE, James H., *The Influence of British Arms*, George Allen and Unwin, London, 1984.

YAEGER, Joseph A, ed., *Non-Proliferation and U.S. Foreign Policy*, The Brookings Institute, Washington, 1980.

YAHUDA, Michael B., *China's Role in World Affairs*, Croom Helm, London, 1978.

DOCUMENTS

Arms Control and Disarmament Agency, World Military Expenditures and Arms Transfers, 1970–1988, ACDA Publications, U.S. Government Printing Office, Washington, D.C.

Council for Arms Control, Faraday Discussion Paper No. 12, Verifying a Ban on Chemical-Warfare Weapons, Julian Perry Robinson, London, 1988.

International Institute for Strategic Studies, Adelphi Paper No. 113, Prospects for Nuclear Proliferation, by John Maddox, IISS, London, 1975.

Rand, The Arms Debate and the Third World, by Robert A Levine, Santa Monica, Cal., 1987.

Strategic Defence Initiative Organisation, Report to the Congress on the Strategic Defence Initiative, U.S. Government Printing Office, 1987.

Appendix One

The Cell Structure of a Terrorist Group

1. Each controller only knows the controller on either side of him. No controller knows the identity of the members at any cell not directly under his or her command.

2. The Surveillance cell carries out very early reconnaissance which might include the preparation of a list of a hundred names for assassination or military bases and their locations. Each member of the cell works on a different day in a different location so none of them even knows of the existence of any other cell member and certainly never meets another operator. Thus, neighbours or even members of the same family could both be working for the same controller.

3. The Planning cell receives the list of likely targets and then examines what support, such as weapons, documents and safe houses, will be required for an attack on any of the targets to succeed.

4. The Operations Controller receives his report from the controller of the Planning cell. He consults with the Central Committee who agree a number of targets.

5. With that target list in mind, Controllers 3, 4 and 5 set up the necessary support network to ensure that a terrorist

group can live and work underground for months or even years.

6. The Operations Controller hands the Planning cell's data to the Target cell who refine the target list and check the information.

7. The Reconnaissance cell prepares a detailed operational plan including precise date and times for the action to happen: where the sniper will fire his rifle and how he will make his escape or where precisely the bomb should be planted and when.

8. This information is passed to the Trigger cell which actually does the job.

The Cell Structure of a Terrorist Group

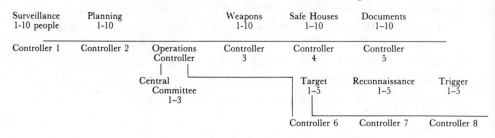

Appendix Two

Interception of Major Arms Shipments intended for PIRA

DATE	AT	ORIGIN	WPNS	AMMO	SPPT	NOTES
Oct 71	Schiphol Airport	Czech	104	Yes	No	Included anti-tank grenade launchers
Mar 73	At sea off Irish Republic	Libya	493	Yes	Yes	Included 250 AK–47s and explosives
Nov 77	Antwerp	Al Fatah	71	Yes	No	Included 2 mortars and explosives
Oct 79	Dublin	USA	160	Yes	Yes	
June 81	New York	USA	23	Yes	Yes	Included 20mm cannon and flame-thrower
June 82	Nantes	Belgium?	33	Yes	No	Included Soviet grenade, and explosives
June 82	Newark, NJ	USA	51	Yes	Yes	
Aug 83	Le Havre	Be/USA	28	Yes	Yes	Included explosives
Sept 84	At sea off Irish Republic (*Marita Ann*)	USA	156	Yes	Yes	Included AA machine gun mounts
Jan 86	Amsterdam	Belgium?	17	Yes	Yes	Included 800 litres of nitro-benzene
Jan 86	Republic	Libya?/ Norway	118	Yes	Yes	
Oct 86	At sea off Brittany	Libya	1000	Yes	Yes	Included first known shipment of SAM–7 missiles
Nov 83	Republic	Australia	10	Yes	No	
June 86	Le Havre	USA	37	Yes	No	
July 86	Paris	France	6	Yes	No	Included 6 grenades

KEY: WPNS = Weapons
      AMMO = Ammunition
      SPPT EQPT = Supporting Equipment

Appendix Three

Trade in Major Conventional Weapons

Table 1. The leading exporters of major weapons, 1984–88

The countries are ranked according to 1984–88 aggregate exports. Figures are in US $m, at constant (1985) prices.

	1984	1985	1986	1987	1988	1984–88
To the Third World						
1. USSR	7,423	8,634	9,136	11,672	9,001	45,866
2. USA	4,905	4,009	4,845	6,229	3,490	23,479
3. France	3,345	3,664	3,420	2,635	1,671	14,736
4. China	1,207	1,011	1,313	2,187	2,011	7,730
5. UK	1,136	849	1,396	1,717	1,464	6,562
6. FR Germany	1,830	395	649	252	482	3,609
7. Italy	811	575	397	317	334	2,434
8. Brazil	271	172	124	466	338	1,372
9. Israel	263	160	242	394	178	1,237
10. Spain	475	139	163	139	205	1,121
11. Netherlands	57	38	132	263	570	1,059
12. Egypt	237	122	164	195	229	947
13. Czechoslovakia	306	124	124	198	146	897
14. Sweden	47	35	141	298	240	762
15. North Korea	36	95	48	98	109	386
Others	740	652	557	566	409	2,921
Total	**23,089**	**20,674**	**22,851**	**27,627**	**20,877**	**115,118**

To the industrial world

1. USA	5,321	4,497	5,128	5,997	5,877	26,819
2. USSR	2,695	4,311	3,769	3,381	3,767	17,923
3. France	507	382	702	438	1,209	3,239
4. FR Germany	705	550	456	464	973	3,149
5. UK	772	797	409	135	122	2,235
6. Czechoslovakia	398	373	373	373	259	1,775
7. Canada	84	99	433	350	41	1,007
8. Sweden	57	117	177	173	286	809
9. Poland	92	92	92	92	92	462
10. Netherlands	41	51	109	2	186	388
11. Switzerland	13	54	46	15	80	208
12. Italy	58	16	6	61	63	204
13. Saudi Arabia	—	—	39	125	—	164
14. Austria	42	42	—	34	34	151
15. Israel	—	59	—	66	8	134
Others	238	170	57	184	95	744
Total	**11,023**	**11,610**	**11,796**	**11,890**	**13,092**	**59,411**

To all countries

1. USSR	10,118	12,945	12,905	15,053	12,768	63,789
2. USA	10,226	8,506	9,973	12,225	9,367	50,298
3. France	3,853	4,046	4,122	3,073	2,881	17,975
4. UK	1,908	1,646	1,805	1,852	1,586	8,797
5. China	1,254	1,082	1,313	2,187	2,011	7,847
6. FR Germany	2,535	945	1,106	717	1,455	6,758
7. Czechoslovakia	704	497	497	570	405	2,673
8. Italy	869	590	404	379	397	2,638
9. Sweden	104	152	318	471	526	1,571
10. Brazil	301	188	140	482	356	1,468
11. Netherlands	98	88	240	265	756	1,447
12. Israel	263	220	242	460	186	1,370
13. Canada	107	132	472	387	67	1,165
14. Spain	475	139	172	139	211	1,136
15. Egypt	237	122	164	195	229	947
Others	1,060	.986	773	1,063	768	4,650
Total	**34,112**	**32,284**	**34,647**	**39,518**	**33,969**	**174,529**

Source: SIPRI data base.

Table 2. The leading importers of major weapons, 1984–88

The countries are ranked according to 1984–88 aggregate imports. Figures are in US $m, at constant (1985) prices.

	1984	1985	1986	1987	1988	1984–88
Third World						
1. Iraq	3,940	2,958	2,179	4,632	2,339	16,048
2. India	1,016	1,876	2,946	5,048	3,378	14,263
3. Saudi Arabia	862	1,447	2,697	2,217	2,066	9,289
4. Egypt	2,322	1,295	1,682	2,335	354	7,987
5. Syria	1,604	1,690	1,508	1,172	1,133	7,107
6. North Korea	654	1,123	1,038	787	2,169	5,772
7. Angola	697	694	974	1,135	890	4,391
8. Pakistan	654	675	616	564	856	3,365
9. Iran	268	739	883	802	656	3,348
10. Libya	425	969	1,359	294	65	3,112
11. Taiwan	378	664	866	642	556	3,105
12. Israel	290	192	446	1,629	327	2,884
13. South Korea	259	388	323	635	736	2,341
14. Afghanistan	210	82	359	435	1,097	2,184
15. Argentina	1,062	388	315	180	160	2,106
Others	8,448	5,494	4,660	5,120	4,095	27,816
Total	**23,089**	**20,674**	**22,851**	**27,627**	**20,877**	**115,118**
Industrial world						
1. Japan	1,529	1,632	1,743	1,615	1,671	8,190
2. Czechoslovakia	818	1,588	1,347	1,228	824	5,804
3. Turkey	563	604	621	1,097	1,090	3,975
4. Spain	36	129	940	1,454	1,362	3,921
5. Poland	424	427	877	952	876	3,556
6. Canada	641	778	747	678	506	3,351
7. GDR	979	609	420	268	808	3,084
8. Netherlands	917	787	676	322	214	2,916
9. Australia	445	352	699	478	628	2,602
10. USSR	481	497	473	497	369	2,317
11. UK	810	420	418	360	247	2,255
12. Hungary	3	759	507	592	—	1,861
13. Greece	264	192	156	98	1,150	1,860
14. Yugoslavia	125	89	89	220	1,209	1,732
15. FR Germany	445	191	431	334	324	1,725
Others	2,543	2,556	1,652	1,697	1,814	10,262
Total	**11,023**	**11,610**	**11,796**	**11,890**	**13,092**	**59,411**

All countries

1. Iraq	3,940	2,958	2,179	4,632	2,339	16,048
2. India	1,016	1,876	2,946	5,048	3,378	14,263
3. Saudi Arabia	862	1,447	2,697	2,217	2,066	9,289
4. Japan	1,529	1,632	1,743	1,615	1,671	8,190
5. Egypt	2,322	1,295	1,682	2,335	354	7,987
6. Syria	1,604	1,690	1,508	1,172	1,133	7,107
7. Czechoslovakia	818	1,588	1,347	1,228	824	5,804
8. North Korea	.654	1,123	1,038	787	2,169	5,772
9. Angola	697	694	974	1,125	890	4,391
10. Turkey	563	604	621	1,097	1,090	3,975
11. Spain	36	129	940	1,454	1,362	3,921
12. Poland	424	427	877	952	876	3,556
13. Pakistan	654	675	616	564	856	3,365
14. Canada	641	778	747	678	506	3,351
15. Iran	268	739	883	802	656	3,348
Others	18,084	14,629	13,849	13,802	13,799	74,162
World total	**34,112**	**32,284**	**34,647**	**39,518**	**33,969**	**174,529**

Source: SIPRI data base.

Picture Credits

The author and the publishers would like to thank the following for their kind permission to reproduce the photographs that appear in this book:

Agence France Press (Rabta chemical plant, customs boarding the *Eksund*); Richard Beeston (Kurdish victims of gas attack); Simon de Bruxelles (Monzer al-Kassar); the *Daily Mail* (SAS in Gibraltar); Network Photographers (Pakistani arms bazaar, Afghan opium field); Novosti/Gamma/Frank Spooner Agency (destruction of Soviet chemical weapons); Rex Features (mujahedeen with missile launcher); Reuters/Popperfoto (Silkworm missiles); the *Sunday Times* (Dimona nuclear plant, Machon 2 bunker, Cheryl Bentov, Mordechai Varunu).

Whilst every effort has been made to trace copyright, this has not been possible in some cases. The publishers would like to apologise in advance for any inconvenience this might cause.

Index